Methods in
Psychological Research

To Marc Daniel

—ANE

To Alison, Amanda, and Andrew

—BR

Methods in
Psychological
Research

Annabel Ness Evans
Concordia University College of Alberta

Bryan J. Rooney
Concordia University College of Alberta

SAGE Publications
Los Angeles • London • New Delhi • Singapore

Original art by Marc Daniel Coldeway.

For information:

Sage Publications Inc.
2455 Teller Road
Thousand Oaks, California 91320
E-mail: order@sagepub.com

Sage Publications Ltd.
1 Oliver's Yard
55 City Road
London EC1Y 1SP
United Kingdom

Sage Publications India Pvt. Ltd.
B 1/I 1 Mohan Cooperative Industrial Area
Mathura Road, New Delhi 110 044
India

Sage Publications Asia-Pacific Pte. Ltd.
33 Pekin Street #02-01
Far East Square
Singapore 048763

Printed in the United States of America

Library of Congress Cataloging-in-Publication Data

Evans, Annabel.
Methods in psychological research/Annabel Ness Evans, Bryan J. Rooney.
  p. cm.
Includes bibliographical references and index.
ISBN 978-1-4129-2485-6 (pbk.)
  1. Psychology—Research—Methodology. I. Rooney, Bryan J. II. Title.

BF76.5.E88 2008
150.72—dc22   2007022693

This book is printed on acid-free paper.

07 08 09 10 11   10 9 8 7 6 5 4 3 2 1

Acquisitions Editor:	Cheri Dellelo/Jerry Westby
Associate Editor:	Deya Saoud
Editorial Assistant:	Lara Grambling
Production Editor:	Laureen A. Shea
Copy Editor:	Gillian Dickens
Typesetter:	C&M Digitals (P) Ltd.
Proofreader:	Jenifer Kooiman
Indexer:	Michael Ferreira
Cover Designer:	Edgar Abarca
Marketing Manager:	Stephanie Adams

Brief Contents

Detailed Contents

2 Understanding the Research Literature   27

3 Research in Psychology: An Ethical Enterprise   51

4 Hypothesis Testing, Power, and Control: A Review of the Basics   76

5 Measuring Variables   97

6 Selecting Research Participants   119

7 Experimental Design: Independent Groups Designs   133

11 Data Collection Methods   219

12 Program Evaluation, Archival Research, and Meta-Analytic Designs   255

13 Your Research Project: Analyzing, Interpreting, and Presenting Your Research   270

14 Communicating in Psychology   324

Preface

Our motivation in writing this book is probably similar to that of most textbook authors. We teach a methods course, and although there are some great books available, none was perfectly suited to our course.

We take an applied approach in our course, and our students are required to complete research projects. As such, Chapter 13 was written specifically for students who are required to conduct or propose a research project as part of their course. Instructors who do not require students to conduct or propose a research project could omit Chapter 13. However, we strongly recommend that students conduct a research project and write it up following American Psychological Association (APA) style. Our students find this exercise to be extremely valuable, and we include a lot of the supporting material we provide our students in Chapters 13 and 14.

In Chapter 13, we discuss, with worked-through examples, basic statistical procedures that students doing research projects would be likely to use to analyze their data. We also cover statistical procedures that students who are reading the literature will need to understand the more complex analyses used by social scientists (Chapter 2), but we have written the book with the expectation that students have taken an introductory statistics course.

Basic statistical concepts for students who have not taken statistics and for those who need a refresher can be found in Chapters 2, 4, and 13.

APA FORMATTING AND STYLE

We have followed the recommendations of the APA as closely as possible in our reporting of statistics, tables, and figures within the confines of Sage's design style. In addition, we discuss the style and manuscript requirements of the association in some detail in Chapter 14. Key terms in each chapter are set in boldface, and most are included in each chapter summary and the glossary at the end of the book.

END-OF-CHAPTER MATERIAL

Answers to Conceptual Exercises

Throughout the text, you will find mini-exercises that ask students to critically think about the material they have just read. We have provided our suggested answers to these questions at the end of each chapter. There may be other good answers to some of the conceptual exercises. Students should not assume, if their answer differs from ours, that it is necessarily wrong. They should be told to consult their instructor.

FAQ

We think the FAQ sections that accompany each chapter will be very popular with students. We compiled the questions most often asked by our students and couched those questions as our students did. We answered the questions as we do in class.

Chapter Exercises and Projects

We have included the chapter exercises and projects that our students have reported, over the years, to be most useful to them.

ANCILLARIES

Student Study Site

This free student study site provides additional support to students who are using *Methods in Psychological Research*. Each chapter in the text is accompanied by a self-quiz on the Web site, which includes true/false questions and multiple-choice questions, as well as e-flashcards and chapter summaries and outlines. The site also includes suggested Web resources that provide students with additional information and support. In addition, the site offers Sage journal articles with discussion questions to get students into original research. Visit the study site at www.sagepub.com/evansmprstudy.

Instructor's Resources on CD-ROM

This set of instructor's resources provides a number of helpful teaching aids for professors who are new to teaching research methods or to using *Methods in Psychological Research*. The CD-ROM includes PowerPoint slides, a computerized test bank, suggested class activities, sample syllabi, and suggested Web resources.

Our students appreciate the student-friendly style of our book, and we hope you and your students do also.

—Annabel Ness Evans and Bryan J. Rooney

Acknowledgments

Marc Daniel Coldeway, son of Annabel Evans, recently completed his BA degree in psychology and art and design. He created the illustrations that accompany several chapters and are found throughout Chapter 6. He worked very hard under demanding time constraints to create these unique designs, and we are extremely pleased with them. Thank you, Marc Daniel.

We are both professors in the Psychology Department at Concordia University College of Alberta, a small institution dedicated to teaching excellence. We want to express our sincere thanks to the administrators at our school who recognized the value of our writing project and gave us the time we needed to complete it.

The people at Sage have been supportive throughout this project, and our occasional changes in focus were taken in stride. Jim Brace-Thompson was our first contact at Sage, and his enthusiasm for our project increased ours immeasurably. Cheri Dellelo and Deya Saoud took us through the preparation and launching of the book with grace and charm.

Gillian Dickens did the copy edit of the manuscript, and Laureen Shea served as the production editor during the production process. We want to express our sincere appreciation to all of you and to the many other employees at Sage who worked on our book.

Several people reviewed the manuscript, and those reviews were invaluable to us as we tried to determine the best direction to take with the material. Many thanks to the following:

Verneda P. Hamm Baugh, *Kean University*

David E. Campbell, *Humboldt State University*

Martin Dempster, *Queen's University Belfast*

Michelle Drapkin, *Rutgers University*

Carlos Escoto, *Eastern Connecticut State University*

Richard Freeman, *London Southbank University, UK*

Alex Haslam, *University of Exeter, UK*

Rolf Holtz, *Ball State University*

Leona M. Johnson, *Hampton University*

Min Ju, *Vassar College*

Robert Lennartz, *Indiana University Southeast*

Keith A. Markus, *John Jay College of Criminal Justice*

Carol A. Miles, *Carleton University*

Jennifer Myers, *University of Michigan*

Todd Nelson, *California State University, Stanislaus*

Robert Proctor, *Purdue University*

Fran Sessa, *Pennsylvania State University–Abington*

H. David Smith, *Northwestern University*

Theodore Steiner, *San Francisco State University*

Harriet R. Tenenbaum, *Brooklyn College and the CUNY Graduate Center*

Burt Thompson, *Niagara University*

Errol Yudko, *University of Hawaii at Hilo*

Over the course of writing this book, we found ourselves in a quandary on several occasions. We would like to thank the people who helped us out. They are Rod M. Cooper, Professor Emeritus of the University of Calgary; Jack B. Kelly of Carleton University; Professor Rob Cribbie of York University; and Professor Alan Law of Trent University.

Of course, we wrote this book for students and would like to acknowledge some special students here.

The students who took our research methods course in 2007 were patient and good-humored "guinea pigs" as we piloted the book. Their comments and suggestions were taken to heart and implemented more often than not. In particular, we want to thank Lisa Okoye, who provided extensive feedback and a valuable student perspective.

Keith Nye allowed us to use his research paper as an example in Chapter 14, an excellent paper, we might add. Thanks, Keith!

Annabel Ness Evans would like to acknowledge the assistance provided by Shane Whippler, who, by agreeing to take on a lot more responsibility than a typical TA, gave her the time she needed to complete this project in a timely manner.

Finally, we want to thank all of our previous research methods students over the years who taught us at least as much as, and very possibly more than, we taught them.

—ANE and BR
Edmonton, 2007

Introduction to Research in Psychology

OBJECTIVES

After studying this chapter, students should be able to

- Describe common sources of belief and identify the likely source of example beliefs
- Describe the critical thinking process
- Describe the objectives of science and identify examples of each
- Describe the tenets of science and identify examples of each
- List the steps of the scientific method and apply them to a problem
- Describe the difference between theory and hypothesis
- List the various reasons why scientists do research
- Describe various approaches to research and classify research examples
- List the steps in planning and doing research
- Generate a research topic from available sources

Vancouver yoga teacher Shakti Mhi has been drinking her own urine every day for the past two decades. Ms. Mhi claims that it not only is rich in nutrients but also offers [and] numerous health benefits, including a boosted immune system. "I drink it first thing in the morning. . . . If I feel my energy level is dropping, I'll drink three cups a day . . . I always heal myself. I haven't seen a doctor in 20 years."

—*Globe and Mail,* Saturday, September 25, 2004

Are you wondering what the basis is for Ms. Mhi's claims about drinking urine? So are we.

ACQUIRING KNOWLEDGE ABOUT THE WORLD

Some expectant mothers play classical music to their growing bellies because they believe this will make their babies more musically talented. Some people believe that dreams predict future events or that a broken mirror can cause 7 years of bad luck. Many people believe all sorts of things that really have no factual foundation.

Why are many people hard-pressed to give up beliefs such as these even in the face of solid evidence to the contrary? Where do these beliefs come from?

Surprisingly, and often unfortunately, we acquire many of our beliefs from flawed sources or in flawed ways.

Tradition or Tenacity: I Believe It Is True Because It Has Always Been True

Good fences make good neighbors. Our fathers believed this so-called truism. So did their fathers. The willingness to accept an idea as valid or as truth because it has been accepted as such for so long or because it has been heard so often is an example of a belief acquired through **tradition.** Psychologists have demonstrated that simply repeating an idea increases the likelihood that people will believe it (e.g., Schwartz, 1982). No proof is necessary—no need to check the accuracy of the idea. Indeed, little intellectual effort is required to acquire knowledge through tradition. Advertisers are well aware of this.

Accepting something as true because it has been traditionally accepted as such is a flawed way of acquiring knowledge. And many traditionally accepted truisms are in fact contradictory. Compare the adage *Out of sight, out of mind* with *Absence makes the heart grow fonder.* These truisms cannot both be correct. What about *Birds of a feather flock together* and *Opposites attract.* You can probably think of more examples. This is not to say that some traditional beliefs are not true; it is to say that we cannot know that something is true simply because it has always been thought to be true. A willingness to do so indicates intellectual laziness.

Consider the following dialogue:

"Grandpa is never going to figure out e-mail."

"What makes you say that?"

"Everybody knows you can't teach an old dog new tricks."

The belief expressed in this example is supported by nothing more than tradition.

Intuition: I Believe It Is True Because I Feel It Is True

Intuitive knowledge or beliefs come to us without any direct involvement of our senses, apparently. Years ago, there was quite a flurry of interest in something called subliminal suggestion. It was thought that we could be influenced by messages sent to our unconscious mind, messages that could not be detected by our normal sensory processes. That there was and still is no evidence that such a process can occur has not deterred some people from continuing to believe it can. The idea that we can perceive things that are purported to exist outside of our senses (i.e., extrasensory perception) continues to thrive today to such an extent that some police forces have been known to consult with psychics.

Consider the following dialogue:

"Same-sex couples do not make good parents."

"How do you know that?"

"I don't care what anybody says; I just know it."

The belief expressed in this example is founded on a feeling or an **intuition,** a belief that is not supported by any evidence.

Authority: I Believe It Is True Because an "Expert" Says It Is True

We professors hear our students make the following kinds of statements all the time. "I read that . . . I heard that . . . I saw somewhere that. . . ." We often reply, "Just because you read it, heard it, or saw it doesn't make it true." Accepting an idea as true because it was claimed to be so by a source we respect is the method of acquiring knowledge by **authority.** This method of acquiring knowledge is pervasive in our world. We learn from our parents, from our teachers, from our religious leaders, and from the media.

Sometimes the authority figures from whom we acquire knowledge are good authorities, and by accepting what they tell us, we avoid having to evaluate the evidence ourselves and save ourselves an enormous amount of work. Unfortunately, often we do not discriminate between good and bad authorities. You have heard the adage *Consider the source.* We often don't consider the source—sometimes we don't even remember the source! Recall our students who heard it *somewhere,* read it *somewhere. . . .*

Consider the following dialogue:

"Women are more emotional and less rational than men."

"How do you know that?"

"My philosophy professor said so."

The belief expressed in this example is a belief acquired through authority. The truth of the belief depends on the credibility of the authority.

Uncritical acceptance of an idea acquired through tradition, intuition, or authority is a flawed method of acquiring knowledge. An intuitive belief that eating pizza late at night will make you dream about dying is probably not going to adversely affect your life. Likewise, not eating pork because your pastor says it is a sin or never wearing white shoes after Labor Day will have few negative consequences in the larger scheme of things. But feeding your infant nothing but eggs for the first year of her life on the advice of your meditation guru (as a relative of one of the authors of this book did) is a decision better made after a more rigorous evaluation of information. Accepting such advice on the basis of this particular authority is doubly flawed: flawed source and flawed process.

Reasoning: I Believe It Is True Because It Is Logically Derived

Rational thought is thinking with reason. Rules of logic are applied so that reasonable conclusions are made. Logical **reasoning** is a more rigorous way of arriving at knowledge. However, logical reasoning requires confirmation from other evidence. A conclusion reached from logical deduction is only as good as the assumptions of the reasoning process. If the assumptions are flawed, then the conclusion, although logical, is still flawed.

Consider the following:

All poodles are dogs. (major premise)

Toast is a poodle. (minor premise)

Therefore, Toast is a dog. (conclusion)

The conclusion is logical and follows from the premises.

However, consider the following:

All poodles are afraid of hot air balloons.

Toast is a poodle.

Therefore, Toast is afraid of hot air balloons.

The conclusion is logically valid, but Toast, the dog of one of your authors, is afraid of just about everything *except* hot air balloons. The premise that all poodles are afraid of hot air balloons must be wrong, or the premise that Toast is a poodle must be wrong. Each premise must be proved to be true in some way other than logical reasoning before the process of logical reasoning will work.

Empiricism: I Believe It Is True Because I Experienced It

Empiricism is acquiring knowledge through our senses or with instruments that extend our senses. Other people can verify such observations and measurements using their senses or their instruments. Directly observing an event or using a machine to measure something are both examples of empirical evidence.

Of course, it would be foolish to always require direct sensory experience before we believe something. For example, just because we have never skied at Park City, Utah, does not mean that the ski resort does not exist. Empiricism must be combined with rational thought to make meaning of our world, and this is what science does.

Science

Science is a way of acquiring knowledge through the continual interaction of empiricism and reasoning. Observation of real events provides the basis for hypotheses that can be tested in methodical and systematic ways. Hypotheses that are not supported by further empirical evidence are abandoned, and new hypotheses are constructed. In this way, general principles are identified and predictions can be made. This is the basis of **theory building**. Hypotheses that have been tested and found to be supported by the available evidence are then encompassed in the body of knowledge of the discipline.

FYI

Interestingly, as its first entry, the Merriam-Webster dictionary lists empiricism as "a former school of medical practice founded on experience without the aid of science or theory **b**: QUACKERY, CHARLATANRY." This is not what we are referring to in our use of the word. Ours is the second entry: "the practice of relying on observation and experiment especially in the natural sciences." Curious how the word refers to both quackery and the natural sciences!

Conceptual Exercise 1A

Consider each of the following beliefs. By what process do you think it is likely the believer acquired the belief?

1. Too many cooks spoil the broth.

2. Boys will be boys.

3. Politicians are corrupt.

4. Capital punishment is immoral.

5. Pedophiles can rarely be rehabilitated.

PSYCHOLOGY—SCIENCE AND ART

Psychology is both a science and an art. The psychologist as scientist might conduct research to determine how best to ask questions of people to encourage sincere dialogue. The psychologist as artist might use that information to help troubled teens in therapy. The science provides the theory; the art of psychology might involve applying that theory in skillful ways to help others.

CRITICAL THINKING

Critical thinking is the ability and willingness to assess claims and make objective judgments on the basis of well-supported evidence. Critical thinking skills can be applied to any topic or problem.

Critical thinkers do the following:

- Ask questions
- Objectively define problems
- Examine the available evidence
- Assess assumptions and biases
- Avoid emotional reasoning
- Separate facts from opinion
- Avoid oversimplifying
- Consider alternative explanations
- Tolerate uncertainty
- Maintain an air of skepticism but be open minded (i.e., not cynical)

Critical thinking is particularly relevant to psychology. Thought and thinking are important areas of study in psychology. Cognitive psychologists in particular study problem solving, concept formation, creativity, and other mental processes we would call thinking. Second, thinking is a topic that interests everybody. We all want to know more about thinking processes. Researchers in psychology generate many competing findings on topics that we find personally interesting or relevant. The fascination by the general public with popular psychology has created a huge market for pseudo-scientists and quacks. As a result, students of psychology must be particularly prudent when it comes to evaluating claims and beliefs. And critical thinking skills help us do that.

Critical thinking skills help us recognize different types of evidence and the kinds of conclusions we can draw from each. For example, limited personal experience and anecdotal evidence are not reliable sources of knowledge. A pervasive habit of many people is to form beliefs on the basis of limited experience. We sometimes call this the *n* of one fallacy. An acquaintance of ours, who should know better, believes in ghosts. Why? Because his father claimed to have seen one. One anecdote was enough for our friend to hold a belief. Limited conclusions can be drawn from such anecdotal evidence.

The popular press is designed to be popular and often dramatizes or overgeneralizes research findings. Critical thinkers are aware that the popular press is a biased sample of information. A critical thinker will view a single report linking urine drinking and improved health with skepticism. A critical thinker will not rely on a newspaper writer's assessment of research (or even the researcher's assessment) but will assess the research for himself or herself.

FYI

Do not confuse skepticism with cynicism. **Skepticism** is a healthy reluctance to accept new information without sufficient evidence, but cynicism is a scornful, negative attitude toward new ideas. A skeptic wants to see the evidence. A cynic is not interested in the evidence; he or she has already decided to not accept the new information.

The Critical Thinking Process

1. **Ask questions:** What makes people happy?
2. **Define the problem:** What does happy mean? How will you know that someone is or is not happy?
3. **Examine the available evidence:** Accepting a conclusion without evidence is not critical thinking.
4. **Analyze assumptions and biases:** Consider an advertiser who claims that medical doctors prefer her pain reliever. The conclusion she wants you to draw is that doctors prefer her pain reliever because it is a better product. But she neither says that nor is it likely to be true. Perhaps doctors prefer it because it is cheaper than other pain relievers. What if she says that no other pain reliever relieves pain better than hers? What does this really mean? It may mean that her pain reliever is as effective as every other pain reliever on the market. Again remember the adage

Consider the source. The advertiser has an interest in persuading you that her product is better, doesn't she?

5. **Avoid emotional reasoning:** Feelings alone are not reliable guides to truth. Set feelings aside as you consider the evidence. Because you feel that something is true does not make it so.

6. **Do not oversimplify:** One dishonest used car salesperson does not mean that all used car salespeople are dishonest—at least we do not think so!

7. **Consider other interpretations:** In general, a critical thinker accepts the interpretation that accounts for the most evidence with the least number of assumptions. Consider the claim that interpersonal attraction occurs when the planets are aligned. This interpretation requires many assumptions about the nature of the relationship between planetary alignment and human behavior. A better interpretation of attraction might be that people like people who are similar to them.

8. **Tolerate uncertainty:** Psychologists know that there may be no good answer. A critical thinker knows this and is willing to accept this uncomfortable situation.

Consider a claim that we have heard many times:

"Eating raw oysters increases libido."

First, let's consider the possible sources of this popular belief. Perhaps someone in author-ity claimed that oysters increase libido. Perhaps this belief has been accepted for so long that it has become part of a general belief system (tradition). Perhaps we have had personal experience with eating oysters and the consequences thereof (empiricism). Perhaps. But we think it is highly unlikely that this belief has come about as a result of scientific inquiry.

So let's analyze this claim as a critical thinker might.

1. **Ask the question:** Does eating raw oysters improve libido?

2. **Define the problem:** How many raw oysters must we eat? How do we measure improved libido?

3. **Examine available evidence:** Is there any scientific empirical evidence about oysters and libido?

4. **Analyze assumptions and biases:** Did the claim originate from oyster farmers?

5. **Avoid emotional reasoning:** Set aside our feelings about oysters.

6. **Don't oversimplify:** Did we have one experience with increased libido after eating some oysters?

7. **Consider other interpretations:** If we have found that there is evidence that libido increases after eating oysters, could there be another explanation for this? Perhaps we only have the opportunity to eat raw oysters at fancy restaurants with candlelight and romantic settings.

All good scientists practice critical thinking and base their scientific beliefs primarily on empirical evidence. Let's now turn to the goals or objectives of science.

OBJECTIVES OF SCIENCE

The **goals of science** are to describe, explain, predict, and control some event(s). A young science first must describe its subject matter. This is the first step, and empiricism is the primary method of doing this. A mature science may be busier with prediction and control. Early astronomers, for example, spent their time describing what they observed in the skies. Only later, when a body of empirical evidence had been gathered, could they begin to explain how planets, stars, and other cosmic entities were formed, died, and interacted.

To Describe

Description of its subject matter is the first objective of a science. The subject matter of psychology is human behavior and mental processes. Describing general laws of human behavior is the work of many researchers in psychology today. Sometimes animal models are used to study human behavior. For example, Frank Epling (deceased) and David Pierce of the University of Alberta have spent several years studying anorexia nervosa in laboratory rats. They have described the phenomenon quite clearly. Rats will develop anorexia if they are given access to a running wheel and if they are given an adequate amount of food for a specific period of time each day. The rats will, over time, spend excessive amounts of time running and will eat less and less even when adequate food is available but only when that food is offered for a limited time each day. Are rats the same as humans? Of course not, but this kind of research may offer some insights into similar processes in humans.

To Explain

Once we have described general laws of our subject matter, we then proceed to try to explain those trends. Epling and Pierce postulated that excessive exercise prompts the body to produce a lot of beta endorphins, which suppress appetite and cause feelings of well-being, sometimes called the *runner's high*. This, then, was their **explanation** for why rats become anorectic under their laboratory conditions. This may not help us explain the problem with humans; humans suffering from anorexia and bulimia have lower levels of beta endorphins.

To Predict

Once a behavior has been well described and an explanation has been offered, the next step is often to make **predictions** from the explanation. If the predictions are not confirmed, then the explanation is considered faulty and must be revised. A prediction that might be made from Epling and Pierce's explanation for the development of anorexia in rats would be that people with anorexia engage in excessive exercise. Epling and Pierce found that excessive physical exercise in anorectic patients was reported quite often and was thought by professionals to be a side effect of the disorder (Epling & Pierce, 1992). Another interesting prediction Epling and Pierce made was that people in some professions would be more likely than others to become anorectic. For example, according to their model, ballet dancers (who are required to be very active) should be more likely to develop anorexia than models. Both groups must control their weight to be successful, but only ballet dancers must also be active. Epling and Pierce (1992) report that the available data support this prediction.

To Control

Once a science has described, explained, and made predictions about its subject matter, **control** of the phenomena can be attempted. Applied psychology has a mandate to take the principles of behavior demonstrated by researchers and use them to help with problems people have. For example, a useful control application based on Epling and Pierce's work might be to treat people with anorexia by reducing the amount of exercise they are getting, rather than trying to change their eating habits.

We have seen that scientists are critical thinkers, their beliefs are founded on empirical evidence, and their goals in doing their science are to describe, explain, predict, and control the subject matter of the discipline. Science, therefore, is a way of thinking and a way of doing things. Scientists view the world differently than many nonscientists. The process of scientific inquiry involves certain assumed principles or tenets about how the world works.

THE TENETS OF SCIENCE

The scientific approach to discovering truth assumes several fundamental principles about how the world works and demands that certain criteria be met. Some people misunderstand some of these tenets of science. Perhaps the most misunderstood is the doctrine of determinism.

Determinism

Determinism is a doctrine of belief that events have natural causes. For psychologists, the events we are interested in are behaviors of humans. When we apply this doctrine to psychology, then, we assume that human behavior is determined or caused by natural phenomena, not supernatural events. In other words, we believe that behavior is neither random nor under the control of nonnatural events. Many people confuse this doctrine with another, *predeterminism*. They are not the same. To say that behavior is determined by natural events is *not* to say that our behavior is somehow predetermined or predestined. Some religious approaches do have a predeterministic bent, but psychology does not.

To say that human behavior is determined is to say that humans behave for reasons that can be understood in terms of natural laws of the universe. We may not know what those laws are in any particular case, but we assume that those laws are operating nonetheless.

Empiricism

Scientists, including psychologists, rely on real evidence, empirical data, to confirm or refute claims. Intuition, faith, and even logic are not enough. There must be empirical support before a scientist will accept a claim.

Replicability

Scientists require that findings be replicable before they are accepted. A single finding may be just a fluke and not reliable. This is of particular importance in psychology because our subject matter, human behavior, is so variable. Behavior varies among people in the same or similar situations. Indeed, the behavior of one person varies even in what appear to be identical conditions.

Falsifiability

For scientists, hypotheses and theories must be **falsifiable** through empirical research. They must be testable such that they could be shown to be false. Some theories are just not refutable. Consider Freud's theory about repression. The assumption is that psychological problems of adults are rooted in childhood trauma. Is this hypothesis falsifiable? We don't think so. If the adult can recall and describe the childhood trauma, the Freudian will conclude that his or her current problems developed because of the trauma. If the adult cannot recall any trauma, the Freudian concludes that he or she has repressed the events into his or her unconscious mind. This hypothesis cannot be proven wrong. This hypothesis, like much of Freud's theory, is pseudoscience. Consider another example of pseudoscience. The psychic who is brought into a laboratory and asked to demonstrate his powers in a controlled setting and who cannot do so claims that the air of skepticism of the researchers is responsible for interfering with the *psychic forces*. The psychic wins either way. His powers are proven when he demonstrates evidence of psychic ability. His powers, however, are not disproved when he does not.

Parsimony

A scientist looks for the simplest explanation for a phenomenon. **Parsimony** means the quality of being sparing or frugal. If two explanations account for similar amounts of data but one explanation requires fewer assumptions, the scientist will favor that explanation. In general, the scientist looks for the explanation that accounts for the most data with the fewest assumptions.

Conceptual Exercise 1B

1. John is a volunteer at a local ER. The medical personnel tell John that on nights when there is a full moon, there are many more shooting and knifing cases in the ER. The workers believe that the moon is the cause. John keeps records and finds that indeed, on full-moon nights, there are many more of these cases that come into the ER than on nights with no full moon. He contacts other ERs and finds that they too report many more of these cases on those nights. He concludes that the full moon has powers that increase criminality in people. What tenet of science has John failed to follow?

2. A student conducted a survey on the Internet to measure attitudes about funding of animal research. She found that people are opposed to the use of animals in research on cosmetic products. Another student used an interview method and learned that her sample had no such opposition to the use of animals in cosmetic testing. What tenet of science is the problem here?

3. Mary, a social worker, has observed that evil people do evil things and good people do good things. She has many examples of this in her practice, and her colleagues report they have too. When a person does evil, Mary claims it is the evil within him or her that caused this behavior. Likewise, good behavior is evidence of goodness. What tenet of science has Mary ignored?

We have discussed the tenets of science, but what makes a science a science? You may have heard the terms *hard* and *soft* science. These terms, which we disapprove of, classify science by its subject matter. Chemistry is considered by some to be a hard science and psychology a soft science. Some people claim that chemistry is a more rigorous science than psychology. Why do they claim this? We think it lies in the variability of the behavior of the subject matter, not in the rigor of the method used. Molecules are less variable in behavior than humans are, but chemistry outside of the laboratory can be just as variable as psychology. A discipline is a science if the **scientific method** is the primary method used in the research process.

THE SCIENTIFIC METHOD

The method of science involves logical steps toward finding truth. The steps are as follows:

1. Assume a natural cause for the phenomenon (i.e., determinism)
2. Make an educated guess about the cause (i.e., generate a testable hypothesis)
3. Test your guess
4. Revise your hypothesis
5. Retest your guess
6. Make a conclusion

Consider a psychology student who lives in a small town in southern Alabama. She has noticed that people of the town often visit a recluse who lives outside of town when they have aches and pains. The townspeople believe that the recluse is a witch who has supernatural healing powers. Our psychology student decides to apply the scientific method to assess the beliefs of the townspeople.*

---

*This example is a variation on one given by the PhD supervisor of Dr. Annabel Evans. Thanks to Dr. Willie Runquist.

Step 1.   She assumes there is a natural explanation for her observation that the townspeople do appear to feel better after they visit the witch.

Step 2.   She has noticed that the witch always gives the townspeople a potion to drink when they visit, and she assumes that the potion contains something medicinal. She has discovered that the potion contains eye of newt, desiccated bat wings, and ground poppy seeds. She decides that the eye of newt might be the active medicinal ingredient.

Step 3.   She finds a way to substitute an inert substance for the witch's supply of eye of newt. For the next week, she observes the effects of the potion on the visitors. She finds that they report they feel better as often as they did before she made the substitution.

Step 4.   She revises her hypothesis and systematically replaces the bat wing ingredient and the poppy seed ingredient.

Step 5.   She observes that the townspeople no longer report they feel better after visiting the witch when the poppy seeds have been replaced.

Step 6.   She concludes that poppy seeds have a medicinal quality that promotes feelings of well-being.

THEORIES, CONCEPTS, AND HYPOTHESES

The objectives of science can be seen in theories. We use theories to describe what is known in an area, present an explanation of those findings, and make predictions for further research. A **theory** is a formal statement of how concepts are related. *Concepts* are the general category of ideas that are represented by our variables. Theories may be very general and account for many phenomena, such as Skinner's behavioral theory, with applications to all of human behavior, or more specific and limited in scope, such as Epling and Pierce's theory of activity-based anorexia.

If we were all-knowing, we would not need theories. We would know how the universe worked, and research would be predictable and boring. Fortunately for those of us who enjoy research, we do not have all the answers, so we construct theories of how we think the world works. The main advantage of a theory is that it provides an explanation of how concepts are related. So rather than having to remember a whole library of specific research findings, we need only to remember and apply the theory. The theory will describe how general concepts are related.

Theories are an integral part of the research process. In addition to explaining what we already know, we use theories to make new predictions that can be empirically tested. By using specific instances of the general concepts, we can derive new testable hypotheses. A **hypothesis** is a prediction of how concepts are related that is often deduced from a theory. We then conduct our research to test the hypothesis. If the hypothesis is supported by the research, the theory is strengthened. On the other hand, if the hypothesis is not supported, then the theory may have to be altered. Theories do not live forever. They start out wonderfully explaining and organizing a whole collection of observations. Over their life, they gain support from some research, they may make surprising new predictions, and they may fail to explain some research findings. When enough research is compiled that does not fit the theory, a new theory will be proposed.

So what is the nature of empirical research? Where do scientists get their ideas, and how do they go about meeting their goals to describe, explain, predict, and control phenomena? Let's look at five common reasons researchers might have for conducting research.

WHY WE DO RESEARCH

To Evaluate a Theory

In psychology, theories abound. Theories, if they are good theories, generate testable hypotheses. Good theories allow us to test hypotheses derived from them. Bad theories often do not. In fact, one criterion of good theory is whether testable hypotheses can be postulated. A great deal of research in psychology is conducted to evaluate current theories about human behavior. In a classic paper, Darley and Latane (1968) offered a theory about why the many people who could hear, from their apartments, a young woman being attacked outside did nothing to help her. They postulated that the responsibility to be good citizens was diffused among the many people, and as a result, no one person felt compelled to help. One hypothesis that can be derived from this theory (called the bystander effect) is that as more people are present, the less likely any one person is to help someone in distress. And indeed, this hypothesis has been confirmed in numerous experiments.

Let's look at another example. Developmental psychologists call the emotional bond between children and their primary caregivers *attachment*. But why does this happen? Behaviorists proposed that attachment develops because the primary caregiver, usually the mother, is associated with food, a strong positive reinforcer to hungry babies. Harlow and Harlow (1966) tested this theory in a classic set of studies. Their results did not support the behaviorists' claim. Contact comfort, not feeding, was shown to be the source of attachment, at least in rhesus monkeys.

Theories provide a wealth of ideas for research topics.

To Satisfy Our Curiosity

Science often develops because scientists are very curious people. We have heard it said that you could get rid of warts by visiting a graveyard around midnight. We will not provide all the details of this activity, but chasing away evil spirits, and presumably your wart, by tossing a cat is involved (see *The Adventures of Tom Sawyer*). The idea that you can rid yourself of warts through some superstitious behavior led one group of researchers to investigate whether you could get rid of warts through hypnosis (Spanos, Williams, & Gwynn, 1990). They conducted a controlled experiment in the laboratory and found that hypnosis was effective. They published their results in a scientific journal. But they were more than a little embarrassed when their study made the cover of *The National Enquirer*—not exactly something you want to brag about at your university.

To Demonstrate a New Technique

As we learn new ways to do things, it is important to determine if those new ways are better than the old ways. Professors are always interested in better ways of teaching. Textbooks these days come with all sorts of fancy supplementary materials. But do they improve learning? At our school, we conducted an experiment to try to answer that question. Different groups of students taking introductory psychology received instruction with various technological accompaniments. Some received traditional lecture instruction. Some received computer-assisted instruction. We measured several variables, including performance and more psychological variables. Are you wondering what we found? Well, very simply, the students with added technology did not learn more, but they had more fun!

To Demonstrate a Behavioral Phenomenon

After observing behavior that tends to recur under certain circumstances, we need to demonstrate it under precise conditions before the phenomenon can be confidently added to the body of knowledge about a discipline. The idea that organisms do things because they receive rewards was known for a long time before Skinner demonstrated this in his laboratory. Indeed, Skinner's career was spent demonstrating the behavioral phenomena of operant conditioning.

Perhaps you have noticed that when you are out walking your dog, people seem a lot friendlier than when you are out walking alone. You could design a simple experiment to see if your perception that people are friendlier is a demonstrable phenomenon. You could take the same walk at the same time each day for several weeks, sometimes with your dog and sometimes without. You might collect data on how many people engage you in conversation and how long they talk to you, for example. If you find that when your dog is with you, more people initiate conversation more often, then you have evidence of a behavioral phenomenon.

To Investigate the Conditions Influencing Behavioral Phenomena

Darley and Latane's (1968) bystander effect has been the focus of numerous experiments. Researchers have studied not only the influence of number of bystanders on helping behavior but also many other factors, such as apparent degree of need of the victim and ability to help of the bystanders. Skinner and others have investigated how size, frequency, and quality of reward (reinforcer) affect behavior, as well as many other conditions affecting operant behavior.

We have discussed some of the reasons why researchers do what they do. Now let's discuss various ways they go about doing what they do.

APPROACHES TO RESEARCH

Over many years of schooling, students are trained to be convergent thinkers, to converge on the one correct answer. But research requires divergent thinking. It is a creative endeavor with many approaches. Here we summarize the diversity of research by organizing various approaches on a number of typical continua you have probably come across in your undergraduate career.

Descriptive Versus Explanatory Research

Descriptive research involves describing a population of measurements. Usually, inferences are made from a representative sample to a population except in the case of censes where entire populations are measured. This is the type of research we see in the media from polling agencies, and the primary interest is in describing how the population thinks. Descriptive research has applications in business, where it is used to understand the consumer, and in social services, where you need to understand the needs of your community.

The focus of **explanatory research** is to answer "why" questions. For example, you may find that there are more women than men in your psychology program. That finding alone is a description, but you may want to know why there are more women than men. In explanatory research, you are interested in explaining why there is a gender difference. You are trying to account for the difference. The simplest explanation would be that there are just more women in the university. You could test this by comparing the gender ratio in psychology to the gender ratio in other disciplines. In this case, you are investigating a relationship between gender and university discipline. Finding a difference may lead to an explanation of why there are more women than men in your psychology program.

Often research may contain aspects that are both descriptive and explanatory. For example, researchers studying drug use in schools may want to describe the prevalence of drug use and also try to account for why some students take drugs and others do not.

Quantitative Versus Qualitative Research

In essence, **quantitative research** in psychology measures differences in *amount* of behavior. What causes people to become *more or less* aggressive? What factors *increase or decrease* interpersonal attraction? Does a particular treatment *reduce* symptoms of depression? Do children diagnosed with autism engage in *less* play behavior than children not diagnosed with autism? In other words, we are measuring the quantity of a behavior often because we wonder what causes the behavior to increase or decrease in quantity.

Qualitative research in psychology, on the other hand, describes differences in *kind or quality* of behavior. What does aggressive behavior *look like* compared to nonaggressive behavior? What is *the nature* of interpersonal attraction? What do depressed people *think or say about themselves?* What *kinds* of play behavior are typical of children diagnosed with autism? It is the nature or quality of the behavior that interests the qualitative researcher.

Quantitative research always involves numbers that reflect amount of behavior. Qualitative research often involves narrative descriptions of what behavior looks like. A tally of how many self-harm behaviors Susie exhibits in a day would be quantitative data. A description of the nature of those self-harm behaviors would be qualitative data.

Basic Versus Applied Research

The distinction between **basic or pure research** and **applied research** is best made by examining the motives of the researchers. In basic research, the researcher may have no application in mind but is interested in answering a question simply to satisfy his or her curiosity. In applied research, the researcher is looking at applying the knowledge to somehow benefit humankind.

Basic or pure research may seem esoteric and may leave people scratching their heads, wondering why this type of research should be funded. Particularly in times of fiscal restraint, should governments be funding research that is only going to increase our understanding of something but has no application in daily life? The answer, of course, is yes! Applied research typically involves the application of basic principles discovered by basic researchers. Without basic research, there is nothing to apply; both are important.

An example of applied research that is becoming more and more common is program evaluation. As the name implies, program evaluation involves the application of various research approaches to measure the effectiveness of a program. Not implied in the name is the importance of objective evaluation in the development of a program and its integration as an ongoing part of the program. This applied research is usually a requirement of any program supported by the government or developed by industry and is discussed in greater detail in Chapter 12.

Cross-Sectional Versus Longitudinal Research

Most research in psychology that looks at age differences is **cross-sectional.** A cross section of different ages is studied at one point in time. The goal is usually to understand developmental or maturational differences between the ages. A potential problem with this research is that there may be other variables that are confounded with age. This problem has been called the *cohort effect* because a cohort of same-aged individuals will share variables related to their history. Differences between age groups, then, are confounded with differences in history. Imagine that we asked 30-, 40-, and 50-year-olds about their attitudes about monogamy. If we found that 50-year-olds have much more liberal attitudes, could we conclude that this is a maturational effect? Probably not. People who are in their 50s today spent their formative years during the 1960s, a very sexually free time in our history.

A solution is to study a single age cohort over a number of years. With **longitudinal research,** everyone has a similar history, but the research is going to take years! This raises problems of cost and the tracking of participants over time.

Field Versus Laboratory Research

The distinction between **field** and **laboratory research** highlights a difference of control. In the laboratory, researchers may have total control over most variables, whereas in the field, they may have difficulty controlling even a few. The control afforded by laboratory research makes it more likely that you will detect a treatment effect or a relationship between variables. But the artificiality of the laboratory may mean that your results do not generalize to the real world. On the other hand, there is nothing artificial about research in the field, but your lack of control of variables may mean that you do not obtain significant results. The decision to conduct research in the laboratory or in the field is a trade-off, then, among artificiality (high in the lab; low in the field), control over variables (high in the lab; low in the field), and generalizability (low in the lab; high in the field).

Conceptual Exercise 1C

1. A researcher has participants rate their mood on a scale after viewing different color combinations. She wonders how color combinations make people feel. How would you classify this research?
   - Descriptive or explanatory?
   - Quantitative or qualitative?
   - Basic or applied?

2. A clinical psychologist, after reading the research on color and mood, decides to conduct his therapy sessions in two rooms, one painted in warm colors that tend to be calming and one painted in colors that have no effect on mood. He hopes that his clients will be more forthcoming in the warm rooms. How would you classify this research?
   - Descriptive or explanatory?
   - Basic or applied?
   - Laboratory or field?

3. A developmental psychologist compares risky decision making of preteens and teens. How would you classify this research?
   - Descriptive or explanatory?
   - Cross-sectional or longitudinal?

We have discussed why researchers do what they do and the general approaches taken by researchers in the social sciences. Regardless of the approach that a researcher takes, the process of planning and conducting research follows a logical series of steps.

STEPS IN PLANNING AND DOING RESEARCH

Most of you will be expected to conduct some sort of research project in your methods course. Here we will discuss how to start thinking about doing research.

Selecting a Research Topic

From Life Experience

Very often, some life event inspires a researcher. Many years ago, one of your authors met a man who could not remember anything he had just learned. She had to introduce herself to him every time she met with him because he could not remember ever having met her before. She found this to be such an interesting phenomenon that she decided, when she began her graduate training, that she would focus on human memory.

Have you noticed that people in elevators rarely make eye contact with you? Have you ever found yourself trapped on the phone by a telemarketer, unable to just hang up? These kinds of personal experiences are a great source of research ideas. As psychology students know, Pavlov did not set out to discover the basic laws of classical conditioning. He was not even interested in psychology. But he noticed something odd in the behavior of his dogs when doing research on digestion. This personal experience led him to begin investigation into an entirely new area.

From Existing Research

Students planning a research project must read the existing literature in the area. After all, you don't want to reinvent the wheel! Once you have an idea about the general area you are interested in, you should read what has been found already. No doubt, as you read the research, you will think of potentially interesting variables, populations, or methods that have not been investigated. The existing research is a great source of ideas for research topics. Understanding empirical research articles can be challenging if you are not already familiar with the topic, but the next chapter (Chapter 2) will provide help. There we will provide you with an overview of the parts of a research article and describe, at a conceptual level, the most common statistical analyses you will likely read about.

Common Sense

Psychology, more so than other sciences, yields research topics based on common sense or folk wisdom. Earlier, we talked about commonsense folk wisdoms such as *Absence makes the heart grow fonder* and *Out of sight, out of mind*. Research topics can be generated from common sense, and indeed, a lot of research has been done to test the veracity of folk wisdom.

A New Technology

New technology can be a source of research topics. Magnetic resonance imaging (MRI), for example, has allowed researchers to investigate what is going on in the brain during various activities. This kind of research was not possible before the development of the technology. The Internet is an obvious example of new technology that has allowed researchers to collect data that they could not easily have collected previously.

In psychology, interesting research topics are all around us. "Why do people do what they do?" is a question we have all asked ourselves. No matter what has inspired your research question, at some point you will need to think about hypotheses that you can test.

Generating Testable Hypotheses

To generate testable hypotheses, you must *operationalize* your concepts, that is, make them measurable. We talked a bit about Harlow's research earlier. One of his research questions was, "Is contact comfort a source of attachment in monkeys?" How did he make the concepts *contact comfort* and *attachment* measurable? Read on!

He created what he called a surrogate "mother monkey" made of wire and a second made of soft fabric. In essence, his operational definition of *high-contact comfort* was the soft, cuddly "mother," and his operational definition of *low-contact comfort* was the cold wire "mother." *Attachment* was operationalized as the "mother" the infant clung to when stressed.

Students often ask us how they can tell if an operational definition is a good one or not. This is an excellent question. Just because one researcher has an operational definition of a concept does not guarantee that it is a good operational definition. We usually advise students to read the literature in the area and see what most researchers tend to do, check whether measures of reliability and validity have been taken, and go from there.

Once you have defined your research topic and generated testable hypotheses, you then must determine which variables you are going to manipulate, which variables you will control, and which variables you will measure.

Classifying Variables

Research in psychology involves various kinds of variables. There are variables you want to manipulate (*independent variables*) to see if they affect other variables (*dependent variables*). Then there are variables you want to control (*control variables*). Researchers must determine how they will define these variables so that they can be measured and controlled. Harlow, as we discussed earlier, in one experiment manipulated the contact comfort of the surrogate mother monkey—this was an independent variable (high- and low-contact comfort). The attachment behavior of the infant (i.e., which surrogate the infant clung to when stressed) was the dependent variable. Size of surrogate mother, type of event that produced stress, and size of cage were controlled variables in that they were constant. Researchers have to consider the potentially important variables when they decide how to test their hypotheses.

You have your hypothesis and you have decided what variables you will measure and control. Now you must select the research design.

Selecting an Appropriate Design

Selecting an appropriate design is a complex task. You will need to consider all sorts of things as you make this decision. Practical factors such as time, money, and facilities; the nature of your research question; and the kinds of variables you intend to measure must be taken into account when you select a design. The research design often dictates the analysis. You must think about how the data can be analyzed given your measures and design. You do not want to find yourself in a position of having collected data that cannot be analyzed the way you intended.

Once the research design has been selected, you need to figure out how to carry it out.

Planning the Method and Carrying It Out

The method should be carefully planned in advance. How will you select your participants? Where and when will you gather your data? How many participants will you need? What are the ethical considerations of your research? Who is responsible for reviewing the ethics of your research? Although the method should be planned in advance, you will need to allow for adjustments if something does not go as you expected. Perhaps you discover that your first couple of participants misinterpreted an instruction. How will you deal with that?

The data have been collected. Now what?

Analyzing Results

The design and the nature of the measures you took will determine the appropriate analysis. We cover the statistical analyses students are most likely to need for their research projects in Chapter 13. Once the data have been analyzed, it is time to interpret the findings and draw conclusions.

Drawing Conclusions

The last step of the research endeavor is to interpret the results and draw conclusions. This is not easy. Researchers must be careful not to go too far from their results. There is a fine line between justifiable conclusions and wild speculation. Your conclusions must include a discussion of how your results fit into the literature. How do your results support the conclusions of other researchers, and how do they disagree? Do they support one theory but not another?

Sharing Your Findings

Of course, researchers do not keep their findings to themselves. Communicating with others is an important part of the research process. Researchers share their work primarily by publishing in journals and presenting their work at conferences. In this way, the research community remains up to date about what is going on in the field. In Chapter 14, we discuss this important part of the research endeavor.

In the above sections, we have tried to give you some idea about how psychologists go about doing research and some tips to help you as a student plan a research project. Our intention was to orient you to a way of thinking before you begin your methods course in depth. Keep these ideas in mind as you study the rest of this book.

CHAPTER SUMMARY

Our knowledge of the world comes from many sources. Believing that something is true because it has always been that way is a belief based on **tradition.** Believing that something is true because an "expert" said so is a belief based on **authority.** Believing that something is true because it feels true is a belief based on **intuition.** Tradition, authority, and intuition are **flawed sources** of knowledge. **Reasoning** (i.e., beliefs based on logic) and **empiricism** (i.e., beliefs based on measured observations) are better sources of knowledge.

Acquiring knowledge via interaction between empiricism and logic is the way of science. Scientists are critical thinkers and apply critical thinking skills in their research. **Critical thinking** is a process involving objectivity and unemotional examination of available evidence. **Alternative explanations** are considered, **uncertainty** is tolerated, and **skepticism** is maintained.

The **goals of science** include **description, explanation, prediction,** and **control.**

Scientists assume that events in the world have natural causes (**determinism**). Scientists are **empiricists;** they rely on real observations to assess claims. Scientific findings must be **replicated** before they are incorporated into the body of knowledge. Hypotheses derived from scientific theory must be refutable through empirical research (**falsifiability**), and scientific explanations should require few assumptions (**parsimony**).

Science is defined by its method of hypothesis testing in the search for truth. **Theories** yield **hypotheses,** which are tested, revised, and retested.

Researchers conduct their studies to evaluate theories, to satisfy their curiosity, to demonstrate a new technique or behavioral phenomenon, or to investigate factors that influence behavioral phenomena.

A researcher's goal may be to describe a population (**descriptive research**) or to explain relationships (**explanatory research**). **Quantitative** researchers in psychology are interested in differences in amount of behavior, whereas **qualitative** researchers are interested in differences in kind or quality of behavior. **Basic or pure research** is conducted to increase the body of knowledge of the discipline; **applied** researchers use that knowledge to improve things in the world. Researchers interested in age differences may study people of different ages (**cross-sectional** research) or may study the same people at different stages in their lives (**longitudinal research**). **Laboratory** research allows better control over variables, but **field** research allows a more natural setting for the behavior.

Planning research involves several steps, including selecting a research topic from theory, previous research, experience, or common sense; classifying variables; selecting the design; carefully considering the ethics; carrying out the research; analyzing the results; and drawing conclusions.

ANSWERS TO CONCEPTUAL EXERCISES

NOTE: There may be other good answers to some of the conceptual exercises. Do not assume, if your answer differs from ours, that it is necessarily wrong. Consult with your instructor.

Conceptual Exercise 1A

1. Although some people may have experienced this, this belief, like all truisms, comes from tradition.
2. As in the first example, this belief is primarily traditional.
3. This belief may have several sources, including tradition and authority.
4. This belief is best described as an intuitive belief based in religion, perhaps.
5. Some people may have acquired this belief from authority. For others, this belief comes from personal experience and, for some, from science.

Conceptual Exercise 1B

1. John has failed to follow the tenet of determinism. He should have assumed a natural cause for the phenomenon. It is likely that on nights when the moon is full, there is more crime committed because there is more light to conduct crime by! This explanation is a deterministic one, a tenet of science.
2. This finding lacks replicability.
3. This example demonstrates lack of falsifiability. The hypothesis is not refutable.

Conceptual Exercise 1C

1. This example is descriptive of how people feel when they look at different colors. It is quantitative; she is collecting ratings. This is basic research. No application has been discussed.

2. This is descriptive. The therapist has not tried to explain why color affects mood. It is applied because he is using the finding to help in therapy. It is field research conducted in the natural therapy setting.

3. This is descriptive and cross-sectional.

FAQ

Q1: Dr. Linus Pauling was the only person to have won two unshared Nobel Prizes; he lived to age 93 and wrote a book about vitamin C and the common cold. If he thinks that taking vitamins makes you healthier, then it must be true. Right?

A1: Wrong! Although he may have been an authority, science requires replicated research before a finding is accepted, and so far, the research on this area has produced mixed results. This does not mean that we should be cynical; amazing discoveries are made all the time. But we should remain skeptical until there is consensus in the literature.

Q2: I believe in auras because I have experienced them. Isn't that empiricism?

A2: Although we cannot argue with your experiences, this is not scientific evidence. In science, the evidence must be based on observations that can be independently verified. This is not possible with your experiences.

Q3: What is wrong with understanding the world through logical reasoning?

A3: Nothing, as long as there are no errors in your reasoning. Indeed, this is how new predictions are formulated from theories. But science also requires an empirical test of logically derived statements.

Q4: The assumption of determinism holds that events have natural causes. Isn't it also possible that there are forces of nature that we are not aware of?

A4: Indeed, before the discovery of atomic particles, nuclear forces were unimagined. Yes, there certainly could be forces that are unknown to us, but that does not mean that we can use them to explain events. Until we have established that they exist, they cannot be used in scientific explanations.

Q5: What is this idea of falsifiability; don't we want to prove things in science?

A5: Yes, we do want to find evidence to support our theory; a theory may only approximate truth. We are interested in discovering the limits of a theory. Where does the theory break down and not account for our findings? That is what motivates us to alter a theory or construct a new theory. Often, research involves pitting two theories against one another, each making a different prediction of outcome. Science moves ahead when we test our theories, and that requires predictions that are falsifiable.

Q6: Is a research hypothesis just a guess of how things will turn out?

A6: A research hypothesis is not just a guess; it is an educated guess. The distinction is important because a hypothesis is a prediction based on a theory, which in turn is based on empirical research. It is a guess based on the scientific literature.

Q7: Which is better, quantitative or qualitative research?

A7: We think the best answer to this is that it is not a contest. Our bias is toward quantitative methods, but we see more and more qualitative research being published. Each approach has its place.

Q8: I'm still not clear on the cohort effect. Can you give another example?

A8: The cohort effect is a problem where age differences are confounded with history. For example, suppose you wanted to look at age differences in people's view of war. You may find that older people have very different views than younger people. This may be an age effect, but it may also reflect the fact that older people have survived World War II and that may have shaped their views. The difference may be the shared experience of the cohort and not an age effect.

Q9: Is it OK to select a research topic based on something you saw on TV?

A9: Absolutely! The most important factor in selecting a research topic is your interest. Researchers are usually motivated by a genuine interest in the topic. Of course, you need to read the scientific literature to get a better understanding of what has been done in the area and what is known about the topic. There is more on selecting a research topic in a later chapter.

CHAPTER EXERCISES

1. For each of the following, indicate the likely source of the belief:
   a. Teenagers are hormonally challenged.
   b. Because all little boys like to play rough, my boy will like to play rough.
   c. Overexposure to sunlight causes skin cancer.
   d. The sun sets in the west.
   e. Men never ask for directions.

2. List and briefly describe the key elements of critical thinking.

3. For each of the following, identify the goal of the research (i.e., description, explanation, prediction, control):
   a. What are violent criminals like?
   b. Is there a connection between children's diet and their school performance?

    c. Are violent criminals more likely than nonviolent criminals to have been abused as children?

    d. Can we develop programs to reduce the likelihood of criminal behavior in victims of child abuse?

4. List and briefly describe each tenet of science. Also include why these tenets are important.

5. Briefly, what is the difference between theory and hypothesis? Can you provide an example for each?

6. Are the following best described as descriptive or explanatory research questions? Why do you think so?
   a. What gambling strategies do men use?
   b. Is parenting style linked to self-esteem in adolescent children?

7. Are the following best described as qualitative or quantitative research questions? Why do you think so?
   a. What are the major themes of the dreams of clinically depressed individuals?
   b. Do clinically depressed people exhibit more negative self-talk than nondepressed people?

8. Are the following best described as basic or applied research questions? Why do you think so?
   a. What learning styles do first-year psychology students use?
   b. Which learning style, typically used by first-year psychology students, is the most effective in performance outcomes?

9. Are the following best described as longitudinal or cross-sectional research questions? Why do you think so?
   a. Do people become more tolerant as they age?
   b. Are young people more tolerant than middle aged people?

10. List one advantage of field research over laboratory research. List one advantage of laboratory research over field research.

CHAPTER PROJECTS

1. Peruse the letters to the editor of your local newspaper. Identify a letter that describes a belief that you suspect is based on each of the sources of beliefs discussed in this chapter. Why do you think so?

2. Obtain a copy of a popular magazine. Find an article of your choice that is opinion based. Identify the sources of belief used by the author. Do you think the writer was a critical thinker? Explain your answer.

3. Select a major psychological theory. Generate three testable hypotheses.

4. Read a research paper in a scientific journal. Generate a testable hypothesis from the research.

5. In our introductory psychology classes, we often do the following demonstration. We ask for eight or so volunteers. Each student is given a coin. We turn our back to the students and instruct them clench the fist holding the coin and place the fist next to their head. We then ask them to try sending thoughts to us about which hand is holding the coin. We hem and haw for a while. We then tell the students to drop the hand and hold out both fists in front of them. We quickly turn around and identify which hand is the one holding

the coin. We are always accurate. The students are required to generate a scientific hypothesis for our ability to do this. Use the steps of the scientific method to plan a way to test your hypothesis. Try to find more than one hypothesis that could explain our "magical" ability and identify how you could test each.

REFERENCES

Darley, J., & Latane, B. (1968). Bystander intervention in emergencies: Diffusion of responsibility. *Journal of Personality and Social Psychology, 8,* 377–383.

Epling, W. F., & Pierce, W. D. (1992). *Solving the anorexia puzzle: A scientific approach.* Toronto: Hogrefe & Huber.

Epling, W. F., & Pierce, W. D. (1996). *Activity anorexia: Theory, research and treatment.* Mahwah, NJ: Lawrence Erlbaum.

Harlow, H. F., & Harlow, M. H. (1966). Learning to love. *American Scientist, 54,* 244–272.

Schwartz, M. (1982). Repetition and rated truth value of statements. *American Journal of Psychology, 95,* 393–407.

Spanos, N., Williams, V., & Gwynn, M. (1990). Effects of hypnotic, placebo, and salicylic acid treatments on wart regression. *Psychosomatic Medicine, 53*(1), 109–114.

Visit the study site at www.sagepub.com/evansmprstudy for practice quizzes and other study resources.

CHAPTER 2

Understanding the Research Literature

OBJECTIVES

After studying this chapter, students should be able to

- Search the literature using common online databases
- Describe what is meant by the term peer reviewed
- List and describe what is contained in each section of a typical research article
- Define independent, dependent, participant, mediating, and moderating variables
- Identify important variables in a research article
- Describe the typical descriptive statistics found in research articles
- Understand at a conceptual level common parametric tests of significance used by researchers in the social sciences
- List common nonparametric alternatives to parametric tests of significance
- Understand how confidence intervals are used in estimating parameters

You have selected your research topic. Now you need to discover what research has *already* been done on the topic. It is time for you to peruse the research literature. You will probably find some research on your topic, but it is unlikely that anyone has done exactly the same study that you have in mind. We often tell our students to think through their topic before going to the literature because it is easier to be creative about your project before you have looked at the other approaches. Indeed, once you have read a few articles in the area, it may be very difficult to think of an original idea!

Although it is unlikely that a study identical to yours has already been done, reading the literature will give you an idea about the kinds of problems that other researchers have had, and you can assess their solutions to those problems. The literature can provide a historical context for your study by describing what has been done and what remains to be explored. You will also find valuable information on how to measure variables, how to control variables, and, in experimental studies, how to manipulate variables. This sounds wonderful, but how do you start to search through all the research to find studies relevant to your topic? In the "good old days," this required many hours (or days) of wading through heavy indexes of research (just imagine a dozen or more telephone directories). Today, there are a number of computer indexes that require no heavy lifting.

SEARCHING THE LITERATURE

There are a number of bibliographic databases for the psychology literature, including Proquest, ERIC, and PsycINFO. We prefer **PsycINFO,** an index that is produced by the

American Psychological Association and is probably the most widely used bibliographic search engine for English-language journals (http://www.apa.org/psycinfo/products/psycinfo.html).

What is the *psychology literature?* When we use this term, we are usually referring to original research published in peer-reviewed journals. These journals can be easily recognized by their common layout. They begin with an **abstract** (a short summary) and include an **introduction**, a **method** section, a **results** section, and a **discussion.** But the literature also includes review articles, books, chapters in books, edited volumes, and chapters in edited volumes. These sources are not usually where original research is published. Rather, they are usually a summary of a collection of research studies in a particular area. Although these sources can be useful by helping you to put the research in context, it is better to read the original research and draw your own conclusions.

Not included in the list above are newspapers, magazines (including *Psychology Today*), or Web sites. There are two reasons that scientific research is not published in these media: (1) the presence of advertising and (2) the lack of peer review. Let's talk about advertising. Newspapers and magazines contain a lot of advertising of products and services. Indeed, these publications would not be viable without advertisers. Editors of newspapers and magazines must keep their advertisers happy; therefore, we, as consumers of the information in these publications, cannot be confident that reporting will be unbiased. Now, we are not saying that all newspaper and magazine reports are biased, but they could be. For example, imagine you have conducted a study that shows that drinking Brand X beer can lead to spontaneous uncontrollable hiccupping. You send your report to a magazine that has Brand X beer as a major advertiser. It's pretty unlikely that the magazine editor will accept your paper for publication. Yes, your research might be terrific, but the potential damage to the advertiser in terms of sales of the product might lead the editor to reject your study for publication. This is why you will not see advertising in journals. Journal editors, by not permitting advertising, avoid the conflict of interest problem that advertising brings.

The second reason that original scientific research is not usually published in newspapers or magazines is that neither of these sources requires review of the research by expert peers. Some sources that you can search are peer reviewed, and some are not. It is important to understand the peer review process because it is a fundamental safeguard of quality in research. As the name implies, *peer review* is a process whereby the editor of a journal sends submitted manuscripts out to be reviewed by other researchers in the same field of study. The manuscript is read and critiqued by peers who have expertise in the area. The review is usually *blind;* this means that the name(s) of the author(s) of the manuscript is removed from the manuscript before the copies are sent to the peer reviewers. Blind review also means that the editor does not reveal the reviewers' names to the author(s) of the manuscript. Blind review helps to guard against any personal conflicts that may be present among researchers and to facilitate a fair review of the research. The editor receives the reviews and decides whether the paper should be accepted as submitted, accepted with minor changes, accepted with revisions, or not accepted at all. If the manuscript is accepted but changes are required, the author(s) is given the opportunity to make the changes necessary to satisfy the editor and to address the concerns of the reviewers. If the study has major flaws, it may have to be redone and resubmitted (of course, the researchers can submit the manuscript to another journal and hope for a more positive review).

Peer review helps to maintain a high standard of quality in research. Without peer review, shoddy, or even fraudulent, research might be published that could send other researchers off on a wild-goose chase that could last for years. Keep in mind that books and magazines (e.g., *Psychology Today*) are usually not peer reviewed.

NOTE: In our courses, we do not permit the use of *Psychology Today* as a source. Students often question this because a lot of psychological research is reported in *Psychology Today*. Along with the advertising and peer review issues, which we discussed above, there are two other reasons for our decision to not permit this magazine as a source for student papers. One reason is simple—we do not want our students to use secondary sources of any kind. Second, the writers for *Psychology Today* are not scientists; they may have some academic background in the area, but they are writing for the magazine as reporters. *Psychology Today,* like any other magazine, needs to sell magazines. Articles written by reporters will not be published unless the editor believes that the report will help sales.

FYI

There are two notable exceptions to the "no ads in journals" rule. Ironically, the two most prestigious scientific journals worldwide are full of advertisements. *Science* and *Nature* are peer reviewed, highly respected, and widely circulated.

When you are ready to use a bibliographic database, your first step is to select the appropriate **search terms.** Often students will complain that they cannot find anything in the literature on a particular topic even though a lot of research is there. Usually, the problem is that they have not used the correct terms when doing the search. Using the correct terms is crucial; fortunately, the databases have a thesaurus of *keywords* to help you.

Imagine you want to find articles on treating seasonal affective disorder (SAD) with light therapy. You can go directly to the thesaurus in PsycINFO and look for "seasonal affective disorder." You will find that the term is used in the database; you will see a brief definition of SAD and the information that the term was introduced in 1991. PsycINFO also provides broader terms that would include SAD and narrower terms that are relevant. One of the narrower terms is *phototherapy.* That sounds useful. You can select "phototherapy" by clicking on the box, and you can similarly select "seasonal affective disorder." The default is to connect these two phrases with "or," but if you want articles that contain both phrases, you should choose the "and" option. When you click "add" and search (DE "Seasonal Affective Disorder") and (DE "Phototherapy"), you will find 276 publications with those keywords. You might want to limit your search to only peer-reviewed articles in English by clicking "refine search" and selecting *peer reviewed journals* under *publication type.* Below that is a box for selecting English language. If you do this and search again, you will get 235 hits. That's a more manageable number, but probably still more than you want to read. Let's limit the search to only *original journal articles* under *document type.* This time the search finds only 25 articles. That seems like a reasonable number. Now you can click on each one and read the abstract of the article. The abstract is a short but comprehensive summary of the article, and based on your perusal of the abstracts, you can decide which articles you want to read in their entirety. If you had done the search the way we have described, you should find that the second article is titled "Light Therapy for Seasonal Affective Disorder With Blue 'Narrow-Band' Light-Emitting Diodes (LEDS)." This might be one you choose to read. If your library has access to the full-text electronic version of the paper, you will be able to download it immediately. If your library does not have access, then you will have to order a copy, called a reprint. You can also write to the principal investigator and request a reprint. This may take a while, so you should begin your **literature search** early. If you leave reprint requests until the last minute, you may not be able to get the articles that are most relevant to your research topic.

Here is another example. Suppose we are interested in how the color of a room might influence mood. A search using the terms *mood* and *room color* produces nothing. Perhaps *room* is too restrictive. A search with *mood* and *color* gives 237 articles. Now let's refine (limit) the search to just peer-reviewed articles in English. Wow, still 167 articles. PsycINFO has a bar that reads "Narrow results by subject:" and in the list is "color." What happens if we click that? We get 31 articles that deal with color and mood—that's perfect! Apparently, this search requires that color be a keyword and not just a word that appears in the title or abstract. The fifth article in the list looks interesting; it is titled "Effects of Colour of Light on Nonvisual Psychological Processes" by Igor Knez at the University of Gävle, Sweden. Again, your library may or may not have access to the full text of the article. Be sure to consult with your reference librarians. These people are well educated and typically underutilized by students. If you have a question, ask your librarian.

THE RESEARCH ARTICLE

Now that you have a research article in hand, let's examine each section of the paper separately. When reading the literature, you need to understand that each section has a purpose and contains specific types of information. Once you know how research articles are written, you will know which section will contain the information you need. The following discussion is presented to help you *read* the literature. You will find information on *writing* a research article in Chapter 14 ("Communicating in Psychology").

The Abstract

The abstract is a comprehensive summary of the article and describes what was done, to whom, and what was found. Online bibliographic search engines such as PsycINFO provide the title and the abstract. If the title seems relevant, you can read the abstract. It should provide you with enough information to decide whether you want to read the entire article.

The Introduction

The introduction directly follows the abstract. Here the author(s) provides background on the research problem. You will find a description of the relevant research (this is the researcher's literature search) and how it logically leads to the research being reported in the article. Usually, near the end of the introduction, you will find a description of the research hypothesis of the author. Again, for information on *writing* an introduction, see Chapter 14.

Knez (2001) has an introduction with a typical layout. He begins with a general statement about the state of knowledge in the research area. He then presents a discussion of the previous research organized by variables. He describes the various independent variables that have been identified as important and discusses various confounding variables and how these should be controlled. He also discusses a theoretical framework that is based largely on his own research. And finally, he defines the purpose of the present research, how it will solve some of the problems identified in the literature review, and why it is important.

Before we continue to a discussion of the method section, it is probably a good idea to review the types of variables you will read about in the introduction of many research articles.

Independent Variable

You will recall that an **independent variable** (IV) is the variable in an experiment that is manipulated by the researcher. The researcher chooses levels of the IV that he or she thinks will have effects on some response measure. The researcher then assigns participants to each level of the IV (or all levels in the case of repeated-measures designs) and compares differences in response measures to see if the IV had an effect. You will recall that some variables are not true IVs. The values of these participant variables may be inherent in the participants. Examples include gender, age, disability type, and so on. Or participants might have self-selected the value of the variable. For example, differences in school success between children attending private and public schools is a comparison on a participant variable where participants have, in effect, assigned themselves to the values of the variable. In either case, studies of group differences on participant variables are not true experiments; rather they are *quasi-experiments*. Remember that a true independent variable is under the direct control of the researcher. The researcher chooses the values of the variable and assigns participants to each and then looks to see if that manipulation has any effect on their responses, the dependent variable. In an experiment, the independent variable can be thought of as the *cause* in a cause-effect relationship.

FYI

Statistical packages such as SPSS do not distinguish between true independent variables and participant (or subject) variables. They refer to both as independent variables.

Dependent Variable

The **dependent variable** (DV) in psychological research is some response measure that we think will be influenced by our independent variable. Reading comprehension might be a dependent variable, and we might measure number correct on a comprehension quiz as our operational definition of reading comprehension. Or we might measure depression by having participants rate how they feel on a scale. In an experiment, the dependent variable can be thought of as the *effect* in a cause-effect relationship.

When we are trying to determine patterns of responding by measuring variables, we are always concerned with the natural variability of participants' responses. Of course, our goal in research is to explain some of this variability. For example, if your research question is "Do students who read a lot understand better what they read?" then you are in a sense trying to account for the variability in student reading comprehension by determining how much they read. This is the variability that you are interested in explaining with your relationship. However, some variability is outside our primary interest. For example, if we are trying to determine if classroom technology improves learning, we are not interested in variables such as temperature of the classroom, time of day of the class, or ability of the instructor. Rather, we want to control or account for these variables so that we can better assess the effect of our primary variable (i.e., technology).

If other variables that might have affected the DV have been controlled in some way, then the researcher can conclude that differences in the DV are a result of, or caused by, the IV manipulation. This is the core of the experimental design, and to the degree that other variables have been controlled, we can be more confident in making causal inferences with these designs than we can from nonexperimental research. We discuss the various ways to control these other variables in Chapter 4.

Conceptual Exercise 2A

1. Identify the independent and dependent variables for each of the following:

   a. Reaction time decreased when more practice trials were given.

   b. Amount of exercise had an effect on depression ratings.

Moderating Variables

Many cold remedies display warnings that they should never be taken with alcohol. It is often the case that these drugs can cause drowsiness, but this cause-and-effect relationship is increased with the consumption of alcohol. In this example, alcohol is acting as a moderating variable by amplifying the drowsiness effect of the drug. **Moderating variables** act to influence the relationship between the independent and dependent variables. A moderating variable can increase, decrease, or even reverse the relationship between the independent and dependent variables. If, as discussed above, the independent variable is the cause in the cause-and-effect relationship, and the dependent variable is the effect in the cause-and-effect relationship, then the moderating variable is a third influence that must be taken into account to clearly describe the cause-and-effect relationship. For example, in his famous studies on obedience, Milgram (1974) found that the actions of a confederate-companion (someone posing as a participant who is actually part of the study) could produce a strong moderating effect. When the companion-participant agreed to shock the learner, 93% of the true participants continued administering shocks, but when the confederate disobeyed the order, only 10% of the true participants continued.

In the Knez (2001) study of the effect of light on mood, gender was identified as a moderating variable. Relative to cool light, warm lighting can produce a more positive emotional response in women than it does in men. Therefore, the influence that lighting has on mood is moderated by the gender of the participant (for more discussion of moderating variables, see the discussion of factorial designs in Chapter 7).

Mediating Variables

Sometimes the relationship between cause and effect is directly linked—your baseball strikes a window and it breaks. However, there are many instances when this relationship is anything but direct—you look at a bright light and your pupil constricts. Certainly, this is a cause-and-effect relationship, but there are many intervening steps. Suppose you just had an eye examination and the doctor used eyedrops to dilate your pupils. What will this do to the cause-and-effect relationship? You leave the office and go into the bright sunlight and . . . nothing, no pupil constriction. Clearly, the eyedrops are acting on some **mediating variable** between the light and the pupil constriction.

Identifying mediating variables may be centrally important to your research or entirely trivial depending on how the research fits into the particular theory. For much behavioral research, the mediating variables may be unimportant. Instead, the focus is on identifying and describing the environmental cues (cause) that elicit behavior (effect). Contrast this position with cognitive research, where much of the focus is on identifying mediating variables.

In the Knez (2001) study, the identification of a mediating variable was an important point. He was trying to show that the characteristics of light do not directly influence cognitive performance but, rather, that the light influences the participant's mood, and that change in mood, in turn, affects the participant's performance.

The introduction gives us a good understanding of the important variables in the study. In the method section, we will find detailed information about how the study was conducted.

The Method Section

Although the variables of the research are defined and discussed in the introduction, it is in the method section where you will read the details of exactly how these variables are measured, manipulated, or controlled. Indeed, if there is a theme to the method section, it would be details, details, details. You should find enough (dare we say it again) details in the method section to replicate the study on your own. That is, you should have all the necessary information to repeat the study as it was done by the authors, with different participants, of course.

The method section is typically divided into a number of subsections usually separated with subheads (for more detail on writing a method section, see Chapter 14). The first section, typically called **Participants,** if human, and **Subjects,** if animal, will provide information about who or what participated in the research. You will read how the participants were recruited into the study or how the animals were obtained. Demographic information will be included such as age, gender, race, and education level. If nonhuman subjects were used, details of care and housing will be described. Of course, you will also read how many participants were included.

You may find a subsection called **Materials** and/or **Apparatus**. Here you will find manufacturers and model numbers of equipment and apparatus, details of tests and measures and the conditions of testing, and often a description of any stimulus materials used. Somewhere in the method section, you will read a description of the research design and the statistical tests. It does not necessarily make for good reading, but the purpose is to provide fine detail, not to entertain. It is in the method section where we find out exactly what was done. The procedure is described in a subsection called, well, **Procedure.** This is often written as a chronological sequence of what happened to the participants. Again, as with all the subsections of the method, it is written in painstaking detail.

In our example article, Knez (2001) tells us he had 54 women and 54 men, all 18 years old, and all in high school. The basic design is described as a factorial between-subjects (his word, not ours) design (see Chapter 7) with three different lights and two genders. He also describes the testing conditions, details of the lighting (the independent variable), and the various dependent measures. He describes the procedure of the experiment, providing the time of day of testing, the information participants were given, and order in which the tests were administered. At the end of the section, we have enough information that we could probably replicate the study exactly as he had done.

After reading the introduction and the method section, we now know quite a bit about the research area, the current researcher's study, and how he or she carried it out. It is time to find out what happened.

The Results

The results section is the part of the paper that is the most exciting. This is where we learn whether or not the data support the research hypothesis. Typically, the section begins with a general statement addressing that very point (i.e., did the data support or fail to support the researcher's hypothesis?). As with the other sections, more detail on writing an article is presented in Chapter 14.

The results section is the most important section of a research paper. Unfortunately, students can become overwhelmed by all the statistics. Even students who have done very well in their statistics courses can find the results sections of most research papers impossible to understand. The problem is that basic statistics courses cover *basic statistics* such as measures of **central tendency** (the mean, median, and mode) and measures of **variability** (the range, variance, and standard deviation). Of course, these statistics will appear in the results section and are widely used for describing and summarizing the data.

The problem is often in the **tests of significance.** Your basic statistics course probably covered the *z* test, *t* test, analysis of variance (ANOVA), and the associated *F* test. You may have also learned about **correlation** and simple regression and perhaps chi-square tests. These are good statistics and are used sometimes in research, but unfortunately, when you go to read the literature, you will face statistical tests that you may have never heard of. We do not intend to teach advanced statistics here, but we do want to provide you with a conceptual understanding of these statistics so that when you read the literature, you will have at least a basic understanding of these procedures. So as briefly as we can, we are going to review statistics. No, you do not need a calculator; this review is at a conceptual level only, but in Chapter 13, we provide more of the nitty-gritty of basic statistics that you may need to do a research project of your own.

In research, statistics are used for two purposes. The first is to *summarize* all the data and make it simpler to talk about the outcome of research. These are typically called descriptive statistics. The second purpose is to *test research hypotheses,* and these are called inferential statistics.

Descriptive Statistics

Descriptive statistics include measures of central tendency, variability, and the strength of the relationship between variables. The mean, median, and mode are the most common measures of central tendency. The **mean** (symbolized as M) is the arithmetic average. It is what we report when talking about the class average on a test, for example. The **median** (symbolized as Mdn) is the value that half the observations (or scores) exceeded and half were below. It is the middle score in a distribution of scores arranged from lowest to highest. The median is often reported when a distribution of scores is not bell shaped (i.e., not a normal distribution). The **mode** (symbolized as Mo) is the most frequently occurring score or value in your data. The mode gives us a measure of the typical value in the distribution. For example, if you were making a "one-size-fits-all" pair of eyeglasses, you would want the mode for head size. Each measure of central tendency uses a different approach to describe the average of a group of scores.

The most common statistics used for describing variability in data are the range, variance, and standard deviation. The **range** either is reported as the highest and lowest score or is reduced to a single value that is the distance between these two scores. On an exam, you may ask what was the highest score attained, and perhaps out of morbid curiosity, you may want to know the lowest score as well. The range is an appropriate measure of variability for some types of data, but it is quite crude. For example, there may be one very high score and one very low score, and the range will not indicate that perhaps all the other scores were concentrated very near the mean. Two related measures of variability do provide this information. The **variance** and its square root, the **standard deviation** (symbolized as SD), provide a measure of the average distance scores are from the mean. Particularly in data that are bell shaped or normally distributed, the standard deviation tells us that about 2/3 of the scores fall between one standard deviation above the mean and one standard deviation below the mean. More detail on the calculation and appropriate selection of these statistics is given in Chapter 13 and Chapter 5.

Often you will read research articles that describe the degree that variables are related to one another. The most common measure of association is the **Pearson product-moment correlation** (symbolized as r). This statistic describes how strongly (or weakly) variables are related to one another. For example, if two variables are perfectly correlated, the r value will be 1 or –1. The sign of the number indicates the direction of the relationship. A **positive correlation** tells us that the variables are directly related; as one variable increases, so does the other, and as one variable decreases, so does the other. A **negative correlation** tells us that the variables are inversely related. That is, as one variable increases, the other decreases, and as one variable decreases, the other increases. The magnitude of r tells us how strongly the variables are related. A zero correlation tells us that the variables are not related at all; as the value increases to +1 or decreases to –1, the strength of the relationship increases. A correlation of 1 (either positive or negative) is called a **perfect correlation.** Be aware that perfect correlations never actually occur in the real world. If they do, it usually means that you have inadvertently measured the same variable twice and correlated the data. For example, you would likely get a correlation of 1 if you measured reaction time in seconds and also in minutes. It would be no surprise to find that the values are correlated because they are the same measure only in different scales. Here is another example: Suppose you measured mood with two scales. It is likely that the measures will correlate highly. Again, this only indicates that you have two measures of the same thing.

These descriptive statistics are used to summarize what was observed in the research. But the idea of a lot of research is to generalize the findings beyond just the observations or participants in the study. We ultimately want to say something about behavior in general, not just the behavior that occurred in the study. To make these generalizations, we need inferential statistics. Before leaping into a list of the various inferential statistics you will likely come across in the literature, we would like to review some of the basic concepts of inference.

Inferential Statistics

Inferential statistics are used to generalize the findings of a study to a whole population. An *inference* is a general statement based on limited data. Statistics are used to attach a probability estimate to that statement. For example, a typical weather forecast does not tell you that it will rain tomorrow afternoon. Instead, the report will indicate the probability of rain tomorrow. Indeed, the forecast here for tomorrow is a 60% chance of rain. The problem with making an inference is that we might be wrong. No one can predict the future, but based on good meteorological information, an expert is able to estimate the probability of rain tomorrow. Similarly, in research, we cannot make generalized statements about everyone when we only include a sample of the population in our study. What we do instead is attach a probability estimate to our statements.

When you read the results of research papers, the two most common uses of inferential statistics will be **hypothesis testing** and **confidence interval estimation.**

"Does wearing earplugs improve test performance?"

"Is exercise an effective treatment for depression?"

"Is there a relationship between hours of sleep and ability to concentrate?"

"Are married couples happier than single individuals?"

These are all examples of research hypotheses that could be tested using inferential tests of significance. What about the following?

"Does the general public have confidence in its nation's leader?"

"How many hours of sleep do most adults get?"

"At what age do most people begin dating?"

These are all examples of research with a focus on describing attitudes and/or behavior of a population. This type of research, which is more common in sociology than psychology, uses confidence interval estimation instead of tests of significance.

The vast majority of psychological research involves testing a research hypothesis. So let's first look at the types of tests of significance you will likely see in the literature and then look at confidence intervals.

Common Tests of Significance. Results will be referred to as either statistically significant or not statistically significant. What does this mean? In hypothesis testing research, a straw-person argument is set up where we assume that a null hypothesis is true, and then we use the data to disprove the null and thus support our research hypothesis. **Statistical significance** means that it is unlikely that the null hypothesis is true given the data that were collected. Nowhere in the research article will you see a statement of the null hypothesis, but instead you will see statements about how the research hypothesis was supported or not supported. These statements will look like this:

"With an alpha of .01, those wearing earplugs performed statistically significantly better ($M = 35$, $SD = 1.32$) than those who were not ($M = 27$, $SD = 1.55$), $t(84) = 16.83$, $p = .002$."

"The small difference in happiness between married ($M = 231$, $SD = 9.34$) and single individuals ($M = 240$, $SD = 8.14$) was not statistically significant, $t(234) = 1.23$, $p = .21$."

These statements appear in the results section and describe the means and standard deviations of the groups and then a statistical test of significance (t test in both examples). In both statements, statistical significance is indicated by the italic p. This value is the p value. It is an estimate of the probability that the null hypothesis is true. Because the null hypothesis is the opposite of the research hypothesis, we want this value to be low. The accepted convention is a p value lower than .05 or, better still, lower than .01. The results will support the research hypothesis when the p value is lower than .05 or .01. The results will not support the research hypothesis when the p value is greater than .05. You may see a nonsignificant result reported as *NS* with no p value included.

You will find a refresher on statistical inference, including a discussion of Type I and Type II errors, and statistical power in Chapter 4.

Researchers using inferential techniques draw inferences based on the outcome of a statistical significance test. There are numerous tests of significance, each appropriate to a particular research question and the measures used, as you will recall from your introductory statistics course. It is beyond the scope of our book to describe in detail all or even most of these tests. You might want to refresh your memory by perusing your stats text, which of course you have kept, haven't you? We offer a brief review of some of the most common tests of significance used by researchers in psychology in the section called "Basic Tests of Significance" at the end of the Discussion section.

Going back to the results section of our example paper, we see that the author has divided that section into a number of subsections. The first section, with the heading "Mood," reports the effect of light on mood. It is only one sentence: "No significant results were obtained" (Knez, 2001, p. 204). The results section is typically brief, but the author could have provided the group means and statistical tests that were not statistically significant. The next subsection, titled "Perceived Room Light Evaluation," provides a statistically significant effect. Knez reports a significant (meaning statistically significant) gender difference. He reports Wilk's lambda, which is a statistic used in multivariate ANOVA (MANOVA; when there is more than one DV), and the associated F statistic and p value for the gender difference, $F(7, 96) = 3.21, p = .04$. He also includes a figure showing the mean evaluations by men and women of the four light conditions and separate F statistics and p values for each condition.

In the subsections that follow, Knez (2001) reports the results and statistical tests for the effect of light condition on the various dependent variables. One of the effects he reports as a "weak tendency to a significant main effect" (p. 204) with a p value of .12. We would simply say that it was not statistically significant, *NS*. Indeed, many of his statistical tests produced p values greater than .05. We bring this to your attention as a reminder that even peer-reviewed journal articles need to be read with a critical eye. Don't just accept everything you read. You need to pay attention to the p values and question when alpha levels are not .05 or .01. You also need to examine the numbers carefully to discern the effect size.

What is noticeably missing from the results section of Knez (2001), our example paper, is a calculation of effect size. *Effect size* gives us some indication of the strength of the effect (see Chapter 4 for more detail). Remember, statistical significance tells us that an effect was likely not due to chance and is probably a reliable effect. What statistical significance does not indicate is how large the effect is. If we inspect the numbers in Knez's paper, we can see that the effects were not very large. For example, on the short-term recall task, the best performance was from the participants in the warm lighting conditions. They had a mean score of 6.9 compared to the other groups, with a mean score of about 6.25. A difference of only 0.65 of a word on a recall task seems like a pretty small effect, but then again, one would hardly expect that lighting conditions would have a dramatic effect on performance.

Once you have finished reading the introduction, method, and results sections, you should have a pretty good idea about what was done, to whom, and what was found. In the discussion section, you will read the researcher's interpretation of the research, comments about unexpected findings, and speculations about the importance of the work or its application.

The Discussion

The dissertation adviser of one of the authors of this book told her that he never read the discussion section of research reports. He was not interested in the interpretation of the authors. He interpreted the findings and their importance himself. We consider this good advice for seasoned researchers but not good advice for students. The discussion section of a research paper is where the author describes how the results fit into the literature. This is a discussion of the theories that are supported by the research and the theories that are not. It is also where you will find suggestions from the author as to where the research should go in the future—what questions are left unanswered and what new questions the research raises. Indeed, the discussion section may direct you in your selection of research project. You may wish to contact the author to see if research is already being conducted on the questions posed in the discussion. Remember that it is important to be a critical consumer of research. Do not simply accept what is said in the discussion. Ask yourself if the results really do support the author's conclusions. Are there other possible interpretations?

In the discussion section of our example paper, Knez (2001) relates the findings to his previous work and the research of others. He discusses the lack of effect of light on mood and questions the mood measure that was used. We think that another possibility, which he does not explore, is that lighting *may not have* an influence on mood. He also describes the effect of light on cognitive performance as being something new to the literature. We could speculate that this small effect might not be a reliable finding. Certainly, the weak *p* values reported in the results section would indicate either that the study should be replicated or that the results were a fluke. Again, as we said before, you need to be critical when reading the literature.

Basic Tests of Significance

t **Test.** The simplest experiment involves two groups, an **experimental** and a **control group.** The researchers treat the groups differently (the IV) and measure their performance (the DV). The question then is, "Did the treatment work?" Are the groups significantly different after receiving the treatment? If the research involves comparing means from two groups, the *t* **test** may be the appropriate test of significance. Be aware that the *t* test can also be used in nonexperimental studies. For example, a researcher who compares the mean performance of women with that of men might use a *t* test.

Typically, a researcher will report the group means, whether the difference was statistically significant, and the *t* test results. In essence, the *t* test is an evaluation of the difference between two means relative to the variability in the data. Simply reporting the group means is not enough because a large difference between two means might not be statistically significant when examined relative to the large variability of the scores of each group. Alternatively, a small difference between two means may be statistically significant if there is very little variation in scores within each group. The *t* test is a good test when you want to compare two groups, but what if you have more than two groups?

F **Test.** The *F* **test** of significance is used to compare means of more than two groups. There are numerous experimental (and quasi-experimental) designs, known as ANOVAs, that are analyzed with the *F* test. Indeed, when we were graduate students, we took entire courses in ANOVA. In general, the *F* test, like the *t* test, compares between-group variability with within-group variability.

As with the *t* test, the researcher will report the group means and whether the differences were statistically significant. From a significant *F* test, the researcher knows that at least two means were significantly different. To specify which groups were different from which others, the researcher must follow the *F* test with post hoc (after-the-fact) comparisons. For example, if there were three groups and the *F* test was statistically significant, a post hoc test might find that all three group means were statistically significantly different or perhaps that only one mean differed from the other two. There are a large number of post hoc tests (e.g., Scheffé, Tukey, LSD, Bonferroni) that have slightly different applications. What is common to all these tests is that each produces a *p* value that is used to indicate which means differ from which.

As indicated above, many designs are analyzed with an *F* test, and they have names that indicate the number of independent variables. You will find a one-way ANOVA used when there is one independent variable, a two-way ANOVA when there are two independent variables, and a three-way ANOVA (you guessed it) when there are three. A null hypothesis is tested for each independent variable by calculating an *F* statistic. The advantage of the two- and three-way ANOVAs is that an interaction effect can also be tested. An **interaction** occurs when different combinations of the levels of the independent variables have different effects on the dependent variable. For example, if we wanted to investigate the effect of environmental noise (silent vs. noisy) on reading comprehension and the effect of different-colored paper (white, yellow, pink) on reading comprehension, we could use a two-way ANOVA to evaluate the effect of each independent variable and also whether the color of paper might interact with the noise to influence reading comprehension. It may be that noise produces a reduction in reading comprehension for white paper but not for yellow or pink paper. The interaction effect is important because it indicates that a variable is acting as a moderating variable. In this example, the effect of environmental noise on reading comprehension is moderated by the color of paper.

There is another type of ANOVA that is used to control for a possible confounding variable. This procedure also uses the *F* statistic and is called analysis of covariance, or ANCOVA. Using our paper color example, suppose we want to test whether the color of paper will influence reading comprehension, but our participants vary considerably in age. This could pose a serious confound because reading comprehension changes with age. If we measured age, we can use ANCOVA to remove variability in reading comprehension that is due to age and then test the effect of color. The procedure removes the variance due to age from the dependent variable before the *F* is calculated for the effect of color. Consequently, we are testing the effect of color after we have taken into account the effect of age.

The statistics described above are useful for comparing group means, but you may come across research where the variables are categories and the data are summarized by counting the frequency of things. When there are frequency counts instead of scores, you may see a chi-square test.

Chi-Square Test. Do people prefer Coke or Pepsi? Perhaps we have offered both drinks and asked people to declare a preference. We count the number of people preferring each drink. These data are not measures, and means cannot be calculated. If people's preference did not differ between the two drinks, we would expect about the same number of people to pick each, and we could use a **chi-square test**, called the goodness-of-fit test, to test our hypothesis. In chi-square, our null hypothesis is that our observed frequencies will not be different from those we would expect by chance.

In the literature, you will likely see the data summarized by reporting the frequencies of each category either as total counts or perhaps as percentages of the total. Then you may read a statement that the frequencies in the groups are statistically significant followed by a report of the chi-square statistic and *p* value.

Chi-square is called a *nonparametric* or *distribution-free* test because the test does not make the assumption that the population is distributed normally. Indeed, hypotheses about the *shape* of the population distribution are exactly what we are testing with chi-square.

There are two common chi-square tests: the **goodness-of-fit test** and the **test for independence**. The goodness-of-fit test is used when there are categorical data on one variable as we had in the soft drink preference example. Perhaps a researcher is interested in the relationship between two **categorical variables**. In this case, you might see the chi-square test for independence. Imagine our researcher has asked cola tasters to indicate their choice of cola and has also categorized them by age. The research hypothesis might be that preference for cola depends on age. The researcher might think that younger people prefer Pepsi, for example, and older people prefer Coke. Or perhaps older people have no preference. The chi-square statistic is the same for this test as for the goodness-of-fit test. The difference is in the hypothesis. The null is that the two variables are independent (i.e., there is no relationship between them). In a research article, you will likely see a table of frequencies (or percentages), a statement as to whether a relationship was found between the variables, and the chi-square statistic and *p* value.

Conceptual Exercise 2B

For each of the following, decide if a *t* test, an *F* test, or a chi-square test might be appropriate:

1. A new teacher decides to put some of the principles he learned in school to the test. He randomly selects half of his class and consistently praises each student for being on task for a minimum period of time. With the other half of the class, he periodically gives praise for on-task behavior. He wants to know if periodic praise produces more on-task behavior than consistent praise.

2. Psychiatric walk-in clients are randomly assigned to five therapists for short-term counseling. One therapist specializes in psychoanalytic techniques, one in client-centered techniques, one in behavioral techniques, and one in cognitive techniques. The fifth therapist is eclectic, using techniques from each of the above therapies. All clients are rated on various scales designed to measure improvement. Mean improvement ratings of the clients for each therapist are compared.

3. A statistics professor wants to know if generally there are more or less equal numbers of psychology, sociology, and business students. She keeps a tally.

Other Nonparametric Tests. In addition to chi-square, there are numerous other nonparametric tests that you will see in the literature. We have not tried to present a complete list here, but instead we have included the more common tests.

A nonparametric alternative to a *t* test for independent groups is the **Mann-Whitney *U* test**, which detects differences in central tendency and differences in the entire distributions of rank-ordered data. The **Wilcoxon signed-ranks test** is an alternative to a t test for dependent groups for rank-order data on the same or matched participants.

A nonparametric alternative to the one-way ANOVA is the **Kruskal-Wallis H test**, used when the data are rank orders of three or more independent groups. When those groups are dependent (i.e., repeated measures), a nonparametric test is the Friedman test.

Pearson's r Test. If you earned a lot of money, would you be happy? Is there a relationship between income and happiness? If a researcher were interested in investigating a linear relationship between two continuous variables, he or she would use the Pearson product-moment test to calculate the correlation, r. If you are getting a sense of déjà vu, it is probably because we talked about r as a descriptive statistic, but here we are talking about it as an inferential statistic. The important distinction is that the r reported as an inferential statistic will have an associated p value. For example, in a research article, you will read that a positive relationship was found between a measure of need for achievement and years of education and that the relationship was statistically significant. If the relationship was statistically significant, then you will also see a p value reported.

Regression. Regression is related to correlation, but in regression, we are interested in using a **predictor variable** to predict a **criterion variable**. Continuing with the example of need for achievement and education, perhaps the researcher was also interested in predicting need for achievement from education level. If the correlation between the two variables is statistically significant, then it is a simple matter of fitting a line through the data and using the equation for the line to predict need for achievement from education level. We say simple matter because the calculations are all done by computer, but certainly the equation for a line is simple.

$$Y = mX + b,$$

(equation for a straight line)

where Y is the criterion variable, X is the predictor variable, m is the slope of the line, and b is the value of Y where the line intercepts the Y-axis. Be sure to keep in mind as you read the research that the accuracy of the predicted values will be as good as the correlation is. That is, the closer the correlation is to $+1$ (or -1), the better the predictions will be.

Important note to students:

If you're reading this material and starting to get anxious, relax! Our intention here is to discuss these inferential statistics at a conceptual level. As we indicated earlier, when you begin reading the literature, it is unlikely that you will see research using t tests or simple ANOVAs. What you will see are complex statistics that may be completely new to you. Our intention here is to give you enough information to understand what is being described in the literature.

Multiple Regression. If predicting someone's performance using one predictor variable is a good idea, then using more than one predictor variable is a better idea. Entire textbooks are devoted to **multiple regression** techniques, but the basic idea is to use more than one predictor variable, X, to predict one criterion variable, Y. As with simple regression, multiple regression requires the fitting of a line through your data, but first, all the predictor variables are combined, and then the linear combination of Xs is correlated with Y. An r value reflects how well the linear combination of Xs predicts Y. Some predictor variables are likely to be better predictors of Y than others, and the analysis produces weights that indicate how well each predictor variable predicts. These values can be used in a regression equation to predict Y. Simply multiply the values of the predictor variables by their respective weights and you have your predicted value.

$$Y(\text{predicted}) = B1(X1) + B2(X2) + B3(X3) + \text{etc.} + \text{Constant.}$$

In addition to the weights used to predict criterion values, multiple regression analysis also provides standardized weights called **beta** (β) **weights**. These values tell us something about each individual predictor in the regression analysis. They can be interpreted much like an r value, with the sign indicating the relationship between the predictor variable and the criterion and the magnitude indicating the relative importance of the variable in predicting the criterion. Thus, in a multiple regression analysis, we can examine the relative contribution of each predictor variable in the overall analysis.

As you just learned, multiple regression is used to determine the influence of several predictor variables on a single criterion variable. Let's look briefly at two useful concepts in multiple regression: partial and semipartial (also called part) correlation.

Partial Correlation. Sometimes we would like to measure the relationship between two variables when a third has an influence on them both. We can partial out the effects of that third variable by computing a **partial correlation**. Suppose there is a correlation between age and income. It seems reasonable that older people might make more money than younger people. Is there another variable that you think might be related to age and income? How about years of education? Older people are more likely to be better educated, having had more years to go to school, and it seems likely that better educated people earn more. So, what is the true relationship between age and income if the variable, years of education, is taken out of the equation? One solution would be to group people by years of education and then conduct a number of separate correlations between age and income for each education group. Partial correlation, however, provides a better solution by telling us what the true relationship is between age and income when years of education has been partialled out.

Semipartial Correlation. As we just discussed, in partial correlation, we remove the relationship of one variable from the other variables and then calculate the correlation. But what if we want to remove the influence of a variable from *only one* of the other variables? This is called a **semipartial correlation**. For example, at our school, we accept senior students into our applied psychology program based on their grades in the first and second years. We have found a strong positive correlation between previous grades and performance in our program. Suppose we could also administer an entrance exam to use as another predictor, but the exam was expensive. We can use semipartial correlation to determine how much the entrance test will increase our predictive power over and above using previous grades.

How do we do this? Well, we correlate entrance test scores and performance in the program after first removing the influence of previous grades on program performance.

This correlation value then will tell us what relationship remains between entrance test and program performance when the correlation with previous grades has been partialled out of program performance but not entrance test scores. In our example, we could decide, based on this correlation, whether an expensive entrance test helped our predictive ability enough for us to go ahead and use it.

Logistic Regression. Suppose you were interested in predicting whether a young offender would reoffend. You measure a number of possible predictor variables, such as degree of social support, integration in the community, job history, and so on, and then follow your participants for 5 years and measure if they reoffend. The predictor variables may be continuous, but the criterion variable is discrete; they reoffend or they don't. When we have a discrete criterion variable, we use **logistic regression**. Just as we used a combination of the predictor variables to predict the criterion variable in multiple regression, we do the same thing in logistic regression. The difference is that instead of predicting a value for the criterion variable, we predict the likelihood of the occurrence of the criterion variable. We express this as an *odds ratio*—that is, the odds of reoffense divided by the odds of not reoffending. If the probability of reoffending is .75 (or 75% chance of reoffending), then the probability of not reoffending is .25 (1 – .75). The odds of reoffending is .75/.25 or 3 to 1, and the odds of not reoffending is .25/.75 or .33. We calculate the odds ratio of reoffending versus not reoffending as .75/.33 or 2.25. In other words, the odds of reoffending is two and quarter times higher than not reoffending.

Factor Analysis. Factor analysis is a correlational technique we use to find simpler patterns of relationships among many variables. Factor analysis can tell us if a large number of variables can be explained by a much smaller number of uncorrelated constructs or factors.

About a hundred years ago, Charles Spearman (1904) thought that measures of mental ability such as mathematical skill, artistic talent, reasoning, language ability, and so on could all be explained by one underlying variable or factor, which he called *g* for general intelligence. He thought that general intelligence was the single common factor to all the various tests of mental ability. Although other theorists disagree with his notion of *g,* his idea demonstrates what factor analysis is all about.

In factor analysis, the researcher is looking for underlying and independent factors that *have not* been directly measured to explain a lot of variables that *have* been measured. The procedure involves identifying the variables that are interrelated. Once the factors have been identified, it is up to the researcher to decide what construct this group of variables is measuring. These underlying factors are hypothetical, that is, inferred by the researcher. The researcher attempts to find the smallest number of factors that can adequately explain the observed variables and to determine the fundamental nature of those factors.

When you read a research report where factor analysis has been used, you will probably see a complicated-looking matrix called a correlation matrix. Don't be discouraged.

Keep in mind that although the mathematics are complex and beyond the scope of this book, the concept is reasonably simple. Can an underlying variable such as general intelligence explain a whole lot of variation in measures of mental abilities?

Cluster Analysis. Cluster analysis includes a range of algorithms and methods used to group similar objects into categories, or clusters. The members of each cluster are thus more similar to each other than they are to members of other clusters. Unlike factor analysis, where the goal is to group similar variables together, in cluster analysis, the idea is to group similar members. Organizing data into meaningful structures or *taxonomies* is a task many researchers face. Cluster analysis is a method that can discover structure in data, but it does not in and of itself have any explanatory function. In other words, the analysis can find structure but does not explain it.

Imagine a hospital where patients are assigned to wards based on similar symptoms or perhaps similar treatments. Each ward could be considered a cluster. A cluster analysis might discover the similarities among the patients in each ward, and the researcher then has the job of determining why the cluster or ward is similar (i.e., symptoms, treatment, age, etc.).

Cluster analysis is often used when researchers have no a priori hypotheses and are in the beginning phase of their research. As such, statistical significance testing often has no role in such analyses.

Structural Equation Modeling. Structural equation modeling is a complex endeavor that can involve various techniques, including factor analysis, regression models, path analysis, and so on. We will just be able to give you an idea of the purpose of structural equation modeling here.

We hope you will remember what happens when we transform a set of numbers by adding a constant to each or multiplying each by a constant. Let's say we multiply all the numbers in a list by a constant c. The mean of that set of transformed numbers will be equal to the old mean times c, the standard deviation of the new set of numbers will equal the old standard deviation times the absolute value (i.e., ignore the sign) of c, and the variance will equal the old variance times c squared. Simple, right?

What is our point, you might be wondering? Well, bear with us. If we suspected that two sets of numbers were related, we could compare the variances of the two sets of numbers, for example, to confirm our suspicions. If one set was related to the other set by the equation $Y = 2X$, then the variance of Y must be 4 times the variance of X. So we could confirm our hypothesis about the relationship between the two sets of numbers by comparing their variances rather than the numbers themselves. We hope you are not too confused by this somewhat odd way of doing things, but we think it might help you understand structural equation modeling. Two sets of numbers could be related in much more mathematically complex ways than by $Y = 2X$, but we hope you are getting the idea. You can determine if variables are related by looking at their variances and covariances.

Structural modeling is a way of determining whether a set of variances and covariances fits a specific structural model. In essence, the researcher hypothesizes that the variables are related in a particular way, often with something called a *path diagram* that shows the interrelationships. Then the researcher figures out what this model predicts about the values of the variances and covariances of the variables. This is the really complex part of the process, and we just can't go there! Then the researcher examines the variances and covariances of the variables to see if they fit the predictions of the model.

As we said earlier, this is a complex procedure well beyond the scope of our book, but we hope our brief discussion gives you some idea of the purpose of structural equation modeling.

Discriminant Function Analysis. As we mentioned earlier, at our school, we offer an applied psychology degree program. One of our objectives is to prepare students for graduate work in applied areas. Imagine that we classified our graduates over the past 10 years into two groups: students who were accepted into graduate school and students who were not. We could use **discriminant function analysis** to predict acceptance into graduate school using grade point average (GPA) and workshop attendance, for example. Our analysis might help us determine how GPA and workshop attendance individually predict acceptance into graduate school and how a combination of both predicts acceptance.

This is the idea behind discriminant function analysis. Of course, we might have many more variables, and the analysis allows us to determine the predictive ability of each variable alone and in combination with other variables. If discriminant function analysis sounds like logistic regression, it is because they are related. They have similar applications, but discriminant function analysis is calculated as ANOVA with more than one dependent variable (MANOVA). The various dependent variables are used to predict group membership.

This analysis, like the others discussed in this section, is much more complex than this, but again we hope our brief discussion gives you an inkling about the use of these techniques so that when you read the literature, you will have some understanding about the research outcomes.

The statistical procedures we have been discussing in the last sections all involve an a priori hypothesos about the nature of the population. Hypothesis testing is used a lot in psychology. Some other disciplines tend to prefer post hoc procedures, and you will find confidence interval estimates quite often in the literature you will be reading.

Confidence Intervals

Confidence intervals are used when we are interested in estimating population parameters. We are still making an inference from a sample to a population, and because of that, we are using probability estimates. But instead of reporting a p value indicating the probability that the null is true, we report the probability that our estimate about the population is true. Pollsters describing political candidates often use confidence intervals. For example, you may have read reports that, based on a poll of 1,000 respondents, 83% say they would vote for X if there were an election tomorrow. These statements are typically followed with a statement such as, "These results are accurate to within 3 percentage points 19 times out of 20." What does this mean? It means that, based on a sample of 1,000, the population support for the candidate is probably somewhere between 83% – 3% and 83% + 3% or somewhere between 80% and 86%. Are they absolutely sure? No, they say the estimate should be correct 19 times out of 20 or 95% of the time (19/20 = .95). So, a p value of .05 from hypothesis testing becomes a confidence interval of .95, and similarly, a p value of .01 becomes a confidence interval of .99 (reported as 99 times out of 100). Again, in hypothesis testing, we report a significance test with a *p* value that indicates the probability that the null is true. In confidence intervals, we report an interval within which we estimate the true population parameter to fall.

We hope that this chapter has prepared you, on a conceptual level, to understand the literature you will be reading as you continue in your social science studies. We now turn to a topic that is so important in social science research, we have devoted an entire chapter to it—research ethics.

CHAPTER SUMMARY

Once a general research topic has been selected, a **literature search** is necessary to determine what research has already been conducted in the area. Various databases are available for the psychology literature. One of the most useful is **PsycINFO.** Review articles, books, chapters in books, edited volumes, and chapters in edited volumes are also found in the research databases. Peer-reviewed journals are the best sources of original research. Searching the literature for relevant research will be more successful if appropriate **search terms** are used.

Original research journal articles generally include an **abstract,** an **introduction,** a **method** section, a **results** section, and a **discussion** section. The purpose of the abstract is to summarize the article. There should be enough information in the abstract for the reader to decide if he or she should read the entire research article. In the introduction, there will be a description of the **relevant research** and a description of the specific **research hypotheses** of the author(s). The **independent** and **dependent variables** are often described in the introduction, as well.

The method section is typically divided into subsections such as **Participants** or **Subjects, Materials,** and **Apparatus.** The method section always contains a subsection called **Procedure.** Enough details of the procedure must be included so that researchers elsewhere could replicate the research.

In the results section, the statistical data are presented. Both **descriptive** and **inferential statistics** will be reported. Descriptive measures of **central tendency, variability,** and the strength of the relationship between variables will be reported. Typically, the inferential statistics follow the descriptive statistics. A lot of psychology research involves testing hypotheses. Any **tests of significance** that were used to assess the research hypotheses will be reported in the results section. Basic tests of significance include *t* tests, *F* tests, **chi-square tests**, **correlation** and **regression** tests, and so on. The authors will indicate whether or not the hypotheses they put forth in the introduction were supported by the statistical analyses.

More complex analyses that are common in the research literature include **multiple regression, partial correlation, semipartial correlation, logistic regression, factor analysis, cluster analysis, structural equation modeling,** and **discriminant function analysis.**

Although hypothesis testing is more common in the psychology research, **confidence interval estimation** is also used. A **confidence interval** is a range of values with a known probability of containing a parameter.

The **discussion section** of a research article contains the authors' interpretation of the statistical findings and suggestions about future research directions.

ANSWERS TO CONCEPTUAL EXERCISES

Conceptual Exercise 2A

1a. IV is amount of practice; DV is reaction time.

1b. IV is amount of exercise; DV is ratings of depression.

Conceptual Exercise 2B

1. Because there are two groups, a *t* test might be appropriate.

2. There are five groups, and so an *F* test might be appropriate.

3. A chi-square goodness-of-fit test would answer this question.

FAQ

Q1: What's a dependent variable dependent on?

A1: We hope it is dependent on our manipulation (the independent variable).

Q2: I have taken an intro stats course and I can't make heads or tails out of the research I am reading.

A2: We understand. The statistics used by most researchers today go well beyond what you learned in your intro stats course. You will need a graduate-level course under your belt to understand a lot of the statistics you will read about, but we hope you will be able to understand on a conceptual level a lot of what you read.

Q3: I just read a research article and they talked about a bunch of correlation stuff and validity and reliability. I have no clue.

A3: Go to Chapter 5 and Chapter 4.

Q4: I just read a paper that talked about stratified sampling. ?????

A4: Go to Chapter 6.

Q5: My prof tells me to use APA style in my report, but the articles I have read don't look anything like the APA manual.

A5: Yes, each specific journal uses its own style. Go to Chapter 14.

CHAPTER EXERCISES

1. Identify the IV and DV for each of the following. Indicate any participant variables being examined.
    a. Does the use of imagery enhance athletic performance?
    b. Are teens more concerned about their bodies than older adults?

    c. Does repetition in advertising improve sales?

    d. Does straight alley training improve the speed of rats in a maze?

    e. Is there a difference in leadership style between men and women?

2. Why are peer-reviewed journals preferable? What does the term *blind review* mean?

3. List two things found in the introduction of a research article.

4. List and describe what is found in typical subsections of the method section of a research article.

5. List two kinds of statistics always found in the results section of a research article.

6. What is the purpose of the discussion section of a research article?

7. Describe the difference between a mediating and a moderating variable.

8. What is the general purpose of a significance test?

9. What is the general purpose of confidence interval estimation?

CHAPTER PROJECTS

1. Locate three research articles from peer-reviewed journals. Briefly summarize the article and describe the IV (or participant/subject variables), DV, control procedures employed (and why they were needed), and the descriptive statistics used. Discuss other ways that the variables could have been operationalized.

2. With a search term of your choice, find three empirical research articles. Describe the methods the researchers used to increase the power of their analysis. Can you think of other ways to increase power in each study?

REFERENCES

Knez, I. (2001). Effects of colour of light on nonvisual psychological processes. *Journal of Environmental Psychology, 21*(2), 201–208.

Milgram, S. (1974). *Obedience to authority: An experimental view.* New York: Harper & Row.

Spearman, C. (1904). General intelligence objectively determined and measured. *American Journal of Psychology, 15,* 201–293.

Visit the study site at www.sagepub.com/evansmprstudy for practice quizzes and other study resources.

CHAPTER 3

Research in Psychology

An Ethical Enterprise

OBJECTIVES

After reading this chapter, students should be able to

- Describe the five general principles that guide psychologists
- Describe the ethical standards of the APA, particularly as they apply to researchers, including confidentiality, informed consent, reduction of harm, privacy, deception, and debriefing
- Describe the standards regarding the use of animals in research
- Define and identify examples of plagiarism
- Identify ethical problems in a research study

We encourage our students to design research projects that interest them. And every year, a group of students propose to do research that has something to do with drinking. They may not be clear on the details of their study, but they are certainly keen to combine their research project with a Friday night out. One of these proposed studies was to determine whether people's judgment of their ability to drive would change as they consumed more alcohol. This project seemed very interesting because one of the problems with drinking and driving is that alcohol affects judgment. Consequently, after you've had too many drinks, you are in no shape to make an accurate assessment of your driving ability. But what are the ethical considerations of this research? What if one of the participants was killed in a car crash on the way home from the bar? Who is responsible for the welfare of the participants? Does it matter who paid for the drinks? What if the drinkers sign a consent form releasing the driver, the bar owner, and even the drink purchasers from responsibility? The answers to these kinds of questions lie in the ethical guidelines that govern researchers.

Because ethical decisions are rarely black-and-white, we need to carefully consider all the possible ethical problems that might arise from our research. Indeed, this is why all universities and colleges that receive government research grants are required to have an **Institutional Review Board** (IRB) or Ethics Review Board (ERB). An IRB consists of a group of people from various backgrounds whose mandate is to apply guidelines to assess the ethics of research proposals.

Be sure to check the requirements of your institution as you plan your research so you do not run into delays obtaining approval. Before you send a research proposal to the members of the IRB, ask which guidelines they suggest you follow in designing your study. Most research disciplines have a code of ethics. Examples of U.S. ethics codes include the American Sociological Association's (ASA's) Code of Ethics, the American Anthropological Association's (AAA's) Code of Ethics, the United States Department of Health and Human Services Office for Human Research Protections, and the Tri-Council Policy Statement: Ethical Conduct for Research Involving Humans. Codes of ethics have been set out by groups in many countries, including the British Psychological Society and the Australian Psychological Society.

In psychology in the United States and Canada, the most widely used guidelines are those of the **American Psychological Association** (APA). After 5 years of discussion, the APA's Council of Representatives published its latest revision of *Ethical Principles of Psychologists and Code of Conduct* (hereinafter referred to as the Code). Published in the December 2002 issue of the *American Psychologist,* the new code became effective on June 1, 2003. Inquiries concerning the Code should be addressed to the Director, Office of Ethics, American Psychological Association, 750 First Street, NE, Washington, DC 20002–4242. The Ethics Code and information regarding the Code can be found on the APA Web site: http://www.apa.org/ethics/code2002.html.

It has been our experience teaching ethics in research that many students read the chapter and then skip or quickly skim the ethical guidelines of the APA. These guidelines were carefully developed to help researchers design ethical studies and conduct their research in an ethical manner. So instead of placing the guidelines at the end of the chapter, we have integrated the guidelines into our discussion of ethics, focusing on issues of particular relevance to students studying research methods. Students should, however, always consult the complete Code before planning and conducting research.

GENERAL PRINCIPLES

General ethical principles are suggested guidelines, not standards or obligations. These are meant to guide psychologists in their research and practice. We will briefly describe some of the general principles provided by the APA.*

---

*Material from the APA Ethics Code is copyright © 2002 by the American Psychological Association. Reprinted with permission. The official citation that should be used in referencing this material is "Ethical Principles of Psychologists and Code of Conduct" (from *American Psychologist*, 2002, *57,* 1060–1073).

Principle A: Beneficence and Nonmaleficence

Psychologists strive to benefit those with whom they work and take care to do no harm. In their professional actions, psychologists seek to safeguard the welfare and rights of those with whom they interact professionally and other affected persons, and the welfare of animal subjects of research. (Code, 2002)

The first principle, and indeed an important principle of most modern ethics codes, arises in part from the unconscionable treatment of humans in research carried out by the Nazis in World War II and made public in the Nuremberg Trials. **Beneficence** means maximizing benefits; **nonmaleficence** means minimizing harm. This principle then directs researchers to design their studies to **minimize harm** and **maximize benefit.** Try to design your study so that your participants are better off after the study than when they began. For example, if you are interested in the effect of mood on mathematics performance, manipulate mood in a positive direction rather than in a negative one. Why not have your participants leave your study in a better mood than when they arrived?

Principle B: Fidelity and Responsibility

Psychologists establish relationships of trust with those with whom they work. They are aware of their professional and scientific responsibilities to society and to the specific communities in which they work. Psychologists uphold professional standards of conduct, clarify their professional roles and obligations, accept appropriate responsibility for their behavior, and seek to manage conflicts of interest that could lead to exploitation or harm. Psychologists consult with, refer to, or cooperate with other professionals and institutions to the extent needed to serve the best interests of those with whom they work. They are concerned about the ethical compliance of their colleagues' scientific and professional conduct. Psychologists strive to contribute a portion of their professional time for little or no compensation or personal advantage. (Code, 2002)

In both research and the practice of psychology, we are given a position of trust. Holding this position of trust means that you have a somber responsibility. Take your position of trust seriously! Typical synonyms for **fidelity** include *loyalty, faithfulness,* and *trustworthiness.* Synonyms for **responsibility** include *dependability* and *accountability.* Fidelity and responsibility in the research context means to be dependable, faithful to, and honest with your colleagues, the community within which you conduct research, and the people you study.

Principle C: Integrity

Psychologists seek to promote accuracy, honesty, and truthfulness in the science, teaching, and practice of psychology. In these activities psychologists do not steal, cheat, or engage in fraud, subterfuge, or intentional misrepresentation of fact. Psychologists strive to keep their promises and to avoid unwise or unclear commitments. In situations in which deception may be ethically justifiable to maximize benefits and minimize harm, psychologists have a serious obligation to consider the need for, the possible consequences of, and their responsibility to correct any resulting mistrust or other harmful effects that arise from the use of such techniques. (Code, 2002)

Several years ago, we were employed to do an independent evaluation of a government-run program. Our employer had a vested interest in a positive evaluation. At the first meeting, we made it very clear to all that we would evaluate the program using the best assessment tools we had and would report what we found, whether those findings were positive or not. Only under those conditions could we, as ethical researchers, accept the contract. Typical synonyms for *integrity* include *honor, veracity,* and *truthfulness.* **Integrity in research** means that the researcher must strive to be truthful, accurate, objective, and fair in all parts of the research process.

Principle D: Justice

Psychologists recognize that fairness and justice entitle all persons to access and benefit from the contributions of psychology and to equal quality in the processes, procedures, and services being conducted by psychologists. Psychologists exercise reasonable judgment and take precautions to ensure that their potential biases, the boundaries of their competence, and the limitations of their expertise do not lead to or condone unjust practices. (Code, 2002)

As a researcher, your findings may be used by policy makers to allocate resources. Researchers must be cognizant of their own limitations and biases because these shortcomings may affect how others are treated. Researchers in psychology have a sense of social **justice** and take steps to ensure that their limitations and biases do not hinder or cause others to hinder the rights of all people to be treated fairly and equally.

Conceptual Exercise 3A

John B. Watson, one of the first behaviorists, stated the following: "Give me a dozen healthy infants . . . and my own special world to bring them up in and I'll guarantee to take any one at random and train him to become any type of specialist I might select—doctor, lawyer, artist, merchant-chief, and yes, even beggar-man and thief, regardless of his talents, penchants, tendencies, abilities, vocations and race of his ancestors" (Watson, 1924, p. 82).

How might Watson's biases lead to unjust practices?

Principle E: Respect for People's Rights and Dignity

Psychologists respect the dignity and worth of all people, and the rights of individuals to privacy, confidentiality, and self-determination. Psychologists are aware that special safeguards may be necessary to protect the rights and welfare of persons or communities whose vulnerabilities impair autonomous decision making. Psychologists are aware of and respect cultural, individual, and role differences, including those based on age, gender, gender identity, race, ethnicity, culture, national origin, religion, sexual orientation, disability, language, and socioeconomic status and consider these factors when working with members of such groups. Psychologists try to eliminate the effect on their work of biases based on those factors, and they do not knowingly participate in or condone activities of others based upon such prejudices. (Code, 2002)

Many researchers work with children and other specialized populations where protection of participants from harm is particularly crucial because often they are less able to protect themselves. It is your ethical duty as a researcher to ensure their safety and well-being. The rights and dignity of all research participants must be protected, and researchers must be especially sensitive when they are working with special populations.

Following these general principles, the APA Code lists the ethical standards of the profession. Ethical standards, unlike general principles, are guidelines that, if violated, could result in sanctions by the APA. These are standards to which psychologists governed by the Code must adhere. The following statement describes who is governed by the Code.

Membership in the APA commits members and student affiliates to comply with the standards of the APA Ethics Code and to the rules and procedures used to enforce them. Lack of awareness or misunderstanding of an Ethical Standard is not itself a defense to a charge of unethical conduct. (Code, 2002)

In the following sections, we will discuss the ethical standards that are of particular relevance to students and researchers.

ETHICAL STANDARDS

NOTE: The heading numbers below start at number two because we have chosen to retain the numbering used in the APA Ethics Code.

2. Competence

2.01 Boundaries of Competence

(a) Psychologists provide services, teach, and conduct research with populations and in areas only within the boundaries of their competence, based on their education, training, supervised experience, consultation, study, or professional experience.

(b) Where scientific or professional knowledge in the discipline of psychology establishes that an understanding of factors associated with age, gender, gender identity, race, ethnicity, culture, national origin, religion, sexual orientation, disability, language, or socioeconomic status is essential for effective implementation of their services or research, psychologists have or obtain the training, experience, consultation, or supervision necessary to ensure the competence of their services, or they make appropriate referrals, except as provided in Standard 2.02, Providing Services in Emergencies.

(c) Psychologists planning to provide services, teach, or conduct research involving populations, areas, techniques, or technologies new to them undertake relevant education, training, supervised experience, consultation, or study.

. . . .

(e) In those emerging areas in which generally recognized standards for preparatory training do not yet exist, psychologists nevertheless take reasonable steps to ensure the competence of their work and to protect clients/patients, students, supervisees, research participants, organizational clients, and others from harm. (Code, 2002)

Researchers must be aware of the boundaries of their **competence**. Doing research on a topic that you know nothing about is hazardous to your participants, the discipline, and you, the researcher. Before you begin designing your research, you must familiarize yourself with the area. Read the literature, take a course, and/or consult with individuals doing research in the area. The e-mail address of the principal investigator is almost always included in published papers. These researchers are often delighted to correspond with an interested student.

Although necessary, knowing the research area may not be sufficient preparation for conducting your research. If your topic involves participants from specific groups, you will need training before you begin your research. For example, if you are interested in the issues faced by Arab immigrants following the terrorist attacks in New York, you would first need a good understanding of Arab culture and a general understanding of the challenges faced by all immigrants. Or perhaps you are interested in how bullying affects gay and lesbian students. You first need a good understanding of these people, and their experiences may be unique. A few decades ago, it was believed that research should be culturally blind. There were some problems with this approach, particularly when much of the research was conducted by Western, white men. It has become clear that it is better to equip yourself with knowledge than try to pretend we can ignore culture as an important factor in many areas of psychology.

3. Human Relations

3.01 Unfair Discrimination

In their work-related activities, psychologists do not engage in unfair discrimination based on age, gender, gender identity, race, ethnicity, culture, national origin, religion, sexual orientation, disability, socioeconomic status, or any basis proscribed by law. (Code, 2002)

Typical synonyms for **discrimination** include *bias, favoritism, prejudice, unfairness,* and *inequity.* This standard is referring to treating people differently solely on the basis of some personal characteristic. An example of discrimination would occur if, during your study, you provide extra help to white male participants and not others. On the other hand, it is not necessarily unfair discrimination to select only participants who have certain characteristics. For example, you may limit your study to only African American women.

Often researchers will select particular participants to limit the variability in their study. This can become problematic if whole groups of people are chronically excluded from study. For example, the medical community was criticized for studying heart attack in men to the exclusion of studies of women. Women suffer heart attacks too, and it is discriminatory to not include them in research. Also, as mentioned earlier, it is a mistake to assume that research that is blind to cultural differences will somehow control for real and important cultural differences. At some point, research needs to be extended to include all participants.

3.02 Sexual Harassment

Psychologists do not engage in sexual harassment. Sexual harassment is sexual solicitation, physical advances, or verbal or nonverbal conduct that is sexual in nature, that occurs in connection with the psychologist's activities or roles as a psychologist, and that either (1) is unwelcome, is offensive, or creates a hostile workplace or educational environment, and the psychologist knows or is told this or (2) is sufficiently severe or intense to be abusive to a reasonable person in the context. Sexual harassment can consist of a single intense or severe act or of multiple persistent or pervasive acts. (Code, 2002)

As a researcher, you are in a position of power over the participants in your study. Always guard against abuses of that power. In the movie *Ghostbusters,* there is a scene where Dr. Peter Venkman (Bill Murray), professor of parapsychology, uses his standing as a researcher as an opportunity to seduce young women. Because many young people, and people in general for that matter, perceive scientists in lab coats to be powerful authority figures, they may comply with inappropriate requests—a coercive situation. Although the movie scene in *Ghostbusters* was intended to be amusing, in real life, such behavior would be considered exploitative.

3.03 Other Harassment

Psychologists do not knowingly engage in behavior that is harassing or demeaning to persons with whom they interact in their work based on factors such as those persons' age, gender, gender identity, race, ethnicity, culture, national origin, religion, sexual orientation, disability, language, or socioeconomic status. (Code, 2002)

Harassment can come in many forms. Physical harassment is the most obvious, but verbal harassment can be equally or even more damaging. The high-powered position you hold as a researcher makes it all the more important that you are very careful in your actions toward and with your words to your participants and colleagues. One of us worked with an individual who, when giving instructions, would say, "Do you know why this didn't work?" The participant would respond, "No, why?" And this person would say, "Because you're stupid." This researcher thought he was amusing! The old adage that "sticks and stones may break your bones, but words can never hurt you" is a "truism" that is simply not true.

3.04 Avoiding Harm

Psychologists take reasonable steps to avoid harming their clients/patients, students, supervisees, research participants, organizational clients, and others with whom they work, and to minimize harm where it is foreseeable and unavoidable. (Code, 2002)

We often work with students who are interested in the effect of the media on women's self-esteem. They usually design a study that involves showing young women photographs of models from fashion magazines and then assessing self-esteem. Their hypothesis is that, compared to control participants who view neutral photographs, the participants who view the fashion models will have lower self-esteem. The research is interesting and topical, but is it ethical to conduct a study when your research hypothesis is that your experimental variable will *reduce* the self-esteem of your participants? As is often the case with ethical issues, you need to consider the relative cost versus the benefits of the research. If this research was allowed, what steps could you put in place to minimize the harm to the participants' self-esteem? In the end, could the study be designed to improve the participants' self-esteem? Perhaps they could be debriefed on the potential dangers of reading fashion magazines.

Conceptual Exercise 3B

One of our students proposed to study the effects of alcohol on social behavior. She intended to have consenting adults drink a specified amount of alcohol (not above the legal limit) and then observe willingness to participate in a karaoke bar by recording things such as how many times did they perform, how loud did they sing, what kinds of songs did they select, and so on. Can you think of any ethical problems with this study?

3.05 Multiple Relationships

(a) A multiple relationship occurs when a psychologist is in a professional role with a person and (1) at the same time is in another role with the same person, (2) at the same time is in a relationship with a person closely associated with or related to the person with whom the psychologist has the professional relationship, or (3) promises to enter into another relationship in the future with the person or a person closely associated with or related to the person.

A psychologist refrains from entering into a multiple relationship if the multiple relationship could reasonably be expected to impair the psychologist's objectivity, competence, or effectiveness in performing his or her functions as a psychologist, or otherwise risks exploitation or harm to the person with whom the professional relationship exists.

Multiple relationships that would not reasonably be expected to cause impairment or risk exploitation or harm are not unethical.

(b) If a psychologist finds that, due to unforeseen factors, a potentially harmful multiple relationship has arisen, the psychologist takes reasonable steps to resolve it with due regard for the best interests of the affected person and maximal compliance with the Ethics Code. (Code, 2002)

One of us had the experience of taking a course where the instructor asked students to tell the class what they did for a living, the instructor's "icebreaker" for this small class. As the instructor went from student to student, he made comments such as "Oh, you're a roofer, eh? I do need some work done on the house," or "You're a psychology professor; I can't see how that can help me." It was all done in jest, but this is exactly what **multiple relationships** are about. What if the instructor had the roofer work on his house? Would the roofer be evaluated objectively in the course? How would the other students feel about the relationship? They might start wishing they too were doing things for the instructor.

Although this ethical standard is directed mostly at educators and therapists, it is equally important that we researchers also remain independent of our participants. As a student, you may be using your friends and family as research participants; could this be problematic? Depending on the research, it certainly could be. Imagine that your study involves measuring intelligence or personality characteristics. How can their participation be anonymous?

Conceptual Exercise 3C

At our school, we professors often employ teaching assistants (TAs) from the undergraduate student body to help us with our courses. What ethical problems do you think might arise from this practice? What might we do to avoid problems?

3.08 Exploitative Relationships

Psychologists do not exploit persons over whom they have supervisory, evaluative, or other authority such as clients/patients, students, supervisees, research participants, and employees. (Code, 2002)

For the same reasons you do not want to be in a multiple relationship with your participants, you should not exploit them. To *exploit* means to take advantage of another. Exploitation can include asking for special favors that are beyond the relationship of researcher and participant. Exploitation in research can also be seen in the treatment of technicians by investigators. To guard against exploitation, it is necessary that all involved understand their roles and responsibilities. It is the purpose of informed consent to make the relationship explicit and clearly understood.

3.10 Informed Consent

(a) When psychologists conduct research or provide assessment, therapy, counseling, or consulting services in person or via electronic transmission or other forms of communication, they obtain the informed consent of the individual or individuals using language that is reasonably understandable to that person or persons except when conducting such activities without consent is mandated by law or governmental regulation or as otherwise provided in this Ethics Code. (See also Standards 8.02, Informed Consent to Research; 9.03, Informed Consent in Assessments; and 10.01, Informed Consent to Therapy.)

(b) For persons who are legally incapable of giving informed consent, psychologists nevertheless (1) provide an appropriate explanation, (2) seek the individual's assent, (3) consider such persons' preferences and best interests, and (4) obtain appropriate permission from a legally authorized person, if such substitute consent is permitted or required by law. When consent by a legally authorized person is not permitted or required by law, psychologists take reasonable steps to protect the individual's rights and welfare.

(c) When psychological services are court ordered or otherwise mandated, psychologists inform the individual of the nature of the anticipated services, including whether the services are court ordered or mandated and any limits of confidentiality, before proceeding.

(d) Psychologists appropriately document written or oral consent, permission, and assent. (See also Standards 8.02, Informed Consent to Research; 9.03, Informed Consent in Assessments; and 10.01, Informed Consent to Therapy.) (Code, 2002)

When conducting research with people, a relationship is created between the researcher and the participant. The purpose of **informed consent** is to clearly define that relationship. The ethical standard of informed consent as it relates to research is described below in Section 8.

FYI

The standard of informed consent indicates that when individuals are legally incapable of giving informed *consent,* we should seek their *assent*. Informed consent means that the individual is able to understand completely the nature of the request and agree or disagree to comply. When the individual cannot do this, the researcher must obtain informed consent, on behalf of the individual, from his or her legal guardian. In such situations, the researcher is still mandated to obtain the individual's agreement to participate (i.e., his or her assent), even though such agreement is not considered to be informed agreement. For example, children are not legally permitted to grant consent for research or treatment. Their parents must grant consent, but children should be asked about their willingness or *assent* to participate in research or treatment after being given information about what they are being asked to do at a level they can understand.

4. Privacy and Confidentiality

4.01 Maintaining Confidentiality

Psychologists have a primary obligation and take reasonable precautions to protect confidential information obtained through or stored in any medium, recognizing that the extent and limits of confidentiality may be regulated by law or established by institutional rules or professional or scientific relationship. (See also Standard 2.05, Delegation of Work to Others.) (Code, 2002)

Any information you gather in your research should remain confidential. You need to understand that it is possible that the data you collect may be disclosed in court. In other words, although it is your responsibility to protect the **confidentiality** of your participant, there may be rare circumstances where you cannot. Probably the easiest way to guarantee confidentiality is to arrange that your participants are anonymous. Ask that they not include names on any materials. If it is necessary to match participants' names to their data, assign numbers to the names and keep the name key file in a safe location. At the conclusion of the study, this file could be destroyed.

4.02 Discussing the Limits of Confidentiality

(a) Psychologists discuss with persons (including, to the extent feasible, persons who are legally incapable of giving informed consent and their legal representatives) and organizations with whom they establish a scientific or professional relationship (1) the relevant limits of confidentiality and (2) the foreseeable uses of the information generated through their psychological activities. (See also Standard 3.10, Informed Consent.)

(b) Unless it is not feasible or is contraindicated, the discussion of confidentiality occurs at the outset of the relationship and thereafter as new circumstances may warrant.

(c) Psychologists who offer services, products, or information via electronic transmission inform clients/patients of the risks to privacy and limits of confidentiality. (Code, 2002)

Again, as indicated above, if you can have your participants remain anonymous, you do not have to be concerned with confidentiality. If this is not possible, then you must explain under what conditions confidentiality can be broken. This needs to be clearly explained as part of the information provided for consent to participate.

4.05 Disclosures

(a) Psychologists may disclose confidential information with the appropriate consent of the organizational client, the individual client/patient, or another legally authorized person on behalf of the client/patient unless prohibited by law.

(b) Psychologists disclose confidential information without the consent of the individual only as mandated by law, or where permitted by law for a valid purpose such as to (1) provide needed professional services; (2) obtain appropriate professional consultations; (3) protect the client/patient, psychologist, or others from harm; or (4) obtain payment for services from a client/patient, in which instance disclosure is limited to the minimum that is necessary to achieve the purpose. (See also Standard 6.04e, Fees and Financial Arrangements.) (Code, 2002)

In the research context, **disclosure** means revealing confidential information to others about a research participant. It is rare that disclosure of confidential information is necessary in research, but there are instances where it is permitted. One of our students conducted a depression survey of her peers at our school. Had she learned that a student respondent had suicidal intentions, we as the supervisors of her research project would be permitted to break confidentiality to get help for that student.

Conceptual Exercise 3D

Students who work with clients in the field as part of their internship at our school meet once a week to discuss their experiences with each other and with their professor. What confidentiality issues are important here?

4.06 Consultations

When consulting with colleagues, (1) psychologists do not disclose confidential information that reasonably could lead to the identification of a client/patient, research participant, or other person or organization with whom they have a confidential relationship unless they have obtained the prior consent of the person or organization or the disclosure cannot be avoided, and (2) they disclose information only to the extent necessary to achieve the purposes of the consultation. (Code, 2002)

Be very careful when discussing your research with your supervisors, teachers, or classmates. Guard against the temptation to gossip about research participants. Certainly you can discuss your research, but not in a way that could lead to the identification of an individual. If you are doing research on a university campus, you quickly learn that it is a small world!

4.07 Use of Confidential Information for Didactic or Other Purposes

Psychologists do not disclose in their writings, lectures, or other public media, confidential, personally identifiable information concerning their clients/patients, students, research participants, organizational clients, or other recipients of their services that they obtained during the course of their work, unless (1) they take reasonable steps to disguise the person or organization, (2) the person or organization has consented in writing, or (3) there is legal authorization for doing so. (Code, 2002)

If, during the course of your research, you discover an individual who is remarkable in some aspect, you may wish to present his or her data in such detail that his or her confidentiality may be at risk. You may proceed to present the information only if you have WRITTEN consent from the individual involved. In order to break confidentiality, verbal consent is not sufficient.

8. Research and Publication

8.01 Institutional Approval

When institutional approval is required, psychologists provide accurate information about their research proposals and obtain approval prior to conducting the research. They conduct the research in accordance with the approved research protocol. (Code, 2002)

At the start of this chapter, we indicated the importance of the IRB in assessing the ethics of research proposals. This standard specifies that you should not misrepresent your research to the IRB. Makes sense!

8.02 Informed Consent to Research

(a) When obtaining informed consent as required in Standard 3.10, Informed Consent, psychologists inform participants about (1) the purpose of the research, expected duration, and procedures; (2) their right to decline to participate and to withdraw from the research once participation has begun; (3) the foreseeable consequences of declining or withdrawing; (4) reasonably foreseeable factors that may be expected to influence their willingness to participate such as potential risks, discomfort, or adverse effects; (5) any prospective research benefits; (6) limits of confidentiality; (7) incentives for participation; and (8) whom to contact for questions about the research and research participants' rights. They provide opportunity for the prospective participants to ask questions and receive answers. (See also Standards 8.03, Informed Consent for Recording Voices and Images in Research; 8.05, Dispensing With Informed Consent for Research; and 8.07, Deception in Research.)

(b) Psychologists conducting intervention research involving the use of experimental treatments clarify to participants at the outset of the research (1) the experimental nature of the treatment; (2) the services that will or will not be available to the control group(s) if appropriate; (3) the means by which assignment to treatment and control groups will be made; (4) available treatment alternatives if an individual does not wish to participate in the research or wishes to withdraw once a study has begun; and (5) compensation for or monetary costs of participating including, if appropriate, whether reimbursement from the participant or a third-party payor will be sought. (See also Standard 8.02a, Informed Consent to Research.) (Code, 2002)

Students often wonder if they need to have their participant complete an informed consent form when doing their research project. The answer is yes! Except when it's no (see 8.05).

The consent form is a contract between the researcher and the participant detailing each point listed in the ethical standard. The consent form is an important document that you should have checked and rechecked to ensure that it contains all the information that your participants will need to make an informed decision to participate. This does not mean that you need to include a complete description of your study. You should provide a brief description of the purpose of the study and what the participants will be expected to do. You should provide a way for participants to find out the results of your study when you have completed it. You might mail them the results, or you could provide a Web site for them to access after completion. In addition, you should explain to your participants how they were selected for study if that is appropriate. We have found that often participants think they have been selected because they are unusual in some way. If you have randomly selected them, you should tell them so.

You want the consent form to be short and written in simple language. Most word processors have a language check function that can estimate the approximate grade level of the document. Try to write the consent form at a Grade 6 to 8 level. If possible, we recommend reading the consent form out loud so the potential participants need only follow along. Also invite questions to ensure the individuals understand the consent form.

The following is a sample consent form.

General Procedure

- Researcher describes the general purpose of the study and explains how participants were selected to participate, and participants sign consent form.
- Participants read scenarios, each describing the behavior of a young child.
- Participants answer a series of questions about each scenario.
- Participants are debriefed, sign debriefing section of consent form, and are given a copy.

A Study of Prognosis and Cause With Acting-Out Behavior in Children

The purpose of this research is to determine what you think is the likely cause of acting-out behavior of children and what you think the long-term outcome of treatment will be for these children. You will read a series of scenarios describing a child who is acting out in class or at home. Then you will be asked to answer several questions about the likely causes of the behavior and the likely result of psychological treatment.

There is no risk to you if you agree to participate in this study, and the Institutional Review Board of the school has approved the research. If you have any questions or concerns, please contact me at. . . .

Consent

I, _____, am at least 18 years of age and I agree to participate in a research study conducted by _____ of the Psychology Department at the University of _____. I have been informed that my participation is voluntary and that I may withdraw at any time without penalty of any kind. Any data I contribute to this study will be confidential. I understand that I will be answering a series of questions about scenarios I will read and that I will receive a complete explanation of the purpose of the research after I have completed the study. I understand that there is minimal risk to me.

_____   _____

Signature of participant   Date

 If you would like to receive a summary of the results of the research, please include a mailing address or go to www. My site after date X.
 At the end of my participation, the nature of the study was fully explained to me.

_____   _____

Signature of participant   Date

8.03 Informed Consent for Recording Voices and Images in Research

Psychologists obtain informed consent from research participants prior to recording their voices or images for data collection unless (1) the research consists solely of naturalistic observations in public places, and it is not anticipated that the recording will be used in a manner that could cause personal identification or harm, or (2) the research design includes deception, and consent for the use of the recording is obtained during debriefing. (See also Standard 8.07, Deception in Research.) (Code, 2002)

 It makes sense that you need to ask permission to record or photograph research participants, but what if they are in a public place? You have probably seen reality TV shows where people are videotaped but their faces are obscured to protect their identity. So, too, in research; you are allowed to make recordings as long as individuals cannot be identified.

8.04 Client/Patient, Student, and Subordinate Research Participants

(a) When psychologists conduct research with clients/patients, students, or subordinates as participants, psychologists take steps to protect the prospective participants from adverse consequences of declining or withdrawing from participation.

(b) When research participation is a course requirement or an opportunity for extra credit, the prospective participant is given the choice of equitable alternative activities. (Code, 2002)

Participation in research should be voluntary. Often psychology research is conducted on "subject pools" obtained from introductory psychology classes where the students are expected to participate for course credit. This is reasonable only if students who do not wish to participate are given an alternative assignment such as an essay on the importance of research in psychology. Some institutions have deemed that even this arrangement is too coercive and have made participation purely voluntary. At our school, senior students often ask to use junior students as participants in their research projects in their methods course. We do not permit the senior students to simply enter the classroom and make their appeal to the junior class. Do you understand why?

8.05 Dispensing With Informed Consent for Research

Psychologists may dispense with informed consent only (1) where research would not reasonably be assumed to create distress or harm and involves (a) the study of normal educational practices, curricula, or classroom management methods conducted in educational settings; (b) only anonymous questionnaires, naturalistic observations, or archival research for which disclosure of responses would not place participants at risk of criminal or civil liability or damage their financial standing, employability, or reputation, and confidentiality is protected; or (c) the study of factors related to job or organization effectiveness conducted in organizational settings for which there is no risk to participants' employability, and confidentiality is protected or (2) where otherwise permitted by law or federal or institutional regulations. (Code, 2002)

Students often wonder whether they have to obtain informed consent when doing survey research or field observations. The answer is no, as long as the research is not going to negatively affect the participants. Imagine that you recognize someone you know while you are observing people at the racetrack. Now imagine that this individual has called in sick instead of going to work and that he or she has a gambling problem. Could this information be harmful? Or perhaps you have asked people to complete a questionnaire with questions about sexual assault and one of your participants has a breakdown recollecting the experience. Dispensing with informed consent should never be taken lightly. It is your responsibility to be certain that your research will not cause distress or harm.

8.06 Offering Inducements for Research Participation

(a) Psychologists make reasonable efforts to avoid offering excessive or inappropriate financial or other inducements for research participation when such inducements are likely to coerce participation.

(b) When offering professional services as an inducement for research participation, psychologists clarify the nature of the services, as well as the risks, obligations, and limitations. (See also Standard 6.05, Barter With Clients/Patients.) (Code, 2002)

There is nothing wrong with offering a small reward for participation, but it can become a problem if the incentive is too large. For example, offering young people iPhones or iPods for their participation would not be ethical. This incentive may be too wonderful for young adults to resist. You do not want your inducement to become too good to refuse! That would be coercive.

8.07 Deception in Research

(a) Psychologists do not conduct a study involving deception unless they have determined that the use of deceptive techniques is justified by the study's significant prospective scientific, educational, or applied value and that effective nondeceptive alternative procedures are not feasible.

(b) Psychologists do not deceive prospective participants about research that is reasonably expected to cause physical pain or severe emotional distress.

(c) Psychologists explain any deception that is an integral feature of the design and conduct of an experiment to participants as early as is feasible, preferably at the conclusion of their participation, but no later than at the conclusion of the data collection, and permit participants to withdraw their data. (See also Standard 8.08, Debriefing.) (Code, 2002)

Experimental **deception** includes any information or action on the part of the researcher that is intended to mislead the participants about the true nature of the research, including omission of information. It is not uncommon for participants in psychology research to ask, "What are you really studying in the experiment?" The question reflects a general mistrust of psychology research because of the widely held view that deception is more often the rule than the exception in research. Although there is no consensus on the harm that may arise from the use of deception, it is agreed that it should be avoided if possible. In the practice of psychology, trust is an important aspect of the psychologist-client relationship. We do not want people to view researchers in psychology as tricksters.

Try to design your research without deception. Often deception is not necessary, but if it is used, be sure to reveal the purpose and importance of the deception when you **debrief** your participants. No one likes to be the object of a practical joke, so be mindful that some of your participants may resent the deception. Your debriefing should set them at ease and make them understand that the study could not have been conducted without deception. After debriefing your participants, you must provide them with the opportunity to have their data excluded from your research. In practice, participants rarely withdraw their data if they understand the importance of the deception.

8.08 Debriefing

(a) Psychologists provide a prompt opportunity for participants to obtain appropriate information about the nature, results, and conclusions of the research, and they take reasonable steps to correct any misconceptions that participants may have of which the psychologists are aware.

(b) If scientific or humane values justify delaying or withholding this information, psychologists take reasonable measures to reduce the risk of harm.

(c) When psychologists become aware that research procedures have harmed a participant, they take reasonable steps to minimize the harm. (Code, 2002)

After your research participants have completed the study, you must debrief them. This is your opportunity to explain all the details of the study that may not have been included in the informed consent form (e.g., your research hypothesis). The debriefing also gives your participants the opportunity to ask questions and clear up any misunderstandings. A lot of damage can occur if your participants provide a distorted account of your research to their friends and family; you want to make sure that your participants are fully informed before they leave. For example, you may decide that making free counseling available to your participants for some period of time following your study is a reasonable step to take to reduce harm.

Conceptual Exercise 3E

In a study of helping behavior, participants were led to believe that another participant, who they could hear but not see, was having a heart attack. The researchers measured whether the participants tried to help by leaving the room and looking for the victim and, if so, the time it took them to act. All participants were told, during the debriefing, that they were deceived and that there was no real victim. Can you think of any ethical problems with this study?

8.09 Humane Care and Use of Animals in Research

(a) Psychologists acquire, care for, use, and dispose of animals in compliance with current federal, state, and local laws and regulations, and with professional standards. (Code, 2002)

Research animals must be purchased from recognized suppliers. Your IRB can provide you with the applicable regulations. Here in Canada, we have the Canadian Council on Animal Care (CCAC) as our regulatory body. It sets guidelines for the care, housing, and treatment of animals in research as well as performing inspections of facilities.

(b) Psychologists trained in research methods and experienced in the care of laboratory animals supervise all procedures involving animals and are responsible for ensuring appropriate consideration of their comfort, health, and humane treatment.

(c) Psychologists ensure that all individuals under their supervision who are using animals have received instruction in research methods and in the care, maintenance, and handling of the species being used, to the extent appropriate to their role. (See also Standard 2.05, Delegation of Work to Others.) (Code, 2002)

Your research proposal must be approved by your IRB before you are allowed to acquire your subjects. Once you accept the animals, their care becomes the responsibility of the supervising psychologist, but of course, all the individuals working with the animals share the responsibility of their care.

(d) Psychologists make reasonable efforts to minimize the discomfort, infection, illness, and pain of animal subjects.

(e) Psychologists use a procedure subjecting animals to pain, stress, or privation only when an alternative procedure is unavailable and the goal is justified by its prospective scientific, educational, or applied value.

(f) Psychologists perform surgical procedures under appropriate anesthesia and follow techniques to avoid infection and minimize pain during and after surgery.

(g) When it is appropriate that an animal's life be terminated, psychologists proceed rapidly, with an effort to minimize pain and in accordance with accepted procedures. (Code, 2002)

Animal rights groups have been known to engage in some pretty radical behavior and make some pretty outrageous statements when it comes to the use of animals in research. Research animals have been released into the wild by antivivisectionist groups. How do you think these animals fared?

Love 'em or hate 'em, these groups have raised our awareness of the treatment of animals in research and probably contributed to the careful guidelines that we now have. Students often comment that the guidelines for ethical research with animals are more extensive than those for humans. When you think about it for a moment, you should realize that this makes perfect sense. Animals have no say in the matter and cannot protect themselves, can they? We must be particularly conscientious when working with animals, which of course have not consented to participate.

8.10 Reporting Research Results

(a) Psychologists do not fabricate data. (See also Standard 5.01a, Avoidance of False or Deceptive Statements.)

(b) If psychologists discover significant errors in their published data, they take reasonable steps to correct such errors in a correction, retraction, erratum, or other appropriate publication means. (Code, 2002)

Researchers recognize the importance of reporting the truth. The research endeavor is a search for truth. That is why fudging data is viewed as such a serious breach of ethics. Research builds on prior findings; if these are fabrications, they can lead researchers down blind alleys that can cost a great deal of time and money. If a data error is discovered, it is the responsibility of the researcher to publish a correction.

A spectacular case of research fraud occurred in the biology department at the University of Alberta (http://www.michenerawards.ca/english/misconduct.htm). A research team with funding from both Canada and the United States was excited by a discovery that appeared to slow the growth of cancerous cells. They published their findings in the *Journal of Biological Chemistry* but later had difficulty replicating their work. Suspicion fell on the lab technician because it seemed to the researchers that they were not getting similar data when the tech was on an extended holiday and was not working in the lab.

The supervising investigator, who was an award-winning biologist, quickly notified the university administration and published a retraction. An investigation concluded that the technician knowingly altered the lab materials, and he was fired. This case underscores the importance of replication in research, and although the damage was controlled by an appropriate response by the investigators, much time and many resources were wasted on work that was valueless.

8.11 Plagiarism

Psychologists do not present portions of another's work or data as their own, even if the other work or data source is cited occasionally. (Code, 2002)

Certainly you can discuss the work of others in your research report. Indeed, that is the purpose of the introduction and discussion sections of journal articles. What is not allowed is the presentation of these ideas as your own. Plagiarism, even if unintentional, is a serious breach of ethics, and we discuss it in detail in Chapter 14.

SPECIAL POPULATIONS

If you are conducting research with special populations, children, or any other population of individuals who require a guardian, the parent or guardian must also provide informed consent. You still must obtain assent or agreement from the participant, but this is not sufficient to proceed. You must have consent from both parties before you can include the individual in your study.

INTERNET RESEARCH

Researchers using the Internet to collect data face a number of ethical dilemmas for which guidelines are not yet fully developed. Online surveys are becoming quite common. You might think that this sort of survey is basically the same as collecting information by interview or over the telephone, but special problems exist with online surveys with respect to ethics. Although confidentiality is not such a problem, informed consent and debriefing are. A consent form might be included with an online survey, but there is no way for the researcher to ensure that the form has been read and understood by the respondent. Furthermore, even if a warning is posted that respondents must be 18 years or older, there is no way to confirm this. Similarly, although a debriefing form might be included, the researcher cannot answer any questions the respondents might have and again has no way of knowing if this form was read.

Some e-researchers study the behavior of Internet users by monitoring frequency of Web site hits or analyzing Web-based interactions in chat rooms. Earlier we said that informed consent may be dispensed with when the researcher is observing behavior in public places. You may think this should apply to the Internet, but there are special problems. Are chat rooms public or private places? This issue has not yet been resolved. If you are planning to do Internet research, we suggest you follow the general principles and guidelines of the code as best as you can. And if you are participating in Internet research, *do not* assume that your data are confidential.

BIAS AND INTELLECTUAL HONESTY

We all have biases. One of the authors of this book is a behaviorist by conviction if not by training. The other's training is in physiological psychology. Our backgrounds and our intellectual convictions bias the way we interpret things, our methods of research, and even the topics we select. This cannot be avoided. However, we can strive to present our research findings objectively so that the reader is free to interpret those findings *with his or her own biases, of course.*

Funding agencies can also bias research. Large pharmaceutical companies routinely fund research. Could this place pressure on researchers to highlight positive outcomes and minimize the negative? We suspect it might. What about the movement within universities to support the commercialization of research by creating spin-off companies from the university; could that also bias the researchers? As an example, in our city, there were a number of billboards advertising that attention-deficit/hyperactivity disorder (ADHD) had been cured. We were skeptical, but the advertising listed a major university as a partner. The message to the consumer was that a respected university had recognized this procedure as an effective treatment. As it turned out, the company had no research evidence to support its claim. The company was created as a spin-off from the university; it sold stock, and a couple of years later, it filed for bankruptcy and all the board members resigned. The problem with these spin-off companies is that they use the name of the university to gain respectability when such respectability may not be warranted. Ultimately, they are accountable to the stockholders to make a profit. The company is motivated to make money and not necessarily to cure ADHD.

What if your research funding is from an organization with an agenda for social change? It would be best if all the interest groups were named when a research proposal is sent to an Institutional Review Board. Certainly, the funding source is included in the published journal article, but perhaps the participants should be told who is funding the research as part of the informed consent process.

Physicians operate under the general guideline of **do no harm.** We think this should guide all researchers who work with humans or animals. Psychologists have, over the years, earned themselves a bit of a reputation for being deceptive. We hope that with our increasing focus on ethical guidelines, we are earning back the respect we may have lost.

Remember—STRIVE TO DO NO HARM.

CHAPTER SUMMARY

The **American Psychological Association** provides general principles and standards as guides for conducting ethical research. Psychologists strive to **minimize harm** and **maximize**

benefits to, uphold standards of conduct with, and behave with **integrity** toward people with whom they work. Psychologists strive to treat all fairly and do not condone unjust practices. They treat people with **dignity** and respect the rights of all people.

Psychologists practice within the boundaries of their **competence,** do not discriminate, eschew **harassment** of any kind, and strive to minimize harm to those with whom they work. Psychologists avoid **multiple** or exploitative relationships. Psychologists ensure that participants and clients have given **informed consent,** and they take steps to protect the **confidentiality** of the data provided by clients and participants in research. Researchers do not coerce participants or offer **inducements** for participation that could be deemed **coercive.**

Researchers obtain institutional approval for all work when required. Researchers provide a full and accurate **debriefing** for all participants, taking care to explain any use of deceptive strategies. Psychologists doing research with animals are fully trained in their care and strive to minimize harm to their subjects. Psychologists report their data accurately, strive to avoid **bias** in their reports, and ensure that fair credit is given. Psychologists working with **special populations** obtain informed consent from participants and their guardians.

Above all, psychologists strive to **do no harm** to those with whom they work.

ANSWERS TO CONCEPTUAL EXERCISES

Conceptual Exercise 3A

Watson's claim that people are a product of their environment *only* is an overstatement. A society that subscribes to this belief might find itself ignoring special needs of certain groups.

Conceptual Exercise 3B

There may be no problems here, but we assume that the researcher thinks that people will be less inhibited in this situation and, as such, is perhaps encouraging such behavior.

Conceptual Exercise 3C

It would be important that the TAs do not benefit from their relationship with the professor (other than being paid, of course), and it would be important that other students did not perceive that the TAs were receiving special treatment.

Conceptual Exercise 3D

The students can discuss their clients but must make sure that the clients cannot be identified. Everyone should agree that all discussions must remain confidential within the group.

Conceptual Exercise 3E

Even though the participants were debriefed, some may have found this experience to be traumatic. The researcher should follow up with the participants and make psychological services readily available.

FAQ

Q1: I'm just doing a research project for a course and I'm using my friends and family as participants. Do I need to have them complete a consent form?

A1: Yes, unless your study is one that does not require informed consent (see 8.05), but you should also check with your institution to see if your study needs approval from an Institutional Review Board.

Q2: What should I do if my institution does not have an Institutional Review Board?

A2: Check with your regional government. They may have an ethics review board that assesses proposals for research institutions in their region.

Q3: Is ethics approval really that important?

A3: Yes, it is really important. Without careful consideration of the ethics of your research, you may cause irreversible harm or injury to your participants.

Q4: I heard that you must report in your research manuscript that ethical procedures were followed. Is that true?

A4: You should report this in your method section, but indeed the publication manual of the American Psychological Association indicates that you must include in your submission letter to the journal editor that your research was conducted "in accordance with the ethical standards of the APA" (American Psychological Association, 2001, p. 19).

Q5: Are there instances where an unethical study is approved because of the importance of the research?

A5: No; unethical research should never be approved. Research may be approved that has higher than minimal risk of harm, in which case the potential participants are well informed and there are measures put into place to address any harm.

Q6: If a study is interesting but it did not get ethical approval, could it still be published?

A6: If the study was not given ethics approval, then it probably would not be accepted by an APA journal. Moreover, it is extremely unlikely that a peer-reviewed journal would publish research that was not ethical.

Q7: When debriefing the participants, what do you do if they are angry that deception was used?

A7: Listen to them and do not discount or minimize their anger, but before they are dismissed, it is important that they understand why deception was used and in particular that the study would not be possible without the deception. They have the right to remove their data from the study, and of course they can complain to the research ethics board at the institution.

Q8: What are the consequences for ethics violations?

A8: If a law has been broken, there can be legal charges. If no law has been broken, then the consequences are determined by the institution(s) that are involved in the research. This can include firing, the withdrawal of research funds, and perhaps the closure of the research institution.

Q9: Should your procedure be reviewed before the study?

A9: Absolutely; the IRB will ask for a complete description of your procedure before it can give ethics approval.

Q10: When we did our research project, people didn't even read the consent form. They just signed it.

A10: One solution to this problem is to read the consent form to your prospective participants as they read along.

Q11: Some of the most important studies in psychology were done long ago. Milgram, Zimbardo, and Watson would not be given ethics approval today. Is it possible to replicate these studies today?

A11: We do not think so. In the three cases you mention, the potential harm to the participants was high and not adequately addressed by the researchers.

Q12: What do you do if you discover ethical problems while conducting your study?

A12: Stop the study and contact the principal investigator. The principal investigator or supervisor of the research will then contact the institution's ethics review board.

CHAPTER EXERCISES

1. Investigate and report the requirements of your institution for research on human and animal subjects.

2. Write an informed consent form for a fictional research project of your creation.

3. Using a recent research article, imagine that you are a member of an IRB that is judging the ethics of the research. What issues would you have to consider and what would be your decision?

4. Many organizations involved in research have written ethics codes. Obtain two or three codes and compare them on specific topics such as informed consent, deception, or participant confidentiality.

5. In small groups, have students select an ethical standard and create a scenario that violates the standard. Have them act out the scenario for the class and have the class identify the problem and offer solutions. Our students have had great fun with this exercise.

CHAPTER PROJECTS

No chapter on research ethics would be complete without a discussion of the following classic examples of *ethics gone wrong*. However, instead of discussing these cases, we prefer to assign them as Chapter Projects. For each question, read the study and identify what ethical standards were broken. Can you suggest ways of improving the studies?

1. Watson, J. B., & Rayner, R. (1920). Conditioned emotional reactions. *Journal of Experimental Psychology, 3,* 1–14.

2. Milgram, S. (1974). *Obedience to authority: An experimental view.* New York: Harper & Row.

3. Zimbardo, P. G., Haney, C., Banks, W. C., & Jaffe, D. (1973, April 8). The mind is a formidable jailer: A Pirandellian prison. *New York Times Magazine,* pp. 38–60.

4. Viens, A. M., & Savulescu, J. (2004). Introduction to the Olivieri symposium. *Journal of Medical Ethics, 30,* 1–7.

5. Rushton, P. (1989). Genetic similarity, human altruism, and group selection. *Behavioral and Brain Sciences, 12,* 503–559.

6. Humphreys, L. (1970). *Tearoom trade.* Chicago: Aldine.

7. Harlow, H. F. (1958). The nature of love. *The American Psychologist, 13,* 673–685.

8. Jones, J. H. (1981). *Bad blood: The Tuskegee syphilis experiment.* New York: Free Press.

REFERENCES

American Psychological Association. (2001). *Publication manual of the American Psychological Association* (5th ed.). Washington, DC: Author.

Watson, J. B. (1924). *Behaviorism.* New York: Norton.

Visit the study site at www.sagepub.com/evansmprstudy for practice quizzes and other study resources.

Hypothesis Testing, Power, and Control

A Review of the Basics

OBJECTIVES

After reading this chapter, students should be able to do the following for a research project they have conducted or proposed:

- Generate conceptual, research, and statistical hypotheses
- List and describe the steps we follow to test a null hypothesis
- Consider the implications of inferential error and statistical significance
- Describe the four outcomes of an inferential decision and provide the probability associated with each
- Discuss power and consider ways of increasing the power of their test of the null
- Discuss the importance of effect size and estimate effect size for a given test of the null
- Discuss the role of replication in research as it relates to power
- Discuss the influence of confounding and extraneous variables on inferential statements
- List and describe common ways of controlling extraneous variables

---

Are outgoing people happier than people who keep to themselves? Do people do better when they think they are being evaluated? Does stress management training help highly anxious people? We use **inferential** techniques to answer these kinds of questions. **Hypothesis testing** is the most common inferential technique used by psychologists.

Hypotheses are educated guesses about the relationships between variables. By educated guesses, we mean that these hypotheses come from previous research, theory, or logic. We categorize hypotheses by the level of the variables specified in the hypothesis.

THREE LEVELS OF HYPOTHESES

As researchers, we first hypothesize about concepts or theoretical constructs. Here are some examples of conceptual hypotheses:

"People work harder when they think they are being evaluated."

"Outgoing people are happier than people who keep to themselves."

"Highly anxious people trained in stress management are less anxious than those not trained."

These are **conceptual hypotheses** because they state expected relationships among concepts such as "work harder, outgoing, happy, and highly anxious." As researchers, we talk about our research using these conceptual terms. To test a conceptual hypothesis, we need to operationalize these concepts, thereby creating the next level of hypothesis—the **research hypothesis.** Our research hypotheses for the three conceptual hypotheses above might be as follows:

"People who are told that experts are rating their performance get higher scores on a test than people who are not told they are being rated."

"People who score high on a standard test of extraversion give higher ratings of happiness in their lives than do people who score low."

"People who score high on a standard test of anxiety have lower resting heart rates after stress management training compared to similar people who have received no training."

These are research hypotheses because we have **operationalized** our concepts such that they are now measurable. We conduct research to test our research hypothesis. But when we do our statistics, we are not testing our research hypothesis directly; rather, we are testing a statistical hypothesis. A **statistical hypothesis,** in parametric hypothesis testing, states the expected relationship between or among summary values of populations, called *parameters.* There are two kinds of statistical hypotheses: the **null hypothesis** (H_0) and the **alternative hypothesis** (H_1). And it is the null hypothesis that we actually test when we use inferential procedures.

NOTE: Statistical hypotheses for nonparametric tests (i.e., tests that are not looking for differences among summary values or parameters of populations) are somewhat different.

Conceptual Exercise 4A

A research methods student hypothesizes that people working in helping professions are more ethical than people working in business professions.
Can you help her restate this hypothesis as a research hypothesis?

Once we have restated our research hypothesis in terms of a null and alternative hypothesis, we can then test the null.

TESTING THE NULL HYPOTHESIS

In science, we recognize that there is much more power in disconfirming a hypothesis than there is in confirming one. For example, let's say you want to show that your spouse is faithful. To demonstrate or confirm this hypothesis, you present the fact that your spouse has never had an affair in your 10 years of marriage. The evidence does seem to confirm that your spouse is faithful, but maybe you should track his or her behavior for another 10 years just to be sure. By using confirmation evidence, it is impossible to know how much evidence is enough—10 years? 20 years? But what if we looked for disconfirming evidence? How much disconfirming evidence would you need to prove that your spouse is NOT faithful? A single affair is all it takes! Just one disconfirming piece of evidence is needed to disprove your hypothesis that your spouse is faithful. Although the null hypothesis is rarely specified in a research article, it is the hypothesis being statistically tested when you use inferential statistics.

You will recall from your statistics course that the null has that name because the researcher hopes to show that the null is not likely to be true (i.e., he or she hopes to *nullify it*). If the researcher can show that the null is not supported by the data, then he or she is able to accept an alternative hypothesis, which is the hypothesis the researcher postulated at the outset of the study. We often tell our statistics students that we cannot prove that our research hypothesis is true; we can only provide evidence that the null hypothesis is probably not!

Let's say our research hypothesis is that people get higher scores on some test when they are told that their performance is being evaluated. Let's follow the steps given below to test this hypothesis:

1. State the null and the alternative. Our null is that the mean score of people who are told they are being evaluated equals the mean score of people who are not told they are being evaluated. The null is a statement of no difference between groups—no treatment effect. This is the hypothesis you hope to nullify. Our alternative hypothesis is that the mean score of people who are told they are being evaluated is higher than the mean score of those who are not told they are being evaluated. This is the hypothesis you hope to confirm. Statistical hypotheses typically use Greek letters to refer to population parameters (i.e., summary values about populations). The Greek letter we use for population mean is μ (mu). In statistical notation, our null and alternative are as follows:

$$H_0: \mu_1 = \mu_2 \quad H_1: \mu_1 > \mu_2$$

2. Collect the data and conduct the appropriate statistical analysis.

3. Reject the null and accept the alternative or fail to reject the null.

4. State your inferential conclusion.

An **inference** is a statement of **probability.** An inference is not a statement made with certainty. It is a leap from a specific instance to a general rule. When we make an inference, we may be wrong, but inferential statistics provide us with an estimate of the probability that our inference is correct. In essence, when we reject a null hypothesis, we are saying that it is *unlikely that the null is true.* It is *more likely that an alternative hypothesis is true.* But remember, inferences are probability statements about the nature of populations that are based on information about samples. And when we make such statements, we can be wrong. After all, it could be that our sample was just unusual or was not representative of the population.

When we say that it is unlikely that the null is true, what do we mean by *unlikely?* How unlikely? This brings us to the heart of the matter—statistical significance!

STATISTICAL SIGNIFICANCE

"People perform *significantly* better when they think they are being evaluated than when they think they are not."

"Outgoingness is *significantly* related to happiness."

"Highly anxious people are *significantly* less anxious after receiving stress management training."

You have no doubt seen many statements such as these during your reading of the research literature. But what do they really mean? Well, *significant* does not mean *important.* Significance is a statistical term, and statements such as these are statements of probability.

Here is what the examples given above really mean.

"It is *highly unlikely* that people perform the same when they think they are being evaluated than when they think they are not."

"It is *highly unlikely* that outgoingness and happiness are unrelated."

"It is *highly unlikely* that highly anxious people who receive stress management training are equally as anxious as those who received no such training."

When we say that there is a significant difference between groups, we are saying that the *probability that the groups are the same is low, very low.* What do we mean by low? Well, researchers have agreed that low is less than 5% or 1%. These two levels are called *significance levels,* and we use the symbol α (**alpha**) to refer to them. Alpha, then, is the level of significance chosen by the researcher to evaluate the null hypothesis. If the alpha level chosen was 5%, for example, then we are stating that the probability that the groups are the same is less than 5%. Therefore, we conclude they are not the same. Seems reasonable, don't you think? Of course, as we have said, any inference is a statement of probability. When we say two groups are significantly different, we are pretty sure they are, but we are not certain. We could be wrong. With any inference, there is some probability that we could be wrong. And if we are wrong, we are making an inferential error.

INFERENTIAL ERRORS: TYPE I AND TYPE II

Imagine we have a coin and we are tossing it. We have tossed it 15 times, and it has turned up heads 15 times. What would you infer from this?

Well, there are two possibilities. One, that the coin is fair, and two, that the coin is not fair. We suspect that you, like us, would infer that this coin is bogus. Even if we have not calculated the actual probability of a fair coin showing heads 15 times in a row, we all know intuitively that this is not very likely to happen. In fact, the probability is close to zero ($p = 1/2^{15}$ or $p = .00003$). We think it is a lot more reasonable to conclude that we have a bogus coin than to conclude we have a fair coin and that it turned up 15 heads in a row by fluke. Of course, it's possible that's what happened—a really rare fluke. And our conclusion that the coin is bogus would be wrong. We would have made the dreaded **Type I error.** So let's examine this coin-tossing situation from a hypothesis testing point of view. We will begin with our null and alternative hypotheses in everyday words.

Null hypothesis in words: *The coin is fair.*

Alternative hypothesis in words: *The coin is bogus.*

Remember our goal in hypothesis testing is to reject the null and accept our alternative. You will recall that **power** in hypothesis testing is our ability to do just that—to reject false nulls. We have already collected our data. We got 15 heads in a row.

There are four possible inferential outcomes in our little study. Here they are:

1. The coin is fair, but we conclude it is bogus—This is a Type I error.
2. The coin is fair, and we conclude it is fair—This is a correct decision.
3. The coin is bogus, but we conclude it is fair—This is a Type II error.
4. The coin is bogus, and we conclude it is bogus—This is a correct decision. This is power.

The last outcome is our goal in hypothesis testing. We want to reject a false null. If our coin is indeed bogus, we want to conclude that it is. Of course, when we make a statistical inference, we never know if we are correct. We could be wrong. That is the nature of the beast. But we can do things to better our chances of being right.

In hypothesis testing language, the probability of making a Type I error is equal to alpha (α), the level of significance chosen by the researcher (typically, α is set at .05 or .01). Displaying an amazing lack of imagination, statisticians call the probability of a **Type II error** beta (β), and because a Type II error can only occur if the null is false, beta is not set by the researcher. Let's put our four outcomes in a table (see Table 4.1).

Researchers do not want to make errors in their inferences, but which error is more important? Well, that depends.

Several years ago, one of us was hired as a statistical consultant to do some research on the state of the terrain at a local ski area. Skiing Louise in Banff, Alberta, had recently put in some snowmaking equipment on the mountain. Parks Canada was concerned that this

TABLE 4.1	Outcomes of an Inferential Decision	
	True State of Affairs	
Our Decision	*Null Is True*	*Null Is False*
Reject the null	Type I error (α)	Correct inference (power)
Do not reject the null	Correct inference	Type II error (β)

equipment might have damaged the mountain terrain. If we wanted to determine the truth of the matter, we would have to assess every inch of the area (the population), but this was impossible. Instead, we sampled the terrain by assessing the density and diversity of the plant growth of randomly determined plots. We knew that there were four possible outcomes of our statistical analysis of the data. They are in Table 4.2.

Skiing Louise was more concerned with Type I error. It did not want us to infer that the mountain was damaged when it was not because it would have to do extensive remedial planting. It wanted us to reduce the probability of a Type I error. Parks Canada, on the other hand, had a different agenda. It was concerned about Type II error. It wanted to make sure that our inference that the mountain was okay was not a mistake. It wanted us to reduce the probability of a Type II error. As you can see, which error is more important depends on the agenda of the researcher. Scientists are objective and so will use procedures to keep both kinds of errors as low as possible.

Are you ready for one of our favorite examples? Romeo made a Type I error when he wrongly rejected the null hypothesis "Juliet is alive." So sad. Julius Caesar made a Type II error when he failed to reject the null hypothesis "Brutus is my buddy." Also, a tragic error (Evans, 2007).

The goal of hypothesis testing is to reject the null when we should, of course, and accept an alternative. After all, the alternative is the research hypothesis that we want to confirm. Techniques and statistical analyses that increase the probability of rejecting false nulls are said to be powerful techniques. Remember that rejecting false nulls is the goal of hypothesis testing. Let's look more closely at power.

TABLE 4.2	Outcomes of Our Analysis of the Mountain Terrain	
	Truth	
Our Decision	*The Mountain Is Okay*	*The Mountain Is Damaged*
The mountain is damaged	Type I error	Correct inference
The mountain is okay	Correct inference	Type II error

Conceptual Exercise 4B

Identify each of the following as a correct statistical decision or an error. If an error has been made, identify which type of error it is.

1. You're disappointed because you found no statistical support for your research hypothesis. You failed to reject your null hypothesis because your inferential statistic was not statistically significant ($p = .07$). [TRUTH: There really is no difference.]

2. You're really excited because you got statistically significant results ($p = .002$). You reject the null and accept the alternative. [TRUTH: There really is no difference.]

3. You're disappointed because your difference was not even close to being significant ($p = .34$). You fail to reject the null. [TRUTH: There really is a difference.]

4. You're pleased because the outcome of your study was statistically significant ($p < .001$). You reject the null and accept the alternative. [TRUTH: There really is a difference.]

POWER AND HOW TO INCREASE IT

For many social scientists, research is all about power. So what exactly do we mean by power?

A powerful test of the null is more likely to lead us to reject false nulls than a less powerful test. As researchers, we want to reject nulls that should be rejected. When we say "powerful test of the null," we are not just referring to the power of the specific statistical test. A test of the null is more powerful when good research techniques are used, good designs are chosen, samples are drawn properly, and so on. However, in this chapter, we are focusing on the role of the statistical procedures in power.

Powerful tests are more sensitive than less powerful tests to differences between the actual outcome (what you found) and the expected outcome (not what you *really* expected but what you stated in the null hypothesis). Remember that β, beta, is the symbol we use to stand for the probability of *not* rejecting a false null, a bad thing—a Type II error. Therefore, power or the probability of rejecting a false null must be $1 - \beta$, a very good thing. Remember our hypothesis that people who think they are being evaluated perform better? If in fact this is true and our analysis of our data led us to conclude this is true, we had a powerful test of our null. So, most researchers want to do things to increase power.

Remember that we reject the null only if the probability of getting the outcome we got was low, less than alpha, our chosen level of significance. Okay, then, let's choose a more "favorable" alpha level and make it easier to reject our null hypothesis. Rather than using the typical significance level of $\alpha = .05$, let's choose $\alpha = .10$. This would surely increase power because we can reject the null if our outcome is likely to occur by chance only 10%

of the time or less, instead of the more standard 5% or 1%. Sounds good, right? Well, yes and no. You surely will increase power this way (i.e., you will reject more false nulls), but sadly you will also increase Type I errors this way—you will reject more true nulls—a conundrum? Maybe not.

Increasing power—that is our mission! First, let's talk about how you measure your variables. Being careful about how you measure your variables can increase power. For example, the level of measurement of your variables will influence the type of statistical analysis that you can use. Remember that some statistical analyses are more powerful than others. Making sure that your variables can be measured on an **interval** or **ratio scale** is wise because then you can use these more powerful parametric procedures. We discuss these scales in detail in Chapter 5.

What about the design itself? Designs that provide good control over the extraneous variables that might be operating on your participants' behavior help increase power by reducing the effects of those nuisance variables on your participants' behavior. If we can get rid of the "sloppy" variation, then we are better able to assess the effect of the variable we really care about (i.e., our independent variable).

Are there any other ways to increase power? Yes there are. We could restrict our sample to only a specific group of individuals. We might select only women between the ages of 18 and 24 years. This group might be more alike in terms of behavior than people in general, and so we might reduce variability that way. There is nothing wrong with this approach, but you need to recognize that you could not generalize your results to the population at large. You really could only make inferences about the population from which you have taken your sample (i.e., women in this age group).

A simple way to increase power without the problems we have just discussed is to increase your sample size. Increasing sample size will tend to decrease "sloppy" variability. More technically, what happens is that what we call *error variance* is reduced, and so the effects of the treatment, the independent variable (IV), are more easily seen. We have some cautions about overdoing this. Check out the FYI below.

Finally, maximizing your treatment manipulation can increase power. For example, if your hypothesis is that exercise will increase academic performance, don't have your participants just walk around the block once; have them engage in vigorous exercise for 45 minutes! You do not want to miss obtaining statistical significance because your treatment was not strong enough.

FYI

Is it possible to have too much power? Yes and no. In testing hypotheses, our aim is to reject the false null hypotheses, and to do that, we need statistical power. But it is possible to increase your power to such a degree that even very small, perhaps trivial, effects become statistically significant. For example, small differences in mean performance between different racial groups can be statistically significant if you increase power by using extremely large samples. But a statistically significant difference does not mean that the difference is important. Put another way, it does not mean that you can predict an individual's performance by knowing his or her race. Why not? Because there is too much variability within each racial group. It is said that men have greater upper body strength than women. Does that mean that if you're a woman, you are not as strong as the average man? Not at all! You may be stronger than 80% of the population of men. So predicting one individual's strength because she is a woman is a mistake. A statistically significant difference does not always mean an important difference; a necessary addition to hypothesis testing is to indicate the size of the effect, which we will talk about now.

EFFECT SIZE

So let's say that we have found that a null hypothesis is false. But how big is the effect? Let's say that in reality, the difference between the hypothesized value and the true value is not exactly zero as stated in the null. What if the true difference is **statistically significant** but, practically speaking, tiny? We need to ask ourselves, how large a difference should we expect? How large a difference really matters?

Powerful tests should be considered to be tests that detect large effects, that is, large differences between the null and the alternative. This brings us back to the difference between important and significant. A statistically significant effect is not necessarily important and may not be worth the attention of researchers. For example, a study might report statistically significant results that eating a chocolate bar 1 hour before an exam will improve your performance. That the researchers found statistical significance (meaning that the results are not likely due to chance) does not tell us anything about the importance of the effect. Imagine that the chocolate bar group had a mean performance of 82% compared to a no–chocolate bar control group mean of 80%. Are two percentage points likely to make much of a difference to anyone's academic career? Is this effect important enough to provide all students with chocolate bars? Researchers should specify the minimum difference that is worth their attention and design their studies with that effect size in mind.

Effect size can be calculated in various ways. The American Psychological Association (APA) *Publication Manual* lists 13 different effect size estimates that are commonly used (APA, 2001). We will describe a couple of common approaches, but for more detail on effect size calculations, you should consult a statistics book. As indicated above, a statistically significant result does not necessarily mean that your effect is large. This is why it is important to report the group means, but it is also important to take variability into account. In the chocolate bar example, there was a mean difference of two percentage points; does that mean that *you* will improve two points? Not necessarily. There was a 2% difference between *averages*. Only if there was no variability in the groups and everyone in the chocolate bar group got 82% and everyone in the control group got 80% could you expect a 2% improvement in your performance, but that is not likely, is it?

Cohen's *d* is a common effect size calculation that looks at the difference between the means of two groups and takes into account the variability, using the pooled sample standard deviation.

$$d = \frac{M_1 - M_2}{SD_{pooled}}.$$

(Cohen's *d*)

The above method is commonly used with a *t* test, but if you are investigating a relationship between variables, you may calculate a correlation coefficient such as Pearson's product-moment correlation. The correlation coefficient *r* tells you the strength of the relationship between your variables. For example, suppose you investigated the relationship between high school performance and performance in first-year university. You obtained the high school records of 500 students who just finished first-year university and you found $r\,(498) = .73, p < .01$. This indicates a pretty strong positive relationship between high school and university performance, but does it apply to you?

Should we use this finding to select students for university based on their high school performance? A simple method to calculate effect size for correlations is to square the correlation. r^2 indicates the proportion of the variance in the criterion variable that is accounted for by the predictor variable. In our example, .73 squared is .53. Therefore, we have accounted for .53 or 53% of the variability in first-year university performance by using high school performance as a predictor. That leaves a lot of unexplained university performance! Indeed, people often want to use correlation research to predict behavior, and they are often surprised when their variables are not very accurate. r^2 is also referred to as the **coefficient of determination** because it indicates how well you can determine the criterion variable by knowing the predictor variable (i.e., how well you can predict).

A related effect size calculation that is commonly used in analysis of variance (ANOVA) is **eta-squared.** Eta-squared is a calculation of the proportion of the total variability of the dependent variable that is accounted for by the independent variable. So, in an ANOVA, it is calculated by dividing the treatment sum of squares by the total sum of squares. It indicates the strength of the effect of the independent variable on the dependent variable, and because it is expressed as a proportion of the total variability, you can move the decimal place to the right two places and see what percent of the dependent variable is influenced by your independent variable.

$$\eta^2 = \frac{SS_{treatment}}{SS_{total}}.$$

(eta-squared)

Yet more effect size estimates include **Cramer's *v*,** which is suitable for the chi-square test for independence, and **Cohen's *w*** for chi-square goodness of fit.

$$v = \sqrt{\frac{\chi^2}{N_{tot}}},$$

(Cramer's v)

$$w = \sum \frac{(P_O - P_E)^2}{P_E}.$$

(Cohen's w)

NOTE: Cohen's w has the same form as chi-square but uses proportions instead of frequency counts.

How large should your effect size be to consider it important? To some degree, this depends on your research question. But some generally accepted guidelines are as follows:

	For Cohen's d	*For r^2*	*For η^2*	*For Cramer's v and Cohen's w*
A small effect	$d = .20$	$r^2 = .01$	$\eta^2 = .01$	$v = .10$
A medium effect	$d = .50$	$r^2 = .09$	$\eta^2 = .06$	$v = .30$
A large effect	$d = .80$	$r^2 = .25$	$\eta^2 = .14$	$v = .50$

See Cohen (1992) for a brief and simple treatment of effect size.

We have shown you a few simple estimates of effect size, and in Chapter 13, we will calculate these for several examples, but in practice, statistical software packages all provide effect size and power estimates if you ask for them. We have included these calculations just to give you an idea of what effect size means and how to interpret the output from the computer programs.

POWER AND THE ROLE OF REPLICATION IN RESEARCH

Students often ask us about the problem that statistical inferences can be wrong. Even with good procedures and good statistical techniques, any inference can be wrong. If we do a study and show that an innovative teaching technique *significantly improves* student performance, we had better be confident in our inference if the superintendent of schools plans to adopt the new curriculum based on our work. This is where **replication** of research comes in. If we do another study and find the same thing, the probability that we have made an error of inference drops in a big way. In other words, our power (i.e., the probability that our rejection of the null is correct) has increased when we replicate the finding in a new study with different participants in a different setting, perhaps.

Many psychology students have heard of the study that involved asking people questions and watching which way they directed their gaze as they thought of the answer. It has long been known that areas in the frontal lobes control movement of the eyes. This research involved monitoring lateral eye movements as people answered questions that required either language processing (left hemisphere) or spatial processing (right hemisphere). Although some researchers have replicated the result, there are many others who have failed to replicate it (e.g., Ehrlichman & Weinberger, 1979).

Could the research have been an example of a Type I error? Perhaps, but at the very least, this underscores the importance of replicability. After all, in 1949, the Nobel Prize in medicine was awarded to Egas Moniz for the transorbital prefrontal lobotomy. It is a real tragedy that practitioners did not wait for independent replication of his claims.

Conceptual Exercise 4C

For each example, indicate if there is a problem of power, effect size, or replication.

1. There was a large difference between the mean for the treatment group and the control group, but we did not achieve statistical significance.

2. There was a small difference between the treatment group and the control group, and we did not achieve statistical significance. Maybe we should increase our sample size.

3. We were amazed that we found a significant difference that has never been reported in the literature.

Research findings, significant or not, that are not replicable may not be important! **Replicability** is a fundamental requirement of research findings in all science. Replicability is one way we have to improve the validity of our research.

EXTERNAL AND INTERNAL VALIDITY

When we have replicated a finding with different participants or in different settings, we have demonstrated that our research has what is called *external validity.*

A study, then, is **externally valid** if the findings can be *generalized to other populations and settings.* Psychologists are typically interested in human behavior—all human behavior. A finding in your laboratory with your participants, your equipment, and your stimuli that does not replicate in other laboratories with other people and other materials does not have external validity. Research carried out under more natural conditions (i.e., in the field) tends to have greater external validity than research carried out under artificial conditions (i.e., in the laboratory) But research studies must also be internally valid. **Internal validity** refers to the validity of the measures *within* our study. Did our independent variable cause the changes we see in our dependent variable? Experiments conducted in the laboratory, where control is high, tend to have better internal validity than studies carried out in the field, where control of extraneous variables is more difficult The internal validity of an experiment or study is directly related to the researcher's control of extraneous variables.

Confounding and Extraneous Variables

An internally valid study is one where the change in the dependent variable is attributable to changes in the independent variable. If a variable that is *not manipulated by the researcher* affects the outcome, the study lacks internal validity.

An **extraneous variable** is a variable that may affect the outcome of a study but was not manipulated by the researcher. Such variables are not a problem as long as they are not systematically related to the IV, but they can be a big problem if they do vary in a systematic way. In one example, we talked about the influence of classroom technology on learning. When we compare two groups of students, one of which receives instruction with technology and the other receives instruction without technology, we do not want variables other than the IV (e.g., type of instruction) to influence learning. Some of these might be related to the students, such as differences in learning ability, motivation, gender, and so on. Others might be related to the instructional environment, such as room temperature, time of day, instructor, and so forth. The researcher is not investigating differences in learning ability, motivation, room temperature, or time of day, but nevertheless, these things are still variables that must be taken into account.

Sometimes, not often we hope, an extraneous variable is not controlled or accounted for and unfortunately gums up the works and produces what we call a *spurious effect*—a researcher's worst nightmare. An extraneous variable can be a **confounding variable** if it is systematically related to the independent and dependent variables and, as a result, offers an alternative explanation for the outcome. The outcome is said to be spurious because it was influenced not by the independent variable itself but rather by a variable that was confounded with the independent variable. For example, consider our classroom technology study. Imagine that we decided to compare a group of students who used classroom technology with a group of students who did not. Imagine further that our tech group met at 8 a.m., and our nontech group met at 4 p.m. If we find that our tech group performed better than our nontech group, can we conclude that technology was the reason for the difference? No, we cannot. Even if we randomly assigned students to the two groups and controlled all sorts of things in this study, we have not controlled something that could be systematically related to both the independent and dependent variables (i.e., time of day). It is possible that early morning is a better time for learning, when students are alert and energetic, than late in the day, when students are tired and want to go home. In other words, the time of day difference between the tech and nontech groups is an alternative explanation for the effect and is confounded (i.e., systematically related) with the independent variable, technology.

Extraneous variables become controlled variables when the researcher takes them into account in designing the research study or experiment. Some of those variables are controlled by good experimental design and good research technique. Differences in room temperature, noise level, and testing apparatus can be controlled by using a soundproof, constant-temperature laboratory. And indeed, many researchers prefer laboratory research because it is easier to control extraneous variables such as these. We want to control extraneous variables because they contribute variance to our dependent measures and cloud the results. We often call these variables *nuisance variables*. The better we can keep these variables out of our results, the better we can estimate the influence of the independent variable on the dependent variable.

Researchers need to think about the variables operating in their experiments that might contribute unwanted variability or, worse, be confounded with the IV. And then they need to control those sources of variance so that they can evaluate the effect of the IV.

As we have said, the internal validity of a research study depends on the researcher's control over extraneous variables. The better we control other sources of variation, the better we can assess the effects of the variables we are interested in. Next we will look at several ways to do this.

Controlling Extraneous Variables

Elimination

One way to control extraneous variables is to get rid of them entirely. For example, if you think that ambient noise might influence the outcome of your study, then eliminate it by conducting your study in a noise-proof environment. The disadvantage of eliminating a variable is that you will not be able to generalize your results to those conditions that you eliminated. Would you have found the same results in an environment where ambient noise was present?

It is easier to eliminate extraneous variables in laboratory settings than in field settings. Laboratories can be soundproofed, but the natural environment cannot.

Lots of extraneous variables, particularly individual differences in ability, motivation, and so on, cannot be eliminated, of course. How would we eliminate room temperature from our study? Well, we couldn't, of course, but we could hold it constant for all groups.

Constancy

Most, if not all, researchers use constancy. Instructions to participants are constant, the procedure (except for the IV) is constant, the measuring instruments are constant, and the questions on a questionnaire are constant. In Chapter 2, we discussed Knez's (2001) study on lighting. He used constancy to control noise and room temperature in his study.

He also kept gender constant by including 54 women and 54 men.

But what if we thought gender might be interesting? Not as interesting as our primary IV but interesting nevertheless. We could make gender another variable to study, which indeed is exactly what Knez did. He included gender as a participant variable and included it as a variable of secondary interest in his analyses.

Secondary Variable as an IV

Often researchers make variables other than the primary IV secondary variables to study. Knez (2001) reported research indicating that men and women respond differently to various light conditions—and he claimed that gender is a moderating variable. He decided it was important to not only control for gender with an equal number of men and women in each group but also to examine how gender differences affect the way the IV acts on the dependent variable (DV). This type of control is not only a design decision but also a statistical decision because the secondary variable will be included in the statistical analysis used to assess the effects of the primary and any secondary IVs on the DV.

Elimination, constancy, and making an extraneous variable a secondary variable are all techniques used to control extraneous variables that might affect the outcome of the study (i.e., variation in the dependent variable).

What if there are extraneous variables operating that we do not know about? This is a good question, and the answer is randomization. Perhaps the most common way to control extraneous variables is random assignment of participants (or subjects, if they are animals) to groups.

Randomization: Random Assignment of Participants to Groups

Before we can conclude that our manipulation of the IV, and nothing else, caused a change in responding, the DV, we must be confident that our groups were equivalent before we treated them. If they were not equivalent at the outset of our study, then it will be no surprise that they are different at the end of our study. Knez (2001) randomly assigned his participants to three light conditions, the three levels of his primary IV. Random assignment of participants to conditions of the study does not guarantee initial equivalence of groups, but we can be reasonably confident that our groups will be more or less similar if participants were truly randomly assigned to groups. This method of controlling extraneous variables is probably the most common procedure used by researchers, particularly when they have large samples. With smaller samples, another common method of dealing with unknown extraneous variables is to test all the participants in all the conditions—the within-participants or repeated-measures design.

Repeated Measures

What better way to control for unknown variation among participants than to use the same participants in all conditions, a **repeated-measures design.** Each participant acts as his or her or its (if we are talking about animals) own control because changes in the DV are compared within each participant (or subject, if we are talking about animals). Gender, IQ, motivation level, and so on are all held constant because comparisons are always made between measures from the same participant. A repeated-measures procedure cannot be used when the treatment conditions may result in lasting changes in responding. For example, you cannot train someone to solve problems using one strategy and then expect that person to forget the first strategy and use a different strategy when solving a second set of problems. Training cannot be unlearned. This issue is discussed in greater detail in Chapters 7 and 8.

What if we discover, after the data have been collected, that the groups were not initially equivalent despite our best efforts? Sometimes statistics can help.

Statistical Control

Sometimes we find that a variable we did not control seems to have affected our outcome. In such cases, we can use statistics to help us. If we are lucky enough to have measured the variable, we can treat it as a covariate and use statistical procedures (e.g., analysis of covariance

[**ANCOVA**]) to remove it from the analysis. Basically, we can use statistical procedures to estimate the influence of the extraneous variable on the dependent measure and remove this source of variation from the analysis. There are statistical techniques that allow us to take into account extraneous variables that have crept into our data that we discovered only after the fact; such techniques would be covered in most upper-level statistics texts.

Conceptual Exercise 4D

What method of control would you suggest for each of the following extraneous variables? Why?

1. Gender of trainer when type of training is IV

2. Breed of rat when diet is IV

3. Intelligence, attitude, capability, and motivation of child when reinforcement strategy is IV

4. Fitness when exercise program is IV

CHAPTER SUMMARY

The most common **inferential** approach in psychology is **hypothesis testing.** A **conceptual hypothesis** is a statement about the expected relationship between conceptual variables. A **research hypothesis** is a statement about the expected relationship between measurable, or **operationalized,** variables. A **statistical hypothesis** is a statement about the relationship between statistical properties of data.

The **null hypothesis** is a statistical hypothesis about the value of a parameter, the relationship between two or more parameters, or the shape of a distribution and is the hypothesis that the researcher hopes to reject. The **alternative hypothesis** specifies something different than what is stated in the null and is the hypothesis the researcher hopes to confirm.

A **statistically significant** finding means that the relationship specified in the null is very unlikely to be true, and so the researcher rejects the null and accepts the alternative. Testing the null hypothesis follows these steps: State the null and alternative, collect the data and conduct the statistical test, reject the null or fail to reject the null, and state the conclusion.

A **statistical inference** is a statement of **probability;** as such, there is always some probability that the inference is incorrect. A **Type I error** occurs when our statistical test leads us to reject a true null. A **Type II error** occurs when our statistical test leads us to fail to reject a false null.

Powerful tests of the null are tests that have a high probability of rejecting false nulls.

Power can be increased by controlling extraneous variables, using interval or ratio scales for the dependent measure, choosing good research designs, using appropriate sampling procedures, choosing powerful significance tests, choosing lenient alpha levels, increasing sample size, reducing participant variability, maximizing the treatment manipulation, and replicating the findings.

   Effect size estimates should be included along with other statistics in any research report. Common effect size estimates include **Cohen's *d,*** suitable for *t* tests; *r*²; the **coefficient of determination,** suitable for Pearson's *r* correlation test; and **eta-squared,** suitable for ANOVA.

   Replicability of research findings is an important part of the research process. A research finding that has been duplicated with different participants or in different settings is **externally valid.** When an IV has been shown to cause change in the DV, the study has **internal validity. Confounding** and **extraneous variables** must be controlled for a study to be internally valid.

   Extraneous variables can be controlled by **elimination, constancy, making a secondary variable an IV, randomization,** using a **repeated-measures design,** and **statistical techniques** such as **ANCOVA**.

ANSWERS TO CONCEPTUAL EXERCISES

Conceptual Exercise 4A

There are numerous ways of operationalizing the variables in this conceptual hypothesis.

   We might operationalize the concept "helping profession" to include clinical psychologists, psychiatric nurses, and psychiatrists, for example.

   We might operationalize "business professions" as bankers, CEOs, and retailers.

   How would we operationalize "ethical"? Well, we could create a series of ethical dilemmas, the solutions to which have already been rated by experts on some scale of ethicality (Is that a word? We are not sure).

   You can see, we hope, that the operational definitions you choose for your research project are up to you. They might be good (i.e., valid), or they might be bad. We suggest you read the literature to find out what other researchers do to operationalize any constructs you want to use in your project.

Conceptual Exercise 4B

1. Your statistical decision was correct. You did not reject the null, and that was correct because the null was true (i.e., there was no difference).

2. Oh dear. You rejected the null, but the null was true. You have made a Type I error.

3. Oh dear again. Your statistical test did not find a significant difference, and so you did not reject the null. Sadly, the null was false. You have made a Type II error.

4. Good on you. The null is false, and your conclusion, based on your significance test, was just that.

Conceptual Exercise 4C

1. Hmm, well, it appears that the treatment effect was large. Probably we have a power problem, which could have been caused by all sorts of things. Perhaps we used a weak

statistical test, or maybe we had poor control over extraneous variables. Probably we need to redo our study with more attention to control of variables and reconsider the significance test we should use.

2. Maybe so, but maybe the effect is not very important. We might achieve a significant result if we increase our sample size in a big way, but would it be important?

3. Aha, time to replicate. Let's not report a finding, even if significant, that is contrary to the existing literature on the topic. If we obtain the same result a second time, with different participants at a different time and in a different setting, perhaps we should go ahead, report our contradictory finding, and feel confident about it.

Conceptual Exercise 4D

1. There are various ways to control for gender. Perhaps the simplest way is to hold it constant.

2. Constancy is probably the best way to control breed of rat.

3. Randomization or repeated measures would be appropriate.

4. Randomization or constancy would be appropriate.

FAQ

Q1: Why do we need inferential statistics?

A1: We need inferential statistics whenever we want to make statements about populations based on sample data. We have not included everyone in our sample, so we cannot be 100% sure that our conclusions will generalize to the population. Inferential statistics provide us with a probability estimate of how likely it is that we are incorrect in our inference. If the probability that our outcome would have occurred by chance is low (e.g., $p < .05$ or .01), we can be more confident that our inference is correct—not 100% certain, but more certain. Only by measuring the entire population can you be certain that you know the true state of affairs.

Q2: Why do we test the null hypothesis and not our research hypothesis?

A2: We test the null hypothesis because it is much easier to disprove than it is to prove. So instead of gathering endless data to confirm our research hypothesis, we set out to disconfirm a null hypothesis. One instance of disconfirmation, and we can reject the null and accept the alternative hypothesis (i.e., our research hypothesis). But perhaps more important, we test the null because the null provides us with a clear expectation of outcomes (called the sampling distribution). We then compare our outcome with what the null would predict. After all, we all know exactly how a fair coin behaves. But a biased coin could be slightly biased toward heads, moderately biased toward tails, extremely biased toward heads, and so on. Remember that our alternative hypothesis specifies that the null is false, and in a one-tailed test in what direction, but it does not specify the expected size of the difference.

Q3: Why is inference always stated as a probability? Isn't science interested in proving things?

A3: In science, we are interested in finding empirical support for our research hypotheses. Because we work with samples and not entire populations, we have to make statistical inferences, and in doing so, there is always a possibility that our inference is wrong. Even research with statistical significance will have a nonzero probability that the results are a fluke and that another outcome may arise using a different sample. That is why the scientific community waits for independent researchers to replicate a finding before getting too excited.

Q4: How can you increase your statistical power?

A4: (1) Increase your sample size, (2) increase your alpha level, (3) decrease the variability among your participants, and (4) increase the magnitude of your treatment.

Q5: Why does the APA publication manual suggest including effect size estimates with your inferential statistic?

A5: Statistical significance tells us that the results are not likely a fluke and that they are probably replicable. However, significance does not indicate the size of the treatment effect or the strength of a correlation. Both pieces of information are needed to assess the importance of a study.

Q6: What is the coefficient of determination?

A6: The coefficient of determination is a measure of effect size that tells us how much variability in the criterion variable we can account for by its relationship with the predictor variable. It ranges from 1, where we have accounted for all the variability and can predict with perfect accuracy, to 0, where we have accounted for no part of the criterion variable, and our predictor does not predict at all (coefficient of determination $= r^2$).

Q7: Why is replication important in science?

A7: A single study that reports statistical significance may be a Type I error. After all, depending on our alpha level, Type I errors are expected to occur about 5% or 1% of the time. Replication is important to reduce the likelihood that a research outcome was just a fluke or Type I error. Having the research replicated by an independent group of researchers also guards against any researcher bias influencing the outcome.

Q8: I remember something about one-tailed or two-tailed t tests. What is the difference?

A8: In performing a t test, you compare two means and test a null hypothesis that they do not differ. Your alternative hypothesis can be either that the means differ and you do not specify which mean will be larger than the other (two-tailed), or you may specify that one mean will be larger than the other (one-tailed). A one-tailed test has more power, so there is strong incentive for using a one-tailed test. In using a one-tailed test, you are only looking for a difference between the means in one direction, so you must have good reason for predicting the direction of the difference (usually based on previous research). The reason a one-tailed test has more power is that the critical value of t is smaller because your region of rejection is all in one tail rather than divided into each end of the t distribution. See Chapter 13 for more detail on one- and two-tailed tests.

CHAPTER EXERCISES

1. What is an inference?
2. What is the relationship between alpha level and statistical power?
3. What are the four outcomes of any inferential decision?
4. List three ways to increase power.
5. Why is effect size important?
6. Your research hypothesis is that women have a keener sense of smell than men. You measure the minimum amount of perfume that can be detected in a room as your measure of olfactory acuity. Based on your sample of women and men, you find that women do have a better sense of smell. Your inferential statistic has a $p < .02$, which means the difference was not likely due to chance. You decide to reject the null hypothesis and accept the alternative. You conclude that women have a keener sense of smell. What are the chances that you made a Type I error? What are the chances you made a Type II error? How would you know for certain that your decision was correct?
7. You read a study that found a strong positive correlation between high school performance and university performance ($r = .68$). Thinking back on your own experience, you did really well in high school but flunked out of your first year in university. Just how well does high school performance predict performance in university?
8. Green hand syndrome is an embarrassing condition where a person's hands turn green in social situations. You have reason to hypothesize that drinking a single cup of tea may be an effective treatment. How would you test this hypothesis? What alpha level would you select (include a rationale)? How would you interpret your results if your effect size is small?
9. What method of control is being used in the following?
   a. A researcher concerned about motivation, fatigue, ability, interests, and so on of her participants randomly assigns them to groups
   b. A researcher concerned about IQ differences decides to select only people with IQs between 95 and 105 as participants in his study
   c. A researcher concerned about gender effects uses only female participants in her study
   d. A researcher concerned about gender effects creates groups with equal numbers of men and women and decides to analyze any differences

CHAPTER PROJECTS

1. With a search term of your choice, find three empirical research articles. Report the inferential statistics from each article and include the degrees of freedom and the p value. Describe why the researchers selected those specific tests. What was the reported effect size? For their statistically significant findings, do you think their effect is important?

2. With a search term of your choice, find three empirical research articles. Describe the methods the researchers used to increase the power of their analysis. Can you think of other ways to increase power in each study?

3. Create a research project of your own and describe how you would operationalize the variables. Describe your IV, DV, and any control procedures you would need to use.

REFERENCES

American Psychological Association. (2001). *Publication manual of the American Psychological Association* (5th ed.). Washington, DC: Author.

Cohen, J. (1992). A power primer. *Psychological Bulletin, 112*(1), 155–159.

Ehrlichman, H., & Weinberger, A. (1979). Lateral eye movements and hemispheric asymmetry: A critical review. *Psychological Bulletin, 85,* 1080–1101.

Evans, A. (2007). *Using basic statistics in the social sciences* (4th ed.). Scarborough, Ontario, Canada: Pearson Education.

Knez, I. (2001). Effects of colour of light on nonvisual psychological processes. *Journal of Environmental Psychology, 21*(2), 201–208.

Visit the study site at www.sagepub.com/evansmprstudy for practice quizzes and other study resources.

Measuring Variables

OBJECTIVES

After studying this chapter, students should be able to

- Describe when it would be appropriate to use a fixed alternative format
- Describe when it would be appropriate to use an open-ended format
- Describe the advantages and disadvantages of fixed and open-ended questions
- Describe a Likert scale and how it differs from other rating scales
- Describe when it would be appropriate to use a semantic differential scale
- Define the term social desirability
- Define what is meant by response set
- Describe ways of avoiding social desirability and response set
- Describe various ways of measuring observable behavior
- Describe the relationship between precision and statistical power
- Define reliability
- Describe the various ways of assessing reliability
- Define validity
- Describe the various types of validity
- Describe the difference between a scale and an inventory
- Describe how to find a test that measures specific variables

In a court case, a witness was asked the following question by the prosecutor: Did you know this person with whom you met on July 7?

The witness responded no.

The prosecutor sat down, confident that the jury members believed that the witness did not know who the person was with whom she had met on July 7.

The defense attorney asked the same witness this question: Did you know who the person was with whom you met on July 7?

The witness responded yes.

Just a few words differed in the question, but the response was very different. Asking questions is a critical part of research in social science. Knowing how to ask questions well has a huge impact on the quality and quantity of the information you receive. Vague questions will get vague replies. But questions that are too specific may fail to get complete answers.

WAYS OF ASKING QUESTIONS

Questions can be asked in many ways. How you ask the question depends in part on your research goal. Different kinds of questions will elicit different kinds of information. **Quantitative** questions provide data that are easy to analyze, but the information may be limited. **Qualitative** questions provide a richness of information that may be harder to analyze.

Fixed Alternative Questions

Fixed alternative questions are questions where the respondent selects his or her answer from a set of specified responses. The simplest fixed alternative question is one where the response choices are YES and NO. This type of question is fine when there are clearly only two choices possible, as in "Are you a student?" But many questions we might want to ask have more than two choices. If we can determine that there is a finite set of answers to our question, we specify those for our respondents. Students know these kinds of questions as multiple choice, which are often used in exams.

For example, consider the following question asked of young adults.

Q: What is your age?

A: 18–22
        23–27
        28–32

If the operational definition of young adults was people between the ages of 18 and 32, then this fixed alternative question is a good one. Everyone sampled could respond accurately. No gray areas here.

But consider the following question asked of single mothers.

Q: Why did you choose to keep your child?

A: Pressured by peers
        Pressured by parents
        Pressured by church

Here is a question where, although some possible responses have been listed, there may be many other factors underlying a woman's decision to keep her child. One way to deal with this problem is to include an "Other" category where the respondent can fill in his or her answer. The disadvantage is that those answers have to be coded in some way, and if you receive many diverse responses, you may have simply created the next type of question—an open-ended question.

Conceptual Exercise 5A

What is wrong with the following items?

What is your age?

____ 10–20

____ 20–30

____ 30–40

____ 40–50

____ Over 50

What is your favorite flavor of ice cream?

____ Chocolate

____ Vanilla

____ Other

Open-Ended Questions

Sometimes, the fixed alternative type of question just cannot quite get at what we want to know. Perhaps we have asked our respondents if they have ever experienced sexual harassment on the job or in school. This could be a simple yes/no question. But what if we wanted to know the details? Given that there are probably too many possible scenarios to specify, we might decide that open-ended questions are the best way to gather information. An **open-ended question** allows the respondent to provide his or her answer in his or her own words. We might ask questions such as the following:

Describe what you did to deal with the harassment.

Did you go to your employer or school official for help? If so, how did they help?

Open-ended questions have the advantage of allowing the respondent to define the answer. As such, you are likely to obtain a lot more information. Responses to open-ended questions are often summarized with a **content analysis.** This is when all the responses are categorized into recurring themes, and the relative frequency of the themes is reported. This is a labor-intensive task that requires reading each and every response; fortunately, a number of statistical analysis programs have been developed to automate the procedure (e.g., SPSS Text Analysis for Surveys).

Rating Scales

Rating scales are essentially fixed alternative questions where we ask the respondent to indicate magnitude on a scale. Rating scales are used to rate movies, restaurants, hotels, and so forth. There is a wide variety of formats for rating scales, but typically, a question is followed by a scale with adjectives that give the respondent a frame of reference for what the numbers mean. Here are some examples:

If you wanted some, how difficult would it be to get:

	Extremely Difficult	*Fairly Difficult*	*Fairly Easy*	*Extremely Easy*	*Don't Know*
Cigarettes?					
Alcohol?					
Marijuana?					
Cocaine (not crack cocaine)?					
Crack?					

Regarding the teacher:

	Completely Unacceptable	*Not Acceptable*	*Acceptable*	*More Than Acceptable*	*Outstanding*
The teacher's explanation of the material was					
The teacher's understanding of the material was					
The level of interest generated by the teacher was					
The teacher's organization was					

Likert Scales

In the early 1900s, Renis Likert invented the **Likert Scale**, a response scale ranging from *strongly disagree* to *strongly agree* that is often used in attitude surveys. Likert scales are easy to construct and use, and they are easy for respondents to understand. Unlike other rating scales that ask respondents a question and provide a scale for the response, Likert items are always statements, and the respondent is asked to indicate the degree to which he or she agrees or disagrees with the statement. Likert items are one of the easiest ways to quantify an attitude or opinion.

A typical Likert item might be the following:

Women should be allowed to enter the priesthood.

1	2	3	4	5	6	7
strongly disagree						strongly agree

The scale is often used with 5 points, but 7 to 9 points provide greater precision. By convention, the left side is always labeled *strongly disagree,* and the right side is always labeled *strongly agree.*

Semantic Differential

Charles E. Osgood developed a derivation of the Likert Scale called the **Semantic Differential**. This scale was designed to measure the psychological distance between the connotative meanings of words (Osgood, Suci, & Tannenbaum, 1957). In other words, the scale measures all the meanings associated with a word that are not, by definition, part of the word. He asked people to tell him the first word that came to mind after they read each word in a list of words that he created. He then determined the opposite word to each of these free-associated words to create a bipolar scale.

Any word then could be rated on a series of bipolar scales. For example, measuring the connotative meaning of the word *mother* with the Semantic Differential would look like this:

Mother:

Hot	1	2	3	4	5	6	7	Cold
Fast	1	2	3	4	5	6	7	Slow
Happy	1	2	3	4	5	6	7	Sad

His findings led him to believe that attitudes could be differentiated on the basis of three factors or dimensions:

1. Evaluative as in good versus bad

2. Potency as in strong versus weak

3. Activity as in active versus passive

Students sometimes think that it would be difficult and possibly silly to try to rate a word on these dimensions, but in fact, once they try it, they find it is actually quite easy to do. Most students rate the word *mother* as good, not so strong, and somewhat passive, whereas *father* is often rated as good, strong, and active.

Osgood thought that this method of measuring attitudes would provide more insight into the relationship between attitude and behavior. The Semantic Differential has been used in personality tests, in marketing, and even to rate psychology courses.

Social Desirability and Response Set

Whenever we ask people questions, we run the risk that they may give answers that they think are appropriate or **socially desirable** or that we might want to hear. In addition, when people respond to a lot of items, they may develop a **response set,** giving only moderate answers or always agreeing or disagreeing.

Here are some tips to help deal with these problems.

- Alter the wording on some items so that an attitude is reflected by agreement on some items and disagreement on others—this helps to reduce the development of a response set.
- Stress anonymity—respondents may be more likely to be honest when they believe they cannot be identified.
- Include irrelevant items—this may help disguise your purpose.

We cannot observe attitudes and feelings directly, and so the above ways of asking questions must be used. Often, however, we do not need to ask questions; we can observe the behavior directly.

MEASURING OBSERVED BEHAVIOR

When the behavior we are interested in is observable, we need to decide how we will measure it. Let's look at some of the typical ways that psychologists measure observable behavior.

When responses are either right or wrong, an obvious measure is **accuracy.** How many questions does Biff answer correctly? How often a behavior occurs in a specified period of time is a very common measure of behavior or response strength, usually referred to as **frequency.** This is the measure of choice for many behavioral psychologists. This measure is suitable when the behavior is discrete. How many times does Cindy-Jo interrupt the teacher during class? Some behaviors are best measured in terms of their speed of onset or **latency.** Reaction time, for example, is a measure of the speed of response to some stimulus. How long did it take Seth to sit after being asked to do so? Other behaviors are best measured in terms of their **duration;** how long do they last? How long did Tally's tantrum continue? **Amplitude** or size of response is yet another measure of response strength. How loud did Selwin scream during his tantrum?

Some researchers are interested in frequency of choice between alternatives, that is, **choice selection.** For example, does Peter prefer small but more frequent rewards or large but less frequent rewards?

Whatever the behavior is that you have chosen to measure, it is important to consider the level of measurement (i.e., nominal, ordinal, interval, or ratio). As you will see below, the level of measure can make the difference between finding a significant result and missing an important discovery.

Conceptual Exercise 5B

Indicate which measure would best suit the following:

1. A road test for elderly drivers

2. Measuring the effectiveness of an intervention for schoolyard bullying

3. Using mental imagery to improve a skier's performance

Levels of Measurement

In the early planning stage of research, you make decisions about how you will measure your variables. As you will learn later in this chapter, it is important that you measure your variables as precisely as possible. Equally important, though, is the type of measurement scale that you use. The level of measurement scale is important because it determines the kinds of statistical manipulations we can perform on the data (see Chapter 13). Some variables carry more information by their very nature. The more quantitative the variable is, the more information we can obtain from it. Quantitative variables differ in terms of amount; different values contain more or less of the variable. Qualitative variables do not; different values of these variables are different in quality, not in quantity. Different levels of measurement reflect the degree of quantification of the measures. Some measures are not quantitative at all; rather, they are qualitative.

Nominal

Nominal variables are qualitative; as the name indicates, values of the variable differ in *name,* not quantity. We can do limited statistical manipulations with these kinds of variables. For example, gender, eye color, occupation, and ethnicity are nominal variables. Even if we code gender as female = 1 and male = 0 to make data recording easier, such coding imparts no quantitative information about gender. Female participants are different in kind, not quantity, from male participants. Blue eyes are nominally different from green eyes. Physicians are not more than or less than lawyers, and Norwegians are not more or less than South Africans; they are just different. There is no quantitative difference between different values of a nominal variable.

Ordinal

When things vary in order of quantity, we use the term **ordinal variable**. Rank ordering of skaters is an example. Win, place, and show in a horse race is another example. Even if we assigned a value such as winner = 1, show horse = 2, and place horse = 3, these values only reflect the order of the finish. The third-place horse might have finished seven lengths behind the second-place horse, and the second-place horse might have lost by a nose to the first-place horse. The intervals between the values are not necessarily equal. When we have an ordinal variable, we only know order from high to low. We do not know anything about the intervals or distance between each value. An example in psychology might be level of depression quantified as mild, moderate, or severe. A criminologist might code offenders by degree of violence: extreme, moderate, or low.

If a researcher has collected information and wants to make inferences about nominal or ordinal variables, he or she must use nonparametric statistical analyses. Nonparametric statistics do not have as much statistical power as parametric statistics, and this can mean that you may need a much larger sample size than you would need if you use an interval or ratio scale measure.

Interval

If the intervals between the values of the variable are equal, we have an **interval variable**. For example, IQ scores are interval. The interval between an IQ score of 100 and 110 is the same as the interval between 110 and 120; both are 10 IQ points apart. Consider a rating scale such as the following:

1	extremely sad
2	moderately sad
3	slightly sad
4	neither sad nor happy
5	slightly happy
6	moderately happy
7	extremely happy

If this were an interval scale, could we say that a person who rated herself as a 6 is twice as happy as a person who rated himself as 3? No, we couldn't. **Interval scales** have arbitrary zero points, and so such comparisons cannot be made. Here is the same interval scale with an arbitrary zero:

–3	extremely sad
–2	moderately sad
–1	slightly sad
0	neither sad nor happy
1	slightly happy
2	moderately happy
3	extremely happy

And the same question: Is a person who rated herself a 2 twice as happy as a person who rated himself a –1?

To make such a comparison, a true zero point is needed. Imagine that we have measured phobic tendencies of three young adults with a test that gives us the following data:

Participant	Degree of Phobia (Scale of 0–6 Where 0 Is Least Phobic)
Megan	2
Robert	6
Mathilda	4

If our test was valid and reliable, we could conclude that Robert shows more phobic tendencies than Megan. But could we say that Mathilda was twice as phobic as Megan? No, we couldn't, because this scale is an interval scale, at best, and has no true zero point. Zero on the scale does not mean absence of phobia; it only means the lowest level of phobic tendency.

Ratio

Twice as many students are enrolled in introductory psychology than in introductory philosophy. My textbook has three times more pages than yours. These statements can be made because number of students enrolled in a course and number of pages in textbooks are both ratio variables. **Ratio variables** are like interval variables but with a true zero point. This does not mean that a zero value is possible. It means that we start measuring from a value of zero. Kelvin temperature is a ratio variable because 0 degrees Kelvin means absence of heat. Eighty degrees Kelvin is twice as hot as 40 degrees.

The level of measurement of variables determines in part what kinds of statistical procedures can be applied to those numbers. We cannot determine a mean for a nominal variable, for example. How would we report mean eye color or mean occupation? We certainly can determine the mean of a ratio variable. The more quantitative a variable is, the more we can do with it and to it.

At this point, we want to discuss the difference between the scale of the measure itself and the scale of the underlying dimension. They may not be the same. For example, I may choose to rank order my students from highest score to lowest score on a test. The rank ordering is an ordinal scale, but the original test scores are ratio. We think of color as being a nominal variable, and most of the time, that is how we treat it. But we could measure wavelength of light reflected by various colors, and we would then have a ratio scale.

Conceptual Exercise 5C

Classify the following variables in terms of the level of measurement:

1. Income

2. Number of children in families

3. Type of mental disorder

4. Gold, silver, bronze at the Olympics

5. LSAT scores

Most researchers try to measure variables on at least an interval level because the statistical analyses of such variables tend to be more powerful. And, in fact, more analyses are permissible with such variables. Let's now look at another important aspect of measurement.

THE IMPORTANCE OF PRECISION IN MEASUREMENT

Precision in measurement is important in all research, whether in the social sciences, physical sciences, or engineering. In descriptive research, precise measurements can improve the accuracy of our description of a population. When testing a research hypothesis, precision increases our chances of finding a statistically significant result. Here is an example to illustrate the importance of precision in hypothesis testing. Imagine that you have developed a drug that you believe will enhance memory. You conduct an experiment by randomly assigning 20 people to take either the drug or a placebo (i.e., 10 in each group). Thirty minutes later, they are given a list of 25 words to study for an hour. Two hours later, their recall of the words (out of 25) is tested with the following results.

Placebo	*Drug*
14	16
18	20
16	18
19	21
18	20
17	19
18	20
18	20
17	19
19	21

Let's compute the means and standard deviations for each group and use a *t* test to compare the means. The drug group remembered more items than the placebo group (drug group $M = 19.4$, $SD = 1.51$; placebo group $M = 17.4$, $SD = 1.51$), and the difference was statistically significant at an alpha level of .01, $t(18) = 2.97$, $p = .008$. Great, you found a statistically significant difference between the groups. You'll probably get rich!

But look at your results if you reduce your precision. Imagine that you rounded the number of words recalled to the nearest 5. Here are the same data as above but rounded.

Placebo	*Drug*
15	15
20	20
15	20
20	20
20	20
15	20
20	20
20	20
15	20
20	20

This time, there is only a small difference between the groups (drug group $M = 19.5$, $SD = 1.58$; placebo group $M = 18.0$, $SD = 2.58$), but more important, the difference is not statistically significant, $t(18) = 1.57$, $p = .135$. The loss in precision changed a statistically significant result into a nonsignificant one. Sigh—not a good thing!

If you can obtain a precise measure, do so because the outcome of your research may depend on it. And never reduce the precision of a measure that you have taken.

We have learned that level of measurement is important. Variables that can be measured on an interval or ratio level are preferred. Our measures must also be as precise as possible. Let's now turn to another important aspect of measurement—reliability.

Reliability of Measurement

Reliable measures are repeatable. This means that participants will produce similar scores when repeated measures are taken. Consider the demo we often use in class. We claim that we are precise measurers of height. We ask several students to stand up, and we "guess" their heights at several inches taller or shorter than the students are. We do this several times, giving the same incorrect estimates each time. When asked, our students eventually agree that we are reliable measurers of height. We are reliable because we provide very similar measures each time. Our measures are reliable but not correct. We will return to this example in the following section on validity.

Researchers use various techniques to determine the reliability of their measures. **Test-retest** reliability is determined by correlating the scores received by a group of participants who were tested at two different times. This produces an estimate of reliability over time, and of course, the assumption is that the trait/behavior you are measuring is stable over time. **Split-half** reliability is determined by correlating half the items on a set of homogeneous questions with the other half. This produces an estimate of internal consistency and is a useful way for measuring reliability when the traits/behaviors are not stable over time. Another measure of internal consistency that is often reported is **Cronbach's alpha.** Generally speaking, this is an average correlation of each item with the other items in a test, but it also takes into account the number of items in the test.

In observation research, when you are measuring categorical variables, reliability of measures is often assessed by measuring **interrater** reliability. For example, if you have two or three observers, are they making the same judgments of behavior? Interrater reliability is often measured using **Cohen's kappa,** which produces a 0 if there is no agreement between raters and 1 if there is perfect agreement.

We began our discussion of reliability by describing our class demo where we estimate height of students. Recall that we gave reliable but incorrect measures. Clearly, reliability is not enough. Our measures must also be valid.

Validity of Measurement

A **valid** measure is one that measures what it says it measures. Measures that are reliable but not valid are useless to researchers; likewise, valid measures that are unreliable are useless.

Face Validity

A measure has **face validity** if, on the face of it, it seems to be a reasonable measure of the variable. We might check for face validity by asking a panel of experts to rate our measure. Head size, for example, would have lower face validity as a measure of intelligence than the number of questions solved per unit time.

Construct Validity

Construct validity is referring to the operational definition of the variable. Does it measure the underlying construct? Imagine that we want to assess the effectiveness of regular aerobic exercise on depression. We randomly select 100 individuals diagnosed with clinical depression and randomly assign half to run for 40 minutes each day; the other half go for a leisurely walk 40 minutes each day. After a month, we measure depression level by asking our participants how often they have gone out with friends over the past week. In this case, we do not have construct validity. How often someone goes out with friends may be correlated with depression, but our measure falls far short of being a valid measure of depression.

Construct validity is determined by how well the measure of a variable fits into a theory. Theories state how constructs are interrelated; a measure has construct validity to the degree that it fits with other constructs in the theory. Our measure of depression, frequency of visiting with friends, is probably correlated with some aspects of depression but would not be the central construct in a theory of depression. A determination of construct validity requires a number of studies and the careful relating of research results to theory.

Content Validity

To the degree that a measure assesses all the dimensions of the construct, it has **content validity**. Suppose that we wanted to measure satisfaction level of students. Imagine that we ask questions that only relate to the library (e.g., open hours, study area, availability of journals). We would measure something about student satisfaction, but aren't we missing important dimensions? Absolutely! What about other factors such as quality of instructors, variety of courses offered, parking availability, sports facilities, number of pubs on campus, and so on?

Criterion and Predictive Validity

If a measure of behavior has **criterion validity**, then it should correlate with another measure of the same kind of behavior, a criterion measure. For example, if IQ score and school performance both measure intelligence, then they should be positively correlated to show criterion validity. In addition, we should be able to predict school success by knowing IQ score. If we can, then IQ would have **predictive validity** for school success.

A special case of criterion validity, called concurrent validity, is used to assess the validity of a measure by correlating it with another, well established measure.

Conceptual Exercise 5D

In a study of the effects of brain lesions on rat behavior, researchers discovered that rats do not groom the side of their body opposite to the side of brain damage. The rats' failure to groom was obvious because their claws grew longer and longer. In normal rats, grooming keeps their nails trimmed. As a measure of nail grooming, the researchers clipped the claws and weighed the clippings. When they correlated the weight with the extent of cortical damage, they found a strong positive correlation. Suppose you wanted to use nail length as a measure of brain damage in rats. Discuss the face, content, and criterion validities of your measure.

Some psychological behavior has been studied long enough that measures have been found that are more or less reliable and valid. Use these available instruments when you can.

TESTS, SCALES, AND INVENTORIES

The terms *test, scale, index,* and *inventory* are used frequently in discussions of psychological measures. The most general term, **test**, refers to many procedures used to measure a variable (e.g., intelligence tests, aptitude tests, and achievement tests). The term **scale** is used to refer to a measure of a specific psychological characteristic. So we can speak of an intelligence scale as a test that assigns a number to your intelligence. Intelligence tests produce a general index of intelligence, but they also have subscales that assign a number to specific aspects of intelligence.

Does it make any sense to assign a number to your interests or personality? No, of course not; your personality is too complex to be reduced or scaled to a single number. Instead, these tests are usually referred to as **inventories** because they are used to describe your interests or personality much as you would take inventory of a warehouse. It is important to point out, though, that within personality or interests, we can scale specific personality traits or interests. For example, a personality test may have many scales, each assigning a number to a particular personality trait (e.g., extraversion or openness to change). Indeed, in some tests, such as the Minnesota Multiphasic Personality Inventory (MMPI), the profile of scores on various scales is interpreted as part of the test.

COMMERCIALLY AVAILABLE TESTS AND INVENTORIES

There are all sorts of tests that have been standardized, and reliability and validity information is available. We will consider here some of the commonly used intelligence, personality, and neuropsychological tests.

Standardized Tests of Intelligence

Probably the intelligence test you are most aware of is the Stanford-Binet test. This test, originally designed by Alfred Binet to detect what was then called retardation, has been revised many times. The most current version is the **Stanford-Binet Intelligence Scale,** Fifth Edition (SBIS-V). This test provides a full-scale intelligence score and subscale scores on fluid reasoning, quantitative reasoning, visual-spatial reasoning, knowledge, and working memory.

The **Wechsler Intelligence Scale for Children,** Fourth Edition (WISC-IV) provides a full-scale intelligence score and subscale scores on perceptual reasoning, processing speed, verbal comprehension, and working memory. This test is designed to assess the intelligence of children between the ages of 11 and 16 years.

The **Wechsler Adult Intelligence Scale** (WAIS), designed to assess intelligence of people aged 16 years and older, provides a full-scale intelligence score and a verbal and performance score. In addition, subscale scores of verbal comprehension, perceptual organization, working memory, and processing speed are provided. The **Woodcock-Johnson III Test of Cognitive Abilities** is suitable for all ages and measures general intelligence, working memory, and executive functions.

Some other less well-known tests of intelligence include the Cognitive Assessment System (CAS), the Comprehensive Test of Nonverbal Intelligence (CTONI), the Universal Nonverbal Intelligence Test (UNIT), and the Kaufman Assessment Battery for Children (KABC).

Tests of Personality

Standardized Tests

The **MMPI-2** is the most commonly used test of adult psychopathology by clinicians for assessment and treatment. Another personality test, based on Dr. Theodore Millon's theory of personality and psychopathology, is the **Millon Clinical Multiaxial Inventory-III** (MCMI-III) assessment from Pearson Assessments that measures 14 personality disorders and 10 clinical syndromes for adults undergoing psychological or psychiatric assessment or treatment. The MMPI-2 and the MCMI-III use the *DSM-IV* categories, and both provide reliability and validity measures.

The **Sixteen Personality Factor Questionnaire** (16PF) is used to assess adult personality. As you have no doubt guessed, the test measures 16 primary traits, including assertiveness, emotional maturity, self-sufficiency, shrewdness, anxiety, tension, rigidity, and neuroticism. The **California Psychological Inventory** (CPI) was designed to measure various personality dimensions, including sociability, self-control, dominance, and achievement.

Projective Tests of Personality

Projective tests are used by clinicians with a more Freudian bent. They are based on the very Freudian notion that we project traits of our personalities when we interpret things. The **Holtzman Inkblot Technique** (HIT) was designed by Wayne Holtzman and his colleagues to improve upon the Rorschach Inkblot Test. The **Thematic Apperception Test** (TAT) consists of a series of pictures of ambiguous scenes. The person being tested describes what he or she thinks is going on in the picture.

It has been difficult to determine the reliability and validity of projective tests because of the lack of standardization in their administration, scoring, and interpretation.

Other Specialized Tests

The **Bayley Scales of Infant Development** (BSID-II) were designed to measure stages of growth at various age levels. Measures include cognitive, language, social, and fine and gross motor development. The **Yesavage Geriatric Depression Scale** (GDS) was designed to assess depression in older adults. The **Young Mania Rating Scale** (YMRS) is completed by the clinician to assess manic symptoms in clients.

There are hundreds, if not thousands, of tests available. However, some can be acquired only by licensed clinicians—contact the publisher for information. Published tests are available from the publisher at a cost, but there are also tests that are published in the literature that may be used for free. Note that even if a test is available for free, you have an ethical responsibility to contact the author and obtain permission to use it.

FYI

Be aware that published tests are not necessarily valid or reliable. Check the literature for reviews of the test and estimates of reliability and validity.

You do not want to reinvent the wheel. Finding a test can be a difficult task, but it is much easier than trying to design your own test. Fortunately, there are a number of test bibliographies available. Many of these bibliographies have test reviews and information on the test's reliability and validity. Check with your reference librarian, but examples include the *Directory of Unpublished Experimental Measures, Tests in Print, Mental Measurements Yearbook, Tests,* and *Test Critiques.* In addition, there are online resources for locating tests. Some examples are the American Psychological Association (http://www.apa.org/science/testing.html), Buros Institute of Mental Measures, Educational Testing Services (http://www.ets.org), Health and Psychosocial Instruments (HAPI), and general literature search engines such as PsycINFO, ERIC, and SocINDEX.

Let's go through an example of how you might go about finding a test for a specific research project.

Finding an Appropriate Test: An Example

Imagine that you were interested in comparing men and women on a measure of body satisfaction. Your hypothesis is that women feel less positive about their bodies than men. A check of the *Mental Measures Yearbook* under "body image" leads to a test for children ages 3 to 6. You are interested in doing your research on university students, so that won't work.

A check of *Tests in Print* produced the *Eating Disorder Inventory-2,* which has a scale called Body Dissatisfaction. You check with the publisher, Psychological Assessment Resources, and learn that the price for an introductory kit is $225, and the company also has restrictions on use. You must have "a degree from an accredited 4-year college or university in Psychology, Counseling, or a closely related field PLUS satisfactory completion of coursework in Test Interpretation, Psychometrics and Measurement Theory, Educational Statistics, or a closely related area; OR license or certification from an agency that requires appropriate training and experience in the ethical and competent use of psychological tests." Good grief, you think. This could be a serious problem.

So, you check the literature using PsycINFO and find an article by Tiggemann (2005), where she describes her study of the effect of television on body image of adolescent boys and girls. Tiggemann used questionnaire items that asked respondents to report their height and weight. She also asked the respondents to rate how overweight or underweight they considered themselves to be on a scale ranging from *extremely underweight* (1) to *extremely overweight* (7) and to rate how satisfied they were with their current weight on a scale from *extremely dissatisfied* (1) to *extremely satisfied* (7), and she used the *Appearance Schema Inventory* (Cash & Labarge, 1996).

A quick search of the Internet finds Cash's Web site, and you discover that he is now selling his measures. Undaunted, you contact Dr. Cash and ask permission to use his inventory, explaining that you are a poor student. He responds immediately with permission to use any of his tests free of charge for student projects or teaching. You have your measure, and it only took a couple of hours. Whew. Well done!

CHAPTER SUMMARY

We can measure behavioral variables by either asking people about their behavior or by observing their behavior. There are many ways to ask questions; some provide **quantitative** data (assign numbers to things), and others provide **qualitative** information (provide a written description). Quantitative data are generally easier to analyze, but qualitative data can provide a richer, more detailed description. When asking our questions, we can ask people to make a selection from a number of **fixed alternatives,** or we can simply make the response **open-ended** and let people create their own answer.

Rating scales are frequently used to quantify a response to a question. Rather than asking people whether they like a program, we can ask them to indicate how much they like the program. A **Likert scale** item asks people to indicate how much they agree or disagree with a statement. The **Semantic Differential** is a rating scale that asks the respondent to indicate, on a continuum between opposite adjectives, the meanings they associate with a word.

When we ask people about their behavior, we need to control **social desirability** and **response set.** Social desirability is the tendency for people to provide answers that make them look good. Response set is the tendency to respond to all questions in a similar way.

Rather than asking people to report their behavior, we could observe behavior directly. When planning to observe behavior, you need to first decide which aspect of the behavior you want to measure—**accuracy, frequency, latency, duration,** or **amplitude.**

No matter what measure you have chosen, **precision** is important. Lack of precision will decrease your statistical power and could cause statistically significant findings to be nonsignificant (i.e., a Type II error).

Reliability is the extent to which a measure produces the same result when repeated. There are a number of ways of assessing the reliability of a measure. The **test-retest** method involves testing people twice and correlating the measures. The **split-half** method measures internal consistency by correlating half the test items with the other half. Reliability of observational measures is determined by the **interrater** agreement.

Validity is the extent to which a measure actually measures what it is supposed to measure. There are a variety of aspects to validity. If a measure looks like it is a reasonable measure, it has **face validity.** If a measure includes all the dimensions that are part of a concept, it has **content validity. Criterion** or **predictive validity** refers to the extent to which the measure correlates or is predictive of an outcome measure. **Construct validity** is how well the measure actually measures the construct and is the most difficult to estimate.

When measuring psychological variables, we use tests, scales, and inventories. Some use these terms interchangeably, but generally, **tests** produce a single score, **scales** provide a number for specific characteristics, and **inventories** indicate, from a wide variety, which characteristics an individual possesses.

Creating a measure of a psychological variable can be an extremely difficult task. Fortunately, tests can be searched in the literature and in catalogs. Some tests are free to use, others can be expensive, and some tests require that that the user have specific training or professional credentials.

ANSWERS TO CONCEPTUAL EXERCISES

Conceptual Exercise 5A

The categories are not mutually exclusive. For example, someone who is 20 years old would fall into two categories.

Including only two flavors of ice cream is not enough, and you will have no idea what the favorite flavor is of all the "other" responses. Either increase the number of choices or make the item open-ended.

Conceptual Exercise 5B

1. The best measure for a driving proficiency road test would be the number of errors.
2. For bullying, a measure of frequency and perhaps amplitude (though this would have to be clearly defined) would be appropriate.
3. The easiest measure of a skier's performance is the time to complete a specified course.

Conceptual Exercise 5C

1. Income is a ratio variable.
2. Number of children is a ratio variable.
3. Type of mental disorder is a nominal variable.
4. Olympic medals are on an ordinal level.
5. The LSAT is on a ratio scale.

Conceptual Exercise 5D

Using the weight of nail clippings to measure brain damage would have little face validity. On the face of it, the measure does not appear to be a valid measure. The measure does have criterion validity because a correlation between nail length and extent of brain injury has been demonstrated. The measure does not have high content validity because nail length reflects only grooming behavior, and there are likely other behaviors that are affected by the brain damage.

FAQ

Q1: When asking questions about sensitive topics such as age or weight, isn't it best to provide a range of age intervals and ask respondents to select one?

A1: The problem is one of precision in measurement. The more precise your measure, the better, but you will have a problem if people leave the item blank. If these items are being collected for demographic purposes, then using intervals is fine, but if these are central variables in your study, you need to get the precise value. One solution for age is to ask date of birth. People seem less bothered by reporting their date of birth than their age. Yes, we agree—it is odd.

Q2: What is the difference between reliability and replicability?

A2: Sometimes people will refer to a study as having reliable findings. What they really mean is that the results are not a fluke, not due simply to chance, and that the research is replicable. When we refer to reliability in this chapter, we are making a statement about a measure, not an entire study. The concepts are related, but *replicability* is usually used to refer to the reliability of the whole study.

Q3: What is the best method for testing reliability?

A3: It is impossible to say which methods are best because they evaluate different aspects of reliability. The test-retest method evaluates the consistency of a measure over time and will only be useful for variables that remain stable over the time interval. The split-half method evaluates the internal reliability of a measure.

Q4: When constructing a semantic differential, how do you determine the opposite word to your target word?

A4: Once you have decided on the continuum, you need only use a thesaurus to find the appropriate antonym. Most word processors have a thesaurus.

Q5: Which is the most reliable—nominal, ordinal, interval, or ratio?

A5: The reliability of a measure is independent of the level of scale. Measures of different levels can be reliable or not.

Q6: What is the difference between construct validity and content validity?

A6: Construct validity is a much larger concept than content validity. Content validity refers to the degree to which a measure evaluates all the dimensions of a concept. So a measure has content validity if it assesses all the content that is included in a concept. Construct validity is much broader and refers to whether a measure is actually assessing the theoretical construct that we think it is measuring.

Q7: Is reliability really possible given that participants may not respond consistently?

A7: A reliable measure may contain items designed to assess whether respondents are being consistent or not. For example, a question may be asked two or three times, with different phrasing at various points in a questionnaire, so that consistency can be determined. A respondent who is not consistent is a problem, but the measure can still be reliable.

Q8: Is it more important that a measure be valid or reliable?

A8: If we had to choose one, we would choose valid. The reason, of course, is that a valid measure must also be reliable. For a measure to be useful, it must be both valid and reliable.

Q9: Why is internal and external validity not discussed with reference to measurement?

A9: Internal and external validity refer to the validity of a research outcome and are discussed in Chapter 4 instead.

Q10: Given that a 9-point rating scale is more precise than a 5-point scale, why not use a 100-point scale?

A10: What a good question! The problem is that the task of rating an item on a 100-point scale is just too difficult. Imagine trying to decide what the difference is between 67 and 68? It is too fine a scale to ask respondents to use.

Q11: Why does it matter if a variable is nominal, ordinal, interval, or ratio?

A11: The scale of measurement determines what can be done with the numbers from an arithmetic, algebraic, and statistical point of view.

Q12: Why isn't number of pages in books an interval variable? You can't have zero pages!

A12: We get this question a lot. It is not a matter of whether a zero level of the variable exists or even can exist. It is a matter of where you begin counting. You start counting pages from zero just as you start counting height from zero. But nobody is zero inches tall, right?

Q13: If nominal and ordinal variables are so bad, why measure them at all?

A13: Some important demographic variables are nominal (gender, country of origin, ethnicity, etc.). You should try to collect data with as much precision as you can, but some variables by their very nature are less quantitative than others. They may still be important variables to study.

CHAPTER EXERCISES

1. A test of mathematic aptitude was administered twice to a group of university students. The reliability of the test was found to be $r = .85$. Can we assume from this that our test is a good measure of mathematical aptitude?

2. You administer a scholastic aptitude test to students as they begin their first year of college. Four years later, you correlate their overall grade point average with their score on the aptitude test. You find the correlation to be $r = .9$. What can you conclude about the test's reliability and validity?

3. You have located a test that measures memory, but you find that it is too long to administer in your study, so you decide to only use half the test. What problem might this create?

4. Explain the following statement: A valid test is always reliable, but a reliable test may not be valid.

5. Explain the difference between construct and content validity.

6. Provide three examples of questions that respondents would likely answer in a socially desirable way. Describe possible solutions to the problem.

7. Classify the following as nominal, ordinal, interval, or ratio variables:
   a. % body fat
   b. psychological disorder
   c. marital satisfaction rating on a scale from 1 to 7
   d. difficulty of ski run (expert, advanced, intermediate, novice)
   e. altitude

CHAPTER PROJECTS

1. Decide on a psychological construct that you wish to measure and locate a test using one of the search procedures available at your library.

2. Locate a journal article on any topic in psychology. Describe the measures that were used and how issues of reliability and validity were addressed. What was the level of measurement of each variable?

3. Describe how you would test the predictive validity of SAT scores on college and university success.

4. Describe how you would construct a measure to determine people's attitudes toward placing bans on smoking in all public buildings. What level of measurement is your variable?

REFERENCES

Cash, T. F., & Labarge, A. S. (1996). Development of the Appearance Schema Inventory: A new cognitive body image assessment. *Cognitive Therapy and Research, 20,* 37–50.

Osgood, C. E., Suci, G. J., & Tannenbaum, P. H. (1957). *The measurement of meaning.* Urbana: University of Illinois Press.

Tiggemann, M. (2005). Television and adolescent body image: The role of program content and viewing motivation. *Journal of Social and Clinical Psychology, 24*(3), 361–381.

Visit the study site at www.sagepub.com/evansmprstudy for practice quizzes and other study resources.

Selecting Research Participants

> ## OBJECTIVES
>
> After studying this chapter, students should be able to
>
> - Define the term sampling frame
> - Describe the difference between random sampling and random assignment
> - Define the term probability sampling
> - Describe the difference between random, systematic, stratified, cluster, and multistage sampling
> - Define the term nonprobability sampling
> - Describe the difference between convenience, quota, and referral sampling
> - Determine the best sampling method for a given research problem
> - Describe the relationship between sample size and effect size
> - Describe the relationship between statistical power and sample size

Have you ever received a phone call from someone who works for some research institute and wants a few minutes of your time? Have you received a questionnaire in the mail or online? Anyone come to your door wanting to know what kinds of products you prefer? We certainly have. How come they picked you, you might have wondered? In this chapter, we discuss methods researchers use to select the people they want to study.

Whether you are surveying people on the street or gathering participants for an experiment, you are selecting a sample from a population of potential participants. Probably the only research that is conducted on whole populations is carried out by government agencies when they conduct a census. We all know that only the government can afford to measure the entire population. The rest of us conduct our research on some sample from a population. We then use inferential statistics to make statements about the population based on the findings from our sample. One of the assumptions of inferential statistics is that the samples were randomly selected from the population. In the real world, this is almost never practiced. Indeed, most psychological research is based on first-year university students enrolled in introductory psychology courses. We knowingly violate this assumption because we are usually not interested in describing a population. Instead, our research goal is to test a theory. We do this by generating a testable research hypothesis, selecting participants, and conducting the study. Unless our theory somehow does not apply to the participants we have selected, we should be safe in using samples that are not randomly selected. On the other hand, if our research goal is to describe an entire population based on our sample (e.g., by surveying), then how we select our sample is critical. And if this is our goal, then the first step is to obtain a list of the population—a sampling frame.

The **sampling frame** is the list that is used to select from a population. For example, if you wanted to select students from a population of all the students at a university, your best sampling frame would be a list of all registered students. If you were interested in sampling from schools, then a list of all the schools in a certain district would be your sampling frame. Keep in mind that a sampling frame may not be complete. For example, a telephone directory will not include households with unlisted numbers or people without phones. Also, when a sampling frame exists, its use may be restricted. For example, it may be that the registrar's office will not allow access to student information. Finally, there are many populations for which a sampling frame simply does not exist.

SAMPLING METHODS

The various approaches to sampling can be broken down into two groups—namely, probability and nonprobability sampling.

Probability Sampling

These techniques are termed **probability sampling techniques** because you can specify the probability that a participant will be selected from a population. By obtaining your sample with probability techniques, you can be reasonably confident that your sample is representative of the population. At the very least, your selection procedure could be replicated by others to obtain similar samples.

Random Sampling

Random sampling is a procedure whereby a sample is drawn such that each member of the population has an equal probability of being included in that sample. The probability that any one individual will be included in the sample is 1 divided by the size of the population. If we had a small population, we could put each member's name in a hat, shake it up, and draw out the number of names we need for our sample. Clearly, if our population is large, this is not going to work. Many statistics texts have a table of random numbers in the appendix. This table can be used to select the members of a sample from the population. Although few researchers use this procedure, many statistical techniques are based on the assumption that sampling has been random. As we discussed previously, this is not really a huge problem for social science researchers who are typically testing theories, not generalizing to entire populations. Our students often have difficulty distinguishing between random sampling or random selection of participants and random assignment of participants to groups. As we just said, random sampling rarely happens in psychological research, and this is not a huge problem, but random assignment of participants to groups is a very common procedure and is an important assumption of several statistical procedures. **Random assignment** means that participants have been independently assigned to groups. Imagine that we have selected 40 participants for a two-group experiment. We could use a table of random numbers to assign 20 participants to the experimental group and 20 to a control group. This would be an example of random assignment of participants to conditions. In Chapter 7, we discuss experimental designs where random assignment has been used to create the groups in a study. Figure 6.1 illustrates the difference between random selection and random assignment.

Systematic Sampling

Perhaps we have a list of all the social workers employed by our city, 600 in all. We could obtain a sample of 100 by selecting every sixth person on the list (i.e., 600 divided by 100 = 6) (see Figure 6.2). The probability that any person will be included in this sample is 1 in 6. When using **systematic sampling**, be sure that the organization of your list cannot bias your sample. Imagine if you were to select every second person from a list of married couples that were organized man, woman, man, woman!

Conceptual Exercise 6A

A researcher randomly selects and telephones 250 homes listed in a city phone book and conducts a survey.
   What is the sampling frame?

Stratified Sampling

Consider the example above where we selected every sixth social worker on our list. Imagine we were gathering opinions about government support for social workers. We might think that social workers with different amounts of experience in the field might have different opinions about this issue. One way to get a fairer assessment of the workers' opinions about this issue would be to stratify the sample by length of experience. Perhaps you learn that 20% of the social workers in this population have 10 years or more of experience, 40% have 5 to 10 years, and 40% have less than 5 years of experience. With **stratified sampling,** you could randomly select 20% of your sample from the most experienced group (your first strata) and 40% from the other two groups (or strata), respectively (see Figure 6.3).

FIGURE 6.1   Random Selection and Random Assignment

In this way, we guarantee that our sample reflects the numerical composition of the social worker population by purposely selecting from each stratum.

Cluster Sampling

What if you do not have a list of the members of your population? Perhaps a list of all social workers in your city is simply not available. You could identify all the agencies in your city

FIGURE 6.2   Systematic Sampling

Every Sixth Person

FIGURE 6.3   Stratified Sampling

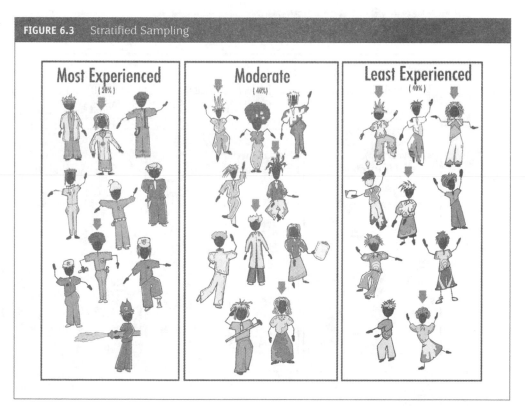

employing social workers and randomly select a number of agencies, called *clusters,* for your sample (see Figure 6.4). You would include all the social workers in each agency/cluster in your sample.

Multistage Sampling

Cluster sampling is often done in multiple stages, going from larger to smaller clusters. Imagine that the city in which you are conducting your social work research is huge. You could begin by identifying boroughs or wards of your city as large clusters and randomly select a number of those clusters. Then, within each borough/ward cluster you have chosen, you would randomly select a number of smaller clusters, agencies, to include in your sample. Cluster sampling is a great way of obtaining a random sample when you do not have access to a list of all members of the population.

The above probability sampling methods are preferred by researchers but are not always practical. Nonprobability sampling methods are easier to use and often cheaper to carry out. No effort is made to ensure that the sample reflects the characteristics of the population.

FIGURE 6.4 Cluster Sampling

Social Services, Inc.   Holistic Health   Youth Services
Wellness Center   Evans Family Center   Crisis Center
Rooney + Associates   Social Support Center   Public Care Center

Crisis Center   Youth Services   Social Services, Inc.

> **Conceptual Exercise 6B**
>
> A researcher is interested in maximum-security inmates. What sampling procedure is she using in each of the following?
>
> 1. She obtains a list of all inmates in maximum-security prisons in the United States and selects every 50th name.
>
> 2. She groups inmates by type of crime, determines the percentage of the total in each crime category, and uses that to randomly select a representative proportion from each group.
>
> 3. She groups maximum-security prisons by state, randomly selects 10 states, and, from those 10, randomly selects three prisons. She includes all the inmates in those three prisons in her sample.

Nonprobability Sampling

These techniques are called **nonprobability sampling techniques** because it is impossible to specify the probability of selecting any one individual. You cannot say that everyone in the population has an equal chance of being selected because you do not know the probability of selection. This is important because it means that your sample may or may not be representative of the population, and this can influence the external validity of your study. This is not usually considered a problem in hypothesis testing, where our primary goal is not to describe a population but to test the prediction of a theory.

Convenience Sampling

Have you ever been approached by someone at the mall with a survey? We have. This approach of grabbing whoever is available is called **convenience sampling** (see Figure 6.5). You might be surprised to learn that convenience sampling is the most commonly used procedure in psychology research. Psychology researchers typically obtain their samples from introductory psychology classes. Why? Because it is convenient. The sample frame then is introductory psychology students.

When students do research projects, they usually just walk around campus and ask people to participate because that too is convenient. The sample frame here is people on campus. Although you might find this a bit peculiar, it is very common. The notion is that university students are fairly representative of young people at large. And remember, most psychological research is about investigating the relationships between manipulated variables and behavior, not about describing the characteristics of the population. This is not true of all research, of course. If you want to describe the attitudes of Americans about free trade, you should not just sample introductory psychology students.

FIGURE 6.5 Convenience Sampling

Quota Sampling

Quota sampling is like convenience sampling, but the goal is to select participants with particular characteristics until you have enough. This would be used, for example, if you want an equal number of Black, White, and Asian participants in your sample. Or perhaps you have identified the population in terms of socioeconomic status (SES) and you want to make sure that you have equal numbers of each SES category in your sample (see Figure 6.6). This is a nonprobability analog to stratified random sampling.

Referral Sampling

If the population you are interested in is difficult to locate, then once you have found one individual, you could ask him or her to refer others to you. This procedure is sometimes called *snowball sampling* because one participant tells his or her friends, and they tell their friends and so on, and so on (see Figure 6.7). Let's say you are interested in studying factors that prevent prostitutes from leaving the street. Obviously, you are not going to obtain a sampling frame, but a **referral** method makes perfect sense.

Conceptual Exercise 6C

A few years ago, we conducted a study trying to determine if technology enhanced learning outcomes in the teaching of psychology.

1. Had we identified all psychology classes and randomly selected four classes to use, what type of sampling would we have used?

2. We did not do that, however. We used the classes we were assigned to teach. What sampling method did we use?

FIGURE 6.6   Quota Sampling

SAMPLE AND EFFECT SIZE

Students always ask, "How many participants do I need?"

This depends on the power of their statistic. Parametric statistics such as the *t* test and analysis of variance (ANOVA) have a great deal of power, but chi-square, a nonparametric procedure, has relatively low power. Consequently, you will need a much larger sample if you are using chi-square.

Your sample size will also depend on your research design. If you want to perform a number of statistical comparisons, you will need a larger sample. For example, if your study has two independent variables, each with three levels, and you also want to compare women and men, you may have $3 \times 3 \times 2 = 18$ groups (three levels of the first independent variable × three levels of the second independent variable × two sexes); with only 10 participants in each group, you can do the math! Similarly, if your chi-square test has many categories, you will need a larger sample.

Students often report that a significant finding might have been more significant if the samples were larger. This is not necessarily the case. We need to consider the **size of the effect.** If the relationship between the manipulated variable and the behavior was strong and control was tight, then a significant result might be found with quite small samples. In

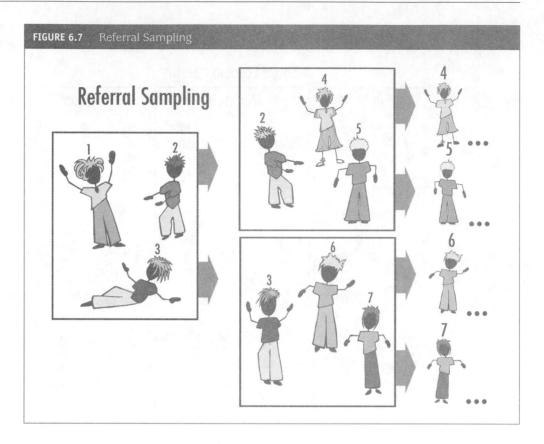

FIGURE 6.7 Referral Sampling

other words, effect size was large. On the other hand, if your manipulated variable has a subtle effect on the dependent variable, then you will require a larger sample to achieve statistical significance.

With larger samples, greater variability in the data may still lead to a significant result. This is why larger samples are used in field research, where we typically have less control than in the laboratory. A larger sample can compensate for greater variability.

The weaker the manipulation and the weaker the experimental control, the larger the samples must be for significance to be reached. In other words, when the effect size is small, larger samples are needed. When it is large, smaller samples are adequate. It is a bit of a trade-off, isn't it?

FYI

Many people think that sample size in a survey, for example, should be a percentage of the population. This is not true. A population of 2,000 and a population of 20,000 could be described as accurately with the same sample size. The important factor is that your sample is representative of the population you want to describe.

POWER REVISITED

One way to increase power is to increase the number of participants in your sample. Imagine that you have collected your data and calculated your statistics, only to find that your results only approach statistical significance. Perhaps your statistic has a p value of .06. It is not statistically significant at an alpha level of .05! What would you do? You do not want to make a Type II error and fail to reject a false null hypothesis! At the very least, you should replicate your study with a larger sample size. Kraemer (1987) provides methods for determining sample size.

We have discussed various sampling methods in this chapter. When you find yourself wondering which method to use, consider what all researchers consider when they ponder the same question: How much time do I have? How much money do I have? How much help can I get? Although the nature of the research question often dictates the best method, let's face it: Time and money must be taken into account. Few researchers have unlimited resources, and certainly it is a rare student who does.

CHAPTER SUMMARY

Measuring entire populations is rarely possible in social science research. Rather, researchers study **samples** selected from **populations**. **Sampling methods** are techniques for selecting samples from populations. The **sampling frame** is a list of the population from which the sample is drawn.

Probability sampling techniques are methods where the probability that a participant will be selected for inclusion in the sample is known. **Random sampling** is a procedure for selecting participants whereby each participant has an equal probability of being included in the sample. **Random assignment** of participants requires that the participants be independently assigned to groups. In **systematic sampling,** the population size is divided by your sample size to provide you with a number, k, for example; then, from a random starting point, you select every kth individual. For example, if your population size was 2,000 and you wanted a sample of 100, you would select every 20th individual. In **stratified sampling,** the population is divided into strata based on some population characteristic, and participants are randomly selected from each stratum. This ensures that each stratum is proportionally represented in the sample. **Cluster sampling** can be used when a population list is not available and researchers simply identify a number of clusters or groups and include all participants in the cluster in the sample. **Multistage sampling** is a cluster technique where smaller clusters are randomly selected from larger clusters previously randomly selected.

Nonprobability sampling methods are easier to use than probability sampling methods but do not provide any way of estimating the probability that an individual in the population will be included in the sample. **Convenience sampling** is the term used when we select any participant who is readily available. When we choose easily available participants who fit a particular criterion, we are using **quota sampling. Referral sampling** involves including participants in the sample who have been referred by other participants.

Determining how many participants are needed in a sample depends on several variables, including the **power** of the statistic, the **research design**, the **size of the effect**, and the **variability** of the data.

ANSWERS TO CONCEPTUAL EXERCISES

Conceptual Exercise 6A

The sampling frame is the numbers listed in the phone book.

Conceptual Exercise 6B

1. systematic
2. stratified
3. multistage

Conceptual Exercise 6C

1. cluster sampling
2. convenience sampling

FAQ

Q1: I just asked people in my class and people in the cafeteria to participate. What kind of sampling procedure is that?

A1: This haphazard method of selection is called convenience sampling.

Q2: I heard that I need more participants if I'm doing a chi-square analysis compared to a *t* test. Is that true?

A2: This is true. For both tests, the number of participants you will need depends on the size of your effect, but generally the chi-square test is less powerful than a *t* test. A statistically significant *t* test depends on the difference between your group means and the variability within your groups. Although increasing your sample size will probably have no effect on your means, it will decrease your variability. However, in the case of chi-square, statistical significance depends entirely on the distribution of your measures and the number of participants. Even with a large effect size, it is difficult to get statistical significance with a small sample size.

Q3: How many participants is enough?

A3: There is no easy answer to this question because sample size is only one of a number of factors that influence your statistical power (your ability to reject a false null hypothesis). Probably the best way to determine your sample size is to collect pilot data. These preliminary data will give you an idea of your effect size, and you can calculate your inferential statistic and substitute various sample sizes into the calculation to get an idea of how many participants you will need. For more information on determining sample size, see Kraemer (1987).

Q4: How can you tell if your sample is unbiased?

A4: The only way to be sure that your sample is representative of the population is to compare your results with those from the whole population. In other words, the only way to be *sure* is to measure the population and compare your sample statistics to the parameters of the population. Of course, you would never do this, and you do not have to. The purpose of probability sampling is to maximize the probability that your sample is representative. For example, in simple random sampling, everyone has an equal chance of being selected; therefore, there is no bias in selection.

Q5: What is the difference between random sampling and random assignment?

A5: Although these concepts sound similar, they are totally different. Random assignment refers to the method used to form your treatment groups in your study. For example, forming experimental and control groups by randomly assigning participants to one condition or the other is random assignment. Random selection refers to the method used to select your participants for the study. For example, you may use random selection to obtain 60 participants by randomly selecting names from a list of the population. Random assignment is used to form groups of participants who are similar. Random selection is used to obtain a sample that is representative of the population.

Q6: How does increasing my sample size increase the power of my statistic?

A6: For parametric tests such as *t* test and ANOVA, when you increase your sample size, you decrease the error variability of your statistic, and that translates into a larger *t* or *F* statistic. In the case of nonparametric tests such as chi-square, a larger sample size makes it more likely that your obtained frequencies can be different from the expected frequencies that the null hypothesis would produce. With few participants, there is little difference between the frequency you expect and the frequency you obtain, and this translates into a smaller chi-square statistic.

Q7: Is it possible to have a sample that is too large?

A7: This does not sound reasonable, but it is possible to have a statistical test that is so powerful that you are able to get statistical significance when you have a very small effect size. The result is a research project that makes a mountain out of a trivial molehill.

CHAPTER EXERCISES

1. What is wrong with the statement "a large sample is always better than a small one"?

2. Why is sampling so important in survey research?

3. Much research in psychology is conducted on students from introductory psychology classes. Is this a problem? Does it matter what type of research is being conducted?

4. Amanda is doing a survey of student opinion on the legalization of same-sex marriage. She believes that students may have different views depending on their area of study and program year. What type of sampling procedure would you recommend she use?

5. Andrew wants to interview homeless people in his city. What type of sampling procedure should he use?

6. A group of students wants to investigate whether men or women are more likely to butt in in a lineup. They chose to observe lineups at a local ski hill. What type of sampling procedure did they use? Is their procedure adequate?

7. You have been asked by your employer to survey the staff on their ideas of how a budget surplus should be spent. With over 1,000 employees, you have decided to select only a sample. Describe how you might obtain your sample.

8. As part of your work in a community outreach center, you want to survey sex trade workers in your area. How would you obtain your sample?

CHAPTER PROJECTS

1. Locate a research article by using one of the sampling procedures (e.g., stratified sampling, referral sampling) as a search term. Describe how the sample was obtained and the researcher's rationale for choosing that technique.

2. Locate three research articles using a probability sampling procedure. Describe the sampling frame and the sampling procedure they used.

REFERENCE

Kraemer, H. C. (1987). *How many subjects: Statistical power analysis in research.* Newbury Park, CA: Sage.

Visit the study site at www.sagepub.com/evansmprstudy for practice quizzes and other study resources.

CHAPTER 7

Experimental Design

Independent Groups Designs

OBJECTIVES

After reading this chapter, students should be able to

- List the steps in conducting an experiment
- Describe the difference between a controlled experiment and a field experiment
- Describe the advantages and disadvantages of controlled experiments and field experiments
- Describe the nature of an independent groups design
- Describe the difference between a completely randomized groups design and a randomized factorial design
- Interpret the statistical outcome of each design, including main effects and interactions in factorial designs
- Design an experiment to assess a given hypothesis

A few years ago, one of the authors of your book read an article in a local newspaper with the headline "Don't take engineering, young ladies, if you hope to marry!" The writer described some data obtained from a major university that indicated that female engineering graduates were less likely to marry than female graduates from other faculties. The reader was left with the impression that women were somehow dooming themselves to singlehood by enrolling in the faculty of engineering. We continue to be amazed to read about the many causal interpretations that are made about data that simply do not permit such interpretations.

We can confidently conclude a cause-and-effect relationship between variables *if and only if* the appropriate study has been conducted. To conclude that being educated as an engineer causes a decrease in marriageability *could* be made if there was a significant difference between the postgraduate marriageability of two groups of women who were *initially* equivalent in marriageability and were then randomly assigned to an engineering group and a nonengineering group. And, of course, it would have to be established that during the course of their education, variables extraneous to the education experience did not differentially affect the groups. Do you think this was the case? We don't either.

WHY WE DO EXPERIMENTS

The **experiment** is the cornerstone of scientific research. The goal when we conduct experiments is to show that an **independent variable** (IV) causes a change in the **dependent variable** (DV). In psychological research, the dependent variable is usually some measure of behavior. Perhaps we would like to know whether technologically enhanced courses compared to traditional course delivery techniques (IV) improve student performance in courses (DV). Or perhaps we are interested in comparing psychotherapy with medical therapy (IV) in the treatment of anorexia symptoms (DV). Conducting an experiment is considered to be the best way to provide us with the answers to these kinds of questions. Not all problems lend themselves to experimental study, but those that do are best approached this way. We will begin this chapter by discussing the basics of the experimental approach.

To be a true experiment, as opposed to a quasi-experiment or a nonexperiment, the independent variable must be *under the control of the researcher.* In other words, the researcher must assign participants to the levels of the independent variable. Consider the example about psychotherapy versus medical therapy in the treatment of anorexia. If our goal is to compare psychotherapy with medical therapy for the treatment of anorexia, we could study people who had been treated with either therapy in the past. We could determine how well they have progressed with each type of treatment. This approach, however, is not an experimental approach because *we* did not assign the patients to the type of treatment (IV). Rather, we compared those who *themselves* had chosen either psychotherapy or medical therapy. This type of study is called a *quasi-experimental design,* and such designs are treated in Chapter 10. For us to conduct a true experiment to study this problem, we, the researchers, must be able to assign the participants to each condition or group in the experiment. We must be the ones to decide who gets psychotherapy and who receives medical therapy. This is crucial because we, the researchers, can then take steps to ensure that there are no systematic differences between the groups before the experiment begins. As a result, we are able to conclude that if we find a difference between the groups at the end of the experiment, that difference is due to the way the people were treated. Imagine that only the most severely affected individuals got medical treatment,

> **Conceptual Exercise 7A**
>
> For each of the following hypotheses, decide if a true or a quasi-experiment is indicated.
>
> 1. Young offenders have poorer impulse control than nonoffending youth.
>
> 2. Children who view a film promoting helping behavior show more altruistic behaviors than children who view a neutral film.
>
> 3. Pigeons on an intermittent schedule of reinforcement emit pecking behavior that is more resistant to extinction than pigeons on a continuous schedule.
>
> 4. Women rate pornography as less interesting than men do.

and those with only mild symptoms chose psychotherapy. In this case, the groups were different at the outset of the study; it would be no surprise to find that they are still different at the end of the study.

As we have said, the true experiment is the foundation of scientific research. Although not all research problems can be studied experimentally, when they can, such an approach is preferable because causal statements about the relationship between variables can be made.

Steps in Conducting an Experiment

Step 1. Formulate a Hypothesis

You will recall, from our discussion in Chapter 4, that a **hypothesis** is a statement about the expected relationships between variables. For example, perhaps we are interested in whether practice in mirror drawing with one hand might transfer to the other hand. In mirror drawing, the participant, while looking in a mirror, attempts to duplicate a figure, number, letter, and so on. Our hypothesis might be as follows:

Positive transfer to the nonpreferred hand will occur with training in mirror drawing with the preferred hand.

As you can see, this hypothesis is a statement about theoretical concepts (i.e., positive transfer and training). The next step is to decide how to measure these concepts. In other words, we have to operationalize, or make measurable, the variables.

Step 2. Select Appropriate Independent and Dependent Variables

In the example given above, the IV is amount of practice (practice vs. no practice) with the preferred hand. There are various ways we could measure (or operationalize) positive transfer. One way would be to count the number of errors on three trials before and after practice. Another way would be to measure the time to complete a trial. Of course, there are questions to answer. What is an error? How much practice?

Deciding which dependent measure is the most valid and reliable way to measure the behavior of interest is a matter of experience and familiarity with the available research. For more detail on measurement, see Chapter 5.

Once we have a testable hypothesis about the expected relationship between our IV and DV, we need to consider what other variables might be involved and find ways to control them.

Step 3. Limit Alternative Explanations for Variation

Remember, the goal of experimentation is to determine cause and effect. Does manipulation of the IV have a causal effect on the DV? Clearly, there is more than one variable influencing behavior at any one time. Let's look at an illustrative, if somewhat obvious, example. An angler wants to know which type of bait is best for trout. *Type of bait* then will be the IV. The *number of trout* caught in 4 hours will be the DV. Our angler goes to a lake and fishes from 8:00 a.m. until 12 noon on Sunday using flies. The following Sunday, he goes to another lake and fishes with worms from 2:00 p.m. until 6:00 p.m. He catches one trout at the first lake and six at the second lake. If we can demonstrate statistically that more fish were caught at the second lake, then we need to ask ourselves, have we demonstrated a *causal relationship* between the IV (type of bait) and the DV? Are there alternative explanations for the difference in number of fish caught that have nothing to do with the IV, type of bait, and, therefore, are confounded with it? We think so. The second lake might have more trout. The weather on the first Sunday might have been less conducive to fishing. Perhaps fish are more likely to bite in the afternoon than they are in the morning. We are sure you can think of other possible confounds. In an experiment (or any research), we want to control as many of these other variables as possible. Once we have done our best to think about, and limit, alternative explanations for our hoped-for effect, we can go to Step 4.

Step 4. Manipulate the IVs and Measure the DVs

In other words, carry out the experiment. We now have our data. What next?

Step 5. Analyze the Variation in the DVs

In the ideal experiment, all the variation in the dependent variable between groups receiving the independent variable (i.e., treatment groups) and groups not receiving the independent variable (i.e., control groups) should be caused by the independent variable. The objective of the exercise is to decrease variation among groups that is not a result of the manipulation of the IV (i.e., error variation). Techniques for reducing error variability are discussed more in Chapter 4.

We now must choose the appropriate statistical technique to analyze the variance in the DV. Which procedure we select depends on the kind of data we have and the questions we wish to answer. In Chapter 2, we discuss common analyses used by researchers in psychology today, and in Chapter 13, we discuss common statistical procedures students might use for their projects. Once we have selected and conducted the appropriate statistical analysis for our data, we can complete the final step.

Step 6. Draw Inferences About Relationship Between IVs and DVs

We use inferential statistical procedures to make statements about populations based on our sample findings. Conducting a true experiment allows us to make causal statements about the relationship between the IV and the DV. We can be confident in saying that the manipulated IV caused the changes in the behavior that we measured if we have carried out our experiment carefully by controlling other variables that could provide an alternative explanation of the changes in the DV, leaving our IV as the only likely causal variable.

Where We Do Experiments

Experiments can be conducted in the laboratory (**controlled experiment**) or in a natural setting (**field experiment**). In both controlled and field experiments, the IV is directly manipulated by the researcher. However, in a natural setting, which is where field experiments are conducted, it is more difficult to control all the secondary variables that might affect the results. As a consequence, many researchers prefer to do their work under laboratory conditions if they can. As you can see, there is a downside and an upside to conducting your experiment in both settings.

Controlled Experiments in the Laboratory

There are three broad advantages to controlled experimentation. First, our ability to control the independent variable is superior under laboratory conditions, improving internal validity. Second, we have superior control over secondary or extraneous sources of variation in the laboratory. For example, we can control noise and temperature. Last, we can more precisely measure our dependent variable under laboratory conditions. This kind of control over the IV, the DV, and secondary variables improves the internal validity of the study—that is, the probability that any changes in the DV are indeed a result of the manipulation of the IV.

Although the experiment is considered by researchers to be the best way to determine cause and effect, there are disadvantages to controlled experimentation. Some phenomena cannot be studied in a laboratory at all. The effect of September 11 on frequency of travel by Americans, for example, is a research topic that does not easily lend itself to laboratory study. Other research topics present ethical problems. For example, it would be unethical to conduct a laboratory study of the effects of sensory deprivation on human infants. There are also practical disadvantages to laboratory investigation. It can be costly and time-consuming.

But perhaps the most serious disadvantage to controlled experiments is that the outcomes may not be applicable to the real world. Behavior that occurs in a laboratory may be idiosyncratic to that environment and may not occur in a natural setting. If we decide to do our experiment in a natural setting, we are conducting a field experiment.

Experiments in the Field

When controlled experimentation is not possible or ethical, a field experiment may be the best choice. A field experiment is conducted in a natural setting (the field) where the experimenter directly manipulates the independent variable. Imagine that we are hired to determine if domestic violence intervention training for police officers reduces domestic assault. We might randomly assign a group of police officers to receive special training and a control group of officers who receive the standard training offered by the police department. We could then take various measures such as number of domestic assaults in areas served by the two groups or satisfaction of families served by those officers. Suppose we find that there was a difference. Fewer assaults and more family satisfaction occurred in the areas served by the specially trained officers. Although we would like to think this outcome was caused by our independent variable (training), we would have to be quite cautious in our inference, in part because in this field experiment, as in all field experiments, we have less control over extraneous, or secondary, sources of variation. The police officers would quickly learn that some of them were in a special training group and some were not. Perhaps the specially trained officers tried harder because they knew they were in the special training group, and it was their extra effort rather than the special training that caused the difference. These "clues" that lead participants to guess about the nature of the study and that may change their behavior are called *demand characteristics*. Researchers must try to anticipate what the demand characteristics associated with their study might be and try to limit their influence on the outcome.

Back to our example. Perhaps there was a factory shutdown in the neighborhoods served by the officers who did not receive special training. When people are out of work, domestic problems probably escalate. It is possible that the greater number of domestic assaults in those neighborhoods might be a result of this factor rather than the training factor. In a laboratory situation, it is often easier to control these kinds of variables by using single- and double-blind procedures.

The outcome we may find in a controlled laboratory setting may not generalize to the external (i.e., natural) world. When you bring a phenomenon into the laboratory, you may be interfering with how it operates naturally. Findings that do not hold true in a natural setting are not **externally valid** and may be of little interest. On the other hand, as you saw in our domestic violence example, field experiments, which may be more externally valid, have a major disadvantage in that they may lack **internal validity** because it is much more difficult to control the IV, the DV, and secondary sources of variation.

Choosing the best setting in which to conduct an experiment requires considerable thought. Some things to think about include pragmatic considerations, including cost, control over variables, and validity considerations. We discuss validity in much more detail in Chapter 5.

As we often say, it is a matter of balance.

Conceptual Exercise 7B

A researcher is interested in the uninhibited behavior she has often observed at rock concerts. She wonders what kinds of variables influence this behavior (loudness of band, proximity of audience to band, etc.). Should she consider a controlled or a field experiment? Why?

We have discussed the steps that researchers follow and the things they must think about as they consider how best to answer the questions they have. The rest of this chapter deals with basic experimental designs where different participants serve in each level(s) of an independent variable(s)—independent groups or between-participant designs.

HOW WE DO EXPERIMENTS: INDEPENDENT GROUPS DESIGNS

We cannot stress enough the importance of the assumption of initial equivalence of groups in experimental design. If we cannot assume that our groups were equivalent prior to treatment (i.e., before manipulation of our IV), then we have no basis at all for any causal inferences about differences after treatment. So, how can we assume that our groups are equivalent at the start?

One common way is to assign participants randomly and independently to conditions—an independent groups or between-participants design. In an **independent groups** or **between-participants design,** participants are randomly and independently assigned to each level of the independent variable. Because the participants were independently assigned to groups or levels of the IV, we can feel confident that the groups were initially equivalent. If we then treat each group differently (i.e., the treatment variable) and find there is a significant difference in the outcome measure (i.e., the dependent variable), then we can confidently infer that the outcome, differences in DV, was causally related to our manipulation (i.e., levels of the IV).

With independent groups or between-participants designs, each score is independent of every other score, hence the name—independent groups designs. Because different participants are assigned to the different levels of the independent variable, their scores are assumed to be independent of each other. The simplest independent groups design is one where the researcher is interested in one independent variable with two or more levels—a completely randomized groups design.

Completely Randomized Groups Designs: One IV

In a **completely randomized design**, research participants are randomly assigned to different levels of *one* independent variable. Figure 7.1 illustrates how we might diagram this type of design.

As you can see, there are four levels of the A independent variable, and *n* participants would be randomly assigned to each group.

The simplest completely randomized groups design would be a two-group design where participants are randomly selected and independently assigned to either an experimental group or a control group (i.e., two levels of one independent variable). Such designs allow us to answer one question: Did the manipulation of the independent variable affect the

---

NOTE: The American Psychological Association recommends that the word *participants* be used when referring to human participants in research. Although the word *subjects* has been used, and typically still is used in many books and published research articles, to refer to various types of research designs such as between-subjects and within-subjects designs, we have followed the recommendation of the APA in this regard. We use the word *subjects* only when we are referring to animals, not humans.

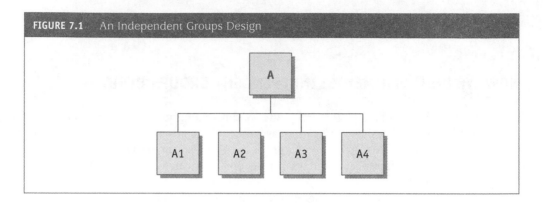

FIGURE 7.1 An Independent Groups Design

dependent variable? Perhaps in more typical language, we might ask, did the treatment of the various groups cause a difference in some response measure, the DV? Let's examine a recently published research paper to see how a between-participants design was used in an effort to answer a specific question.

Randomized Groups Design: One IV With Two Levels

The Research Problem. We have all heard the phrase "conflict of interest." We expect a person who is making a judgment about the value of something to be fair, impartial, and objective. A conflict arises when a person's judgment about a primary interest (such as which drug works better) is influenced by a secondary interest (such as ownership of shares in a drug company).

Chaudry, Schroter, Smith, and Morris (2002) were interested in how readers of a medical research periodical judge the scientific value of that research. Specifically, they wanted to know if readers would judge a research study as less interesting, important, and valid if they believed that the researchers who conducted the study had a conflict of interest.

Hypotheses. Chaudry et al. (2002) hypothesized that readers who believed that a research study had been conducted by researchers with competing interests would judge the study as less interesting, important, relevant, valid, and believable than readers who had no such belief.

Selection of Participants and Assignment to Conditions. Chaudry et al. (2002) randomly selected 300 readers of the *British Medical Journal.* All readers were sent a short report about the substantial impact of pain on the lives of sufferers of herpes zoster (cold sores). For half the readers, the authors of this paper were declared to be employees of, and held stock options in, a fictitious pharmaceutical company. For the rest of the readers, the authors of the paper were claimed to be employees of a care center with no competing interest.

The IV and DVs. The independent variable was the information about the authors, whether they had competing interest (held company stock) versus no competing interest. Readers rated the study described in the paper on several variables, including interest, importance, relevance, validity, and believability on a 5-point scale. These ratings were the dependent variables.

The Design. Because the readers were randomly assigned to receive each version of the research paper and could only be assigned to one condition, this is an independent groups design. Table 7.1 illustrates the design.

The Statistical Analyses. The researchers chose to compare the means of their groups with independent *t* tests.

The Results. Some of the descriptive statistics reported by Chaudry et al. (2002) are presented in Table 7.2.

Because Chaudry et al. (2002) had two independent groups, they chose independent *t* tests as their inferential analyses. The outcome of these tests indicated that readers in the competing interest group rated the research paper as significantly less interesting, relevant, valid, and believable (all *ps* < .001) and less important (*p* < .02) than did the readers in the no competing interest groups.

TABLE 7.1 Independent Groups Design

Group	
Competing interest	No competing interest

Source: Adapted from Chaudry et al. (2002).

TABLE 7.2 Descriptive Statistics: Reader Perceptions of Research Study

	Group	
	Mean Ratings (Standard Deviations)	
Variable	*Competing Interest*	*No Competing Interest*
Interest	2.59 (0.87)	2.99 (0.91)
Importance	2.59 (0.90)	2.94 (0.96)
Relevance	2.70 (1.10)	3.15 (1.10)
Validity	2.53 (0.99)	3.04 (1.00)
Believability	2.73 (1.10)	3.33 (0.92)

Source: Chaudry et al. (2002).

Note: Low scores indicate low interest, importance, and so on.

The Conclusions. The authors concluded that readers judge scientific research findings as less credible when they perceive that the people conducting the research have a conflict of interest.

An independent groups design with two groups is a basic design where the researcher is interested in comparing an experimental group, which received some sort of treatment, with a control group, which did not. Often we are interested in more levels of the independent variable. Rather than comparing a group of participants who received drug treatment with participants who received a placebo, we may want to compare groups of participants who received various dosages of a drug to determine which dosage is more effective in treating some disorder. In this case, we would have an independent groups design with *several levels of one independent variable.* Here is an example from the literature.

Randomized Groups Design: One IV With More Than Two Levels

The Research Problem. Teachers are not likely to use classroom interventions that they think are unacceptable. Jones and Lungaro (2000) noted that, although many studies have revealed that teachers find reinforcement-based intervention to be more acceptable than punishment-based interventions, little research had been done to examine the nature of the reinforcement strategy. Specifically, they wondered if reinforcement strategies that were clearly connected to the assessment of the problem would be seen as more acceptable than strategies where the reinforcer was not clearly connected to the problem (i.e., more arbitrary).

Consider a child who is acting out in class and receives attention from his or her peers for this behavior. A differential reinforcement procedure could be used where acting-out behavior is ignored by the teacher (rather than the peer group), and desirable behavior is rewarded by points that could be traded in for rewards. In this case, the reinforcers (i.e., teacher attention and points) are not linked to the original problem situation where the behavior seemed to be reinforced by *peer attention,* not *teacher attention.* On the other hand, a differential reinforcement procedure could be used where acting-out behavior is ignored by peers and desirable behavior is rewarded with attention from peers. Given that the acting-out behavior had probably been reinforced by attention from classmates originally, this procedure then links the reinforcer (i.e., peer attention) to the problem situation. This was the basic procedure that Jones and Lungaro (2000) used. Their interest was in the reinforcer itself. If peer attention was reinforcing acting-out behavior, then withdrawing peer attention rather than some other event such as teacher attention might be a more acceptable strategy. And likewise, teachers might feel that rewarding desirable behavior with peer attention rather than teacher attention is a better strategy. This was the problem that Jones and Lungaro decided to investigate.

Hypotheses. Jones and Lungaro (2000) expected that teachers would rate treatments linked to an assessment of the behavior problem to be more acceptable than treatments not linked to such an assessment. They were also interested in the likelihood that teachers would use such strategies. Although they did not specifically say so, we suspect they expected teachers to say they were more likely to use strategies that they perceived as being more acceptable.

Selection of Participants and Assignment to Conditions. One hundred and eleven public school teachers volunteered to participate in the experiment. The teachers were randomly assigned to one of three conditions with 34, 38, and 39 teachers in the groups. All of the teachers read vignettes about a child, Jesse, who was disruptive during class by getting out of his seat. They read that the school psychologist observed the behavior and noted that Jesse was out of his seat about once every 10 minutes and that 90% of the time when he was out of his seat, classmates talked to, laughed at, or teased Jesse. The vignette went on to describe a differential reinforcement strategy recommended by the psychologist in one of three ways.

Teachers in the peer attention group (PA) read that the strategy recommended was that classmates were instructed to ignore Jesse when he was out of his seat. In addition, they were told that Jesse would receive a point for every 10-minute interval that he remained in his seat. At the end of the class, Jesse could have 1 minute of free time with a classmate for every point he had earned during class. This strategy then was linked to the problem situation; peer attention, which seemed to be reinforcing the out-of-seat behavior, was used to reinforce in-seat behavior.

Teachers in the teacher attention group (TA) read that the strategy recommended was that the teacher would ignore Jesse when he was out of his seat. Points were given for in-seat behavior as in the PA group, but those points could be traded in for free time with the teacher, not a classmate, at the end of the class period. This strategy then was linked to the attention part of the problem but used teacher rather than peer attention.

Teachers in the tangible reinforcer group (TR) read that Jesse could earn points for remaining in his seat and that those points could be traded in for desirable items in a grab bag. The reinforcer in this condition, then, was not linked to the problem. Rather, the reinforcer was arbitrary.

The IV and DVs. The independent variable was type of reinforcement strategy. Jones and Lungaro (2000) compared three strategies: peer attention, teacher attention, and tangible reinforcer.

Jones and Lungaro (2000) measured two dependent variables: acceptability of strategy and likelihood of use.

The Design. The design, an independent groups design with three levels of the IV, is illustrated in Table 7.3.

TABLE 7.3 Independent Groups Design		
Group		
PA	TA	TR

Source: Jones and Lungaro (2000).

The Statistical Analysis. Because the design was an independent groups design with three levels of one independent variable, the researchers analyzed each DV with a separate one-way analysis of variance (ANOVA).

The Results. The descriptive statistics from Jones and Lungaro's (2000) experiment are presented in Table 7.4. Jones and Lungaro did not provide descriptive statistics for the likelihood of use dependent measure.

Because Jones and Lungaro (2000) had three levels of one independent variable, they used a one-way ANOVA to analyze each dependent measure and a Tukey HSD test to compare pairs of means. You will recall, we hope, from your statistics course that a significant *F* from an ANOVA tells us only that at least two means are significantly different. The Tukey test tells us which pairs of means are different. The outcome of the ANOVA that Jones and Lungaro conducted was significant on the acceptability of the strategy dependent measure, $F(2, 108) = 6.66$, $p < .01$. Jones and Lungaro reported that the acceptability scores for the peer attention group were significantly higher than those in the teacher attention and tangible reinforcer conditions (inferential statistics were not reported for the comparisons).

The outcome of the second ANOVA, conducted on the likelihood of use measure, was also significant, $F(2, 108) = 4.20$, $p < .01$, and again, the Tukey comparisons indicated that teachers in the peer attention group said they were more likely to use the procedure than teachers in the other two groups (they reported the finding to be significant but did not report the Tukey statistics).

The Conclusions. The authors concluded that teachers report that a behavioral intervention strategy is more acceptable and that they are more likely to use that strategy if it is linked to an assessment of the problem behavior situation than if it is not linked. Although the strategy used in the teacher attention condition seems more linked to the behavior problem than the strategy used in the tangible reinforcement condition, there were no significant differences in acceptability or likelihood of use scores between these two groups.

To this point, we have talked about independent groups designs where participants have been assigned to two or more levels of one independent variable. But what if we are interested in a second or a third or more independent variables? As you will see in the next sections, there are important benefits to including more than one IV in a single experiment.

TABLE 7.4   Descriptive Statistics: Acceptability of Intervention Strategies

	Group		
	Mean Score Out of 90 (Standard Deviation)		
Variable	*PA*	*TA*	*TR*
Acceptability	61.1 (11.9)	48.3 (17.5)	49.3 (18.5)

Source: Jones and Lungaro (2000).

Note: Higher scores indicate greater acceptability.

Randomized Factorial Groups Designs: More Than One IV

How were your grades in high school? Do you think they accurately reflected your level of achievement? Perhaps your classmates, teachers, or textbooks influenced your grades. Human behavior is complex and influenced by all sorts of variables. Experiments designed to assess the effects of more than one independent variable on performance are probably more like the real world and more likely to be externally valid (i.e., generalize to real-world settings and situations).

In a **randomized factorial design,** participants are randomly assigned to each level of *more than one* independent variable (or factor). These designs allow us to assess the effects of more than one independent variable and to assess the interaction between independent variables. A *simple randomized groups design* provides the answer *to one* question: Did the independent variable affect the dependent variable? *Factorial designs* allow us to find answers to *several* questions. What effect, if any, did each independent variable have on the dependent variable, and how did the combination of levels of the independent variables affect the dependent variable? The statistical analysis of a factorial design, then, allows us to assess the effects of each independent variable on the dependent variable (called the **main effects**), and it will indicate the interactions between those independent variables (called the **interaction effect**). Interaction effects are very important; indeed, if significant interactions between independent variables are present, the interpretation of the effects of those independent variables becomes more complicated. Figure 7.2 illustrates how we might diagram a randomized factorial design.

As you can see, this design has two IVs: A has four levels, and B has two levels. Participants would be independently assigned to one of the eight groups.

Before we look at some real randomized groups experiments, let's examine a hypothetical experiment. Many people, including us, find that reading under incandescent light is easier on the eyes than reading under fluorescent light. But is text easier to read (i.e., more legible) under incandescent light? Word processors offer many different fonts. We find certain fonts to be easier to read than others. Perhaps some fonts are easier to read under incandescent light and others under fluorescent light. We could design an experiment to determine if our anecdotal experience with light and fonts is supported empirically. We

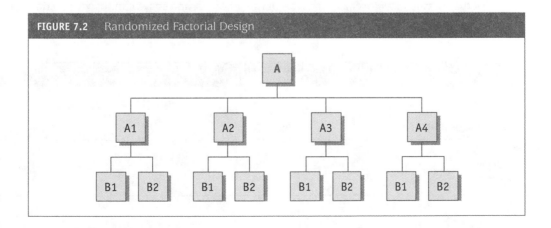

FIGURE 7.2 Randomized Factorial Design

might randomly assign readers to incandescent light conditions and others to fluorescent light conditions, and we might have them read text typed in three different fonts under each type of light condition. With two levels of our first independent variable (light) and three levels of our second independent variable (font), we would have six different conditions in our experiment. If we randomly assigned different readers to each condition, we would have a 2×3 randomized factorial design (i.e., two levels of one IV and three levels of a second IV) that might look like the following (see Table 7.5).

As you can see, readers in the IT condition would read text in the Times font under incandescent light, and readers in the FG condition would read the same text in the Geneva font under fluorescent light. Following the reading part of our study, perhaps we have asked our participants to rate the text for readability. In a randomized factorial design, we have three questions. In our hypothetical experiment, the first question to ask is, "Did the first independent variable (i.e., light) affect the dependent variable (readability)?" In other words, forgetting about the different fonts used for the moment, did light condition affect readability overall? We could examine the mean readability ratings calculated over all font conditions. We would simply determine the mean readability rating for *all* the participants who read the text under incandescent light regardless of the font used and compare those ratings with the mean readability ratings of *all* the participants who read the text under fluorescent light. Let's plot these ratings in a graph. Figure 7.3 shows the main effect of light for our hypothetical experiment. Higher ratings indicate the text was more readable.

It seems that text is more readable under incandescent than under fluorescent light. In a real experiment, we could analyze these data with a two-way ANOVA to determine if the difference was statistically significant.

Our second question is, "Does our second independent variable (i.e., font) make a difference, overall?" Now, we will look at the readability scores for each level of font calculated over both light conditions. In other words, we will find the mean score for *all* the readers who read the Times font, *all* those who read the Courier font, and *all* those who read the Geneva font, regardless of light condition. Figure 7.4 is a graph of the main effect of font.

Our graph indicates that the Times font is easiest to read and the Courier font is the hardest to read. Our two-way ANOVA would tell us if the groups differ significantly.

In a randomized factorial design, the main effects must be interpreted in light of any interaction effects. When we examine a main effect, we are looking at means for each level of that IV calculated over all the levels of the other IVs, and so we cannot see any differences

TABLE 7.5 Hypothetical Randomized Factorial Design Comparing Different Kinds of Light and Font

	Light (First IV)	
Font (Second IV)	Incandescent	Fluorescent
Times	IT	FT
Courier	IC	FC
Geneva	IG	FG

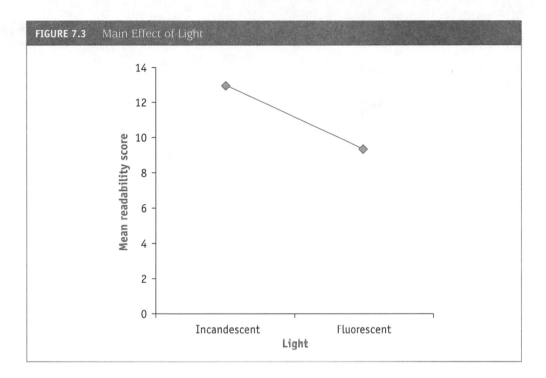

FIGURE 7.3   Main Effect of Light

that might exist at the different levels of the other IVs. The following is our third question: "Is the dependent variable affected by the combination of levels of each IV?"

Let's now graph the mean readability scores for *each* level of each IV to see if there is an interaction effect (see Figure 7.5).

You can see that things are not quite as simple as they seemed when we looked at the graphs of the two main effects. If the two independent variables did not interact, we would see two more or less parallel lines. These lines are not parallel, so it seems that we have an interaction going on here. Of course, the statistical analysis would tell us if the interaction is statistically significant, but let's examine our graph. Readability of the Times and Geneva fonts seems to be little affected by light conditions. Readability of text in these two fonts is not much affected by the light conditions, but this is not the case for the Courier font. It seems to be much harder to read the Courier font under fluorescent light than under incandescent light. The interaction effect tells us that the dependent variable (readability) is affected differently under the different combinations of the independent variables. This is the great advantage of a factorial design. We can determine how different combinations of levels of two (or more) independent variables affect the dependent variable. We could not determine this effect with a simple independent groups design.

Are you ready for a real experiment?

The Research Problem. Benzodiazepines are central nervous system depressants that tend to reduce aggressive behavior in animals, but some researchers have found the opposite

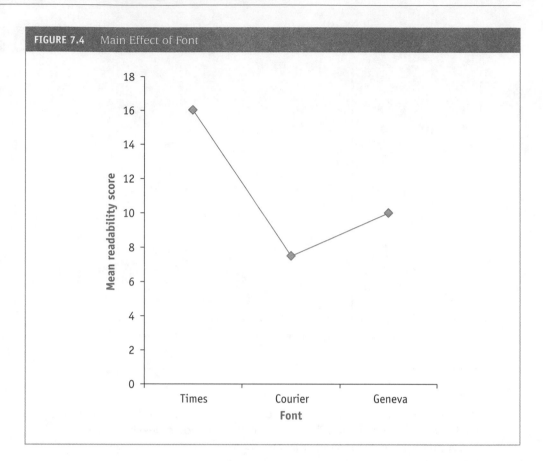

FIGURE 7.4 Main Effect of Font

effect, increased aggressiveness, when sustained low doses are used (e.g., Fox, Webster, & Guerriero, 1972, as cited in Renzi, 1982). Renzi (1982) decided to examine the effects of single versus repeated doses of a depressant drug on aggressive behavior of mice that had been induced, by a low-voltage shock, to fight with each other. Renzi was also interested in whether size of dose would make a difference in aggressive behavior and whether size of dose would interact with the number of doses variable.

The Hypotheses. Renzi (1982) did not specifically state his hypotheses, so we will simply specify the three questions his research was intended to answer.

1. Is aggressive behavior affected by number of doses of drug? (Main effect of number)

2. Is aggressive behavior affected by dosage (amount of drug given)? (Main effect of dose)

3. Is aggressive behavior affected by different combinations of dosage and number of doses? (Interaction effect)

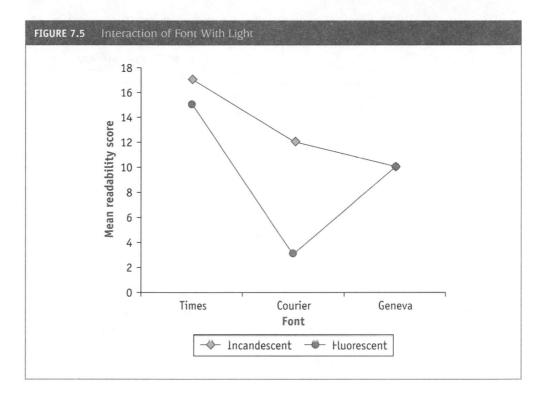

FIGURE 7.5   Interaction of Font With Light

Selection of Subjects (Mice, Not People) and Assignment to Conditions. Renzi (1982) reported that mice were assigned to six conditions, with 16 mice in each condition. He did not specify how they were assigned, but it seems likely that they were randomly assigned.

The IVs and DVs. One independent variable in this experiment was dosage or amount of drug given. The IV had three levels: 0, no drug (saline); 2.5 mg/kg of body weight of depressant; and 5 mg/kg of depressant.

A second independent variable was number of doses, and this variable had two levels: single dose (S) and repeated dose (R) (one dose a day for 10 days).

The dependent variable was aggressive behavior, and Renzi (1982) measured number of bites during a specified period of time.

The Design. Renzi (1982) assessed all combinations of all levels of each variable. This particular design, like our hypothetical design, was a 3 × 2 randomized factorial design. There were three levels of the first independent variable (dosage) and two levels of the second independent variable (number of doses). Three groups of mice received a single dose, with one of the three groups receiving saline, one receiving 2.5 mg/kg of drug, and one receiving 5 mg/kg of drug. Three other groups of mice received repeated doses, with one of the three receiving saline, another group receiving the lower dose, and the third group receiving the higher dose. Table 7.6 illustrates the six conditions in this experiment.

TABLE 7.6 Randomized 3 × 2 Factorial Design

	Dosage Group (mg/kg)		
Number of doses	0	2.5	5
S (single)	S0	S2.5	S5
R (repeated)	R0	R2.5	R5

Source: Renzi (1982).

Mice in the S0 group received a single dose of saline with no depressant, and mice in the R5 group received repeated doses (one per day for 10 days) of 5 mg/kg of the drug.

The Statistical Analysis. This design has two independent variables, and different mice were assigned to each of the six conditions. An appropriate statistical analysis is a two-way ANOVA, which is the analysis Renzi (1982) used.

The Results. Some of the descriptive statistics from this experiment are presented in Table 7.7. We estimated these statistics from a graph included in the report.

The two-way ANOVA provided answers to the three questions of interest to the researcher: Does number of doses affect the behavior? Does dosage level influence aggressive behavior? And, do dosage and number of doses interact?

To address the first inferential question, we examine the outcome of the ANOVA for the first main effect. The ANOVA revealed that there was a significant main effect of number of doses, $F(1, 42) = 29.78$, $p < .001$. Figure 7.6 illustrates this main effect.

As you can see, there was certainly more aggressive behavior when the mice were given repeated doses of the drug.

The second question was, "Does aggressive behavior differ depending on the dosage level given?" The statistical analysis revealed that dosage level did make a significant difference in the aggressiveness of the mice, $F(2, 42) = 13.52$, $p < .001$. Let's examine Figure 7.7, the graph of the main effect of dosage.

We can see that the mice that received the highest dose of the drug were the most aggressive. The mice that received the saline did not bite at all, it appears. The significant F from the ANOVA tells us that at least two means are different, so we know that the 5-mg group

TABLE 7.7 Descriptive Statistics: Aggressive Behavior (Mean Number of Bites)

	Dosage Group (mg/kg)		
Number of doses	0	2.5	5
Single	~0	~3.5	~90
Repeated	~0	~1	~3

Source: Renzi (1982).

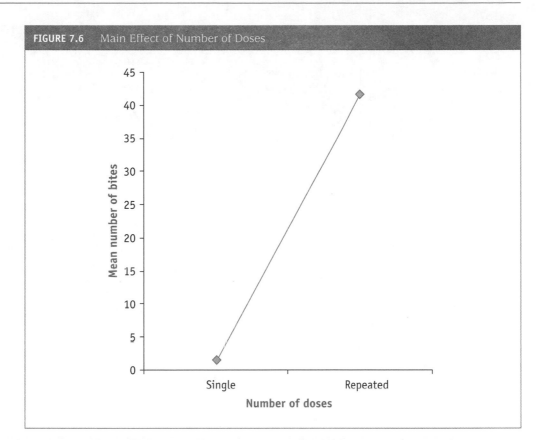

FIGURE 7.6   Main Effect of Number of Doses

was more aggressive than the 0 group, but Renzi (1982) did not include a post hoc comparison between the 2.5 mg and the 5 mg groups, so we do not know if those two groups are significantly different.

To really understand how the two variables operated, we must examine the interaction illustrated in Figure 7.8.

Renzi (1982) reported that the interaction was significant, $F(2, 42) = 11.43$, $p < .01$, and as you can see, the lines are not parallel. A single dose, either saline or the depressant drug, had little effect on the behavior of the mice regardless of the amount of drug given, but when repeated doses of the depressant were administered, aggressive behavior *increased* with the dosage level.

The Conclusions. Renzi (1982) speculated that effects of the depressant drug on aggressive behavior might be a result of an accumulation of the drug or its active metabolites that would only occur with its repeated administration.

You can see that the interpretation of the main effects must be made in light of any interaction. The factorial design allows us to investigate these more complicated and often more interesting relationships between variables.

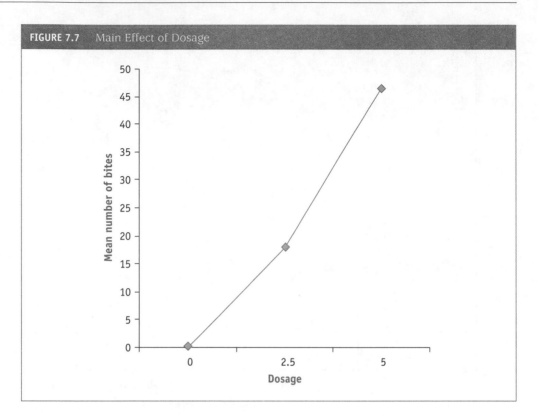

FIGURE 7.7 Main Effect of Dosage

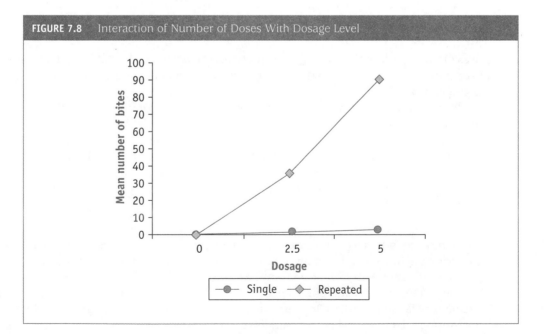

FIGURE 7.8 Interaction of Number of Doses With Dosage Level

Renzi's (1982) 3 × 2 factorial design involved two variables with three and two levels, respectively. The complexity of a factorial design increases with the number of levels of each variable and with the number of independent variables. With only two variables, the design yields two main effects and one interaction effect. With three independent variables, the design yields three main effects, three two-way interaction effects, and one three-way interaction effect. As you can imagine, the more variables, the more complicated the interactions, and the more difficult it is to interpret the findings. But given the complexity of human behavior, designs involving multiple variables are the rule in social science research today.

In addition to increasing complexity, the number of participants also dramatically increases with the addition of each new variable. Renzi (1982) had 16 single-dose mice and 16 repeated-dose mice in each of the three dosage-level conditions: 96 mice in total. What if he were to add a third independent variable; perhaps he also wanted to see if level of shock used to induce aggressive behavior made a difference. If he tested the mice under two shock conditions (high vs. low, perhaps), he would be adding six more groups to the experiment. If he used 16 mice per group, he would have needed 192 mice in his design!

Between-participants designs where participants are randomly and independently assigned to conditions are excellent experimental designs, particularly if there is any concern that one treatment condition might contaminate another. However, just because participants have been randomly assigned to conditions does not guarantee initial equivalence of groups. Nevertheless, random assignment of participants to conditions is the most common technique researchers use to deal with initial differences between participants. Another approach to ensuring equivalence of groups is addressed in Chapter 8.

CHAPTER SUMMARY

Experiments are the first choice of most behavioral researchers because they allow us to infer a **causal relationship** between a manipulated **independent variable** and some measure of behavior, the **dependent variable.** We conduct experiments to evaluate theories, satisfy our curiosity, and demonstrate behavioral phenomena and the factors influencing them.

When we conduct experiments, we begin with a **hypothesis.** We select appropriate independent and dependent variables to test our hypothesis. We make every attempt to control alternative sources of variation, and then we carry out our experiment. After analyzing the data, we are then in a position to draw **inferences** about the relationship between our manipulated independent variable and the observed behavioral change.

Experiments can be conducted in a laboratory and are called **controlled experiments.** When we conduct experiments in a natural setting, these are called **field experiments.** Controlled experiments tend to have greater **internal validity** than field experiments, but field experiments may have greater **external validity.** Some research problems are better examined in a natural setting, whereas others are better examined in the controlled conditions of the laboratory.

Independent groups or **between-participants designs** are used to compare different groups of participants, all of whom have been independently assigned to treatment groups. The simplest of these is the **completely randomized design** with one independent variable with two levels. When participants have been independently assigned to all combinations of more than one independent variable, we have a **randomized factorial design.** Factorial designs allow the simultaneous assessment of more than one IV and the interactions between IVs. The effects of each IV on the DV are called **main effects,** and the effect of combinations of levels of IVs on the DV is the **interaction effect.**

ANSWERS TO CONCEPTUAL EXERCISES

Conceptual Exercise 7A

1. Comparisons between offending and nonoffending youth are participant comparisons; this is a quasi-experiment.
2. We might assume that the children were independently assigned to each type of film, and so this would be a true experiment.
3. It seems reasonable to assume that the pigeons were independently assigned to groups—a true experiment.
4. Gender is a participant variable; this is a quasi-experiment.

Conceptual Exercise 7B

This research problem is probably best studied in the field. It would be difficult to simulate rock concert conditions in a laboratory setting. And it is doubtful that the same kinds of behavior would occur in a laboratory as those in the natural setting.

FAQ

Q1: Most psychology research is conducted on psychology students. Is that a problem?

A1: Using psychology students in research is a problem that affects the external validity of your study. To the degree that these participants are different from the population you want to generalize to, your study lacks external validity. Practically speaking, most researchers do not consider this a problem because their focus is on testing a null hypothesis. Whether experimental results conducted on university students will generalize to other groups is perhaps the topic of another experiment.

Q2: What is the difference between random assignment and random selection?

A2: Random assignment is a procedure that is used to assign participants to treatment groups (or levels). The goal is to form groups of participants who are initially equivalent on measures of the dependent variable. That is, if you were to measure the dependent variable at the start of the experiment, the groups should not differ. Random selection is a procedure for selecting a sample from a population. The goal is to make your sample representative of the population. Random assignment affects the internal validity of your study, and random selection affects the external validity.

Q3: Why is random assignment so important?

A3: Random assignment of participants to treatment groups (or levels of treatments) is crucial to the internal validity of the experiment. As mentioned in Question 2, random assignment is used to ensure that the groups are equivalent on any variable that may influence the dependent variable. For example, if your treatment and control groups differ on measures of the dependent variable, then it cannot be said that the difference was caused by the independent variable.

Q4: What is the difference between an experimental and a nonexperimental design?

A4: The main difference between an experimental and a nonexperimental design is control of the independent variable. In an experiment, the researcher has control over who receives the treatment. In a nonexperimental design, the participants have, in a sense, already been assigned to their group. For example, if you were conducting an experiment on the effects of alcohol on cognitive ability, you would assign sober participants to consume two, four, or six drinks and also assign some individuals to a nonalcoholic drink control group. Once everyone had consumed his or her assigned amount, you would administer your dependent variable measure. This is an experiment because *you* have formed the groups. If you were to do this study using a nonexperimental design, you could simply enter a bar and ask people how many drinks they have had and then administer your dependent variable measure. In the experiment, you could make causal statements about how the alcohol had influenced cognitive ability. In the nonexperimental design, you could make statements of relationship but not statements of causation. This is because you did not assign the participants to the conditions; they assigned themselves. And it could be that the individuals differ on cognitive ability even before they began drinking (i.e., perhaps their differences in cognitive ability are driving them to drink excessively).

Q5: If the experiment is the cornerstone of scientific research, why use any other approach?

A5: Some research problems simply do not lend themselves to an experimental approach. Psychologists are interested in many variables that are inherent in the participants and, therefore, cannot be manipulated. Developmental psychologists, for example, often study variables such as gender and age. Such participant variables can only be studied with a quasi-experimental design. In addition, there may be ethical problems or practical reasons that cause the researcher to choose a nonexperimental approach.

Q6: Are treatment levels used in both experimental and nonexperimental designs?

A6: There are treatment groups in quasi-experimental designs; however, the researcher does not form them. When the researcher does not have control over the assignment of participants to groups, such a design is not considered a true experimental design, and strong statements of causal relationship cannot be made.

Q7: When doing field experiments, do you have to tell people they are being observed?

A7: Although you must have your research examined by an Institutional Review Board, generally you do not have to obtain consent when observing people in a public setting. However, you must be able to guarantee anonymity of those observed. In other words, if you use video, it must be done in such a way that no one can be identified.

CHAPTER EXERCISES

1. What are the main reasons for doing experiments?

2. What are the steps involved in conducting an experiment?

3. What is the difference between a controlled laboratory experiment and a field experiment?

4. Describe the advantages and disadvantages between controlled and field experiments.

5. How are participants assigned to groups in independent groups designs, and what is the purpose of that method?

6. What does it mean when we say there is a significant main effect?

7. What does it mean when we say there is a significant interaction effect?

CHAPTER PROJECTS

1. A social psychologist is interested in the effects of video games on children's hand-eye dexterity. Design a controlled experiment to investigate this research problem.
   a. Specify IV (operationalize).
   b. Specify DV (operationalize).
   c. What is your research hypothesis?
   d. Specify how you will select participants and assign them to conditions.
   e. What is your statistical hypothesis and how will you test it?

2. Design a field experiment to investigate the research problem described in Question 1.
   a. Specify IV (operationalize).
   b. Specify DV (operationalize).
   c. What is your research hypothesis?
   d. Specify how you will select participants and assign them to conditions.
   e. What is your statistical hypothesis and how will you test it?

3. Design an independent groups experiment to evaluate the following conceptual hypothesis: Children diagnosed with attention-deficit disorder (ADD) are more distractible on group tasks than on individualized tasks.
   a. Specify IV (operationalize).
   b. Specify DV (operationalize).
   c. What is your research hypothesis?
   d. Specify how you will select participants and assign them to conditions.
   e. What is your statistical hypothesis and how will you test it?

4. You have conducted an experiment to determine how children diagnosed with ADD perform on group and individualized tasks. In addition, the tasks are classified as difficult or easy. The children were independently assigned to each of the four conditions (difficult group, easy group, difficult individualized, easy individualized). You have measured mean performance of the groups on talk solution.
   a. What kind of design have you used?
   b. What are the IVs and what is the DV?
   c. Using the data on the next page, graph each main effect and the interaction using group means. Describe what seems to have occurred. Higher scores are better.

	Task Difficulty	
Type of Task	*Easy*	*Difficult*
Individual	10.0	7.0
Group	9.0	2.0

REFERENCES

Chaudry, S., Schroter, S., Smith, R., & Morris, J. (2002). Does declaration of competing interests affect readers' perceptions? *British Medical Journal, 325*(7377), 1391–1392.

Fox, K. A., Webster, J. C., & Guerriero, F. J. (1972). Increased aggression among grouped male mice fed nitrazepam and flurazepam. *Pharmacological Research Communications, 4,* 157–162.

Jones, K. M., & Lungaro, C. J. (2000). Teacher acceptability of functional assessment-derived treatments. *Journal of Educational & Psychological Consultation, 11*(3/4), 323–332.

Renzi, P. (1982). Increased shock-induced attack after repeated chlordiazepoxide administration in mice. *Aggressive Behavior, 8,* 172–174.

Visit the study site at www.sagepub.com/evansmprstudy for practice quizzes and other study resources.

CHAPTER 8

Experimental Design

Dependent Groups and Mixed Groups Designs

OBJECTIVES

After reading this chapter, students should be able to

- Describe the difference between dependent groups, independent groups, and mixed designs

- Describe the difference between matched groups and within-participants designs

- Describe carryover effects associated with within-participants designs

- Describe three methods to control for carryover effects

- Describe advantages and disadvantages of independent and dependent groups designs

- Design an experiment to assess a given hypothesis

In Chapter 7, we discussed independent groups designs, where participant differences are controlled by independently assigning participants to each group. Another way to handle participant differences between groups is to use a **dependent groups design.** Often researchers use a combination of independent and dependent groups. Such designs are called **mixed designs.**

Consider the following questions:

Do women feel safer after they have taken self-defense classes?

How do married couples evaluate their satisfaction with their relationship after the first, third, fifth, and seventh years of marriage?

Do persuasive messages change people's attitudes?

How might we examine these questions? We could ask women how safe they feel before and then after they have taken self-defense training. We could have our couples rate their satisfaction at each point in time. We might measure attitudes of people before and after they hear persuasive messages. In all three examples, we are measuring responses of the *same* people under different conditions, a dependent groups approach.

DEPENDENT GROUPS DESIGNS

There are two kinds of dependent groups designs. In the **matched-groups design,** matched sets of participants are assigned in such a way that one member of each matched set is randomly assigned to each treatment condition or group. Because the participants are similar to each other (i.e., matched), the groups are initially equivalent, at least on the **matching variable.** In the **within-participants design,** the same participants are used in all treatment conditions. These designs eliminate the problem of nonequivalent groups by "reusing" the same participants.

Dependent groups designs reduce the between-participant variability, thereby reducing the error variance. Most of the error variance in social science research is due to differences between the participants (i.e., individual differences). You will recall that we discussed power in Chapter 4. Because dependent groups designs reduce this error variance, they are generally more powerful than between-participants designs. You may be wondering why we do not always use dependent groups designs. Well, there are several reasons. In the matched groups approach, we may not know what the important variables are that we should match our participants on. And if we lose one member of a matched set (perhaps one participant just quit), then we must eliminate the other members of the matched set from our analysis.

In the case of the within-participants approach, some research problems simply do not lend themselves to this kind of design. For example, if one of the treatment conditions permanently affects behavior (e.g., learning a skill), then this type of design cannot work. Participants cannot unlearn the skill in the control condition, for example. However, dependent groups designs, when they are appropriate, usually provide more powerful tests of the hypotheses than independent groups designs.

Within-Participants Designs

Within-participants or repeated-measures designs have another advantage over between-participants designs. They are economical in terms of the number of participants needed to complete the design. Because the participants serve in all conditions, we need fewer of them. For example, a 2×2 randomized factorial design with 20 participants in each group would require a total of 80 participants to complete the design (i.e., four treatment combinations with 20 participants per group). If we were to use a factorial within-participants design, on the other hand, we would need only 20 participants in total because all participants would serve in all treatment combinations. Often, a repeated-measures or within-participants design involves taking measures on the dependent variable at different times. In these cases, the time that the measure was made serves as an independent variable.

Like independent groups, designs discussed in the previous chapter, dependent groups designs can involve one independent variable or more than one independent variable. If all combinations of all levels of each independent variable were included in the design, then this would be called a **within-participants factorial design.**

FYI

Statistical analysis computer program packages have made our lives much easier. Rarely do researchers do analyses by hand these days. With the availability of these packages come some disadvantages. Different software companies use different terms to refer to the same thing. For example, the term *repeated-measures design* rather than *within participants* is used by some software manufacturers, including SPSS. Some common statistical packages include SPSS, Systat, SAS/STAT, and Minitab.

When the same participants serve in all conditions, we must be concerned about **carryover** or order effects such as fatigue and practice. Such effects are also sometimes called *transfer effects.*

Dealing With Carryover Effects in Within-Participants Designs

Clearly, it would be unwise to have the same order of treatment conditions for all participants if there was any possibility of one treatment affecting or carrying over to another. For example, if we were interested in determining whether abstractness of verbal items affects learning time, we would be foolish to have our participants learn the items in the same order. Consider an experiment where all participants learned a list of highly abstract items (HA) first, followed by a list of moderately abstract items (MA), and finally followed by a list of the most concrete (least abstract) items (LA). By the time our participants got to the third list of the most concrete items, they might be tired, a variable that is confounded with our independent variable (abstractness). Or they might do better on this third list because of the practice they have had learning the previous two lists. Practice, then, sometimes called transfer of training, would be another potentially confounding variable.

There are various ways to handle this problem. We could randomly determine the order of treatments. This technique is difficult to do unless you have a large number of participants. More common is a counterbalancing strategy. A **completely counterbalanced** approach requires that each condition occur equally often and precede and follow all other conditions the same number of times. Table 8.1 illustrates one replication of a completely counterbalanced order of conditions for our single-variable design.

TABLE 8.1	Completely Counterbalanced Scheme for a Three-Group Design		
Participant #	**Order of Conditions**		
1	LA	MA	HA
2	MA	HA	LA
3	HA	LA	MA
4	LA	HA	MA
5	MA	LA	HA
6	HA	MA	LA

As you can see, it takes six participants to complete the scheme one time. As the number of conditions increases, the number of participants required for a completely counterbalanced design increases dramatically. **Incomplete counterbalancing** is the more reasonable approach if the design involves a large number of conditions. Such a modification usually involves ensuring that each condition occurs equally often but does not necessarily precede and follow all other conditions the same number of times.

FYI

There are several other ways of balancing order effects, including the use of Latin squares. Readers can find information by consulting an upper-level statistics text.

Counterbalancing controls for various **carryover effects,** which we must address in within-participants designs. Be aware, however, that **differential order effects** are not controlled for by this technique. By this, we mean that some treatment effects are not reversible. If one particular order of treatment affects performance in a particular way, then this confounding variable will not be controlled with counterbalancing. For example, if we were interested in the effect of lighting on reading comprehension, we could test half the participants in bright conditions followed by dim, and the other half could be tested in the reverse order. Counterbalancing would control for practice effects or participant fatigue. However, if we were interested in the effects of alcohol on reading comprehension, a repeated-measures design would fail miserably. Half our sample could be tested sober and then tested after consuming a drink (oh, let's maximize our effect; let's say four drinks). The other half would get the reverse order; they would consume four drinks, be tested, and then be tested in the sober condition. What? The problem of differential order is obvious.

Whenever a treatment condition affects a second treatment condition differently than it does when it follows any other treatment condition, then counterbalancing will not eliminate this confound. Prudent researchers must consider such potential confounds when designing their study.

TABLE 8.2	Within-Participants Design	
Group		
Natural	Laboratory	Rest

Source: Focht and Hausenblas (2003).

Note: Order of conditions was counterbalanced.

Let's look at an example from the literature of a within-participants dependent groups design where counterbalancing was used to control the order of conditions.

The Research Problem. Regular exercise has both emotional and physical benefits. Focht and Hausenblas (2003) wondered if people who are anxious about their appearance might avoid exercise in public settings where others have an opportunity to evaluate their appearance. They may feel threatened in health clubs, for example, in the presence of other people who are perhaps more attractive than they are. Focht and Hausenblas included several variables in their study. We have selected only part of the experiment to present here.

The Hypothesis. One of Focht and Hausenblas's (2003) hypotheses was that participants would rate settings where the potential for evaluation by others is high as more threatening than settings where the potential for evaluation is low.

Selection of Participants and Assignment to Conditions. Thirty female college students were recruited from university classes to participate in this experiment. All of the women met two criteria: high social physique anxiety and low physical activity levels. Each woman participated in all three experimental conditions.

Independent Variable and Dependent Variable. One within-participants independent variable was the activity/setting: laboratory exercise, natural environment exercise, and rest control. The natural environment was a university fitness facility during times when others were exercising. Exercise in the laboratory condition took place in a private laboratory with no other exercisers present. In the rest condition, participants sat quietly in a room. Each session lasted for 20 minutes.

One dependent variable was ratings of perceived evaluative threat.

The Design. Because all of the women participated in all three conditions, the design was within participants. The researchers were concerned about possible order effects, always a concern with within-participants designs. They counterbalanced the order of the conditions to control for such effects, and each session took place on different days. The design is illustrated in Table 8.2.

The Statistical Analysis. A one-way analysis of variance (ANOVA) with repeated measures was used to compare the ratings of evaluative threat of the three conditions.

The Results. Some of the descriptive statistics of this study are presented in Table 8.3.

The inferential statistical analysis revealed that there was a significant difference between the three conditions, $F(2, 86) = 35.28, p < .001$. Focht and Hausenblas (2003) reported that participants rated the natural environment as more threatening than the laboratory environment, and they rated both exercise conditions as more threatening than the rest condition. They did not include the statistics for these comparisons.

The Conclusions. Focht and Hausenblas (2003) concluded that women with high social physique anxiety feel more threatened by exercise environments where others are present and perceived as likely to be evaluating their appearance. They suggested that the relationship between exercise and anxiety warrants further research.

Conceptual Exercise 8

Mnemonic schemes are often used to help us remember various things. You know the "thirty days has September" scheme. A researcher wants to investigate the use of mnemonic schemes in the learning of lists of words. Participants will be trained to use a rhyming scheme to learn one list, an imagery scheme to learn another list, and no scheme to learn yet another list. She hypothesizes that the imagery scheme will produce the fastest learning, and no scheme will produce the slowest learning. Which design (i.e., within participants or between participants) should she use and why?

Within-participants designs are not appropriate for some research problems. A treatment condition that carries over to another is such a situation. The researcher may choose to use another dependent groups design such as a matched groups design in these cases.

Matched Groups Designs

A matched groups design provides the added power of dependent groups designs and eliminates the problem of carryover effects. In a matched groups design, participants are

TABLE 8.3	Mean Ratings of Evaluative Threat of the Three Conditions	
Group (Activity/Setting)		
Natural	**Laboratory**	**Rest**
2.55	1.60	0.965

Source: Focht and Hausenblas (2003).

Note: Ratings on 5-point Likert scale—higher ratings indicate more perceived threat.

matched, or made equivalent, on a variable or variables that correlate with the dependent variable, thus reducing the error variance due to individual differences. It is important that the matching variables do correlate with the dependent measure. Otherwise, the power of the design is in fact reduced because the loss of degrees of freedom associated with dependent groups designs is not counteracted by the reduction in error variance. Consider a situation where a researcher has matched participants on IQ and assigned one member of each matched pair to an experimental group and to a control group. The dependent measure is performance on a stimulus discrimination task after the experimental participants have been trained in discrimination and the control participants have not. If discrimination ability is unrelated to IQ, then there is no reduction in variability of discrimination scores because participants were not matched on a variable that contributes to such variability. But there is a loss of degrees of freedom because the design is a dependent groups design, and as a result, there is an overall loss of power. The test of the hypothesis then will be weaker, and significant differences will be less detectable. The power of a matched groups design will only be enhanced if the matching variable is correlated with the dependent measure. Let's see how Ozonoff and Cathcart (1998) used a matched groups design in their study of children with autism.

The Research Problem. Autism is a developmental disorder of children. Children with autism have difficulties communicating, and many exhibit behaviors that interfere with learning. Ozonoff and Cathcart (1998) were concerned that much of the research examining intervention strategies with these children lacked appropriate control conditions, making it very difficult to know if these programs were effective. They decided to conduct an experiment to determine the effectiveness of a particular home-based intervention program called TEACCH (Treatment and Education of Autistic and Related Communication Handicapped Children), a program developed at the University of North Carolina.

The Hypotheses. Although not specifically stated by Ozonoff and Cathcart (1998), we will speculate that they expected that the TEACCH program would be effective in improving the performance of children with autism compared to no treatment.

Selection of Participants and Assignment to Conditions. Twenty-two children with autism were recruited to participate in the experiment. The children were matched on age, severity of autism, and scores on a developmental test that measured functioning in domains such as imitation, perception, motor skill, and so on (PEP-R: the Psychoeducational Profile–Revised).

The Independent Variable and Dependent Variables. The independent variable in this experiment was treatment (TEACCH) and a no-treatment control. Dependent variables were changes in score on the developmental subtests from pretest to posttest.

The Design. This matched groups pretest/posttest design is illustrated in Table 8.4.

The Statistical Analysis. A 2×2 ANOVA with repeated measures was used to analyze the test scores. One variable was treatment condition (TEACCH and control), and the other was time of testing (before and after).

TABLE 8.4	Matched Groups Design	
Group	*Pretest*	*Posttest*
TEACCH		
Control		

Source: Ozonoff and Cathcart (1998).

The Results. Some of the descriptive statistics are presented in Table 8.5.

The main effect statistics were not reported because the interest of the researchers was in the interaction between group and time of test. They did not expect improvement in the control children beyond perhaps a slight pretest/posttest effect. Improvement was expected only in the treated children.

Ozonoff and Cathcart (1998) reported a significant interaction between group and time of testing on the fine motor measure, $F(1, 20) = 7.93$, $p < .01$; the cognitive measure, $F(1, 20) = 9.37$, $p < .01$; and the total PEP-R score, $F(1, 20) = 4.57$, $p < .05$. The treated children showed significant improvement over the control children on all three measures. These three interactions are illustrated in Figures 8.1, 8.2, and 8.3.

The Conclusions. Ozonoff and Cathcart (1998) concluded that the TEACCH program was effective in improving the development of various skills in young children with autism.

As we have seen, there are advantages and disadvantages of within-participants and between-participants designs. Between-participants designs require a lot of participants and, as such, can be impractical. Within-participants designs often are not suitable for certain research problems. One way to maximize the benefits and minimize the drawback of each design is to use a mixed design.

TABLE 8.5	Descriptive Statistics, Mean (*SD*)		
Subtest	*Pretest*	*Posttest*	*Difference*
TEACCH			
Fine motor	28.8 (7.7)	38.7 (14.6)	9.9
Cognitive	15.6 (6.4)	26.2 (12.5)	10.6
Total PEP-R	21.4 (6.0)	28.7 (11.5)	7.3
Control			
Fine motor	30.6 (8.9)	32.9 (9.6)	2.3
Cognitive	20.5 (7.7)	22.4 (10.9)	1.9
Total PEP-R	24.2 (7.6)	26.9 (10.4)	2.7

Source: Ozonoff and Cathcart (1998).

Note: Difference = post/pretest score: Higher difference scores indicate improvement.

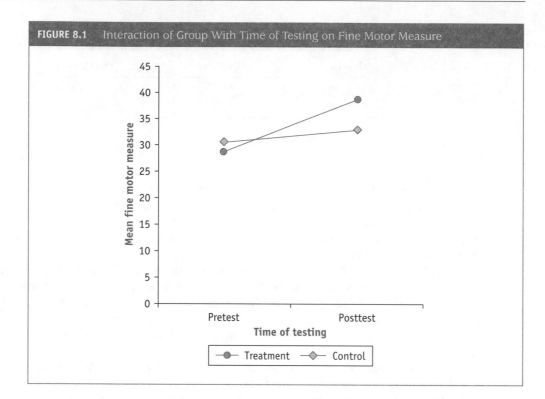

FIGURE 8.1 Interaction of Group With Time of Testing on Fine Motor Measure

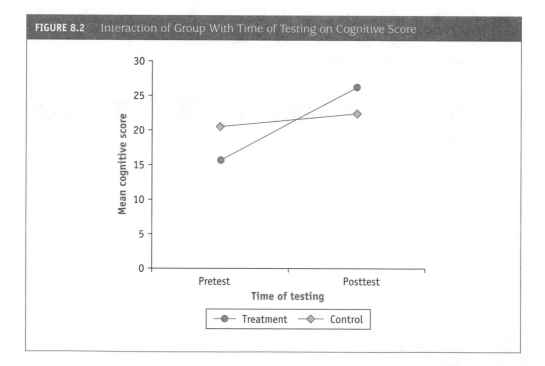

FIGURE 8.2 Interaction of Group With Time of Testing on Cognitive Score

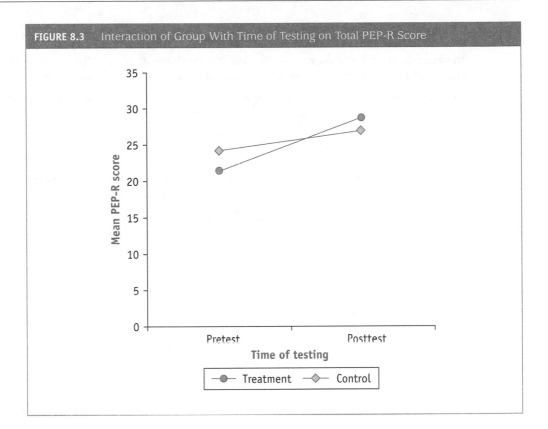

FIGURE 8.3   Interaction of Group With Time of Testing on Total PEP-R Score

MIXED DESIGNS

In a mixed design, a variable (or variables) is assessed *between* participants, and another variable (or variables) is assessed *within* participants. A variable that the researcher thinks might produce carryover effects can be assessed between participants with other variables, with no such potential problems assessed within participants. Although mixed designs are quite common in the social sciences, the statistical analyses of such designs can be quite complex. In the following example, we will see how a mixed design was used to examine how powerful people affect our behavior.

The Research Problem. We have all been in positions where we have power over others and in positions where others have power over us. How people in positions of power affect the behavior of others is a question of interest to many researchers. van Knippenberg, van Knippenberg, and Wilke (2001) were particularly interested in how factors such as the cooperative/competitive nature of the task, task competence, and confidence in their ability affect how people use power. They defined power for the purposes of their study as "the capacity to influence the outcomes or behavior of others."

The Hypotheses. The hypotheses with respect to task competence were as follows:

> In cooperative settings, power holders who are more competent at the task than the others involved use their power more often than less competent power holders.

> In competitive settings, task competence of the power holder has little effect on the frequency of the use of power by the power holder.

The hypotheses with respect to confidence in ability were as follows:

> In cooperative settings, power holders who are more confident in their ability use their power more often than power holders who are less confident in their ability.

> In competitive settings, the confidence of the power holders has little effect on their use of power.

Selection of Participants and Assignment to Conditions. Sixty-six university students were randomly assigned to different levels of two of the three independent variables in this experiment. The first independent variable was social context. van Knippenberg et al. (2001) used two levels of this variable: cooperation and competition. The second independent variable was task competence, also with two levels: high and low. The third independent variable was confidence in ability, and it also had two levels: high and low. The effect of this third independent variable was assessed within participants. Therefore, the participants were randomly assigned to the levels of two independent variables and provided repeated measures on the third.

The Independent Variables and Dependent Variables. Participants in this experiment played a game with another person where they had to estimate the number of black squares in a checkerboard grid that was presented for a brief period of time. Participants worked at computers and could not see the other player (in fact, the other player's responses were simulated). The first between-participants independent variable was social context. Participants in the cooperation context were told that their score and the other player's score would be combined and compared to the score of another pair of players (there were no other players, however). The pair with the highest combined score would earn a payoff. Participants in the competition context were told that they were playing against the other player and that the player with the highest score would receive a payoff.

The second between-participants independent variable was task competence. To manipulate this variable, the researchers gave the participants a 10-trial pretest. Feedback regarding their performance was given following this test. Participants in the high-competence group were told that they did better than the other player, and participants in the low-competence group were told that they did worse than the other player.

The third independent variable, confidence, was a within-participants variable. The researchers used grid presentation time to manipulate this variable. Grids were presented for either 25 seconds (high confidence) or 5 seconds (low confidence). The researchers expected that when participants had more time to study the grid, they would feel more confident about their estimates.

van Knippenberg et al. (2001) measured several dependent variables. We will discuss only one—the use of power. Participants were told that they had been randomly selected by the computer to decide what estimate they wanted their partner/opponent to make. They were told that if they decided to use this power, the estimate that the participant selected would replace the other player's answer, and they were told that the other player would be aware of this. Participants were told that if they did not use this power, the other player's estimate would stand. The researchers measured the number of times the participant used power by forcing the answer of the other player.

The Design. The design was a $2 \times 2 \times 2$ mixed design with social context (cooperation vs. competition) and task competence (high vs. low) as between-participants factors. Confidence in ability was the within-participants factor (high vs. low). The design is illustrated in Table 8.6.

The Statistical Analysis. A three-way ANOVA was used to assess the effects of the three independent variables and the interactions.

The Results. Some of the descriptive statistics are presented in Table 8.7.

The three-way ANOVA provided several findings. The researchers discussed the main effects and 2 two-way interactions. They reported no main effect of social context, $F(1, 62) = 1.65, p > .05$. Overall, then, there was no difference between the cooperation and competition contexts in the number of times participants used their power opportunity. There was a main effect of task competence. Participants who were led to believe they were very competent at the task used their power more often than participants who believed they were less competent, $F(1, 62) = 6.04, p < .05$.

The confidence main effect was also significant. On trials where participants had more time to view the grid and presumably felt more confident, they used their power more often than on those trials where they felt less confident, $F(1, 62) = 12.61, p < .001$.

TABLE 8.6   Mixed Design

	Between Factor	
Social Context	*High Task Competence*	*Low Task Competence*
Cooperation		
Competition		
	Within Factor	
Social Context	*High Confidence*	*Low Confidence*
Cooperation		
Competition		

Source: van Knippenberg et al. (2001).

TABLE 8.7   Descriptive Statistics: Mean Number of Times Power Was Used/10 (*SD*)

Social Context	Between Factor	
	High Task Competence	**Low Task Competence**
Cooperation	6.88 (3.56)	2.82 (3.03)
Competition	3.88 (3.39)	3.50 (4.56)

Social Context	Within Factor	
	High Confidence	**Low Confidence**
Cooperation	3.06 (2.44)	1.73 (1.86)
Competition	2.03 (2.30)	1.67 (2.09)

Source: van Knippenberg et al. (2001).

As always, these main effects must be interpreted in relation to any interactions, and van Knippenberg et al. (2001) reported two significant interactions. There was a social context by competence interaction. Let's examine the graph of this interaction (see Figure 8.4).

FIGURE 8.4   Interaction of Social Context With Competence

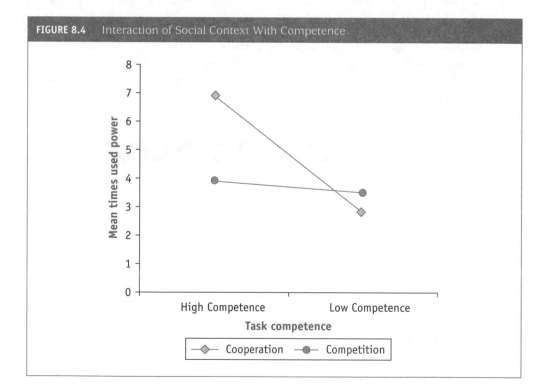

As we can see in Figure 8.4, high-competence participants used their power more often than low-competence participants in the cooperation context but not in the competition context, $F(1, 62) = 4.13, p < .05$ (these means are in the upper part of Table 8.7).

van Knippenberg et al. (2001) also reported a significant social context by confidence interaction. This interaction is illustrated in Figure 8.5.

On trials with longer exposure times where participants felt more confident in their estimates, they used their power more often only in the cooperation context, $F(1, 62) = 4.41$, $p < .05$. These means are in the lower part of Table 8.7.

The Conclusions. van Knippenberg et al. (2001) concluded that competent and confident power holders use their power in cooperative but not in competitive situations. They pointed out that it is often easier to determine what hinders others from reaching goals (needed to succeed in a competitive context) than it is to determine what helps others to reach goals (needed to succeed in a cooperative context). They speculated that factors such as task competence and confidence, which increase the power holder's ability to bring about positive outcomes for the other, would affect the use of power only in a cooperative context.

Mixed designs are useful in many research situations. Some variables are best assessed between participants, whereas others are best assessed within participants.

In this chapter and the previous chapter, we have presented various experimental designs where treatment effects are evaluated between groups. Another way of evaluating

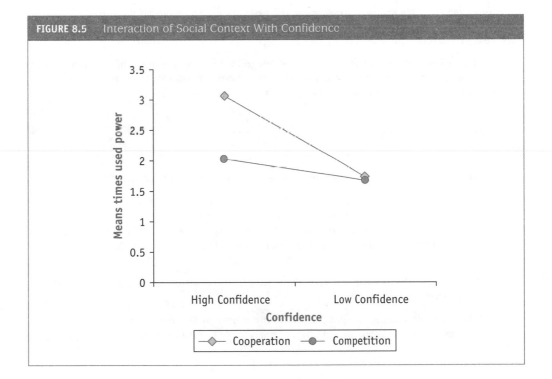

FIGURE 8.5 Interaction of Social Context With Confidence

treatment effects is the approach used by a field of psychology called the experimental analysis of behavior. Behavior analysts follow the tradition of operant psychology and evaluate treatments using what is typically called a single-subject or single-participant design, the topic of the next chapter.

CHAPTER SUMMARY

Dependent groups designs are designs that control for participant differences by either reusing the same participants or assigning matched participants to groups. Dependent groups designs can be more powerful than independent groups designs. **Within-participants designs** are not suitable for certain research problems where **carryover effects** might mask the effect of the treatment. It is important that the **matching variable** in a **matched groups design** be correlated with the dependent variable, or power will be lost.

A **within-participants factorial design** is one where participants serve under all combinations of all levels of each independent variable. Methods for controlling carryover effects in such designs include **randomization, complete counterbalancing**, and **incomplete counterbalancing.** Counterbalancing does not control for **differential order effects,** however. **Mixed designs** may have an advantage over others in that some variables can be assessed between participants and others within participants.

ANSWER TO CONCEPTUAL EXERCISE

Conceptual Exercise 8

She should use a between-participants design in this case. Because the independent variable is the learning of a skill (i.e., using a mnemonic scheme), participants cannot unlearn the skill once it has been taught (e.g., when they are in the control condition).

FAQ

Q1: If I choose to use a dependent groups design, can I use fewer participants?

A1: Often you can use fewer participants in a dependent groups design. By using a dependent groups design, you can drastically reduce the error variability in your study, making it easier to achieve statistical significance. However, it is a trade-off because you have fewer degrees of freedom in a dependent groups design, and that makes it more difficult to get significance.

Q2: When either design could be used, should I do a within-participants design or a between-participants design?

A2: The better of the two designs is the within-participants design because you reduce the error variability in your study. However, carryover effects often make this design impossible.

Q3: Why do you lose power if your matching variable is no good?

A3: If your matching variable has little or nothing to do with the dependent variable, then you will not have reduced error variance. You will have fewer degrees of freedom in your significance tests and thus lost power.

CHAPTER EXERCISES

1. Describe the major difference between dependent groups, independent groups, and mixed designs.
2. Describe the difference between matched groups and within-participants designs.
3. Describe two potential carryover effects that could confound the independent variable in a within-participants design.
4. Describe two ways to deal with carryover effects in a within-participants design.
5. Describe the power advantage of matched groups and within-participants designs over between-participants designs.

CHAPTER PROJECTS

1. Design a dependent groups experiment to evaluate the following conceptual hypothesis: Children diagnosed with attention-deficit disorder (ADD) are more distractible on group tasks than on individualized tasks.
   a. Specify IV (operationalize).
   b. Specify DV (operationalize).
   c. What is your research hypothesis?
   d. If you choose a matched groups design, what is your matching variable?
   e. Specify how you will select participants and assign them to conditions.
   f. What is your statistical hypothesis and how will you test it?

2. Use a mixed design to evaluate the following conceptual hypotheses:
   - Children diagnosed with ADD are more distractible on group tasks than on individualized tasks.
   - Children with ADD are less distractible when the tasks are concrete rather than abstract.
   - Children with ADD are most easily distracted when they are in a group and required to complete an abstract task and least distractible when they are alone and required to complete a concrete task.
   a. Specify between-participants IVs.
   b. Specify within-participants IVs (operationalize).
   c. Specify DV (operationalize).
   d. What are your research hypotheses? Specify the main effects you expect. Do you expect an interaction?
   e. What are your statistical hypotheses and how will you test them?
   f. Sketch each expected main effect and interaction.

REFERENCES

Focht, B. C., & Hausenblas, H. A. (2003). State anxiety responses to acute exercise in women with high social physique anxiety. *Journal of Sport & Exercise Psychology, 25*(2), 123–144.

Ozonoff, S., & Cathcart, K. (1998). Effectiveness of a home program intervention for young children with autism. *Journal of Autism and Developmental Disorders, 28*(1), 25–32.

van Knippenberg, B., van Knippenberg, D., & Wilke, H. A. M. (2001). Power use in cooperative and competitive settings. *Basic and Applied Psychology, 23,* 293–302.

Visit the study site at www.sagepub.com/evansmprstudy for practice quizzes and other study resources.

Experimental Design

Single-Participant Designs/The Operant Approach

OBJECTIVES

After reading this chapter, students should be able to

- List similarities and differences between multi- and single-participant experimental design
- Describe the basic concepts used in the experimental analyses of behavior
- Describe the ABA and the ABAB designs, as well as their strengths and weaknesses
- Describe the multiple baseline design and provide examples of three types of multiple baseline designs
- Describe the alternating treatments design
- Describe the changing criterion design
- Provide an example of a research problem that would be suited to study with each of the designs in this chapter
- Describe the advantages and disadvantages of single-participant experimental design
- Design a single-participant experiment to treat a given problem

---

A few years ago, Tod, one of our students, decided that, as his course research project, he would try to break a habit of his younger brother that he found extremely annoying. That habit was nail biting—excessive nail biting. Tod was not interested in nail biting in general, although it bothered him to see people chewing away. But his brother's habit was really getting on his nerves, and that was the behavior Tod wanted to change. He designed an experiment to see if he could reduce or, better yet, eliminate this behavior.

Prolonged study of a single individual has a long history in psychology. Wilhelm Wundt, for example, used a carefully trained participant to study sensory processes. Hermann Ebbinghaus studied his own memory for long lists of what he called nonsense syllables. Ivan Pavlov's original work was conducted on a single dog. Single-participant research was the rule in psychology until 1935, when Fisher published his experimental design book where he introduced statistical methods for analyzing data from experiments on many participants. This publication changed the way many psychologists did research.

Today, the debate continues about the relative merits of single-participant research and group research. Both can be experimental, and this chapter is devoted to experimental single-participant research. It is important to note that the single-participant research designs discussed in this chapter are *not* case studies. Single-participant research designs adopted by B. F. Skinner, which are the focus of this chapter, are used to examine the behavior of a single individual under highly controlled conditions with the goal of determining the effectiveness of a particular treatment on changing the strength of a specific behavior. Case studies are quite a different kettle of fish and are discussed in Chapter 10. We think it would be fair to say that **single-participant design** as discussed here is a quantitative approach, whereas the case study is better described as a qualitative approach.

SINGLE-PARTICIPANT DESIGN AND THE EXPERIMENTAL ANALYSIS OF BEHAVIOR

Although many researchers in psychology have adopted the multiparticipant approach to studying behavior, B. F. Skinner is perhaps the most well-known exception to this trend. He and his followers developed an approach to studying behavior that is known as the **experimental analysis of behavior** and focuses on studying the behavior of an individual rather than group averages. The individual's behavior is studied over time as the researcher changes the independent variable, and then the experiment is replicated several times with other participants on an individual basis. Researchers who use this experimental method are called *behavior analysts*.

As we have discussed several times, individual differences are the largest source of experimental error or error variance. Statistical procedures take this error variance into account in the analysis of group data based on averages or means. Operant designs are carried out to show experimental control (not statistical control) at the level of individual behavior. The individual then serves as his or her own control, and if the experimental environment is adequately controlled and precise measurements of the dependent variable are made, the researcher can, with confidence, evaluate the effects of the independent variable on behavior. Skinner devoted his research career to doing just this, and from his work, we have learned much about human behavior.

CONCEPTS IN THE EXPERIMENTAL ANALYSIS OF BEHAVIOR

Operant

You will recall that the response in classical or Pavlovian conditioning that is strengthened by the conditioning process is called the *conditioned response*. The process of classical conditioning involves bringing a response under the control of a stimulus (called the *conditioned stimulus*) that did not control that response before conditioning took place. In operant or Skinnerian conditioning, the response that will be strengthened (or weakened) is called the operant. An **operant** is any behavior that operates on the environment to produce effects or consequences. The effects of operant behavior feed back and increase (or decrease) the likelihood of this behavior. The process of operant learning or conditioning involves bringing the operant behavior under the control of its consequences, the reinforcer (or punisher).

Phase

In operant research, the individual is studied over time to see how his or her behavior changes when different treatments are introduced, withdrawn, or changed. These periods of time are called **phases.** Before we can show that a particular reinforcer has strengthened a behavior, an operant, for example, we must determine what the natural or baseline level of that behavior is.

Baseline

During the **baseline** phase of a single-participant experiment, we measure the free level of the operant or response. We need to know how strong the target behavior is before we can assess any changes that might occur in its strength when we introduce a treatment. Baseline measurements are made for a period of time long enough that we have a good idea of what the operant level is prior to treatment. Recall our student who wanted to treat his brother's nail-biting behavior. He kept careful records of how often his brother bit his nails for a specific period each day. He was gathering baseline data on the operant.

Treatment

In the treatment phase of the experiment, the independent variable is introduced, and of course, the behavior is carefully measured and recorded. The treatment in these kinds of experiments usually involves some sort of reinforcement or punishment procedure. In your introductory psychology course, you learned that a *reinforcement procedure* is one where the operant response is followed by a stimulus (the reinforcer) intended to increase its strength. In punishment, the behavior is followed by a stimulus (the punisher) intended to reduce the strength of the behavior. Our student decided to use a punishment procedure to treat his brother's nail biting. During the treatment phase, he painted his brother's nails with a concoction that tasted dreadful. This is a punishment procedure because the consequences of the behavior of nail biting (i.e., dreadful taste) were intended to reduce nail biting.

Length of Phase

How long each phase lasts depends on the stability of the behavior being observed. In general, each phase continues until the target behavior is stable or consistent over time.

Changing Phase

Over time, behavior does tend to stabilize such that we see a consistent level of responding. Once this has occurred, we can then introduce, withdraw, or change a treatment. Our goal is to show that our treatment causes a change in the operant level. You may be wondering how much change indicates that our independent variable was effective. This is a good question. The answer is there is no single answer. The experience of the researcher is crucial when it comes to interpreting the outcome of single-participant research. Obviously, the interpretation of the results of single-participant research is more subjective than that of multiparticipant research, where the statistical analysis provides more objective answers. But keep in mind that a treatment effect seen in a single-participant experiment will be replicated with other individuals.

Measuring the Response

In single-participant research designs, various measures of response strength are used, but perhaps the most common measure is **rate** or frequency of responding in a specific period of time. Researchers typically measure the total frequency of the operant behavior and the time when each response occurred. This is called a cumulative record of the response. This record is often made by a machine called a cumulative recorder, but in some cases, a researcher simply records when the response occurs over units of time. In either case, the cumulative record tells us the total number of responses in the given observation period and the time each occurred. Researchers using these designs often display the data in a cumulative response graph, such as the one shown in Figure 9.1.

The backslashes help us see when a response was made. By looking at the top of the curve, we can see the total number of responses that were made. During baseline, very few responses occurred. Once treatment began, responding started to increase. Examination of the cumulative record, called *graphic analysis*, is typically how researchers using such designs decide whether the independent variable or treatment had an effect. There are now statistical procedures for analyzing these kinds of data, but graphic analysis is still the most common method used.

ABA AND ABAB WITHDRAWAL DESIGNS

In single-participant research, the baseline phase is usually referred to by the letter A and the treatment phase by the letter B. The term *withdrawal* refers to the withdrawal of the treatment in the second A phase. For example, an **ABA design** means that we have gathered **baseline** data (A), then introduced a **treatment** (B), and then withdrawn the treatment

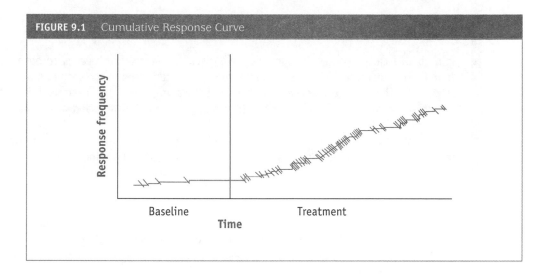

FIGURE 9.1   Cumulative Response Curve

and measured response again (A). You may be wondering why researchers withdraw treatment at all. This is a critical part of single-participant research designs. Remember we are trying to show that our treatment (B) changed the strength of the behavior. If we simply introduced a treatment after the baseline phase (AB), we could not establish a causal relationship. Even if the behavior did increase in strength after the treatment was introduced, we do not know what the behavior rate would have been had we not introduced our treatment. We are assuming that because the rate increased, our treatment was responsible. Perhaps the behavior increased simply because of practice, for example. This AB approach is analogous to a before-after multiparticipant design with no control group.

Remember, in single-participant research, the individual serves as his or her own control. We must go back to baseline conditions to establish that the treatment was responsible for any change in response strength. If the response weakens in the second baseline phase, then we can conclude that it was our treatment, not something else, that strengthened the behavior. If, on the other hand, we find in the second baseline phase that the response is still strong, then we have a problem relating the change in response strength to our treatment.

The ABA design is often used in basic research to demonstrate the effectiveness of an independent variable on behavior. Like some other kinds of psychologists, behavior analysts are often called upon to apply their principles to help real people with real problems. This application of the experimental analysis of behavior is part of the general psychotherapeutic approach called *behavior modification*. The goal of behavior modification is to change a behavior to help the individual. Some behaviors are desirable, and the goal is to maintain or increase their strength, whereas other behaviors are undesirable, and the goal is to weaken them or eliminate them. In these applications of behavioral principles, the ABA design is not used. We are sure you can see why. We want to change the behavior, not return to the way it was. Adding a second treatment phase solves the problem. This withdrawal design is called an **ABAB design**.

> ## FYI
>
> Some books call these two designs we have discussed *reversal* or *reversal to baseline designs*. The idea is that there is a reversal to baseline condition in the second A phase. Others use the term *reversal design* to refer to designs where the treatment is not withdrawn in the second A phase but rather is applied to a different and incompatible behavior.
>
> We think the second use of the term *reversal* seems to be an example of a multiple baseline design across behaviors (see our discussion of multiple baseline designs below).

Let's examine some work Christie Fyffe did as part of her master's degree (Fyffe, Kahng, Fittro, & Russell, 2004). She and her associates used an ABAB design to modify the inappropriate sexual behavior of a little boy.

The Research Problem. Matt was a 9-year-old boy who had suffered from traumatic brain injury. He was in a wheelchair and used picture cards to communicate. He had several problems, including aggressiveness, destructiveness, and inappropriate sexual behavior. In fact, he was placed in a residential facility because of his inappropriate sexual behavior toward his siblings, and this was the problem behavior addressed by Fyffe et al. (2004).

Objectives. Fyffe et al. (2004) noted that treatment of inappropriate sexual behavior has typically been reinforcement based but not necessarily functionally based. Fyffe et al. wanted to analyze Matt's behavior from a functional point of view and tie the treatment to that functional assessment.

The Independent Variable and Dependent Variable. Matt's inappropriate sexual behavior was observed under various conditions, and the researchers determined that adult social attention was the reinforcer maintaining Matt's behavior. For example, when inappropriate sexual behavior resulted in a brief reprimand, the behavior was quite frequent (about six behaviors per minute). Remember that consequences that we might think are negative, such as reprimands, often in fact reinforce behavior. Getting some attention, even negative attention, might be better than no attention at all.

Given that the function of Matt's inappropriate sexual behavior seemed to be to get attention from adults, the researchers chose attention as the independent variable. The dependent variable, inappropriate sexual behavior, included touching or attempting to touch the groin, buttocks, or breasts of others.

The Design. Fyffe et al. (2004) used an ABAB design. They withdrew treatment in the second A phase to demonstrate that the behavior was indeed under the control of the independent variable, and then they returned to treatment in the second B phase.

During the baseline phases, inappropriate sexual behavior resulted in a brief reprimand. This was thought to be similar to how Matt's behavior was treated in general by others. During the treatment phase, Matt received 30 seconds of attention from adults when he handed an attention card to the experimenter. Handing the attention card to the experimenter then functioned to get him the attention he seemed to need. Inappropriate sexual behavior was basically ignored. The researchers then were trying to extinguish the inappropriate sexual behavior and at the same time reinforce a desirable behavior (i.e., communicating with the researchers).

The Results. Fyffe et al. (2004) reported that the mean number of inappropriate sexual responses per minute was 6.7 across both baseline conditions and 0.4 across both treatment conditions.

Figure 9.2 illustrates the response rate during each phase of the study.

You can see that during the first baseline phase, Matt showed a certain amount of inappropriate behavior (about six behaviors per minute). During the first treatment phase, where Matt was allowed to use the card to get attention from adults, his inappropriate sexual behavior disappeared. The second baseline phase shows that the inappropriate behavior came back when the treatment was withdrawn. The researchers had demonstrated that their independent variable was effective, and had that been their goal, they could have stopped after doing so (an ABA design). But of course, their goal was twofold: first to demonstrate the treatment was effective and then to eliminate the undesirable behavior. So these

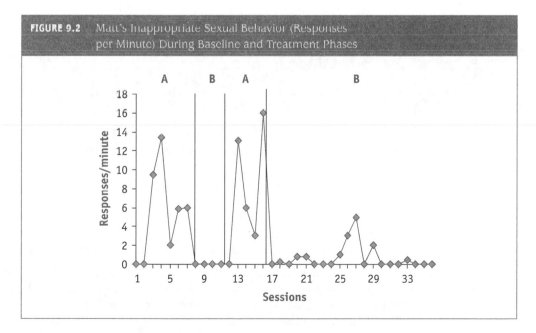

FIGURE 9.2   Matt's Inappropriate Sexual Behavior (Responses per Minute) During Baseline and Treatment Phases

Source: Adapted from Fyffe et al. (2004).

researchers, like most behavior analysts using behavioral techniques to help people, reintroduced the treatment for a second phase and continued for a period of time, at the end of which they were confident the behavior was eliminated (or extinguished).

The Conclusions. Fyffe et al. (2004) concluded that behavioral interventions that are tied to a functional analysis of the problem behavior can be effective. They note that the functional analysis of Matt's behavior led them to conclude that attention was the reinforcer maintaining that behavior. They then used that information to design a reinforcement strategy rather than a punishment procedure for Matt.

Withdrawal designs from a basic research point of view are preferable over designs where no second baseline is taken because control of the behavior by the treatment variable is demonstrated. However, in practice, there are situations where returning to baseline conditions is not possible or not ethical. If the treatment produces permanent changes in the participant, then clearly such changes are not reversible. For example, something that has been learned during the treatment phase cannot be unlearned. Imagine that you are using a reinforcement strategy with a dyslexic child to help her discriminate between the letters *d* and *b*. Once she has learned to discriminate between the two letters, her discrimination behavior will not return to baseline just because you withdraw the reinforcer.

Withdrawal of treatment is ethically unacceptable in cases where such withdrawal might cause harm to the client. Imagine you are working with a suicidal client, and you have been successful in reducing your client's suicidal symptoms. You can see that returning to baseline is not a consideration. In situations such as these, a multiple baseline design may be a good option.

Conceptual Exercise 9A

Would you suggest an ABA or an ABAB design for each of the following? Why?

1. Susan suffers from anorexia. A behavior analyst has been called in to treat her.

2. Does continuous reinforcement produce faster bar pressing in rats than reinforcing only some of the time?

MULTIPLE BASELINE DESIGN

With the ABAB design, the replication of the effect is seen in the second treatment phase. In **multiple baseline designs,** the replication of the effect is seen in another behavior, another individual, or another setting. Perhaps we have two or more individuals with the same target behavior. If we can establish a change in behavior in both individuals when our treatment is introduced, then we have confidence that it was our treatment that was responsible. This is a **multiple baseline across-participants design**.

Perhaps we have an individual with more than one behavior that we have targeted for change. We could introduce our treatment for the first behavior and then later introduce the same treatment for the second behavior. If each behavior changes only when the treatment is introduced, then we have confidence that our treatment caused the change. This is a **multiple baseline across-behaviors design**.

Last, we might measure our targeted behavior in different settings and apply our treatment in one setting at a time. This would be a **multiple baseline across-settings design**. Multiple baseline designs allow us to assess our treatment by comparing its effect on different behaviors, settings, or people rather than by withdrawing treatment.

Children with autism typically do not play like other children do. Finding ways to increase play skills for these children is a challenge; D'Ateno, Mangiapanello, and Taylor (2003) tackled this problem with a child named Rachel.

The Research Problem. Rachel, diagnosed with autism, was almost 4 years old when D'Ateno et al. (2003) started working with her. She attended the Alpine Learning Group in New Jersey, an education center for children with autism. Like many children with autism, Rachel did not talk very much and spent a lot of time manipulating toys in a repetitive manner rather than playing with the toys as most children would.

Objectives. D'Ateno et al. (2003) were interested in video modeling as a training procedure for play behavior. They noted that many treatment programs using video modeling also use a reinforcement procedure. They wanted to determine if video modeling alone would be effective in training play behavior.

The Independent Variable and Dependent Variables. The independent variable was the video model. Rachel viewed videotapes of a model playing. Three play sequences were modeled: tea party, shopping, and baking.

Several dependent variables were measured. We will discuss modeled motor responses here. A modeled motor response was a movement that matched the movement of the model in the video, in that the outcome of Rachel's behavior was the same as the outcome of the model's behavior. For example, if the model in the tea party video had picked up two plates and simultaneously placed them on a table, a correct modeled response would be counted if Rachel picked up two plates and put them on the table one at a time.

The Design. Three sets of play behaviors were targeted in this study: tea party, shopping, and baking. During baseline phases, Rachel was presented with toys associated with each category of play and told to play tea party, shopping, or baking. Each baseline session was 5 minutes. For treatment phases, Rachel viewed a video of a model demonstrating the play sequence. Later, Rachel was again given the play materials that had been shown in the video. Each experimental play session was 5 minutes. Once Rachel had reached the criterion response rate determined by the researchers, the next treatment condition was introduced. This, then, was a multiple baseline design across three kinds of responses (tea party, shopping, and baking).

TABLE 9.1	Summary Statistics: Modeled Responses per Session			
	Baseline		**Treatment**	
	Mean	**Range**	**Mean**	**Range**
Tea party	2.0	2–2	9.8	3–11
Shopping	4.2	1–7	9.8	7–11
Baking	0.5	0–2	4.4	0–7

Source: D'Ateno et al. (2003).

The Results. A summary of some of the results are presented in Table 9.1.

The modeled response rate across sessions for each type of play is illustrated in Figure 9.3.

You can see that during the baseline phase, Rachel made very few to no responses. During each treatment, she began to mimic the behavior of the model she had viewed in the video. Because the number of responses increased only after the treatment was introduced in each case, the researchers could be confident that it was the video treatment that caused the behavior to increase in frequency.

The Conclusions. D'Ateno et al. (2003) concluded that video modeling can be effective in training play behavior even without any reinforcement contingencies in place.

The multiple baseline design has a distinct advantage over withdrawal designs because baseline conditions are not reintroduced after treatment has begun. This makes the design particularly useful for studying treatments that we expect to be permanent or long-lasting. When a multiple baseline design across behaviors is used, it is important that the behaviors be independent. If they are not, then the treatment used to modify one behavior may also modify the other behaviors, an occurrence that would compromise the experiment's validity. Although this might be a good thing from a clinical point of view, it is not good from a scientific point of view. The researcher must show that only the treated behavior changes for the experiment to be credible.

In the designs we have discussed so far, only one treatment was used. As with multiparticipant research, single-participant researchers are often interested in more than one treatment. Does positive reinforcement or modeling work better in training developmentally delayed kids to tie their shoes? Perhaps a combination of the two is the best strategy. An **alternating treatment design** can be used to assess these kinds of questions.

ALTERNATING TREATMENT DESIGN

For reasons we do not understand, there seems to be more than the usual confusion about terminology in behavioral research. We have seen the alternating treatment design called multielement, discrete trials, multitreatment, and interaction design. We have simply selected the term that was used most frequently in the books on research methods we found on our shelves.

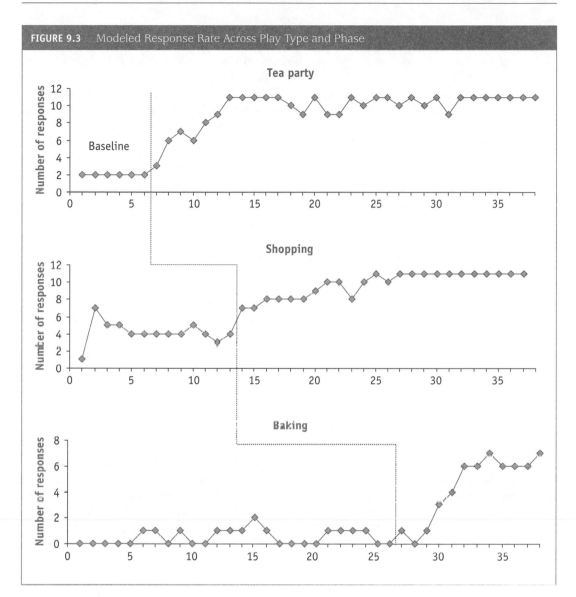

FIGURE 9.3   Modeled Response Rate Across Play Type and Phase

Source: Adapted from D'Ateno et al. (2003).

The alternating treatment design is useful for evaluating the effect of more than one kind of treatment on one individual within the same experiment. After the baseline phase, different treatments are alternated several times. The order of the treatments is randomly determined or counterbalanced to control carryover effects. You will recall that in the ABAB design, the treatment effect is replicated in the second treatment phase. In the multiple baseline design, the treatment effect is replicated in other people, in other settings, or with other behavior. In the alternating treatment design, each treatment effect is replicated each time it is introduced. A treatment may be applied a few times or many times. Let's look at an example.

As any teacher of young children knows, getting kids to pay attention during group activities is a challenge. Research has shown that active involvement in classroom activities is important in academic performance (e.g., Heward et al., 1996), and so teachers must find effective techniques for encouraging this kind of behavior. Godfrey, Grisham-Brown, Schuster, and Hemmeter (2003) were interested in comparing different strategies for getting kids to be more involved in classroom activities.

The Research Problem. Five children attending a preschool in rural Kentucky were the participants in Godfrey and her colleagues' (2003) study. These five children had various difficulties when the class of 14 students in total was engaged in group activities. They had trouble sitting at their desks, following directions, and completing tasks, and they often disrupted others.

The Objectives. Godfrey et al. (2003) wanted to find the best intervention technique to help these kids attend better in class. They decided to examine choral responding, where students respond in unison to a question from the teacher, and the response card technique, where each student holds up a card with his or her response depicted. Godfrey et al. chose these two techniques because, as they note, both have been shown to be effective in various studies.

The Independent Variable and Dependent Variable. Three conditions were used: two active responding treatments and the traditional technique of hand raising. The hand-raising condition was included as a control.

Several dependent variables were included. We will discuss only one: active responding. Active responding was defined as showing the behavior that fit the treatment condition. For example, if the treatment condition was hand raising, a response from a target child would be recorded if the child raised her or his hand in response to a question. If the condition was response card and a target child raised his or her response card with an answer to the question, this would be recorded. Eight questions were asked in each condition, and responses were counted whether they were correct or not.

The Design. The design was an alternating treatments design with the three conditions (i.e., hand raising, choral, response card) randomly alternated across 15-minute sessions.

The Results. Godfrey et al. (2003) recorded data for five students and three dependent variables. We have chosen to present some of the active responding data for two of the students in the experiment (see Figure 9.4).

Eight questions were asked per session, and the treatments were alternated. Both Andrea and Bobby responded to all the questions in the response card (RC) condition. The children responded the least in the hand-raising (HR) condition.

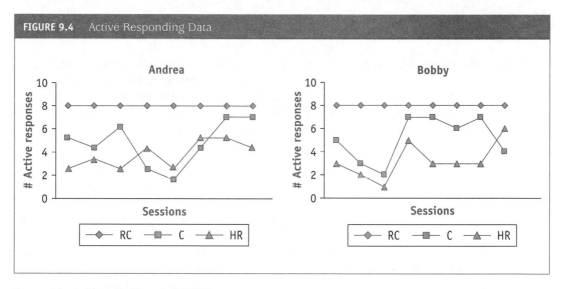

FIGURE 9.4   Active Responding Data

Source: Adapted from Godfrey et al. (2003).

The Conclusions. The authors concluded that the response card method is an effective way of increasing active participation with preschool-age children who have problems attending during group activities. They point out that this technique is useful for nonverbal children and others with special needs.

Have you ever tried or watched someone try to quit smoking? How about losing weight? Often, these kinds of goals are best attempted in small steps. *Shaping* is the operant term for a procedure where closer and closer approximations to the final goal are reinforced. In everyday terms, we are talking about reinforcing improvement in behavior. A single-participant research design that shapes behavior toward a final goal is called a changing criterion design.

CHANGING CRITERION DESIGN

When a goal behavior can be quantified into different target levels, a **changing criterion design** might be a good choice. When the behavior reaches the targeted level, the criterion is changed, and the behavior must meet the new criterion. The final goal behavior then is reached in a stepwise fashion.

One of many problems children with autism can have is extreme sensitivity to sound. For some children, it seems that certain sounds can even be painful. Koegel, Openden, and Koegel (2004), at the University of California in Santa Barbara, used a changing criterion design in their investigation of hypersensitivity to sound in three children with autism.

The Research Problem. Lori, Jamie, and Jeff were toddlers who were severely hypersensitive to certain sounds. All had been diagnosed with autism and were referred to the researchers for treatment for this problem. Koegel et al. (2004) decided to use systematic desensitization to treat these children.

The Objectives. Lori was hypersensitive to the sound of the school toilet flushing. Jamie would scream and run away when playing with toys that made animal sounds. Jeff reacted badly to vacuum cleaners, blenders, and hand mixers. For all three children, this sensitivity was creating problems in their lives. The objective was to use systematic desensitization to treat the extreme reactions to these sounds to the point where the child was no longer uncomfortable hearing these sounds.

The Independent Variable and Dependent Variable. The independent variable was desensitization training, and one dependent variable was the level of anxiety as rated by observers.

The Design. Each child was systematically desensitized to a sound stimulus in a changing criterion design. Lori was treated in her school. Hierarchical steps were defined. For example, in the first step, Lori was expected to enter the hall when the bathroom door was closed. When she could do this without feeling anxious, she moved to the next steps where the door was gradually opened wider. The criterion was two to four 3-minute intervals during which Lori was observed to be unaffected by the sight or sound of the toilet. This process continued until Lori was able to be close to the bathroom when the toilet was flushing. A similar process was followed with the other two children.

The Results. The systematic intervention worked well for all three children. Some of the data for Lori are presented in Table 9.2.

Baseline measures were taken with Lori at the bathroom door while the toilet was flushed. This was so difficult for Lori that baseline sessions were terminated, and intervention was started on Day 3. At the end of Day 4, Lori could be in the stall while the toilet was continually flushed. She remained comfortable with the sound of the toilet during follow-up 2 weeks later.

The Conclusions. Koegel et al. (2004) concluded that because the intense reaction of these children to the noise stimuli was reduced with systematic desensitization, the problem may have been phobia. They noted that it has been suggested that noise causes actual pain for these children and pointed out that if this were the case, their treatment would not likely have been effective. The fact that the intense reactions of all three children were quite easily modified by the procedure led the researchers to conclude that a learned phobia was most likely the problem.

TABLE 9.2 Number of Steps Completed Over Days

Day	Steps Attempted	Steps Completed
1-baseline		
2-baseline		
3	1–5	5
4	6–13	13

Conceptual Exercise 9B

Choose a multiple baseline, alternating treatment, or changing criterion design for each of the following. Why did you make your choice?

1. A behavior analyst is helping a developmentally challenged adolescent learn how to cook.

2. A behavior analyst is dealing with a young child with several problem behaviors that are interfering with learning in school.

ADVANTAGES AND DISADVANTAGES OF SINGLE-PARTICIPANT DESIGNS

Single-participant designs are particularly well suited to clinical settings. Researchers can establish a causal link between a treatment and a behavior with only one individual and then put this into practice with other people. The advantage of being able to demonstrate cause and effect with a single individual can also be seen as a disadvantage. The treatment that works for one individual may not work for others. The study then would lack external validity. This is not usually a serious problem because most important findings are replicated with other individuals and in other settings.

With single-participant designs, conditions can be tailored to the individual being studied rather than standardized for a group. The researcher can easily modify the design even after the study has begun without jeopardizing its integrity. If Johnny is still interrupting the teacher after a reprimand for interruption has been applied, then the teacher can quickly change the design and praise Johnny for every 5 minutes he does not interrupt her.

The experimental analysis of behavior traditionally uses response rate as the primary dependent measure. This is a disadvantage of the single-participant approach because other measures of behavior such as number correct, reaction time, rating, and so on are excluded.

In research with groups, statistical analysis determines whether the treatment was effective. In single-participant research, statistical analysis has been used, but more often, the researcher examines the data and determines if the treatment was effective, a seemingly more subjective approach that relies on the experience and integrity of the researcher.

FYI

There is some evidence that visual inspection is superior to statistical analysis for detecting treatment effects in single-participant research. Fisher, Kelley, and Lomas reported in their 2003 study that visual inspection resulted in lower error rates and more power (recall that power is the capability of the technique to detect true effects) than two statistical methods.

This difference can be seen as both a strength and a weakness. Some argue that the use of statistical procedures masks the true effects of an independent variable on the behavior of people by averaging behavior over groups. Observing behavior in an individual change in strength as the result of treatment introduction and withdrawal, for example, could be argued as a better method of determining treatment effectiveness. Behavioral analysts argue that small treatment effects are of limited value whether they are statistically significant or not. This may be true from a practical point of view. Clinicians are probably not likely to select a treatment that has only a small effect on behavior. Experimentalists, on the other hand, would argue that such effects, though small, might be important from a scientific point of view. We do not see this as a strength or weakness of either approach. Clinicians and basic researchers often have different goals, and as such, a comparison of the designs used by each may be inappropriate.

Clinicians and others in applied settings (e.g., teachers) sometimes find themselves using treatment strategies that they have learned about from case studies or quasi-experimental research and that have never been demonstrated to be effective. The single-participant approach offers the best of both worlds to clinicians: Treatment can be provided at the same time that cause and effect is demonstrated. This meshing of experimental research and clinical practice is perhaps the biggest strength of single-participant designs.

CHAPTER SUMMARY

The **experimental analysis of behavior** is an **operant** approach, and its followers focus on the behavior over time of a single individual, **a single-participant research design.** **Replication** with other individuals is common with the operant approach. Basic concepts used by operant researchers include **operant, phase, baseline, treatment, length of phase,** and **changing phase.** The most common measure of response strength is **rate** or **frequency.**

Basic operant designs include the **ABA** and the **ABAB withdrawal designs,** where A refers to **baseline** conditions and B refers to **treatment.** In **multiple baseline designs,** replication is conducted across behaviors, individuals, or settings. **Alternating treatment designs** are useful for evaluating the effect of more than one treatment on the behavior of an individual. **Changing criterion designs** are useful when the target or goal behavior can be broken down into steps.

Single-participant designs are well suited to clinical settings where treatment conditions can be tailored to each individual and modified as needed.

ANSWERS TO CONCEPTUAL EXERCISES

Conceptual Exercise 9A

1. An ABA would not be appropriate because we want Susan to end up in the treatment phase.
2. Either design would be fine for this research problem.

Conceptual Exercise 9B

1. Cooking involves many steps, so perhaps a changing criterion design is best.
2. A multiple baseline design across behaviors might be useful.

FAQ

Q1: Where did the word *operant* come from?

A1: We believe that Skinner coined this term. He thought it was a good term for behavior that operates on the environment.

Q2: What does *behavior modification* mean?

A2: Behavior modification generally refers to operant and classical conditioning techniques that are used to help modify the behavior of humans (or perhaps animals also).

Q3: I tried positive reinforcement to get my boyfriend to be more considerate. It didn't work, so I think this stuff is useless.

A3: Well, a good behavior analyst would tell you that you did not choose an effective reinforcer or perhaps you were inconsistent.

Q4: I am a student teacher and I have a kid who constantly talks out in class. I have reprimanded her many times and she keeps doing it. Why?

A4: You might consider the possibility that your attention to her when she talks out is in fact reinforcing her behavior. You might try giving her attention when she is behaving properly and ignoring her talking-out behavior.

CHAPTER EXERCISES

1. How are single and multiparticipant experimental designs similar? How are they different?
2. Why is the baseline phase important in single-participant designs?
3. The ABA design is used to demonstrate control over the operant. Explain.
4. The ABAB design has a distinct advantage over the ABA design. What is that?
5. Describe the difference between a multiple baseline design across participants, settings, and behaviors.
6. When is a multiple baseline design useful?
7. Describe an alternating treatment design. Give an example of a problem suitable to this design.
8. Describe a changing criterion design and give an example of a problem suitable to this design.
9. What are some of the advantages of single versus multiparticipant research? What are some of the disadvantages?

CHAPTER PROJECTS

1. Henry has a serious visual problem. He has special glasses that will help keep his vision from deteriorating. Unfortunately, Henry hates his glasses and refuses to wear them. Design an intervention to treat Henry's problem. Justify your choice of design.

2. Lucas has problems in school. He is out of his seat a lot. He pulls the girls' hair, and he interrupts the teacher often. Design an intervention to treat Lucas's problem behaviors. Justify your choice of design.

3. Three friends have decided to quit smoking together. Design an intervention and justify your choices.

REFERENCES

D'Ateno, P., Mangiapanello, K., & Taylor, B. (2003). Using video modeling to teach complex play sequences to a preschooler with autism. *Journal of Positive Behavior Interventions, 5*(1), 5–11.

Fisher, W., Kelley, M., & Lomas, J. (2003). Visual aids and structured criteria for improving inspection and interpretation of single-case studies. *Journal of Applied Behavior Analysis, 36*(3), 387–406.

Fyffe, C., Kahng, S., Fittro, E., & Russell, D. (2004). Functional analysis and treatment of inappropriate sexual behavior. *Journal of Applied Behavior Analysis, 37*(3), 401–404.

Godfrey, S., Grisham-Brown, J., Schuster, J., & Hemmeter, M. (2003). The effects of three techniques on student participation with preschool children with attending problems. *Education and Treatment of Children, 26*(3), 255–272.

Heward, W., Gardner, R., Cavenaugh, R., Courson, F., Grossi, T., & Bargetta, P. (1996). Everyone participates in this class: Using the response card to increase active student response. *Teaching Exceptional Children, 28*(2), 4–11.

Koegel, R., Openden, D., & Koegel, L. (2004). A systematic desensitization paradigm to treat hypersensitivity to auditory stimuli in children with autism in family contexts. *Research and Practice for Persons With Severe Disabilities, 29*(2), 122–134.

Visit the study site at www.sagepub.com/evansmprstudy for practice quizzes and other study resources.

CHAPTER 10

Finding Relationships Among Variables

Nonexperimental Research

In Chapters 7, 8, and 9, we discussed various experimental designs. We do experimental research to determine cause and effect. The experimenter wants to determine if some treatment (i.e., the independent variable) affects some measure of behavior (i.e., the dependent variable). Finding causal relationships is an important research activity. And the true experiment offers the most control over variables and therefore is the best approach for ruling out alternative explanations for any outcomes that are found. But not all research focuses on causal relationships. There are other important questions to ask about human behavior. And not all research problems can be investigated experimentally.

Are boys more aggressive than girls?

How effective are the various smoking cessation programs offered by local hospitals?

What about the relationship between trans fats and heart disease?

What makes serial killers such as Paul Bernardo and Karla Homulka, as well as Jeffrey Dahmer, tick?

These kinds of research problems are of wide interest but in many cases do not lend themselves to experimental research either because the researcher cannot control the variables or the nature of the question is not causal. To answer these kinds of questions, the researcher may turn to nonexperimental approaches.

In general, a nonexperimental design includes research where the researcher does not manipulate an independent variable, has limited or no control over the nature or timing of the treatment, or when causal relationships are not the primary focus of the research. In this chapter, we examine a number of nonexperimental designs, including case studies and correlational research. We also look at how nonexperimental research is used in longitudinal research. First, let's explore various designs that are considered quasi-experimental designs: interrupted time-series, multiple time-series, and nonequivalent groups designs.

QUASI-EXPERIMENTS

We use the term **quasi-experiment** for designs that look a lot like true experiments and that are statistically analyzed in similar ways. But there are important differences between quasi-experiments and true experiments in the interpretations that can be made of the findings. In quasi-experiments, although the researcher wants to compare groups, he or she does not control the nature and/or the timing of the treatment or comparison variable. In some cases, the treatment variable is not a treatment at all but rather is a participant variable.

> **FYI**
>
> Because the statistical analysis of a quasi-experiment is often the same as the analysis of a true experiment, the comparison variable is called an independent variable in most statistical software packages. But keep in mind that these are not true independent variables, despite the fact that the analysis treats them as if they are. The analysis is the same, but the inferences that can be made are not.

Quasi-experiments take on a number of forms, but what is common among them is that the researcher has little or no control over the independent variable or variables.

Earlier we asked whether boys are more aggressive than girls. Although we cannot randomly assign children to gender conditions, we *can compare* girls with boys. Gender, then, is a participant variable, specifically an **organismic** variable. We can certainly say, if indeed this is what we find, that boys are more aggressive than girls, and we can offer ideas about why that might be the case. Describing differences in behavior between groups who differ on participant variables is a worthy subject of research, and indeed, there is a wealth of research focusing on just that.

In other cases, the participants, not the researcher, have "assigned themselves" to the different levels of the treatment. Earlier we asked how effective are different smoking cessation programs offered by local hospitals. We can examine the treatment outcomes of the people who participated in these programs, but because they, not us, chose the program they wanted to take, we cannot make causal inferences about program effectiveness.

The problem is a lack of initial equivalence of groups. Because we have not randomly assigned participants to conditions, we cannot assume the groups were similar at the start of our study. Do you remember the example we gave at the beginning of Chapter 7? We described an article that cautioned young women from studying engineering if they hoped to marry. We suspect that the writer was reporting data that indicated that a smaller percentage of female engineering graduates were married at some specified age than a similarly aged group of female nonengineers. Do you suspect that women who choose engineering might be different from women who choose other disciplines? So do we. If they are different before their training, we should not be surprised to find that they are different at the end. Perhaps women who choose to be engineers are "not the marrying kind."

Conceptual Exercise 10A

Does scouting produce better citizens? A researcher compared good citizenship behaviors of a group of scouts with a group of nonscouts. What problems do you see with this study?

Although claims that changes in some measure of behavior can certainly be made with the use of a quasi-experimental design, claims about the cause of those changes cannot. And some will argue that it may not matter. The fact that a measured behavior has improved in some way when a treatment or program was introduced may be good enough; some might argue that the cause of the improvement is of secondary importance. But perhaps we might feel more confident in our conclusion if we measured behavior more than once both before and after the treatment was introduced, a time-series design.

Time-Series Designs

A **time-series design** is a quasi-experimental design where participants who have been exposed to a treatment are tested more than once both before and after the introduction of that treatment. This, then, is a within-participants design, but the researcher does not control the nature of the treatment or the time that the treatment was introduced. Indeed, although we call the event we are interested in studying a treatment, it is best thought of as an event because we do not *treat* the participants; instead, it is something that happens to them—an event. A time-series design usually involves several pre- and posttest measures and may include a comparison group; both are methods to try to control extraneous variables. A diagram of such a design is in Table 10.1. 01 is the first observation taken.

FYI

We have noticed that some texts include as a quasi-experimental design the one-group pretest-posttest comparison where the researcher measures some aspect of behavior of a single group of participants once before and once after treatment. Such an approach has a serious flaw because there is no control group, and so we cannot determine if any changes in behavior after treatment are related to the treatment. Perhaps the change might have occurred without treatment. We have no way to assess this possibility. As such, we do not consider this to be a research approach of value.

Let's take a look at a couple of examples of time-series designs: the interrupted time series and the multiple time series.

Interrupted Time-Series Design

In an **interrupted time-series design,** we take several pretest measures and several posttest measures. By measuring behavior at different times before and after some event/treatment occurred, we can determine the natural fluctuation in scores. By knowing how the scores fluctuate naturally, we can better assess any posttreatment changes. This design might look like the AB design we discussed in Chapter 9, but it is different in two key ways. First, we are studying a group rather than a single individual. Second, we did not introduce the treatment. Rather, the behavior being measured was "interrupted" by some, often naturally occurring, event.

Imagine that the state of California introduced a helmet law for motorcycle riders in 2000. We could obtain injury data for 5 years preceding the introduction of the law and for

TABLE 10.1	Time-Series Design			
Pretest		*Treatment*	*Posttest*	
O1	O2	X	O3	O4

Note: O = observation; X = "treatment."

5 years following it. Because we have five pretest and five posttest measures, we can determine how injuries fluctuate from year to year both before and after the new law was put into effect. This design is illustrated in Table 10.2.

TABLE 10.2 Interrupted Time-Series Design		
Pretest (1995–1999)	*Treatment (Helmet Law)*	*Posttest (2000–2004)*
O1 O2 O3 O4 O5	X	O6 O7 O8 O9 O10

Note: O = observation; X = "treatment."

Let's look at some real research.

The bombing of the Murrah Federal Building in Oklahoma City in April 1995 was a devastating event for the city and the country. Because this terrorist attack was a "naturally occurring event," studies of its impact on the citizens of Oklahoma are nonexperimental in nature; some, like the example below, are quasi-experimental designs.

The Research Problem. Nakonezny, Reddick, and Rodgers (2004) noted that there has not been a lot of research on the effect of community disasters on family and marital relationships. They were specifically interested in the effect of the Oklahoma City bombing on the divorce rate of Oklahomans. They decided to examine divorce rate information over several years following the bombing.

The Hypothesis. Nakonezny et al. (2004) described two theories that led to their hypotheses. According to terror management theory, people will want the comfort of their spouse and family after they have experienced a terrorizing event. The researchers describe how attachment theory makes similar predictions. According to attachment theory, people who have been traumatized will want to be closer to their spouses. Therefore, the researchers hypothesized that divorce rates in Oklahoma would decrease after the bombing.

The Measured Variables. The researchers obtained divorce rate statistics from 1985 to 2000 for all 77 counties in the state of Oklahoma.

The Design. The researchers used an interrupted time-series design to investigate their hypothesis. The researchers had 10 years of divorce statistics preceding the bombing and about 5 years of divorce rate data following the bombing.

This design is illustrated in Table 10.3.

The Statistical Analysis. The time-series data were first analyzed with a polynomial regression model, which is used to evaluate the nonlinear relationship between variables. There are times when the relationship between variables is better described with a curve than a straight line. Fitting a curve to the data is called **polynomial regression.** The prebombing measures were

TABLE 10.3	Interrupted Time-Series Design														
Premeasures (1985–1995)										*Bombing*	*Postmeasures (1996–2000)*				
O1	O2	O3	O4	O5	O6	O7	O8	O9	O10	X	O11	O12	O13	O14	O15

Source: Nakonezny et al. (2004).

Note: O = observation; X = "treatment."

used to determine the average yearly change in divorce rate before the bombing occurred. This rate of change was then used to estimate the divorce rate that would have occurred had the bombing not happened. And this was done for each county in the state. Dependent *t* tests were used to compare the predicted rates with the actual rates after the bombing.

The Results. Nakonezny et al. (2004) examined the average change in divorces per 1,000 across the state. In other words, they computed the observed postbombing rate minus the predicted postbombing rate obtained from the regression analysis. Some of the descriptive statistics are presented in Table 10.4.

The inferential *t* test analyses used by Nakonezny et al. (2004) supported their hypothesis for the year following the bombing. The researchers did not report the *t* values but said that the divorce rate was significantly lower than predicted in 1996 ($p < .05$). The effect was short-lived, though, because there were no significant differences between the actual and predicted divorce rates for the years following 1996.

The Conclusion. The researchers concluded that their hypothesis that divorce rates, at least immediately following the Oklahoma bombing, would be lower than expected was supported.

The multiple observations before and after the event permit us to be reasonably confident that the effect is not due to random fluctuations. However, a problem with the interrupted time-series design is that we really cannot be confident that any changes we see in the posttest scores were related to the "treatment." Because there is no control group, we

TABLE 10.4	Descriptive Statistics (Observed Rate – Predicted Rate)	
Year	*Mean*	*Standard Error*
1996	−0.228	0.130
1997	−0.202	0.147
1998	−0.1212	0.130
1999	−0.106	0.129
2000	0.008	0.166

Source: Nakonezny et al. (2004).

do not know if something else was responsible for the changes in scores. In the research example above, the treatment is the bombing. Nakonezny et al. (2004) acknowledged this weakness of the design but commented that this event was so catastrophic that it seems unlikely that anything else going on in Oklahoma at the time (i.e., history effects) could have had more of an effect on the divorce rate than the bombing. The researchers used another quasi-experimental design in this study, a **nonequivalent groups design,** and we return to this research when we discuss that design a bit later on in this chapter.

Multiple Time-Series Design

Let's return to our motorcycle example. Recall that we were comparing injury data before and after a helmet law was introduced in California. What if we collected injury data from another state, perhaps New Mexico, where no helmet law was introduced in 2000? With the inclusion of **multiple time-series** data, we now have a control group of sorts that was not exposed to the treatment (i.e., the helmet law).

Our design is illustrated in Table 10.5.

Although the inclusion of a comparison time series makes this a better design than an interrupted time-series design, we still must be cautious in our conclusions. Let's say that we find fewer injury accidents in the California group after the new law was introduced. Can we conclude that this effect was a result of the law? No we cannot. Perhaps something else occurred at the time. Maybe massive road repairs were done that year in California. New Mexico might have had unusually foggy and rainy weather in 2000. Researchers can and do attempt to account for alternative explanations for any effects they find with such a design, but like all quasi-experimental research, inferential conclusions must be made very cautiously.

Conceptual Exercise 10B

A researcher examined the number of hits on a computer security Internet site for 2 weeks preceding Y2K and for 2 weeks following Y2K. She found that the number of hits on the site decreased following Y2K. What type of design is this, and what kinds of problems do you see with her conclusion that Y2K was responsible for the effect? Can you think of a better design?

TABLE 10.5   Multiple Time-Series Design

	Pretest					*Treatment*	*Posttest*				
Experimental group	O1	O2	O3	O4	O5	X	O6	O7	O8	O9	O10
Control group	O1	O2	O3	O4	O5		O6	O7	O8	O9	O10

Note: O = observation; X = "treatment."

In an experimental design, the researcher creates the experimental and control groups often by random assignment or a matching process. Great care is taken to ensure that the groups are equivalent at the start of the experiment. However, there are many instances in research where creation of the treatment and control groups is not possible, and in those cases, we take whatever control group we can. Let's have a look at these nonequivalent groups designs.

Nonequivalent Groups Designs

Often, researchers want to compare groups that they know, or suspect, are different at the outset of the study. As we have said, differences between a treated group and a nontreated group are hardly surprising when the groups were different to begin with. So comparing the groups on some posttest would not be useful. But what if we compared *changes* in behavior between the groups? By comparing change in behavior between the groups, we can control for initial group differences. This approach is common in educational research where students taking different programs are compared. As long as we have no reason to suspect that the behavior of our groups might change at different rates, this can be a useful design. Indeed, much **program evaluation research** uses a nonequivalent control group design.

We discussed the research of Nakonezny et al. (2004) on divorce rates in Oklahoma following the Oklahoma City bombing of the federal building in 1995. The researchers predicted that divorce rates would drop based on two theories about how people respond after experiencing a terrorist event. They referred to attachment theory to make a second hypothesis about divorce rate.

The Research Problem. According to attachment theory, people who are closer to a terrorizing event will show more attachment behavior than people who are farther away.

The Hypothesis. Nakonezny et al. (2004) hypothesized that divorce rates following the bombing would be lower in areas closer to Oklahoma City than in areas that are farther away from the city.

The Design. This part of the study was a nonequivalent control groups design. The researchers compared divorce rates for counties close to Oklahoma City with rates for counties farther away. The design is illustrated in Table 10.6.

The Statistical Analyses. The researchers used *t* tests to analyze differences between observed and expected divorce rates (based on the polynomial regression analysis) as part of their inferential analysis.

The Results. The researchers compared the difference scores (between the actual divorce rates after the bombing and the predicted divorce rates based on the polynomial regression analysis) of counties close to Oklahoma City with counties farther away, averaged

TABLE 10.6	Nonequivalent Control Group Design
Difference Scores
Experimental group (counties close to city)
Control group (counties farther from city)

Source: Nakonezny et al. (2004).

Note: Measure: Difference scores = observed postbombing divorce rate − predicted postbombing divorce rate for 5 years following the bombing.

TABLE 10.7	Descriptive Statistics	
	Observed Rate – Predicted Rate	**Standard Error**
Counties close to the city	−0.939	0.344
Counties farther from the city	−0.048	0.127

Source: Nakonezny et al. (2004).

over the 5 years following the bombing. Some of the descriptive statistics are presented in Table 10.7.

The inferential analysis included a *t* test comparison between the closer and farther counties. There was a significantly greater decrease in divorce rate in the counties closer to Oklahoma City than in those that were farther away, $t(*) = -2.14, p < .03$.

*df were not reported—Oklahoma City counties, $n = 7$; non–Oklahoma City counties, $n = 70$.

The researchers noted that this design could have internal validity problems; other influences on divorce rates may have been operating. As such, they examined various demographic variables that have been shown in other research to affect divorce rate. They reported that age, education, income, employment status, and race, in the period following the bombing, were not related to the postbombing divorce rates.

The Conclusions. The authors concluded that their hypotheses based on terror management and attachment theory were reasonable. They were very careful to point out the weaknesses of this design and to describe the measures they took to rule out many possible threats to the internal validity of the study.

The nonequivalent control groups design is useful in situations where the researcher cannot randomly assign participants to groups but can compare groups of initially different participants by examining changes between pre- and posttest measures.

Conceptual Exercise 10C

A researcher compared learning outcomes of behavior-disordered, attention-deficit, and developmentally delayed children after they had all received computer-assisted instruction (CAI) in reading comprehension. He found that the behavior-disordered children had the best reading comprehension scores on a test given after the CAI treatment. What problems do you see with his conclusion that CAI is more effective for behavior-disordered children than for attention-deficit and developmentally delayed children?

FYI

Longitudinal research: Many methods books include longitudinal research as a separate research design, implying that it is fundamentally different from other research designs. Although longitudinal research studies are sometimes conducted over long periods of time, unlike much research, they need not be fundamentally different from other designs. For example, a longitudinal study could be experimental, quasi-experimental, or correlational in design. We discuss it here not as a separate design but as a research method.

LONGITUDINAL RESEARCH

Sometimes our interest is in studying a group of individuals over a long period of time to determine how characteristics measured earlier in life relate to behavior later in life. Longitudinal research is frequently used by developmental psychologists who are interested in factors that affect the development of children over time. Perhaps we want to know if a traumatic experience in early childhood predicts problems later in life. No treatment may be involved; rather, the researcher is often trying to determine **risk factors**—factors that can be identified as predicting later problems. Because this kind of research is conducted over long periods of time, loss of participants is a real problem. As you can imagine, it is not easy to keep track of people over many years.

Sexual abuse is an abhorrent and devastating event in the life of a child. What are the factors that increase the probability that someone might commit such heinous acts on a child? This is the problem that Salter et al. (2003) of the United Kingdom decided to investigate.

The Research Problem. Salter et al. (2003) noted that much research in the area of child sexual abuse has been **retrospective.** In other words, adult abusers provide information about their childhoods, and researchers attempt to find common factors or events among those childhood experiences to better understand what leads someone to abuse children. Often they find that adult abusers were abused as children.

Salter et al. (2003) approached this problem somewhat differently. They obtained information from the treatment clinic about male children who had been sexually abused. Their objective was to identify factors in these abused children that increased the risk that they also would abuse children when they became adults. This study was conducted over a 7- to 19-year period.

Selection of Participants. The participants in this study were boys who had been referred to a sexual abuse clinic between 1980 and 1992. Most were between 8 and 14 years of age at the time of the referral. None had at that time committed any abusive acts themselves. Rather, they were all victims of sexual abuse.

The Objective. The purpose of this study was to examine characteristics of the sample of abused children to try to identify risk factors and predict abuse by these children when they became adults. The researchers examined a large database provided by various agencies in the United Kingdom to determine potential risk factors for later sexual abuse by abused male children. They identified several factors, including physical abuse, antisocial behavior, cruelty to animals, fire setting, bedwetting, and so on. And they examined their sample of boys for these factors. They were also interested in factors, called **protective factors,** that seem to reduce the influence of risk factors. They then collected data on the adult behavior of their sample 7 to 19 years later.

In this longitudinal study, the researchers used the information they had about the child victims to try to predict which victims would become abusers as adults and which factors reduced that likelihood.

The Statistical Analyses. A multiple logistic regression analysis was the primary inferential analysis. This analysis allowed the researchers to construct a risk index from the risk factors thought to be important (from previous research) in predicting adult abuse and a protective index from factors thought to reduce the risk of becoming abusive.

The Results. A small portion of the descriptive statistics from this study is presented in Table 10.8. Victim-abusers are people who were abused as children and went on to abuse others when they became adults. Nonabusers are people who were abused as children but did not become abusers themselves.

The inferential analyses revealed that the risk index score did predict whether abused children would become abusers ($\beta = 0.19$, $SE = 0.07$, $p = .005$), but the protective index score did not ($\beta = -0.12$, $SE = 0.08$, $p = .16$).

NOTE: As we discussed in Chapter 2, β indicates the relative importance of a variable in regression analysis. The sign (positive or negative) indicates the direction of the relationship, and the value indicates the strength of the relationship.

The Conclusions. One conclusion was that the probability that childhood victims of sexual abuse will themselves become abusers as adults is lower than previously thought. The researchers note that their results are consistent with retrospective studies that showed that parental emotional neglect and experiencing or witnessing violence seem to be risk factors. They discuss several limitations of the study, including the lack of a nonabused comparison group and other difficulties associated with longitudinal research of this kind, including missing data.

Longitudinal research is difficult and expensive to conduct. One serious problem is **attrition.** When a researcher attempts to follow a group of people for many years, it is

TABLE 10.8 Descriptive Statistics (in Percentages)

	Victim-Abusers	Nonabusers
Percentage of sample	12	88
had been abused by a female person	38	17
had witnessed family violence	81	58
had been physically neglected	71	42
had been cruel to animals	29	5

Source: Salter et al. (2003).

inevitable that some will move away or even die. Indeed, the loss of research participants used to be called *experimental mortality*. Attrition can seriously affect the internal validity of your study, particularly if you have high attrition in one group relative to the others. One way to preserve the internal validity of your study is to carefully compare data from those who dropped out with those who remain in the study. The hope is that they do not differ in any systematic way from those who remain.

In longitudinal research, a group of participants is followed over time to determine how that group changes over time. Another way to study differences in behavior at different ages is to study groups of people who are different ages. Rather than comparing one group of people when they are 5, 10, 15, and 20 years old, we could study five different groups of people of those ages. This is called cross-sectional research because we study a cross section of age groups at one point in time.

CROSS-SECTIONAL RESEARCH

As the "baby boom" generation ages, there is growing interest in research with older people. At the University of Colorado, Miller, Segal, and Coolidge (2001) were interested in age-related changes in suicide rates and how people's thoughts of suicide might change with age.

The Research Problem. Miller et al. (2001) note that we often think that suicide is more common among young people than among older people. They point out that this in fact is not the case. Suicide is more common among older rather than younger adults. Furthermore, older adults are more likely than younger adults to succeed in suicide attempts. Miller and colleagues wanted to identify age-related differences in the extent of suicidal thinking and in reasons for committing suicide.

The Hypothesis. The researchers expected that older adults are different from younger adults in their suicidal thinking and in their reasons for considering committing suicide because of differences in socialization, life history, and coping strategies.

The Participants. Older adults (60–95 years) were matched with younger adults (17–34 years) on gender and ethnicity, and most were also matched on religion and self-reported health status. All the participants were either students at the university or their family members and friends.

The Measured Variables. The Beck Scale for Suicide Ideation (BSS) was used to measure suicidal thinking. The Reasons for Living Inventory (RFL) was used to measure beliefs that distinguish between suicidal and nonsuicidal people (Linehan, Goodstein, Nielsen, & Chiles, 1983). These are both self-report scales.

The Design. This was cross-sectional research with two groups: older and younger adults.

The Statistical Analyses. The researchers used various inferential procedures, including *t* tests, to compare their two groups.

The Results. Some of the descriptive statistics are presented in Table 10.9.

The researchers used *t* tests for some of their inferential comparisons. They found no significant differences between the older and younger adults on the types and levels of suicidal ideation from the BSS.

On the RFL, inferential analyses revealed two significant differences between the groups. The older adults had significantly stronger moral concerns about suicide than the younger adults, $t(159) = 2.70$, $p < .01$, and the older adults reported more child-related concerns as reasons for not committing suicide than the younger adults, $t(140.4) = 3.07$, $p < .01$.

The Conclusions. Miller et al. (2001) noted that suicidal thinking in older adults is not different from that of younger adults but that older adults report moral objections and child concerns as stronger reasons for not committing suicide than younger adults. They went on to suggest that this information might be helpful for planners of prevention programs.

TABLE 10.9   Descriptive Statistics

BSS Suicidal Thinking (score on a 3-point scale)

	Older		*Younger*	
	Mean	*SD*	*Mean*	*SD*
Active suicidal desire	0.13	0.47	0.29	0.04
Wish for death	0.44	1.03	0.83	1.54
Preparation	0.99	1.58	1.34	2.10

RFL (score on a 6-point scale)

	Older		*Younger*	
	Mean	*SD*	*Mean*	*SD*
Child-related concerns	4.95	1.27	4.19	1.79
Moral objections	4.26	1.40	3.63	1.54
Fear of social disapproval	3.14	1.55	3.11	1.37

Source: Miller et al. (2001).

A potential problem with cross-sectional research is that there may be other variables that are confounded with age. As we mentioned in Chapter 1, this problem is called the *cohort effect* because a cohort of same-aged individuals will share variables related to their history. Longitudinal researchers address this problem by studying a single age cohort over a number of years, a costly endeavor. Why not combine the two? **Sequential research** does this by selecting a cross section of ages over a number of years. This way, cohort effects are controlled by following a number of age cohorts (cross-sectional) over time (longitudinal).

Robert Siegler (1995) comments that although both cross-sectional and longitudinal studies help us understand changes in behavior over time, neither provides much information about how those changes occur (i.e., the process underlying changes). He discusses a method for studying the process of change called the **microgenetic method.** This method involves carefully observing behavior during periods when rapid change is occurring and collecting both quantitative and qualitative information. He uses Piaget's classic stage model of conservation as an example. He argues that stage models that describe transitions from one stage to another may not adequately reflect what is going on cognitively. In his 1995 study, children were asked not only to *solve* various problems but to *explain* their reasoning. For example, when children reported that there was more water in the tall, narrow glass than in the short, fat glass, they were asked why they thought that was so. Siegler continues to use his method for studying how children learn (e.g., Siegler & Svetina, 2006).

The methods we have discussed so far in this chapter have involved groups of participants. The researchers were focused on finding patterns of behavior. In Chapter 9, we discussed single experimental designs where individuals, rather than groups, are studied. In single experimental designs, a treatment is introduced, and a dependent variable is measured to assess the effect of that treatment. Sometimes, a researcher is interested in studying a single individual on many variables where no treatment is being assessed. Rather, a description of that individual, not some treatment, is the purpose of the research. These studies are called case studies.

Conceptual Exercise 10D

A researcher found that his group of older adults (> 75 years old) performed significantly worse than younger adults (< 30 years) on a memory test where recall was measured after participants viewed a computer screen displaying 15 common words for 5 seconds. Participants had 1 minute to write down as many of the words as they could remember. What problems do you see with her conclusion that memory is impaired in older adults?

CASE STUDIES

Case studies are in-depth studies of a single individual. Unlike the single-participant designs discussed in Chapter 9, case studies are *not* experimental designs. Case studies are very common in clinical research where a physician, psychiatrist, or psychologist has extensive experience with a client and wishes to report the case. A case study is *descriptive* because the objective is to describe the characteristics of the individual case, *not to* generalize to a population of similar cases. Freud developed his theory of personality based only on case studies, something he has been soundly criticized for, we might add. Case studies may provide interesting ideas and hypotheses that other clinicians might explore in their treatment efforts. Case study research may not involve statistics of any kind. Often, case studies are descriptive narratives that are *qualitative, not quantitative.* You can see why it is difficult to generalize from case studies; the point is to describe what *can* happen and not what *generally* happens.

Ready for an example?

The Research Problem. Blazina (2004) illustrates how psychoanalytic theory describes masculine identity development as a process whereby a boy has to break ties with his primary caregiver (usually his mother) and identify with a male role model (usually his father). *Disidentification* is the term used for the process of breaking ties with the mother, and *counteridentification* is the term for the process of identifying with the father. He notes that the theory is that these steps must occur if the boy is to become securely masculine as an adult. Blazina suggests that this traditional model needs some changes in light of our modern society. He suggests that it is more appropriate to think of the restrictive gender role behaviors of boys as a form of gender conflict that can cause problems with the developing male self. He proposes that to deal with this conflict, some men might adopt stereotypical male patterns of behavior, whereas others might become overly dependent, patterns he called fragile masculinity. As examples of these patterns, he presents two case studies. We will discuss the case study he used as an example of the stereotypical man.

The Description of the Case. The individual Blazina (2004) discusses was a man in his mid-40s who came for help with speech phobia, extreme anxiety when giving speeches. The therapist learned that he had a history of displaying stereotypically male behaviors, some of which the client seemed to feel he had to, rather than wanted to, display. Although the client was not totally cooperative with attempts by the therapist to explore any deep psychological reasons for his phobia, Blazina was able to learn about the client's difficult relationship with his father. Eventually, the client came to realize that his speech phobia was related to his need for his father's approval. When he had to give speeches, he would become anxious and imagine that his father was listening and criticizing him; as a result, he doubted his own masculinity. To protect himself, he would behave in overly masculine ways, including risk taking, not showing emotion, and taking up "he-man"-type hobbies.

During the course of the therapy, he learned to deal with his grief at not receiving his father's approval, and he attempted to bond with his father in a more emotional way.

Blazina (2004) suggested that his client's phobia about giving speeches was how his fragile masculine self displayed itself. Because the overly masculine role that he took on was not enough to protect him from his doubt about his masculinity, the phobic symptoms occurred.

As you can see, case studies are very different from the other approaches we have been discussing. They are often descriptive qualitative narratives about a single individual. Not all case studies are like this, however. Some case studies are more quantitative. Neuropsychologists, for example, use case studies to describe individuals with abnormal brain function, and these descriptions almost always include both qualitative and quantitative data.

The Research Problem. Earlier in the chapter, we presented research on the effects of the Oklahoma City bombing. Following such traumatic events, some people experience a collection of problems called posttraumatic stress disorder (PTSD). People suffering from PTSD relive the traumatic experience through nightmares and flashbacks; consequently, their sleep is disrupted, and they are anxious and depressed. Health care professionals are aware of PTSD and look for symptoms in people following such events. But it is unlikely they would be on the lookout for people suffering from PTSD as a result of their experience during World War II or their survival of the sinking of the *Titanic.* Yet this is exactly what has been described in some patients with dementia (van Achterberg, Rohrbaugh, & Southwick, 2001). Grossman, Levin, Katzen, and Lechner (2004) described the following case study of two Holocaust survivors who began to experience PTSD following a neurological illness.

The Description of the Case. Grossman et al. (2004) presented two cases of PTSD in men who had experienced a recent neurological illness. The neuropsychological assessment included a battery of tests to measure cognitive functioning. By making careful comparisons of the test results, they found common features that may be responsible for the onset of PTSD in these early survivors.

Both men showed impaired performance on measures of executive functions (e.g., Wisconsin Card Sorting Test, Design Fluency). A deficit in executive functioning is typical of neurological damage that includes the prefrontal cortex and results in an inability to regulate thought processes. The result is a person who has trouble inhibiting thoughts and is tormented with perseverate thoughts and behaviors. For these individuals, those thoughts were of their early experiences of the Holocaust.

The Conclusions. Grossman et al. (2004) concluded that health care providers must be aware that PTSD can emerge in patients many years after the event. Previous case studies have shown that patients with dementia can experience PTSD; Grossman et al.'s research extends this finding to include individuals who have suffered a neurological injury.

Have you ever wondered if more attractive people are more successful? Have you wondered if intelligence and mental health are related? How about the relationship between the size of the ozone layer and global warming? These are questions about relationships between variables, or correlations, and we turn to this area of research now.

CORRELATIONAL RESEARCH

We once read a newspaper article reporting that skiers who drink more tend to have fewer skiing accidents than those who drink less. We are sure that some readers were left with the impression that somehow drinking a lot *causes* fewer skiing accidents. We think skiers who spend a lot of time in the resort bar have fewer opportunities to hurt themselves on the slopes.

Did you know that better educated men have less head hair than less well-educated men? We are sure that you do not think that education causes hair to fall out. We know you have all heard the warning: Correlation does not infer causation. Unfortunately, we often see causal interpretations of correlational relationships. Correlation has an important place in research, but we must understand its limitations. Let's consider an example we often use in our statistics classes to explain why correlational findings cannot provide cause-and-effect information.

A relationship has been found between drinking during pregnancy and birth weight of the newborn. More drinking is associated with smaller babies. Just because this relationship has been demonstrated does not mean that the relationship is a causal one. Many variables other than the amount of alcohol could be responsible for the birth weight effect. For example, perhaps women who drink a lot during pregnancy also smoke a lot. Perhaps they do not eat as well as women who drink less or not at all. Perhaps women who drink during pregnancy have poorer prenatal care. We are sure you can think of other potentially confounding variables. Could we do research that would allow us to make a causal statement about drinking during pregnancy and birth weight? Not with humans. It would not be ethical to randomly assign pregnant women to a drinking or a nondrinking condition, would it? And that is what is required to demonstrate cause and effect (i.e., conducting a true experiment). What could we do? Well, if we think that smoking might be a potential confound, we could control for this variable by finding women whose smoking habits are similar. We could do the same for the other variables we think might confound the relationship. We could find women who are of similar health, receiving similar care, and so on. By carefully controlling for potential confounds, we can be more confident in our finding that the drinking and birth weight relationship remains. We still have to be careful because there may have been a variable that we did not think of. This is a limitation of **correlational research**.

NOTE: We want to emphasize that the relationship between alcohol ingestion during gestation and birth weight has been demonstrated experimentally with lower animals. And careful correlation research confirms the relationship between drinking during pregnancy and problems with fetal development. Pregnant women should never drink alcohol.

A great deal of medical research is quasi-experimental or correlational because of the ethical problems that arise with experimental research into these problems. A researcher who is interested in the relationship between smoking and lung disease, brain damage and memory loss, or depression and suicide cannot use an experimental approach with humans as participants. Smoking, brain damage, and depression are all participant variables and cannot be manipulated experimentally with humans. Of course, experiments into these kinds of problems have been done with lower animals, and we have learned much from that research. But with the human population, research on these problems must be nonexperimental. As long as we use good research techniques and are careful in our interpretation, correlational designs are important sources of knowledge about relationships between variables. Take the next topic, for example.

Have you ever thought that people seem to pick partners who are similar to them in physical attractiveness? Or have you thought that we try to date the most attractive people we meet? From a biological point of view, we could argue that greater physical attractiveness might be a cue that the person is healthy and therefore in better reproductive condition. For women, then, who are seeking a long-term mate, more masculine facial characteristics might be important. For a short-term relationship, perhaps these factors are less important to women. This is the general area that Penton-Voak et al. (2003) decided to investigate. We discuss a small part of their study here.

The Research Problem. Penton-Voak et al. (2003) were interested in preference of women for male faces differing in masculinity. They noted that the research in this area is somewhat confusing. Some researchers have reported that women prefer more masculine faces, but others have not found this preference.

They were also interested in whether the attractiveness of the woman affects her preferences for attractiveness in men. For example, perhaps women who are less attractive themselves are not as "picky" as women who are more attractive.

The Hypothesis. One of Penton-Voak et al.'s (2003) hypotheses was that rated facial attractiveness of women predicts their preference for masculinity of male faces.

The Participants. Eighty-two women, mostly undergraduates, volunteered to participate.

The Measured Variables. To obtain measures of the participants' attractiveness, ratings of the women by another group of students on a 7-point Likert scale were collected.

The participants were presented, by a counterbalanced scheme, with pictures of male faces that they could adjust, by digital editing, to be more feminine or more masculine. They were to adjust each face until it was close to what they would find attractive for either a short- or a long-term relationship.

The Design. Several comparisons were made, but the primary design was correlational.

The Results. Some of the descriptive statistics from this research are presented in Table 10.10.

The inferential analyses included t tests and correlations. In the long-term condition, there was a significant preference for more feminized faces than for average faces, $t(35) = 3.25, p < .01$, but in the short-term condition, the preferred faces were not significantly different from average.

The researchers used correlational statistical analyses to determine if rated physical attractiveness of the women was related to their preferences for male facial masculinity. In the long-term condition, as facial attractiveness of the women increased, so did their preference for masculinity, $r(33) = .405, p < .05$. There was no significant correlation between rated attractiveness and preference in the short-term condition.

The Conclusions. The researchers concluded that, overall, women prefer some femininity in the features of male faces. And women who are rated as less attractive prefer more feminine

TABLE 10.10 Descriptive Statistics	
	Mean Preference (% Face Was Feminized From Zero)
Long-term condition	7.70
Short-term condition	1.02

Source: Penton-Voak et al. (2003).

male faces when they are considering a long-term relationship but not when they are considering a short-term relationship. These preference differences were not seen with women who were rated as attractive. The researchers speculate that less attractive women choose more feminine men for long-term relationships because they perceive these men as less likely to abandon them. They go on to speculate that perhaps in short-term relationships, where abandonment is not such a concern, less attractive women prefer more masculine men. The preferences of attractive women, on the other hand, do not show these differences, perhaps because attractive women may have fewer concerns about abandonment.

How are you feeling right now? Happy? Sad? Bored? Anxious? Now once you've determined how you are feeling, try to think about the cause for your present state. There may be one major factor that is influencing you at this moment, but it may also be a combination of a number of things. If we are interested in what influences behavior, we will probably have to take into account a number of variables at a time. This is exactly the idea of **multiple correlation analysis.** Multiple regression analysis is a powerful technique that allows us to look at the relationship between a number of predictor variables and a single criterion variable. It tells us not only if the predictor variables are positively or negatively correlated with the criterion variable but also the relative importance of each variable in determining behavior.

FYI

Statistical software packages typically refer to predictor variables in a regression analysis as independent variables, and the criterion variable is called a dependent variable. We do not use this terminology because regression is not an experimental technique. We reserve the terms *IV* and *DV* only for experimental designs where the researcher directly manipulates the IV.

Earlier in the chapter, we presented a case study of two people who suffered from PTSD many years after the event. In a general discussion of PTSD, we noted that not everyone experiences this disorder following a traumatic event. Indeed, some people experience positive change in their lives as a result of their ordeal, a phenomenon termed *posttraumatic growth* (PTG). The following research is an example of multiple correlation analysis used to examine PTG in men whose wives have survived breast cancer.

The Research Problem. Weiss (2004) was interested in determining what variables influence the experience of PTG in husbands of breast cancer survivors. In his literature review, Weiss notes that PTG has been studied in female cancer survivors, but no one has looked at PTG in their husbands. Previous research had identified a number of social context factors as important determinants of PTG in women, and Weiss set out to investigate whether these factors also influenced men.

The Hypotheses. Weiss (2004) made four hypotheses based on four social context variables that had been shown to be important for women's experience of PTG. He hypothesized that emotional support, the quality of the marital relationship, exposure to individuals model-ing PTG, and the wife's experience of PTG would all be positively correlated with the husband's experience of PTG.

The Participants. Seventy-two couples were recruited through information that was on hot-line and support services, was mailed, appeared in the newspaper, or was available in the surgeon's office. All the women had survived 1 to 5.5 years since initial diagnosis of early stage breast cancer.

The Measured Variables. This multiple correlation design required measuring a number of proposed predictor variables and a single criterion variable. An adaptation of the Posttraumatic Growth Inventory (Tedeschi & Calhoun, 1996, as cited in Weiss, 2004) was used to measure both husbands' and wives' experience of PTG. The husband's PTG was the criterion variable, and the wife's PTG was a predictor variable.

Social support was measured with the Brief Social Support Questionnaire (Sarason et al., 1987, as cited in Weiss, 2004). The quality of marital relationship was assessed with the Quality of Relationship Inventory (Pierce et al., 1991, as cited in Weiss, 2004). Exposure to models of PTG (other than the wife) was measured by asking, "During your struggle with your wife's breast cancer, did you have contact with a person who experienced a similar trauma and who perceived benefits from the experience?" and obtaining a yes/no response.

The Design. This was a correlational study using multiple regression analysis.

The Results. Pearson product-moment correlations were used to assess the relationship between each variable and the husband's PTG.

The number of supporting people in the husband's social network was positively corre-lated with the husband's PTG, $r(65) = .28$, $p = .01$.

The quality of the marital relationship was also related to the husband's PTG. Positive correlations were found for the amount of support in the marital relationship, $r(65) = .36$, $p = .001$, and the depth of commitment to the relationship, $r(65) = .38$, $p = .001$.

Exposure to individuals (other than the wife) who have modeled PTG was not related to the husband's PTG. A t test revealed a difference that only approached statistical signifi-cance, $t(67) = 1.54$, $p = .06$, between the PTG of husbands who were exposed to models ($M = 53.6$, $SD = 23.4$, $n = 20$) versus those who were not ($M = 44.3$, $SD = 22.3$, $n = 49$).

Although modeling of PTG by someone other than the wife was not a significant factor, experience of PTG by the wife was. The wife's experience of PTG was positively correlated with the husband's PTG, $r(67) = .20$, $p = .04$.

Weiss (2004) computed a multiple regression analysis using all the factors that were statistically significant in the Pearson product-moment correlations. Multiple regression analysis indicates how much of the total variability in the husbands' PTG can be accounted for by using all the variables as predictors. By using all the variables to predict the husbands' PTG, the multiple correlation accounts for 42% of the variance in the husbands' PTG mea-sure, $R = .65$, $p < .005$, $N = 61$.

Multiple regression analysis also tells us which variables are accounting for unique vari-ance in the criterion variable, that is, variance that is not already accounted for by another predictor variable. For example, if we wanted to predict university performance by using IQ score and a measure of reading comprehension, we would find that IQ and reading comprehension account for the same variability. Because reading comprehension is a part of the IQ test, it would not account for any variance that was not already accounted for by the IQ test.

When Weiss (2004) computed a multiple regression analysis using all the variables that were significant in the Pearson correlations, he found that only the depth of commitment measure of marital quality ($\beta = .33$, $p < .05$) and the wife's experience of PTG ($\beta = .24$, $p < .05$) accounted for unique variance. A third variable that was significant in the analysis was whether or not the husband's experience of his wife's breast cancer met the *DSM-IV* criteria for a traumatic stressor ($\beta = .32$, $p < .01$). Almost half the husbands' experience constituted a traumatic event by *DSM-IV* criteria.

The Conclusions. To varying degrees, Weiss (2004) found support for his research hypotheses. He concluded that the number of individuals in a husband's support network is positively related with a husband's experience of PTG. However, this relationship disappeared in the multiple regression analysis, indicating that other factors are more important, particularly the experience of the wife.

It is clear that the depth of commitment to the marriage is an important factor in PTG. This portion of the quality of the marital relationship measure was significant alone and in the multiple regression analysis. This means that it is an important determinant of the husband's PTG.

It was hypothesized that husbands who were exposed to individuals modeling PTG would be more likely to experience it themselves. However, this did not appear to be an important factor. This was a weak effect that only approached statistical significance. On the other hand, the husband's PTG was strongly associated with his wife's PTG. This relationship was significant when examined alone or in the multiple regression analysis. For husbands, the wife's experience is the most important model of PTG. Weiss (2004) concluded by indicating that both husband and wife are affected by breast cancer and that interventions to support personal growth should include both individuals. For husbands of breast cancer survivors, the social context is an important determinant of their experience of PTG. Weiss suggested that further research should include personality measures that may influence the husband's experience of PTG.

In this chapter, we have discussed several nonexperimental approaches commonly taken by many social science researchers. Although you know by now that we prefer experimental designs, we are well aware that true experiments are not always possible, ethical, or practical.

Conceptual Exercise 10E

A researcher found a significant positive correlation between the amount of pornographic material available and number of sexual assaults. In cities where pornography was more readily available, sexual assaults were more frequent. What problems do you see with her conclusion that pornography is responsible for sexual assault?

CHAPTER SUMMARY

In a **quasi-experiment,** the researcher does not control the nature and/or the timing of the treatment variable. Although quasi-experiments allow comparisons between groups, causal interpretations cannot be made. **Time-series designs** are quasi-experimental designs in which measures are taken both before and after a treatment or event has occurred. In an **interrupted time-series** design, several pretest measures are taken before the occurrence of some event, often a naturally occurring event, and then several posttest measures follow. **Multiple time-series designs** have an advantage over interrupted time-series designs in that a comparison group is available that did not experience the treatment/event. Because the comparison group is not a true control group, inferential conclusions are limited.

In a **nonequivalent groups design,** changes in behavior among groups that differ at the outset of the study are compared. Because changes in behavior are compared, initial group differences are taken into account with this design.

When we study a group of individuals over a long period of time, we are conducting **longitudinal research.** Because the research is carried out for long periods, **attrition** or loss of participant data is a real problem. When we study groups of individuals of different ages, we are conducting **cross-sectional research.** Both longitudinal and cross-sectional research is common in education and developmental psychology.

Case studies are detailed studies of a single individual. Case studies reported by clinicians are often descriptive narratives but can be more quantitative as in the case of a neuropsychological case study.

When we are interested in relationships among variables, we may choose to conduct **correlational research.** Variables that are systematically related are said to be correlated. **Multiple regression analysis** is a correlational technique for evaluating the relationship between several predictor variables and one criterion variable.

ANSWERS TO CONCEPTUAL EXERCISES

Conceptual Exercise 10A

The problem here is with initial equivalence of groups. Children who join scouts may be different at the outset from children who do not. As such, these differences are not related to the scouting experience.

Conceptual Exercise 10B

This is an interrupted time-series design. Because there is no control group, we cannot be sure that the change in number of hits was related to Y2K. It may be that hits on all Internet sites routinely drop in the New Year. A better design would include measures of hits at other Internet sites over the same time period, a nonequivalent groups design.

Conceptual Exercise 10C

As with any nonequivalent groups design, there is a problem with initial equivalence of groups. We have no way to determine if CAI had anything to do with the outcome. The behavior-disordered group may be superior in reading comprehension to begin with. We just don't know.

Conceptual Exercise 10D

The problem here is with the measurement of the dependent variable—memory performance. The stimulus items were presented visually. Do you think older people might have more vision problems than younger people? They got 1 minute to write down their answers. Do you think older people might write more slowly than younger people? So do we.

Conceptual Exercise 10E

There are probably all sorts of other variables operating here. Why would pornographic material be more available in some cities? Perhaps the residents of cities where pornography is tightly controlled are more conservative in general and have a zero-tolerance policy for all crime. Perhaps the cities where the material is easily available are large cities where crime in general is higher. We are sure you can think of other variables that might be involved.

FAQ

Q1:   If you can't generalize the findings from case studies, what good are they?

A1:   Clinicians report interesting cases for several reasons. For example, a clinical case study might provide support for a theory or hypothesis about a psychological disorder. Another clinician with a client with similar symptoms might get some ideas about treatment from a case study. Case studies contribute information to the knowledge body of the discipline.

Q2:   If multiple correlation approaches allow us to assess the relative contribution of a number of independent variables on a dependent variable, why not include as many IVs as you can think of?

A2:   Theoretically, this is a good idea, but it has a problem. The amount of unique variance that can be accounted for in the dependent variable becomes smaller and smaller as you add more independent variables. Eventually, there is such a small amount of unexplained variance that you are accounting for less and less by adding more and more variables. You reach a point where it becomes more effort to measure these variables than it is worth. Usually, researchers include the variables that are judged to be the most important.

Q3:   What is the difference between a pre- and postmeasure pseudo-experiment and a time-series design?

A3:   A one-group pre- and posttest design does not include a control group. As such, it is not possible to determine if posttest changes are related to the treatment. Perhaps the behavior being measured fluctuates naturally. Time-series designs typically measure behavior several times before and several times after treatment. In this way, the natural fluctuation in scores can be examined and compared to posttest changes. Some time-series designs include control groups and are considered superior to those that do not.

Q4: I'm interested in how attitudes toward spanking have changed over time. Should I do a longitudinal or cross-sectional study?

A4: If your interest is in whether societal norms regarding the use of physical punishment in child rearing have changed, you should use a longitudinal design. A cross-sectional approach would be useful if your interest was in how people (perhaps parents) of different ages view the use of punishment today.

Q5: If you can't make causal inferences from quasi-experimental designs, then why use them?

A5: Many interesting research problems cannot be investigated experimentally. A carefully designed quasi-experiment can provide information that we might follow up later with an experiment. In addition, some clinical researchers are interested in outcomes, not causes.

Q6: Time-series designs look like repeated-measures experiments. How are they different?

A6: Certainly, repeated measures are taken in time-series designs. The difference is that the researcher does not control the nature and/or timing of the treatment in a time-series design.

Q7: What is the difference between a case study and an $n = 1$ study?

A7: A case study is a narrative description of one individual. No quantitative measures may have been taken, and a treatment may not have been introduced. An $n = 1$ study is an experiment where the participant serves as his or her own control. A treatment is introduced after baseline measures of behavior have been made, and the no-treatment/treatment comparison is replicated in some way so that the researcher can infer a causal relationship between the independent variable and the dependent variable.

Q8: Without random assignment, can the nonequivalent control group really be called a control group?

A8: Well, the term *control* as used here refers to the fact that the control group did not receive the treatment or received a different level of the treatment. The term *nonequivalent* means that no attempts were made to ensure initial equivalence of the groups on the behavioral variable being measured. Perhaps *comparison group* might be a better term than *control group*.

Q9: What is *interrupted* in an interrupted time-series design?

A9: The interruption is in the environment really. Measures of something were being taken in a systematic way, and then something happened. A new law was introduced, a disaster occurred, or perhaps a war broke out.

Q10: I want to measure how alcohol affects judgment. I have visited a bar and had people complete a judgment test after each drink. What design is this?

A10: This is a one-group posttest design with several posttest measures. It is seriously flawed for many reasons. There is no control group. The environment cannot be controlled. The dosage of alcohol is not systematic. The sample is biased.

Q11: Why are case studies used so often in clinical psychology?

A11: It is the nature of the discipline. Clinicians treat people one client at a time, often for extensive periods of time. The problems are often unique to each individual. Psychological disorders, even those clearly described, manifest themselves differently in different individuals.

CHAPTER EXERCISES

1. From 1985 to 1997, motorcycle rider training was mandatory in Quebec. In 1997, training was no longer a requirement for licensing, and motorcycle fatalities shot up by 46%. What kind of design is this? What conclusions can be drawn? Mandatory rider training was reintroduced in 2000. What could this add to our conclusions? Is there anything else we could do to increase the validity of our study?

2. What is the main difference between experimental and nonexperimental designs?

3. As the name suggests, a quasi-experimental design shares many of the features of an experiment, but how are they different?

4. Describe the advantages and disadvantages of an interrupted time-series design.

5. In a nonequivalent groups design, something like a control group is used. How is this group similar to a control group in a true experiment, and how are they different?

6. What are the advantages and disadvantages of longitudinal research?

7. If we cannot make causal inferences from correlational research, then why do it?

CHAPTER PROJECTS

1. Is using crack cocaine during pregnancy related to neonatal problems?
   a. Design a nonequivalent groups study to assess this research question.
   b. Design a correlational study to assess this research question.

2. Are there any differences between children reared by same-sex parents and children reared by opposite-sex parents? Describe how you would investigate this research question using cross-sectional research and longitudinal research. Include the advantages and disadvantages of each approach.

3. Torture survivors can suffer devastating psychological trauma.
   a. Describe how you would investigate the effects of torture.
   b. Describe the advantages of your design over other possible designs.

4. No one who is getting married would imagine that the marriage might end in divorce, yet many do. You are interested in identifying the factors that predict a successful marriage.
   a. Design your research project using a longitudinal approach.
   b. Design your project using a correlational approach.
   c. What are the advantages and disadvantages of each?

REFERENCES

Blazina, C. (2004). Gender role conflict and the disidentification process: Two case studies on fragile masculine self. *Journal of Men's Studies, 12*(2), 151–161.

Grossman, A. B., Levin, H. L., Katzen, H. L., & Lechner, S. (2004). PTSD symptoms and onset of neuro-logic disease in elderly trauma survivors. *Journal of Clinical and Experimental Neuropsychology, 26*(5), 698–705.

Linehan, M., Goodstein, J., Nielsen, S., & Chiles, J. (1983). Reasons for staying alive when you are think-ing of killing yourself: The Reasons for Living Inventory. *Journal of Consulting and Clinical Psychology, 51,* 276–286.

Miller, J., Segal, D., & Coolidge, F. (2001) A comparison of suicidal thinking and reasons for living among younger and older adults. *Death Studies, 25,* 357–365.

Nakonezny, P. A., Reddick, R., & Rodgers, J. L. (2004). Did divorces decline after the Oklahoma City bombing? *Journal of Marriage and Family, 66,* 90–100.

Penton-Voak, I., Little, A., Jones, B., Burt, C., Tiddeman, B., & Perrett, D. (2003). Female condition influ-ences preferences for sexual dimorphism in faces of male humans (Homo sapiens). *Journal of Comparative Psychology, 117*(3), 264–271.

Salter, D., McMillan, D., Richards, M., Talbot, T., Hodges, J., Bentovim, A., et al. (2003). Development of sexually abusive behaviour in sexually victimised males: A longitudinal study. *Lancet, 361*(9356), 471–476.

Siegler, R. S. (1995). How does change occur: A microgenetic study of number conservation. *Cognitive Psychology, 28,* 225–273.

Siegler, R. S., & Svetina, M. (2006). What leads children to adopt new strategies? A microgenetic/cross sectional study of class inclusion. *Child Development, 77,* 997–1015.

van Achterberg, M. E., Rohrbaugh, R. M., & Southwick, S. M. (2001). Emergence of PTSD in trauma sur-vivors with dementia. *Journal of Clinical Psychiatry, 62(3),* 206–207.

Weiss, T. (2004). Correlates of posttraumatic growth in husbands of breast cancer survivors. *Psycho-Oncology, 13,* 260–268.

Visit the study site at www.sagepub.com/evansmprstudy for practice quizzes and other study resources.

CHAPTER 11

Data Collection Methods

OBJECTIVES

After reading this chapter, students should be able to

- Briefly define observational research
- Describe the differences between naturalistic observation and participant observation
- Describe the advantages and disadvantages of naturalistic and participant observation
- List special concerns with participant observation
- Describe how laboratory observation differs from both naturalistic and participant observation
- Describe the advantages and disadvantages of laboratory observation
- Describe how survey research differs from observational research
- Describe the difference between a survey and a questionnaire
- Describe the advantages and disadvantages of face-to-face versus telephone interviews
- Describe the advantages and disadvantages of self-administered versus group-administered questionnaires
- Describe the advantages and disadvantages of mail-out versus Internet questionnaires
- Describe a focus group and indicate why a researcher might use this method
- Design a study to address a given research question

In the United States, certain families are given special television equipment so that their viewing habits can be monitored. These families provide what are known as the Nielsen ratings, and television program developers use these ratings to make decisions about which television programs will be continued and which will be dropped. Do you wonder how these decisions are made, exactly?

Have you ever wondered what the TV ad proclaiming that "8 out of 10 dentists prefer Crest" really means?

Have you ever wondered how Kinsey got the data he did in his study of sexual attitudes of men and women?

Well, the Nielsen people clearly have some sort of information about the popularity of TV shows. The Crest people must have some sort of information from dentists about their opinions about toothpaste. Did Kinsey really ask people such private questions?

Where does this information come from? How was it gathered? These are the questions we will address in this chapter.

The most obvious way to collect data is to just watch people and record their behavior, and indeed, this is the basis of **observational research.** Sometimes, though, it is difficult or impossible to actually observe the behavior we are really interested in; perhaps it only occurs under limited conditions, or perhaps it only occurs in private. In the same vein, if we are interested in attitudes or opinions of people, observing their overt behavior may tell us little or nothing about their real attitudes or opinions. Often, we find that we need to ask people questions—**survey research.** But how do we ask our questions? Should we ask them in person? Should we develop a questionnaire? Maybe the best way to answer our specific research question is to get a group (or groups) of people together and facilitate a discussion of our research topic—**focus group research.** Let's look at each of these approaches in detail.

OBSERVATIONAL RESEARCH: OBSERVING THE BEHAVIOR OF INDIVIDUALS

Who doesn't like to watch people from time to time? It's interesting to watch people even if we are only passing the time while waiting for the bus. Our interest in watching people is the same as the researcher's. We want to learn more about human behavior. In observational research, we study behavior by directly observing it. The distinction between research and casual people-watching is that research includes systematically recording behavior.

Observational methods can be used to collect data in both experimental and nonexperimental research. In this chapter, we are focusing on observational research as it is used in nonexperimental research. The independent variable, then, is not under the control of the investigator. We will look at three observational research methods: naturalistic observation, participant observation, and observation in the laboratory.

Observation Behavior From the Outside: Naturalistic Observation

Naturalistic observation researchers might ask questions such as the following:

What does a porpoise reared in a marine zoo do when released into the ocean?

How does a special education student fare in a regular classroom?

Who attends gun shows, and what do they do there?

As the name indicates, naturalistic observation involves making systematic observations of behavior in the environment where it occurs naturally. It is a favorite approach of **ethologists,** researchers who are interested in animal behavior in its natural setting. Probably the best-known ethologist is Jane Goodall, whose studies of the chimpanzee have spanned decades.

Naturalistic observation is used whenever we wish to study behavior as it naturally occurs and in a way that is as unobtrusive as possible. It is particularly well suited for studying behaviors that we fear would be altered or not occur at all if the participants knew they were being observed. The tendency for people to alter their behavior when they know they are being observed is called the **reactivity effect.** To demonstrate how people react to being observed, ask a friend to walk down the hall and tell her you are interested in watching exactly how she carries herself as she walks. Did she alter her behavior? She was probably very self-conscious and felt that she was walking funny. This highlights one of the important features of naturalistic observation. You do not want your participants aware of your presence. You want to be unobtrusive in your record taking and inconspicuous in your presence.

Imagine that it's Friday night and you are at the bar with your friends. You see someone across the room sitting at a table with friends. You are pretty sure that person is interested in you, so you decide to make contact. With the exception of physical appearance, you know nothing about this person, and she or he knows nothing about you. How do you know if the person you are interested in is interested in you? Should you just saunter right up to the table and use your best line? Will you be shot down in flames or accepted with enthusiasm?

One indicator of your potential paramour's interest, which can be noticed from a distance, is body language. Does she occasionally glance at you? Does he smile? Does she blush just a little? Does he smooth his hair? Nonverbal behaviors such as these have been identified and studied in women, but do men engage in nonverbal behaviors that women can read from a distance? This is the general focus of Renninger, Wade, and Grammer (2004).

The Research Problem. Renninger et al. (2004) wanted to determine if men give off nonverbal signals prior to initiating contact with women. And they wondered whether men who are successful in these encounters exhibit behaviors that are different from those of men who are unsuccessful.

Hypotheses. The researchers hypothesized that men who are successful in making contact with women engage in nonverbal behaviors prior to contact that differ from the behaviors of men who are not successful.

Selection of Participants. Thirty-eight men were unobtrusively observed in three bars located in Pennsylvania. Men were randomly selected for observation. However, they had to be surrounded by 10 or more people, not sitting in a booth, and not accompanied by a woman. Participants were debriefed after exiting the bar, and all signed a consent form. (One wonders if the participants' alcohol consumption may have influenced their decision to participate. Nevertheless, this project was given approval by an internal ethics review board.)

The Variables. The variables in this study were occurrences of specifically defined behaviors over the course of the 30-minute observation period. Based on previous research and their own preliminary observations, Renninger et al. (2004) created four main categories of behavior with 18 subcategories. The main categories were glancing behavior, physical space changes, gesturing, and touching. It is important to note that the observers were clear on all the behavioral definitions before the study started. You can imagine the difficulty in remaining inconspicuous if you had to keep referring to a list while trying to record ongoing behavior.

The outcome variable was the successful contact with a woman. This was a categorical variable, with success defined as the participant engaging a woman in conversation for 1 minute or longer. Those who did not establish contact for this duration were scored as unsuccessful.

The Design. Renninger et al. (2004) employed naturalistic observation. Given they were interested in how men behave in a courtship setting, it is unlikely their participants would behave in a natural way if observations took place in a laboratory setting. And it is equally unlikely the men would act naturally if they knew they were being watched. Consequently, observations were made in a bar, and the participants were unaware they were being studied. Two observers were positioned in remote locations and made audio recordings of their observations. Two observers were used so that measures of interrater reliability could be calculated for the various behaviors. Also, one of the observers was blind to the research hypothesis as a guard against research bias in the recordings.

From a group of people in the bar, a focal man was chosen at random, and behaviors were observed for 30 minutes. If within the observation period, the man made contact with a woman, he was scored (pun intended) as a success; otherwise, he was recorded as unsuccessful. Observers then waited for another group of individuals and again selected a single man.

The Statistical Analysis. Both descriptive and inferential statistics were used in this study. The descriptive statistics included the mean frequency of each behavior during the 30-minute observation periods averaged across all the men who were successful and those who were unsuccessful.

For inferential statistics, Renninger et al. (2004) used a one-way analysis of variance (ANOVA) to make comparisons between the men who were successful and those who were unsuccessful in making contact with a woman.

The Results. Of the 38 men included in the statistical analysis, 11 made contact and 27 did not. Some of the differences between the successful and unsuccessful men are shown in Figure 11.1. ANOVA was used to test for statistical significance between the successful and unsuccessful groups of men. All these data are presented as frequency of the behavior observed within 30-minute observation periods.

The main differences between successful and unsuccessful men were as follows: Successful men made short, direct glances at the women more frequently, $F(1, 37) = 24.22$, $p < .001$. They made more space-maximizing movements, $F(1, 37) = 16.59, p < .001$. They made more nonreciprocal touches with other men, $F(1, 37) = 8.62, p < .006$, and made fewer closed-body movements, $F(1, 37) = 14.30, p < .001$.

The Conclusions. The researchers concluded that there are differences in nonverbal behavior between men who are successful at making contact with women in a bar and those who are not. Successful men make large movements that maximize their space, they glance at

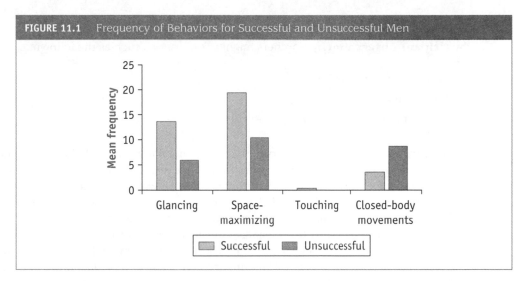

FIGURE 11.1   Frequency of Behaviors for Successful and Unsuccessful Men

Source: Adapted from Renninger et al. (2004).

the woman more frequently, they touch their male friends more often, and they avoid making movements close to their body.

Now before you men start practicing these behaviors, we should remind you of the limitations of nonexperimental research. You cannot make strong causal inferences. Just knowing these are the behaviors that successful men engage in does not mean that they will work for you. Why not? Well, these may be common behaviors of friendly, outgoing, cheerful men—men who are fun to be around. These behaviors may be indicators that women use to judge you from a distance. Engaging in these behaviors may or may not work for you. Moreover, just because this study shows a relationship between the nonverbal behaviors and successful contact does not mean that one leads to the other. It could be that men with these mannerisms just happen to also be the men most likely to approach women at a bar (and engage her for a minute or longer). To test the causal relationship that these nonverbal behaviors increase your chances of successful contact with women, you would need to conduct an experiment. You would need to independently assign men (of all types) to behave as the successful and unsuccessful men in this study and observe the outcome. Furthermore, to our male readers—once you have made contact, you will have to rely on your *verbal* behavior as well. Good luck!

A strength of naturalistic observation is high external validity. There is nothing artificial about this research; it occurs in the real world. Of course, this is also a disadvantage because the real world does not operate on your schedule. In naturalistic observation, we do not influence the environment, and as a consequence, we may have to wait a long time for the behavior to occur. Also, studying the behavior where it occurs and when it occurs means that you must go to the natural setting at times that may be inconvenient (who wants to sit in a bar night after night observing men?).

Sometimes we are interested in behavior that may not be observable by a third party. We must experience the behaviors ourselves. This is the idea behind participant observation.

Observing Behavior From the Inside: Participant Observation

Participant observation researchers might ask questions such as the following:

What goes on in cults?

What happens in AA meetings?

What is life like in Olympic villages?

Research using participant observation is often qualitative. Instead of counting the frequency of behaviors in a given time, rich narratives are written about the experiences of the observed and the observer. Here the researchers enter the world of the people they are interested in studying and maintain field notes chronicling their observations. These may include verbatim quotations, closely recalled quotations, or general recollections.

This type of research has the advantage of introducing us to the world of others. For example, Erving Goffman (1961) described the inner world of mental hospitals by working in institutions and making observations. Important in its own right, qualitative information that is discovered in this type of research can be valuable in giving direction for quantitative researchers about what variables are important.

Obviously, this type of research requires that you gain entrance to the group you are trying to study. This may be very easy or almost impossible depending on the group. Similarly, it may also be very safe or very dangerous depending on the group. Our example of participant observation research also takes place in a bar, but in this study, the researcher was a participant. Although entrance to the group was relatively easy, it was a dangerous world.

Have you ever wondered what it would be like to be a bouncer? Perhaps you have considered, if only in passing, the kind of punishment bouncers (or door staff) can deliver to misbehaving patrons. But have you ever considered the kind of abuse that these individuals must deal with? Monaghan (2003) did.

The Research Problem. Lee Monaghan (2003) worked as a bouncer, recording the experiences of his fellow door staffers and making observations of his own. Monaghan had no specific research hypothesis. Instead, he was interested in describing the dangers that are inherent in work as a bouncer.

Selection of Participants. Monaghan (2003) obtained work in seven establishments located in southwest Britain and made observations between 1997 and 2001. The premises varied on a number of dimensions such as size, mood, appearance, and opening times. For example, one was a sports bar; another was a dance club. The researcher's large build and history of weight lifting and boxing helped him gain employment at these places. He never concealed his academic interests, but his fellow workers considered him primarily to be a bouncer. This is an occupation with a high turnover, and most people were employed either part- or full-time in other occupations.

In participant observation, the individuals who are observed are called **key informants.** The researcher had some contact with more than 60 door staffers, of whom only a few were women. Nevertheless, he maintained regular contact with five doorwomen.

The Variables. Although Monaghan's (2003) field notes may allow him to study a number of different research questions, the focus of this study was a description of the factors that affect bodily risk for door staffers. From his field notes, Monaghan focused on 15 factors that he identified as being associated with either increasing or reducing bodily risk. Some of these factors included the type of venue, door staff/customer ratio, and gender of the staffer.

The Design. To be able to characterize the world of bouncers, Monaghan (2003) chose to use participant observation. Although he could have simply asked bouncers about hazards in their occupation, these reports may be unreliable. Indeed, Monaghan points out that workers may either exaggerate the dangers in a bid to have their salary increased or may minimize the risk in a show of bravado.

Although the author did not detail his data collection methods, it is likely that he completed his field notes as soon after his shift as possible.

The Statistical Analysis. This type of qualitative research does not include statistical analysis. Instead, Monaghan (2003) maintained field notes of his observations and reread his notes numerous times to identify common or characteristic observations (i.e., content analysis). He presents representative narratives to illustrate his main observations.

The Results. Monaghan's experiences confirm that indeed being a bouncer can be dangerous work. Some bouncers tried to reduce their risk by carrying weapons such as metal batons and threatening to use them if necessary. Of course, Monaghan points out that the risk reduction may be illusory because weapons can be used against the bouncer. Certain occasions were deemed more dangerous. For example, important football (soccer) games would attract a potentially more dangerous crowd. Here is one of his observations on this topic.

> Because there was a football match in the city, football supporters congregated in the pub. Most were having a (noisy) drink before the game. Male customers outnumbered the women by ten to one. The men were rowdy and many appeared drunk. One of the doormen, after telling a disruptive group of men to calm down, came over and warned: 'It's not like rugby. It's a different crowd. They're sneaky, sly bastards. They're the type that'll try to bottle or knife you.' (Wednesday 29 March 2000: Uncle Sam's) (Monaghan, 2003, p. 16)*

Another factor was the customer-to-door staff ratio, which is judged to be about 100 customers per bouncer. But here is an excerpt describing what really happens.

> I stood on the front door with Paul and several other members of the door team. Paul complained about the number of doorstaff working at this sports bar during a recently televised rugby match. There were eight doorstaff and approximately 1600 customers in the club at any one time. Paul commented: 'If it kicks off big

---

*Excerpts are from Monaghan, L. F. (2003). Danger on the doors: Bodily risk in a demonised occupation. *Health, Risk, and Society, 5*(1), 11–31.

time we'd have no chance. It happened at Asterix [another local venue]. The only reason why we could handle it was because a lot of the boys [other known doormen] were out drinking and they helped us out. We could have twenty, thirty doormen here and it still might not be enough . . . you just have to hope for the best.' (Thursday 23 March 2000: Uncle Sam's) (Monaghan, 2003, p. 19)

Interestingly, he found that female bouncers (who are very much in the minority) could stop patrons from fighting without using violence.

I talked to Julie, who reportedly has a black belt in karate, about the risks of doorwork. Did she feel these were magnified by her female gender and slight physical build (she was no taller than 5'2" and weighed less than nine stone [126 pounds])? Similar to other doorwomen, she rationalized the possible risk of doorwork. She did this both in relation to her female gender and her use of physical self-defence techniques: 'If there's two men fighting and I go over they're often more likely to stop than if a doorman went to sort it out. I think so, anyway. I think I'm less likely to inflame the situation. Saying that, I always keep my hands high and to my chest, ready to clonk [hit] them just in case they try to clonk me.' (Saturday 30 June 2001: Oceanic) (Monaghan, 2003, p. 22)

The Conclusions. Monaghan (2003) concluded that his ethnography of door staffers in southeast Britain is an important contribution to the literature because there is a glaring lack of empirical evidence on the sociology of the body. His descriptions of how bouncers act and are acted upon give a rich sense that these people are more than social actors; they are "actual flesh and blood bodies" (Monaghan, 2003, p. 29). This conclusion brings to light one of the important aspects of qualitative research. The narratives bring the subject matter to life in a powerful and moving way. In a manner similar to the way we can empathize with the characters in a novel, we get a glimpse at the truly human aspects of the subject matter in qualitative research. Monaghan gave us an understanding of the importance of the situation in the actions of people in this high-risk occupation.

Like naturalistic observation, participant observation has high external validity. You are making observations in the real world, not in an artificial setting, and so it cannot be claimed that your observations do not apply to the real world. However, there are obvious limits to our ability to generalize from this research. For example, we do not know if Monaghan's (2003) observations in Britain would generalize to North America.

The goal of naturalistic observation is to try to remain hidden, or at least unobtrusive, while you observe. Participant observation takes the opposite approach, where you actually join in the action. This has the advantage that you can experience the same environmental conditions as your participants. You will be able to describe your subjective experiences as well as the experiences of others. Another advantage is that you can collect information on factors that may not be overtly observable. Both through your own experiences and by listening to the experiences of others, you can address areas of interest that include people's opinions, attitudes, and emotions as well as their overt behavior. In addition, once accepted by the group, you may be privy to information that group members would not share with researchers carrying clipboards and tape recorders. You will be able to collect information that would otherwise be kept secret.

Subjectivity is a major advantage of participant observation, and it is also a major disadvantage. Although an important strength of participant observation is that you can subjectively experience the world of those you are studying, at some point you must be able to maintain (or regain) your objectivity. You are a researcher, and it is expected that you will not misrepresent or bias your observations as a result of your experiences. Something that may help you in your quest for objectivity is that, unlike the people you study, you are going to eventually leave the group and situation. They will not.

Participant observation studies can take a lot of time. Monaghan worked, on and off, as a bouncer for over 3 years, a sizable investment not only in time but also financially and personally. Participant observation can also be dangerous. You must consider the risks to your safety. This may not be an issue if you are studying librarians, for example, well known for their pacifistic leanings, but it certainly was a factor in Monaghan's (2003) research. This leads us to another issue, that of entrance into a group. Do you have the qualifications to become a participant? Monaghan already was a big man who liked weight lifting and boxing, so he was readily hired as a bouncer. This was also facilitated by the high staff turnover in the occupation. How well do you think he would be accepted if he were interested in day care workers? Motorcycle club members? How about emergency ward surgeons? Clearly, entrance to some groups is easier than to others.

There are important ethical issues that need to be considered in this type of research. If you are planning to enter a formal institution, you may need permission from high-level staff. This may be a formality or it may be impossible depending on the institution. You must protect the anonymity of your informants. Monaghan (2003) changed the names of the people and the venues in his report. But there are instances when this may not be sufficient, when people may be recognized. This could lead to a loss of employment, social harm, or even physical harm. The responsibility lies with you to see that your contacts are protected.

Finally, like the other methods in this chapter, this is nonexperimental research, and so you must be careful in drawing inferences. You cannot make strong causal inferences from this research. The research can certainly suggest possible causal relationships, but these remain, to some extent, speculative until supported by experimental research.

Observing Behavior in a Controlled Setting: Laboratory Observation

Laboratory observation researchers might ask questions such as the following:

How do people respond to someone in apparent distress?

Do children mimic aggressive models?

When given a choice, do girls and boys cooperate or compete in a game?

Conducting observational research in the natural setting is not always the best approach. If you are interested in a behavior that only occurs under specific conditions, you may be waiting a long, long time. However, in the laboratory, we can create the situations we need. In Chapter 9, we discussed the field experiment where an independent variable(s) is manipulated by the researcher in a natural setting. That approach provides the power of the true experiment to determine cause and effect in a natural setting. We can make causal inferences because the researcher controls the independent variable, and we have increased external validity because the research takes place in the real world. Here we take a different approach by bringing observational, nonexperimental research into the laboratory. We make a trade-off between external validity and level of control. In bringing our observational research into the laboratory, we lose some external validity, but we gain control over the situation so that we can create the conditions necessary for our study.

Cast your mind back to when you were 10 years old. You were playing with your best friend when a new kid comes along and wants to join in. What did you do? Can you remember the phrase "Two is company, three's a crowd"? We hope that you would happily invite the newcomer, but sadly, that doesn't always happen. Sometimes children exclude others from their play by things they say and the way they act, as Underwood, Scott, Galperin, Bjornstad, and Sexton (2004) found.

The Research Problem. Underwood and her colleagues (2004) were interested in the behaviors that children use to exclude a newcomer. Their research on social exclusion provides a good example of observational research in the laboratory. Although the research contained both true independent variables (manipulated by the researchers) and participant variables (the gender of the child), we will focus on the description of behavior and the relationships between the measured variables.

Hypotheses. The researchers were interested in determining the types of behaviors children use to exclude a newcomer. The behaviors they specified included social exclusion, verbal aggression, verbal assertion, and exclusionary gestures. One of their hypotheses was that girls would engage in social exclusion in a more polite and less direct way than boys.

Selection of Participants. Children in Grades 4, 6, and 8 were recruited from five elementary and two junior high schools. The researchers had teachers send home parental request letters. If consent was given, the child was contacted by telephone and asked to identify his or her three closest friends. If a close friend had also given consent, the pair was scheduled to participate. The study ran over two summers and included 175 play sessions. The final number of participants was 292, or 146 pairs or dyads.

The Variables. Gender of the child was the participant variable, and the frequency of each observed behavior was measured.

The Design. Underwood et al. (2004) were interested in the types of behaviors children display to exclude a newcomer from their activity. If you wanted to observe this behavior in the natural setting, you might have to watch children for a very long, time. Consequently, they chose to stage an artificial situation in a laboratory that was scripted to facilitate this type of response. The children were studied in groups of three. Two were the participants who were good friends, and the third was a child actor of the same gender and age, trained to behave in a belligerent manner. The children were given a tour of the laboratory prior to the study so they were aware that their behavior was being videotaped. They were reminded of their rights as research participants throughout the study and, particularly because deception was used, they were fully debriefed at the end.

The procedure involved having the children play the game "Pictionary." The children played for a while, but following a cue from the researchers, the actor began acting in a provocative manner by criticizing, boasting, being bossy, and being a poor game player.

Recording of behaviors was done from the videotape by a number of research assistants (6 one year and 4 the second year). Instead of recording all events, they chose to code behaviors in 10-second intervals. To guard against researcher bias, the coders were blind to the research hypotheses. Reliability estimates were calculated for each behavior category, and all were high.

The Statistical Analysis. Both descriptive and inferential statistics were used in this study. The descriptive statistics included the mean frequency of each behavior reported separately for girls and boys. For inferential statistics, ANOVA was used to assess gender differences for each behavior.

The Results. Some of the descriptive and inferential statistics from Underwood et al. (2004) are shown in Table 11.1. Data from each pair of children were combined as the units of analysis. This was necessary because one of the assumptions of ANOVA is that the units of measure are independent. This was clearly not the case in this study because the children were acting together in the same situation.

When the actor was absent, girls and boys did not differ in their frequency of social exclusion. Indeed, there were no differences among any of the behavior categories. When the provoking actor was present, there were still no gender differences in overall rates of social exclusion, but there were subtle differences between boys and girls in their expression of social exclusion. Girls were more likely to express social exclusion through gestures such as hostile glares, rolling of eyes, tossing of hair, and turning away in disgust. Boys, on the other hand, showed social exclusion through verbal responses, which included gossiping, planning to exclude the other, and so on. But take a look at the means and the effect sizes ($\eta^2 = SS_{effect}/(SS_{effect} + SS_{error})$)! These are not large differences. They are *statistically* significant, but they are small.

TABLE 11.1   Mean Frequencies of Verbal and Gestural Responses During the Actor Provoking, by Gender

Type of Behavior	Gender		F(1, 139)	η^2
	Girls (n = 74 dyads)	*Boys (n = 72 dyads)*		
Verbal responses				
Social exclusion	1.49	2.39	4.78*	.03
Verbal agression	4.14	11.85	10.29**	.48
Verbal assertion	0.86	5.14	8.18**	.15
Gestures				
Social exclusion	17.28	12.15	11.98***	.08

Source: Underwood et al. (2004).

Note: * $p < .05$; ** $p < .01$; *** $p < .001$.

However, more impressive differences were observed in rates of verbal aggression and, to a lesser extent, verbal assertion. In both behaviors, boys showed significantly (in both senses of the word) higher rates. Statements of "verbal aggression include[d] mockery, sarcasm, and openly critical comments" and "verbal assertion included saying 'shhh!' to the actor, telling the actor to stop cheating or to stop bragging, or disputing the actor's comments" (p. 1545).

The Conclusions. The researchers concluded that girls are not more socially exclusive than boys but that boys and girls employ different techniques when they engage in social exclusion. Girls are more likely to use nonverbal behaviors such as making mean faces. Boys tend to use verbal behaviors of social exclusion as well as verbal aggression. The authors remind us that all the children were aware that they were being videotaped and were probably trying to be on their best and most polite behavior. In that regard, it may be that the girls engaged in subtle facial gestures in an attempt to socially exclude without being detected. Perhaps this is an artifact of the laboratory; on the other hand, it is equally possible that this is the case in the real world too. As parents, we know that social exclusion is painful for children, and as the authors conclude, "A better understanding of the social process involved in girls' and boys' social aggression could guide the development of interventions that are sensitive, focused, and effective in helping more children refrain from breaking each other's hearts" (Underwood et al., 2004, p. 1553).

When we observe behavior in the laboratory, we can create the conditions necessary to make the behavior occur. As would be the case in the example above, we might have to wait a long time to observe an occurrence of social exclusion in the real world. Certainly, the behavior occurs, but will you be there watching when it does? This strength also produces the main weakness of this research. The artificiality of the laboratory may influence the way the participants behave. Of course, we cannot determine to what extent the laboratory setting will influence behavior, but the possibility is there. As a result, our research may (or may not) lack external validity. In other words, our findings may be as artificial as our setting.

In Underwood et al.'s (2004) research, for example, the children knew they were being videotaped and may have tried to be as polite as possible to the new child. Indeed, the authors point out that this may be why the gender differences (though statistically significant) were so small. Of course, it is equally possible that this is exactly how boys and girls behave in the real world. After all, in the real world, a parent or a teacher might be watching them play.

ADVANTAGES AND DISADVANTAGES OF OBSERVATIONAL RESEARCH

In all types of observational research, it is important to form clear definitions of the behaviors you are interested in observing. These definitions may be based on previous research or pilot observations. They could be done before the data are collected, as was the case in the courtship example. Or they may be formed after the observations are made after careful reading of field notes, as was the case in the bouncer study.

Reliability of the behavioral coding can be calculated only if you have more than one observer or coder. In the research on courtship behavior and social exclusion, calculations of reliability were included. Obviously, you want your reliability estimates to be as high as possible, and in the study of men's behavior in bars, behavioral categories with reliability estimates less than .5 were excluded.

How you observe behavior in these types of studies really depends on the nature of your research. In the social exclusion study, observations were made from videotapes. Then, after the fact, observers coded behavior in 10-second intervals. By deciding to code in time intervals, the researchers could be assured that coders were observing the same behaviors. On the other hand, the behavior of men in the bar was coded and audio recorded as the events occurred. This requires that you be well practiced in coding the behaviors before you go out in the field. And in the case of the bar study, the observers sat with someone so they did not appear to be talking to themselves.

In observational research conducted outside the laboratory, you might think that you do not have to be concerned with ethical issues. However, it does not matter where the research is conducted; the researcher must be accountable for any harm to the participants. Whether the research is participant research, naturalistic, or laboratory, steps can and must be taken to guard the rights of those involved. For more discussion on ethics in research, see Chapter 3.

Observational research is often time-consuming and requires observers who are trained to carefully record behavioral observations. The objective is to observe the behavior as it occurs. Many research problems involve attitudes or opinions, things that are not readily observed. In such cases, a survey might be the best approach.

Conceptual Exercise 11A

A young researcher is curious about the claim of her female friend that auto repair shops rip off women more than men. She decides to observe the behavior of auto mechanics in a selection of shops in her city. She obtains permission from the owners to observe the goings on for several weeks. She records comments by the mechanics about the car problems, being careful to note whether the car was brought in by a woman or a man, and she notes the cost of each repair. Being a cautious young researcher, she sits in a far corner and never makes comments to anyone in the shops. At the end of her study, she finds no difference between the average cost of repairs and no obvious difference in the kinds of comments the mechanics make about cars brought in by women or men. What do you have to say about her intention to write in her report that auto mechanics do not discriminate in any way between men and women?

SURVEY RESEARCH: ASKING PEOPLE QUESTIONS ABOUT THEIR BEHAVIOR

Survey researchers might ask questions such as the following:

How do people feel about corporal punishment in the schools?

Should prisons be rehabilitative or punitive?

How do Canadians feel about the recent lobby to legalize gay marriage?

"When I was in England, I experimented with marijuana a time or two, and I didn't like it. I didn't inhale, and I never tried it again." These are the famous words of Bill Clinton during his 1992 presidential campaign. Bob Dole ran a number of television advertisements that highlighted this statement, but Clinton won the election. Could that be because many Americans have experimented with this drug at least once in their life? Indeed, many political leaders (e.g., Jean Chrétien, former prime minister of Canada) believe that possession of marijuana should not be a criminal offense.

Is marijuana use widespread? How many people have tried it? Have you tried it?

FYI

Questionnaires can be used in nonexperimental and experimental research. Questionnaires are often discussed in the context of nonexperimental research, where the goal is to describe some characteristic of the people who are surveyed. And we will discuss questionnaire construction in this chapter because questionnaires are often used in surveys. However, we want to make it clear that they can also be used to measure the effects of a manipulated independent variable in an experiment. For example, we might be interested in how attitudes toward smoking are influenced by watching a television commercial featuring an emotionally charged testimonial by a cancer patient. We can randomly assign participants to watch either the cancer commercial or an equally emotional commercial about famine victims. Following our treatment conditions, we could give all participants a questionnaire to assess their attitudes on smoking. In this case, we are using a questionnaire in an experiment.

By its very definition as a discipline, psychology is the study of human behavior. In the previous section, we looked at observation techniques as ways of understanding behavior. In other words, we discussed understanding behavior by watching it. Now instead of observing behavior, we will discuss how to ask people about their behavior. Besides assessing self-reported behavior, we can use surveys to measure people's opinions and attitudes, variables that may be difficult or impossible to observe directly.

To venture out and ask people about their behavior, attitudes, and opinions seems simple, but often novice researchers discover that the apparent simplicity of this approach is deceptive. Not for a minute would any of us consider it simple to develop a new intelligence scale or a new measure of brain activity. Yet we might be quite pleased with the survey we developed on the back of a napkin while we ate dinner. The major problem with survey research is that it appears to be a simple and easy endeavor. Of course, brain surgery is simple too if you are not too concerned about whether the patient lives or dies. And survey research is simple too, unless you are worried about whether or not you will find an answer to your research question.

Success in any research endeavor begins with careful planning, and survey research is no exception. We must consider what we will ask, how we will word the questions, and how we will administer the surveys. We have to decide who we will ask and how many. And so that we don't put the cart too far in front of the horse, we must also plan how the data will be analyzed. We do not want to be in the unfortunate situation where we have collected a lot of survey data only to find that there is no way to analyze them.

Defining Your Research Question

A practice that improved the baseball swing of one of the authors of this book was to always keep his eye on the ball. This is sound advice in research as well. From start to finish, your research question or hypothesis must guide you. Perhaps we want to determine how many people have tried marijuana. We may want to limit the scope of the research to young people, high school students, or university students. We may not want to limit our focus to just marijuana; we might want to include other drugs, and we might also want to relate the use of such drugs to levels of alcohol use. At this early planning stage, we have to decide if we are satisfied with just describing drug use or if perhaps we might want to test a number of hypotheses. Perhaps there are psychological or social factors that predispose people to try drugs. Conversely, there may be factors that influence youth to avoid drugs. If so, we may wish to go beyond a description of drug use and analyze relationships between variables. At this stage, it may be that we are not sure of our purpose. It is important to spend some time thinking about it before moving on, because if you are not sure of your purpose, the next step will be extremely difficult.

How Will You Ask Your Questions?

The terms *survey* and *questionnaire* are paired so often that it is easy to start using them interchangeably. However, they are not synonymous. **Survey** refers to the action of collecting information, whereas a **questionnaire** is a list of questions that are asked when you are collecting the information. The distinction is important because the form of your questionnaire will be very different depending on how you do the survey. For example, you could conduct a telephone survey where you call your fellow students and ask them a few questions such as their age, major, how often they drink alcohol, and, when they do, how much. If you have a written list of questions to ask, and that seems like a reasonable thing to do, then you are conducting a survey, but you are not using a questionnaire. Your list of questions would be considered a **structured interview schedule.** The major difference between an interview schedule and questionnaire is that a trained interviewer will read a schedule, but your respondent reads a questionnaire.

At this stage, you need to determine the kinds of information you need and the best method of obtaining that information. You will also need to consider who are your respondents. Specifically, can they read or can they follow written instructions? For example, if your respondents are young children, then it is unlikely that a self-administered questionnaire will be the method of choice. It is not impossible to design a child-friendly questionnaire, but an interview may work better. The choice you make will depend on many factors. The best method may be the cheapest or the fastest or the most reliable. Your decision will have to involve a weighing of these factors. Because the type of questions you ask will depend on whether you are asking them over the telephone or having someone read the questions, you must decide how you will administer the survey before you can write the questions. As you may have guessed, there are advantages and disadvantages to each survey method. Time, money, literacy, and respondent honesty are all factors that need to be considered when making the choice.

Interviews

Interviewing can be very expensive and time-consuming, and it requires trained interviewers. However, an **interview** gives us that human contact that we can use to develop a relationship with our respondents. This relationship may be particularly important if we are interested in exploring sensitive topics. However, this rapport can be a double-edged sword. It can work to our advantage by allowing probing questions as a result of a particular response. But it can also work against us if we consciously or unconsciously influence the respondent to answer in a particular way.

Face-to-Face Interview

One way to conduct a survey is to just walk up to a potential respondent and ask your questions. You may have experienced this approach in shopping malls. Someone approaches you and says, "Good afternoon, my name is Alison and I'm conducting a survey for Mattel. The survey takes only 5 minutes. Would you care to participate?" As a researcher, you hope that the person will agree. You may run into problems of sampling bias if only a small minority of the people you approach agree to participate. Well, do you participate? Can you spare 5 minutes?

If you are interested in obtaining information about consumer opinions or attitudes, it makes a lot of sense to ask people shopping (and consuming) at a mall. Generally, if the population you want to study is available at a particular location (e.g., mall, airport, emergency waiting room) and your questions do not take more than about 5 minutes, then the simplest approach is to go to where your group is and interview them in person. On the other hand, if your interview takes more time, you may have to arrange for the respondents to meet you somewhere.

Although you do not need to have respondents complete an informed consent form before they answer your questions, you still need to consider the ethics of consent. As a researcher, you must consider what your respondents will need to know before they decide if they want to answer your questions. It is good practice to be honest with your potential respondents and tell them who the survey is for and how long it will take. This way, if they agree to participate, they are giving their informed consent, and it makes it more likely that once they start, they will continue to the end.

Advantages and Disadvantages of Face-to-Face Interviews

One advantage of the **face-to-face interview** is that you gather information directly from the people you are interested in. For example, if you want to find out what university students think about drugs, simply position yourself on campus and ask them. This works very well if the population you are interested is regularly available in a particular location. Be aware, though, that your sample may be biased depending on where you position yourself on campus. You may get very different results if you ask students in the library rather than the campus pub. It is important to consider specifically where you will approach respondents, and it may be best to gather data from a number of locations. For more information on sampling and ensuring that your sample is representative, see Chapter 6.

Another advantage of the face-to-face interview is that you can explore complex issues that do not lend themselves to multiple-choice answers. Particularly in early stages of research, you may not know what the important questions are; in this case, it is useful to ask **probing questions.** Probing questions are open-ended questions that permit the whole range of possible responses. For example, following a question with the query, "Is there anything else?" or "Why is that?" might yield useful information. But be careful that your probing does not influence your data. It is easy to use these probe questions to lead the respondent in one direction or another, so it is very important that the probes be neutral. It may also be a good idea to script the probe questions beforehand to guard against bias.

A disadvantage of face-to-face interviews is that they can be very time-consuming. For example, if your interview takes 5 minutes, you will be able to conduct only 12 interviews in 1 hour (and that is in an ideal world, not the real world). To solve this problem, you must hire many interviewers, which leads to another disadvantage—they can be very expensive.

A potential drawback to a face-to-face interview is that people may not feel comfortable discussing personal or embarrassing topics. Although it is possible to establish good rapport with the respondent, it is unlikely that anyone will feel comfortable revealing intimate information to a stranger (and those who do may not be representative of the population). Imagine asking people detailed questions about their sex lives!

Durant and Carey (2000) investigated whether young women would give different responses to questions asked in a face-to-face interview (FTFI) compared to a self-administered questionnaire (SAQ). Participants kept a diary for 8 weeks where they recorded their sexual- and health-related behaviors. To ensure anonymity, participants used code names of their own choosing. The diaries consisted of recipe cards that the women deposited weekly in a secure drop box. On the cards, they recorded their activities over the week and their code name. Of the women recruited from an introductory psychology course, only those who were sexually active continued. These women were randomly assigned to retrospective measures of their sexual activity either with a face-to-face interview or by completing a self-administered questionnaire. A discrepancy score was calculated for each behavior by subtracting the frequency reported retrospectively (interview or questionnaire) from the diary data. Given that the participants were aware that their reporting could be checked against their diaries, it is not surprising that there was a high level of agreement between the diaries and the retrospective reports. But even given this limitation, Durant and Carey found that, at least for some behaviors, SAQ produced more accurate responses than FTFI. Actually, as the authors note, it is surprising that they found any difference between FTFI and SAQ for the following reasons. First, the participants were assured anonymity in both conditions. Second, well-educated women are more comfortable responding to questions about sexuality than women recruited from community outreach programs. Third, the interviewers were well trained in sexual behavior interviewing. All these factors should have worked against finding a difference between the modes of survey, but still an advantage for SAQ was found.

The fact that some people are hesitant to discuss embarrassing topics is one problem with the face-to-face interview. Another is **social desirability.** This is the tendency for people to respond in a manner that makes them appear better than they are. In other words, in a face-to-face interview, people may engage in response management by answering in ways that may not be totally honest but that make them look good. Consider our example of drug use in high schools: A face-to-face interview might be disastrous. Imagine asking Grade 10 students whether they had ever smoked marijuana. Do you think they would answer truthfully? Do you think they might alter their response if their teacher was hanging about? How about if a parent was there or if you asked them while they were standing with a group of friends? Clearly, it is important to consider how people will react to your questions and also exactly under what conditions you will conduct your interviews. Indeed, it may be the case that your topic is too embarrassing to ask in a face-to-face interview, and perhaps a more anonymous approach is better.

Anyone who has children knows what a wonderful and rewarding experience it can be. There are times, though, when it is frustrating, difficult, and heart wrenching. It is at those times when we wonder (hopefully not out loud) why we ever had kids! The cost is enormous both financially and emotionally. So why have them? The following research addressed this very question using face-to-face interviews.

The Research Problem. Langdridge, Connolly, and Sheeran (2000) wanted to determine why people had children. More important, though, they were interested in whether couples undergoing in vitro fertilization would have different reasons than fertile couples.

The Hypothesis. The researchers were not interested in testing a specific hypothesis. Instead, their goal was to examine how people rank the importance of various reasons for having children and then to compare the ranks across three groups.

Selection of Participants. Thirty-four couples were recruited from three clinics in Sheffield, United Kingdom. There were 10 expectant couples (E), 10 couples who were about to receive in vitro fertilization (IVF), and 14 couples who were undergoing donor insemination (DI).

The Variables. The variables in this study were the category of the couple (IVF, DI, E) and their reasons for having children. Individuals ranked the relative importance of 24 reasons. The researchers had previously generated these reasons, but the respondents were encouraged to add reasons of their own if the list was not sufficient.

The Design. Langdridge et al. (2000) had a number of reasons for choosing face-to-face interviews to collect their data. Sex and reproduction are sensitive topics, and they believed that the personal approach would yield better results than an over-the-telephone questionnaire. Moreover, the sensitive nature of the topic is likely magnified for groups having trouble conceiving. Now before you point out that Durant and Carey (2000) found that self-administered questionnaires are probably better for this type of research question, we hasten to add that Langdridge et al. had other reasons for using face-to-face interviews. One reason was related to their data analysis. In addition to looking at differences between the groups on the reasons for having children, they were also interested in constructing a model network illustrating how the reasons are related. This **network analysis** required that the participants not only select reasons and rank their importance but also construct diagrams showing how they think their reasons are linked. Clearly, to explain such a complicated procedure and to explore such a sensitive topic required the rapport that is best achieved with a face-to-face interview.

The Statistical Analysis. Both descriptive and inferential statistics were used in this study. The descriptive statistics were the mean rankings of the 24 reasons for having children. For inferential statistics, the Kruskal-Wallis *H* test was used to make comparisons across the three groups of the ranks given to each reason. This is a nonparametric statistical procedure that has similarities to one-way ANOVA but is used with ordinal data. Comparisons of the mean rankings were made across the three groups, and sex differences were investigated by comparing the rankings given by men and women.

The Results. Some of the descriptive statistics from Langdridge et al. (2000) are shown in Table 11.2. Data from women and men were combined because there were no gender differences in the rankings.

Instead of listing all 24 reasons for having children, we show only the top six as ranked by the expectant group. There were some differences among the groups, but only two reasons showed group differences that were statistically significant. Among the top six reasons, there was a difference between the expectant and the DI groups on the reason "to make a family." The DI group ranked it third (*M* = 5.32), and the expectant group ranked it sixth (*M* = 9.85), Kruskal-Wallis *H* = (2) 6.57, *p* < .05.

The Conclusions. The researchers concluded that the main reasons for having a child were similar across the three groups. The top reasons were "to give and receive love" and "to have something that is a part us." The authors noted that their results were similar to earlier findings. They also point out the reason "to have something that is a part of us" poses a real challenge to groups working for adoption and donor insemination. Interestingly, this reason was ranked number two by the donor insemination group in this study. It is surprising that this group would not rank social ties as more important than biological ones.

TABLE 11.2	Descriptive Statistics: Reasons for Wanting Children, Mean Rank (Rank Position)		
		Group	
Reason	***Expectant***	***IVF***	***DI***
To give love to a child	2.70 (1)	4.25 (1)	3.46 (1)
Enjoyment a child could give	4.85 (2)	4.85 (3)	6.04 (4)
To have something that is a part of both of us	7.95 (3)	4.75 (2)	4.32 (2)
One of the most worthwhile things a person can do	9.30 (4)	10.55 (7)	8.04 (5)
To receive love from a child	9.45 (5)	7.56 (5)	10.04 (9)
To make us a family	9.85 (6)	6.95 (4)	5.32 (3)*

Source: Langdridge et al. (2000).

Note: *p* < .05 between Expectant and DI.

Face-to-face interviews have some real advantages, but they are labor intensive, and, as such, there are practical limitations in terms of the number of people who can be included. In addition, it is very difficult to include people who are not in the immediate vicinity of the researchers. One way around this problem is to conduct the interview over the telephone.

Telephone Interview

Survey by telephone is your best choice if your research question requires interviewing a large number of respondents who are spread over a large geographical area. Although this approach can be expensive and does require trained interviewers, it will certainly be cheaper and faster than conducting face-to-face interviews. Of course, the interview itself will take the same amount of time, but contacting your respondents can be much faster. Rather than chasing after people, you can let your fingers do the walking.

Telephone interviews must be shorter than face-to-face interviews. In a face-to-face interview, it is unlikely that your respondent will get up and leave partway through, but if your telephone questions run too long, watch out. It is probably best to keep your interview to about 10 minutes. This is certainly an important consideration and restricts the type of research question that can be adequately investigated by telephone.

If you are doing research on a specific population, such as physicians, for example, you might be able to obtain a list of telephone numbers through an organization. However, large-scale population studies may require specific samples, and often these lists are purchased from survey sampling companies.

Often data are coded and entered into a computer directly by the telephone interviewer. Computer-aided telephone interview programs display the interview questions on the screen for the interviewer and permit direct entry of each response. These programs also provide probe questions on screen and branch to questions that follow as a consequence of a certain response. These programs can certainly reduce training time for interviewers.

Advantages and Disadvantages of Telephone Interviews

The most important advantage of the telephone interview is that you do not have to be in the same location as the respondent. This means that your interviewers have no travel time, and you can interview people from across a wide area.

Face-to-face interviews allow us to select the specific individuals we are interested in, but this is not always the case with the telephone interview. Indeed, a major disadvantage of telephone interviews is related to **selection bias.** Early telephone studies were flawed because not everyone had a telephone listing; today, selection bias results from people screening their calls with answering machines or call display.

To ensure that someone will be home when you call, the dinner hour is used as the prime time for data collection. However, with the increasing number of telephone solicitors interrupting our dinner, a market has emerged for devices that block automatic dialer calls. Indeed, you can now purchase a telephone accessory that has a button that you press and hang up. The device then sends an automatic message saying that you do not take these types of calls and to remove this number from the caller's list.

On our campus one year, we heard a very sad story from our student counselor. A student had gambled away all her tuition money in a single afternoon. She thought she could cover the cost of her books and tuition if she won. Unfortunately, she lost and lost and lost. Gambling is the focus of the next research example.

The Research Problem. Gambling can be a great recreational pastime for some, but for others, it can spell disaster. Desai, Maciejewski, Dausey, Caldarone, and Potenza (2004) report that pathological and problem gamblers suffer high rates of social, financial, personal, and health problems but that these individuals are in the minority of gamblers. They were interested in looking at the health and well-being of recreational gamblers. Specifically, they compared younger and older recreational gamblers on these factors.

The Hypothesis. In their previous research, Desai et al. (2004) had found that recreational gamblers had "higher rates of alcohol abuse/dependence, substance abuse/dependence, depression, and incarceration. However, they also had higher rates of good to excellent subjectively rated general personal health" (p. 1672). One of the relationships they investigated was the difference between young gamblers and older gamblers on health and well-being measures. Given their previous findings, they did not propose a directional hypothesis but instead were just looking for differences.

Selection of Participants. The participants were contacted by random-digit dialing of telephone numbers purchased from Survey Sampling, Inc. Of the 3,160 interviews attempted, 2,417 were completed, giving a response rate of 76%. Of the completed surveys, 1,486 individuals reported gambling in the previous year. Because the focus of this study was on recreational gamblers, 51 individuals who were pathological or problem gamblers were excluded from the sample.

The Variables. The participant variable, age, was categorized into two groups: younger (18–64) and older (> 64). The measures of health and well-being included alcohol use and abuse, substance abuse, depression, whether they had sought treatment for mental health in the past year, and subjective general health rating.

The Design. Telephone interviews were used to gather the information.

The Statistical Analysis. Separate chi-square tests were used to compare young and older respondents on each health and well-being variable.

The Results. Subjective rating of health was the only statistically significant difference between the younger and older respondents. As shown in Figure 11.2, there was little difference between a rating of good or excellent health for young gamblers and nongamblers, but there was a difference between older gamblers and nongamblers, $\chi^2(1, N = 387) = 16.33, p < .001$. The interaction suggests that older gamblers are healthier than nongamblers!

The Conclusions. Does this mean that once you hit 65, you should head to the casino? What do you think? We think maybe and maybe not. It is possible that gambling gives older people an opportunity to socialize and get out of the house, and that is beneficial to their general health. But there are other equally possible interpretations that were not overlooked

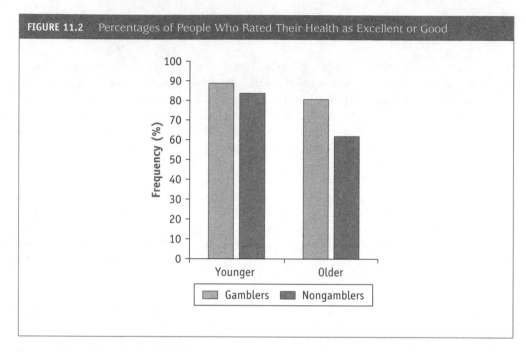

FIGURE 11.2   Percentages of People Who Rated Their Health as Excellent or Good

Source: Adapted from Desai et al. (2004).

by the researchers. If you examine Figure 11.2, you notice that the frequencies are uniform among all the groups except the older nongamblers. This could indicate that this group may contain individuals who are too sick to go out and gamble, giving the appearance that older gamblers are healthier. Again, this is nonexperimental research—we cannot say that gambling causes older people to feel healthier. It could simply be that sickness causes older people to not gamble. To make strong causal inferences, you would have to do an experiment and would probably have to provide the gambling money.

Telephone surveys allow us to contact a lot of people over a large geographic area. But they do require trained interviewers, and they do take time. Another way to gather a lot of data from a lot of people is to give them questionnaires and let the people respond at their convenience.

Conceptual Exercise 11B

For his master's thesis, Mark has decided to conduct a survey about teachers' views of administrative interference in curriculum decisions. Some of the questions he wants to ask are a bit sensitive, so he is torn between a face-to-face interview and a telephone interview. What is your advice?

Questionnaires

Self-Administered Questionnaires

Self-administered questionnaires (SAQs), as the name implies, are survey questions that are read and answered by the respondent with little or no direct contact with the researcher. Relative to the interview, self-administered questionnaires have two major advantages: They are cheaper and faster. If your research question can be answered by a self-administered questionnaire, then it is probably your best choice. Of course, there are limitations to SAQs. Because respondents complete a questionnaire on their own, they must be able to read and follow instructions. For the respondent, this requires literacy, and for the researcher, this means that the questionnaire must be well written.

Another advantage that was mentioned earlier is that SAQs give respondents a stronger feeling of anonymity than the interview methods or focus groups (which we will look at later).

If you decide to use self-administered questionnaires to survey, your next decision is how to distribute and collect them. If it is possible to gather your respondents into groups (e.g., students in classrooms), then group administration is probably your best option. However, if your respondents are not available in groups, you could mail your questionnaires. Another option is to post your questionnaire on the Internet and invite people to complete it online.

Group-Administered Questionnaires

This survey method requires that you send people out to distribute and collect the questionnaire, and as mentioned above, it only works if your respondents can be brought together into groups. If we were interested in drug use by high school students, a **group-administered questionnaire** is the most reasonable approach. Our participants are already grouped for us in their classrooms, so we have only to select the classrooms and administer the questionnaires.

At the beginning of our discussion of surveys, we asked whether marijuana use is widespread. This is an important question for policy makers, educators, parents, and people working in the area of drug addiction and rehabilitation.

The Research Problem. In 2002, the Alberta Alcohol and Drug Abuse Commission (AADAC) used a group-administered questionnaire to survey students in junior and senior high schools in Alberta, Canada (Archibald, 2002; George, Dyer, & Levin, 2002). The survey included questions on a variety of behaviors, but we will only focus on marijuana use.

The Hypothesis. The purpose of the research was to describe the prevalence of drug use in students and to identify any factors that may make drug use more or less likely.

Selection of Participants. A multistage stratified sampling procedure was used to randomly select 89 schools throughout the province. The sample included 3,394 students in Grades 7 to 12.

The Variables. The questionnaire contained questions about drug use and variables that had been identified as possible risk factors and possible protective factors for drugs. The 15-page questionnaire had 84 questions.

The Design. A group-administered survey was used to ask students in Grades 7 to 12 about their use of drugs, particularly over the past 12 months.

The Statistical Analysis. Descriptive statistics were calculated on prevalence by grade and gender. Simple and multiple regression procedures were used to identify risk and protective factors and drug use.

The Results. The prevalence of cannabis use (marijuana or hash) in the past year among students was 27.6%, and there were no gender differences. When asked if they had ever tried cannabis, 56.7% of Grade 12 students reported that they had.

The rate of cannabis use increases dramatically with grade (see Figure 11.3). By Grade 12, more than 40% of those surveyed had used cannabis at least once in the past year.

A number of potential risk factors and potential protective factors were correlated with cannabis use (see Table 11.3). The risk factors that were identified with regression analysis included age, history of family substance abuse, family discord, grade at first use of cigarettes, and grade of first use of cannabis. Some of the factors that were identified as protective were parental monitoring, social skills, availability of prosocial activities, connection to school, and positive adults in the neighborhood.

The Conclusions. The report concludes that cannabis use in Alberta (27.6%) is lower than that reported in other provinces (Ontario [29.8%] or Nova Scotia [36.5%]). This may or may not be the case due to methodological differences among these studies. Both the Ontario and Nova Scotia studies used **passive consent** to participate. That is, all students were included in the study unless the consent form was returned with a parental refusal. The Alberta researchers were required to achieve **active consent;** students were only included in the study if their parents returned the consent form. This small difference in handling

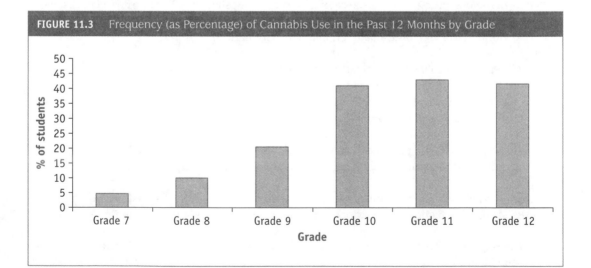

FIGURE 11.3   Frequency (as Percentage) of Cannabis Use in the Past 12 Months by Grade

TABLE 11.3 Correlations Between Risk/Protective Factors and Cannabis Use	
Risk Factors	*r*
Peer risk behavior	.638
Ease of access (cannabis)	.460
Ease of access (cigarettes)	.340
Age	.293
Parental approval of smoking, drinking, and using drugs	.282
School marks	−.281
Early signs of leaving school	.270
School disconnect	.265
Family history of abuse	.248
Protective Factors	*r*
Parental monitoring	−.430
Social skills	−.425
School marks	−.281
School connection	−.260
Adult neighbors	−.240
Participation in prosocial activities	−.151
Peer influences	−.141

Note: All correlations are $p < .01$.

of informed consent may make comparison of these studies misleading. Alberta may show a lower prevalence of use because the students who are using cannabis were not included in the study. Why? Perhaps because their consent forms were never brought home from school. After all, one of the risk factors is school disconnect.

The factors that have been identified give a clear direction for action on the part of the schools, community, and parents. Schools can focus on engaging students to become integrated members of school life, particularly for students who are struggling. The community needs to promote pro-recreational activities, and parents need to monitor their children and help them develop good social skills.

Relative to interview methods, group-administered questionnaires save time and money. We can obtain information from a large group of respondents in the time it would take to complete one interview. Another advantage arises from the fact that someone is present while the participants complete the questionnaire. This makes it possible to give verbal instructions and to answer questions.

Last but not least, group-administered questionnaires produce very high response rates. As we will see below, response rate is a real problem with mailed surveys but a real strength of the group-administered approach. Given that *you* distribute and collect the questionnaires, you can achieve a response rate close to 100%. This is an important consideration because the validity of your study depends on having a high response rate.

Mail-Out Questionnaires

Mail-out questionnaires are a quick and economical method for distributing your questionnaire to a large number of people spread over a large area. They also have the advantage of giving respondents a confident feeling of confidentiality and anonymity. People may feel more at ease answering personal questions in their own home and at their own pace. Sounds like the perfect method—why not use mail surveys all the time? Mail surveys are very popular; in fact, you have probably received one yourself, or perhaps one was sent to your house (it may not have been specifically addressed to you). Did you complete it? Did you return it? These two questions address the main problem with mail surveys—a problem of response rate. There is a further problem in that, as a researcher, you do not have control over who completes the questionnaire. You must rely on the recipient to read your cover letter and follow the instructions you have included.

If you received a mail survey, completed it, and returned it, congratulations! Congratulations because you are in the minority. Although the response rate for a group-administered questionnaire may be close to 100%, you can expect that only 10% to 20% of your mail surveys will be returned. For example, the Alberta government conducted a large-scale mail survey of all households in the province and got a response rate of only 12%.

This is a serious problem: Not only does it increase the cost (you may have to print and distribute five times the number of surveys that you need), but it directly casts doubt on the validity of your survey. Who are these respondents? Those who respond are likely the people for whom the questionnaire is most salient, people who feel strongly about the issues addressed in your study, or people who may have an axe to grind. Are these people truly representative of the entire group to whom the questionnaire was mailed? There is really no way to know, and because of this, certain measures must be taken to maximize the response rate. In the appendix are some suggestions for ways of increasing response rates to mail-out surveys.

Today, most people have access to the Internet. In the next section, we will look at research using the Internet, a method that promises to be easier and faster than other survey procedures.

Conceptual Exercise 11C

Clair, an undergraduate student in psychology, mailed a questionnaire asking undergraduate students to report their feelings about the recent decision by their university to increase tuition fees the following year by 10%. She discovered that the students were incensed about this decision. What cautions would you give to Clair before she reports that the students as a whole object vigorously to the decision of the university?

Internet Questionnaires

We discussed the problem of anonymity earlier in this chapter. Respondents may be more willing to answer honestly when they feel confident that they remain anonymous. **Internet questionnaires** provide a strong feeling of anonymity.

Posting your questionnaire on the Internet means no paper, and it saves having to pay someone to enter the responses into a computer. Another advantage of using the Internet to gather your data is that you can target special groups. For example, if you were interested in issues related to animal rights, you could post your questionnaire on an animal welfare Web site. This way, you are reaching those people who are interested in the topic.

Internet questionnaire research has many of the same problems as other questionnaire research. People who do not use or cannot be reached by telephone will not be included in a telephone survey. Similarly, people who do not use the Internet will not be included in an Internet survey. Social desirability and other kinds of response bias must be considered in any kind of interview or survey research. But Internet research has special problems. For example, the government of Alberta conducted a survey asking how it should direct government spending. It sent 1,163,055 questionnaires to households across the province and asked for a mailed response. It got a low response rate of 12%, but it also invited people to respond at its Web site. The response it got on the Internet survey was almost as high as the paper version: 114,000 for the Internet compared to 144,000 by mail. Wonderful, except it had to carefully screen the Internet submissions. Here is the problem. Let's say you want the government to increase funding of postsecondary education. You think that perhaps the government should remove tuition for university and college. So you and all your friends go to the Web site and complete as many surveys as you can. Your plan is to flood the government with surveys that support your view. It sounds like a good plan, but the researchers had already considered this problem. To guard against you and your friends (or special interest groups) trying to manipulate the outcome of the survey, they checked all Internet submissions that came from the same Internet provider and were received at a similar time. If the responses were identical and the submission time was consecutive, only two responses were accepted. With these rules, they excluded only 478 Internet submissions. Multiple submissions can also occur with a paper surveys, and they also excluded 310 paper submissions that they thought were suspicious.

As access to the Internet at home becomes more common, this method may become an important method of survey research. Also, using e-mail to reach people may become useful, particularly for groups or institutions that want to survey their members.

General Guidelines for Writing Survey Questions

The wording of your questions is important for all types of surveys, whether interview or questionnaire. Before we discuss writing the questions, we emphasize that the most important step you can take to ensure that your questions are asking what you intend them to ask is to pretest your items. Do this by recruiting some volunteers to read and answer your questions while you monitor them to note any problems that might arise. If they are uncertain about what you are asking or how to answer, it is best to catch it before you begin your research. After the pretest, it is a good idea to do a pilot study. A pilot study is conducted exactly the same as your research project but on a limited number of respondents. The pilot study gives you one last chance to catch problems that you missed in pretesting.

The following are important points to consider when you start writing your questions:

- **Keep your questions short and simple.** This is not a place to practice your literary flamboyance. You want to be sure that your participants clearly understand your questions.

For example, "Would you be inclined to the practice of locating electronic gaming machines in local drinking establishments?" can be simplified to "Are you in favor of placing video lottery terminals in local bars?"

- **Avoid using _and_ in your questions.** This is related to the first point on keeping your questions simple. You want to be sure that you are measuring no more than one dimension with each question. For example, the statement, "I prefer working with colleagues who are pleasant and competitive" is measuring attitudes on two dimensions. Break this item into two separate statements.

- **Do not use biased wording in your questions.** For example, no one will agree to the statement, "I support the killing of innocent Iraqis." But you may find agreement with the statement, "I support the war in Iraq."

- **Be sure you avoid using double negatives.** This may seem obvious, but we have seen instances of less obvious negation-type survey items. For example, in 1998, our city held a plebiscite to decide whether video lottery terminals should be removed. The question was, "Are you in favor of Bylaw No. 1853 which says, City Council requests the Government of Alberta through the Alberta Liquor and Gaming Commission to remove Video Lottery Terminals from the city of Edmonton?" If you wanted to vote against video lottery terminals (VLT) and you were prepared to vote NO to VLTs, you had better be careful because a NO meant YES to VLTs. On the same issue, another region had a much better question: "Should the Province of New Brunswick continue to permit the legal and regulated operation of video gaming devices (commonly known as video lottery terminals or VLTs)?"

Type of Questions

Questions can be of two types: open-ended or forced choice. **Open-ended questions** are items that simply have a blank space for the response. They allow the respondents to answer in any way they wish (provided you have given enough space). Open-ended questions are the best choice if you are not sure how people will answer a question or if you are looking for diverse responses. A disadvantage of open-ended questions is that they may be difficult to analyze. Usually, content analysis is used to identify recurring themes in the responses and then count the frequency of each theme. This provides a measure of the prevalence of each response. On the other hand, you may be more interested in the unique and creative responses than in the most common. Either way, open-ended questions require a lot of reading, which can be time-consuming and costly. It should be noted that software is available that can automatically analyze open-ended responses (e.g., SPSS Text Analysis for Surveys), and there is also software that can scan written responses (e.g., SPSS MRScan).

Forced-choice or **closed-ended questions** are items that include response categories. This makes them easier to analyze and easier to answer because you have already created the response categories. The only problem with forced-choice items is that you must be sure that the response choices include all the possible responses people can make. You do not want to frustrate your respondents by not providing a category for their response. You also need to provide clear instructions that only one response may be selected. A common practice is to include an OTHER category. If you decide to include OTHER as a category, be sure to leave a blank for people to enter their response. But be warned, if too many people select

OTHER, you have essentially created an open-ended question, and you will have to analyze it as an open-ended question.

General Rules for Self-Administered Questionnaires

If you are conducting a survey with questionnaires, it is very important that it looks professional. Take the time to format the final questionnaires so they are easy to read and organized in a way that is easy to follow.

If your questionnaire is being mailed, you should include a cover letter with sufficient information for your participants to decide whether or not to participate. Similar to the informed consent form discussed in Chapter 3, your letter should describe the purpose of the study, who is doing the research, and what will be done with the information. Include also an estimate of how long the survey takes and provide contact information if they have any questions. You should also indicate that participation is voluntary and, if the information is to be shared, how you will keep the respondent's information confidential.

Your questionnaire should have a clear organization so that your respondent does not get lost filling it out. Place simple demographic questions at the beginning where people expect them to appear. When asking age, your respondents may be more comfortable reporting their date of birth rather than their age in years. People may also be sensitive about questions of income, so instead of asking people to specify an amount, provide income ranges that they can select.

For the rest of your questionnaire, try to organize the questions by topic. You do not want to annoy your respondent with questions that jump from one topic to another.

Often questionnaires contain branching questions (e.g., if you have a dog, then proceed to Question 15). Try to arrange your questions to keep branching to a minimum, but when branching is necessary, make it easy for your respondent by using boxes or arrows such as the following:

Have you played a video lottery terminal within the last year?

Yes ☐
No ☐

If yes, have you enjoyed your experience?   Yes ☐
No ☐

There are many different ways to format a question on a survey. Let's say you want to measure people's attitudes toward premarital sex. You could ask a simple yes/no question.

Are you in favor of premarital sex?   Yes ☐   No ☐

Or you could use a Likert-type scale, where the question is phrased as a statement.

Indicate on a scale of 1 to 7 your opinion of the following statement:
I think premarital sex is good for a couple.

1	2	3	4	5	6	7
Strongly disagree	Disagree	Somewhat disagree	Neither agree nor disagree	Somewhat agree	Agree	Strongly agree

For more details on measurement and scales, see Chapter 5. Let's turn to yet another way to find answers to your research questions.

OBSERVING GROUP BEHAVIOR: THE FOCUS GROUP

Focus group research is conducted by recording the discussion of a small group of people. Think of it as a structured interview with 12 people. Typically, questionnaires are completed, and a **moderator/facilitator** gives a presentation on the topic. By asking questions and directing the conversation, the facilitator can probe for answers and explore relevant lines of conversation. Unlike an interview, where the discourse is between the interviewer and interviewee, in a focus group, the moderator can fade into the background and let the discussion develop on its own. Focus groups often result in lively and fast-paced banter, and they are usually recorded so the content of the discussion can be analyzed later. The discourse is analyzed with qualitative techniques that involve identifying relevant themes and examining how they are interrelated.

The purpose of focus group research is not to investigate the prevalence of opinion but instead to identify and explore variables that are relevant to the research question. Often, the research is used as a starting point for questionnaire development and qualitative research. In addition, focus groups are often used in marketing to test advertising campaigns.

Focus group researchers might ask questions such as the following:

What are the service needs and experiences of persons with traumatic brain injury?

How can we reduce the student dropout rate?

What are good strategies for health care professionals to use when reporting injuries from child abuse?

Focus groups are like an interview except the participants can interact and generate ideas from one another. This can give you information that you might miss from interviewing people one at a time. In a focus group, someone may respond to a question, and spontaneously others may agree or disagree, but the discussion that follows can produce important information.

The dynamic nature of focus groups can also lead to problems. It is possible to have a few assertive or aggressive participants take over the discussion. If they control the discussion, you may never hear the views of the less assertive. A facilitator must be skilled in mediating these situations so that everyone gets a chance to talk. Let's look at an example of the use of a focus group to explore the lifestyle of young drivers.

The Research Problem. The insurance companies have the data: Young drivers (younger than 25) are more likely to crash than any other age group. Much of the psychology literature has focused on variables related to driving performance, but recently interest has turned to variables related to lifestyle. The idea is that your lifestyle reflects your attitudes and motivations, and it is these factors that have an important influence on driving behavior.

The Hypothesis. In his review of the literature, Møller (2004) indicated that correlations have been found between lifestyle factors and driving behavior. However, his interest was in understanding how and why this relationship exists. To address this question, he conducted focus groups with young drivers to explore how aspects of their lifestyle might influence their driving behavior.

Selection of Participants. Twenty-nine young drivers (18–24 years) who had their license for at least 6 months were recruited to participate.

The Design. Four same-sex focus groups were conducted with participants from two education levels. The moderator used a loosely structured guide to address the various aspects of lifestyle and driving behavior.

The Statistical Analysis. The focus groups were videotaped and later transcribed for qualitative analysis.

The Results. Some of the results of the qualitative analysis procedure are shown in Figure 11.4.
Aspects of lifestyle that were related to driving behavior were assigned to three categories, each with two dimensions. Leisure time included their interests and the degree to which these interests were planned in advance. An example of leisure time activities at one extreme is, "I party with my friends, that's all I do." Others reported more organized activities, "I do sports, gymnastics. . . ." Within friends was group structure and social life. For some, the activities determined the group structure. For example, they would meet their teammates for a sporting activity. For others, the group of friends was unplanned, and selection of activities was impulsive. This latter group used the car as a focus of their activity: "A

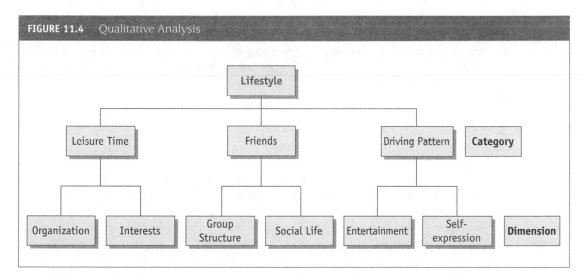

FIGURE 11.4   Qualitative Analysis

Source: Adapted from Møller (2004).

friend of mine drives a [Volkswagen] Golf, yeah, and then we drive into town on Friday nights. Then we stop maybe three times to whistle at some girls. . . ." You get the idea. Driving pattern was broken into entertainment and self-expression. Some talked about their adventures of handling the car in difficult and dangerous situations or as a tool in self-expression, as in showing off and competing for attention through risky driving behaviors.

The Conclusion. Although Møller (2004) indicates that his study is not intended to be representative of young drivers, he points out that a next step would be to test these relationships in a large-scale study. Indeed, the strength of focus group research is to explore the variables that are important to your research question. In this research, Møller identified that "a lifestyle with few planned activities, few hobbies and meeting with friends as the centre of activities seems to facilitate the use of the car in a way that leads to risk-taking behaviour" (p. 1087).

CHAPTER SUMMARY

In **observational research,** the researcher is mainly concerned with making systematic observations of behavior. **Naturalistic observation** involves making systematic observations of behavior in the environment where it occurs naturally. This method has high external validity because observations are made in the natural setting, and it also limits **reactivity** because observations can be made unobtrusively. Sometimes it may be impossible to observe a behavior without becoming a participant ourselves; in this case, we are conducting **participant observation.** Unfortunately, some behaviors may only occur in specific situations or under certain conditions. In those cases, we may want to create those conditions by conducting **laboratory observations.** In the laboratory, we may be trading off some external validity by bringing our research into the artificial environment of the laboratory, but this may be worth the cost by permitting the observation of behavior that might otherwise be impossible.

Observational research is well suited for studies of overt behavior, but sometimes it may be preferable to ask people about their behaviors by conducting a survey. **Surveys** involve asking people questions, either verbally, as in an **interview,** or in writing, by having them complete a **questionnaire.** Besides measuring self-reported behavior, surveys permit us to ask respondents about their attitudes and opinions. **Face-to-face interviews** are time-consuming and expensive but permit the development of rapport between the interviewer and respondent that may be necessary for exploring sensitive research topics. **Telephone interviews** permit surveys of large geographical areas without wasting time on travel, but they must be relatively short.

Another approach to surveying is to ask people to complete a questionnaire. **Group-administered questionnaires** allow rapid data collection and a very high response rate but are only useful if the respondents can be found in groups (such as students in classrooms). **Mail-out questionnaires** are used to survey people over a large geographical area. They can be relatively economical but suffer from low response rate. **Internet questionnaires** are economical and are useful for surveys of specific populations (e.g., people visiting a Web site).

Focus groups could be described as face-to-face interviews of a small group of people. They are often used to measure attitudes, opinions, or self-reported behavior of select groups (e.g., attitudes of young people on the use of condoms). Focus groups have the advantage of revealing information that may not surface in face-to-face interviews. This is a result of the dynamics of the groups. Although this is an advantage of focus group research, it may also be a disadvantage (e.g., if a few forceful members dominate the discussion).

ANSWERS TO CONCEPTUAL EXERCISES

Conceptual Exercise 11A

The concern here is reactivity. Because the researcher is visible to the workers and clearly collecting data about their behavior, there is a high probability that the mechanics, knowing that they are being observed, will behave differently than they would in normal circumstances. Our researcher might have considered a more unobtrusive way of gathering her data. Or she might have considered participant observation.

Conceptual Exercise 11B

The simple answer is that Mark should survey his teachers by telephone. They might be more likely to give Mark honest answers to his questions on the telephone.

Conceptual Exercise 11C

The students who took the time to respond to this mail-out questionnaire may be those who have strong feelings. As a result, the sample that Clair is using to infer the attitude of the student body at large may be biased.

FAQ

Q1: Isn't it almost impossible to guard against reactivity?

A1: Reactivity occurs when people alter their behavior as a reaction to being measured. This is the main advantage of naturalistic observation. The hope is that your observations will not be noticed by those being observed, and thus you avoid the problem of reactivity.

Q2: How can you guard against bias when doing observational research? Won't you just see what you want to see?

A2: Bias can be controlled by clearly defining your behaviors before making observations. It is also a good idea to keep your observers "blind" to the research hypothesis and to use more than one observer so you can calculate measures of interobserver agreement.

Q3: Can a researcher rely too much on qualitative data or quantitative data? Is there a balance?

A3: It is probably not an issue of reliance on one type of data over another, but rather that some research questions are better suited to quantitative and others to qualitative data analysis. It is not a matter of achieving a balance but rather the appropriate use of different approaches.

Q4: People's words and actions aren't always the same. Given this, how can we be sure that self-reported behavior is a valid indicator of true behavior?

A4: Self-reported behavior may not be a valid indicator of people's true behavior, and as such, we must always be cautious of our interpretation of self-reports.

Q5: How can you be sure that people are answering questions honestly?

A5: Again, as in Question 4, we must be cautious in interpreting our research. You can include questions more than once in a survey to check that people are at least consistent in their responses. Of course, this may only indicate a good liar.

Q6: Wouldn't an introductory statement on a questionnaire immediately create a bias in the responses?

A6: The introductory statement should provide the potential participant with enough information to make a decision to participate, but it does not have to reveal the research hypothesis. You should be able to write an informative introduction without biasing the participant.

Q7: In observational research, do you always know what behaviors to observe before you begin?

A7: Usually, you do make clear definitions of what is, and what is not, the behavior of interest. However, these definitions should be based on a review of the literature and/or some pilot research. If, once in the field, you find that your definitions are not adequate, it is probably best to stop and make changes before continuing.

Q8: In participant observation, isn't there a risk that your observations will not be objective? After all, you are a participant.

A8: This is a real concern because one of the advantages of participant observation is that you can become a member of the group and relate your subjective experiences but report them in an objective manner. A useful safeguard is to have others, who have not been participants, read and critique your observations. They may be in a better position to objectively challenge your observations and force you to be objective about your observations.

CHAPTER EXERCISES

1. What is the difference between naturalistic observation and participant observation?
2. What are the advantages and disadvantages of laboratory observation studies?
3. What are some of the problems with conducting participant observation research?
4. For what type of research question would laboratory observation be preferred to naturalistic observation?
5. What is the distinction between a survey and a questionnaire?
6. What advantages do interviews have over questionnaires?
7. What are the advantages and disadvantages of mailed questionnaires?

8. What advantages do group-administered questionnaires have over mailed questionnaires?

9. What are some of the problems with mailed questionnaires?

10. You have a short questionnaire and you want to survey people across a wide area. What approach is best?

11. What are the advantages and disadvantages of open-ended questions?

12. How are focus groups and interviews similar? How are they different?

CHAPTER PROJECTS

1. Provide an example research question for each research approach listed below. For each example, include an explanation of why you think this is the best approach: naturalistic observation, participant observation, laboratory observation.

2. You are interested in the experiences of people living on the street. Discuss the advantages and disadvantages of the various approaches presented in this chapter as they relate to answering your research question.

3. Conduct a literature search to find an example of research employing each of the approaches described in this chapter. For each example, discuss the advantages of the design and the feasibility of using a different research method.

4. Search the Internet for an example of an Internet questionnaire. Evaluate the effectiveness of this questionnaire.

APPENDIX: WAYS TO INCREASE RESPONSE RATES TO MAIL-OUT SURVEYS

NOTE: We do not have empirical data to support our suggestions. We gathered them from other writers and researchers.

- Hand address and stamp your envelopes. If your house is like ours, you probably receive your share of junk mail. We have all become experts in identifying junk mail before we even open the envelope. The computer-generated label and the metered postage are usually good indicators. It is much more likely that a hand-addressed envelope with a real stamp will be noticed. It was important enough for someone (a real human being) to address and mail to your house, so it's probably important enough to complete and return.

- Include a good cover letter. This may be your only contact with the respondent, so make sure the letter is clear, concise, and persuasive. For more on the cover letter, see the section on general rules for self-administered questionnaires.

- Include a self-addressed stamped envelope. Only the most motivated respondents will go to the trouble of providing their own envelope and postage.

- Paying your respondents can increase your response rate. Research has found that including $1.00 in cash with a statement thanking respondents for their time can increase your response rate (Whiteman, Langenberg, Kjerulff, McCarter, & Flaws, 2003).

It is hard to believe that such a small amount would make a difference, but it probably reflects the operation of the principle of reciprocity. If you give people something, they feel they must reciprocate.

- Send a reminder out about a week after you have received your first bunch of questionnaires. This will remind those who have not returned their surveys and thank those who have. Be sure to include a telephone number if a questionnaire needs to be re-sent.

REFERENCES

Archibald, J. (2002). *The Alberta youth experience survey 2002: Technical report.* Edmonton, Alberta, Canada: Alberta Alcohol and Drug Abuse Commission.

Desai, R. A., Maciejewski, P. K., Dausey, D. J., Caldarone, B. J., & Potenza, M. N. (2004). Health correlates of recreational gambling in older adults. *American Journal of Psychiatry, 161*(9), 1672–1679.

Durant, L. E., & Carey, M. P. (2000). Self-administered questionnaires versus face-to-face interviews in assessing sexual behavior in young women. *Archives of Sexual Behavior, 29*(4), 309–322.

George, S., Dyer, A., & Levin, P. (2002). *The Alberta youth experience survey 2002: An overview of risk and protective factors.* Edmonton, Alberta, Canada: Alberta Alcohol and Drug Abuse Commission.

Goffman, E. (1961). *Asylums: Essays on the social situation of mental patients and other inmates.* New York: Anchor.

Langdridge, D., Connolly, K., & Sheeran, P. (2000). Reasons for wanting a child: A network analytic study. *Journal of Reproductive and Infant Psychology, 18*(4), 321–338.

Møller, M. (2004). An explorative study of the relationship between lifestyle and driving behaviour among young drivers. *Accident Analysis and Prevention, 36,* 1081–1088.

Monaghan, L. F. (2003). Danger on the doors: Bodily risk in a demonised occupation. *Health, Risk, and Society, 5*(1), 11–31.

Renninger, L. A., Wade, T. J., & Grammer, K. (2004). Getting the female glance: Patterns and consequences of male nonverbal behavior in courtship contexts. *Evolution and Human Behavior, 25,* 416–431.

Underwood, M. K., Scott, B. L., Galperin, M. B., Bjornstad, G. J., & Sexton, A. M. (2004). An observational study of social exclusion under varied conditions: Gender and developmental differences. *Child Development, 75*(5), 1538–1555.

Whiteman, M. K., Langenberg, P., Kjerulff, K., McCarter, R., & Flaws, J. A. (2003). A randomized trial of incentives to improve response rates to a mailed women's health questionnaire. *Journal of Women's Health, 12*(8), 821–828.

Visit the study site at www.sagepub.com/evansmprstudy for practice quizzes and other study resources.

Program Evaluation, Archival Research, and Meta-Analytic Designs

OBJECTIVES

After studying this chapter, students should be able to

- Describe the purposes of program evaluation
- Discuss why a needs analysis is required in program evaluation
- Discuss why it is important to use objective measures in program evaluation
- Describe how ethics can influence design selection
- Define archival research
- Explain how archival research differs from other types of research
- Describe what archives are used for research
- Define meta-analysis
- Describe how meta-analysis and a literature review differ

Sometimes writers of textbooks discover that they want to include material that is important but does not seem to fit nicely within the structure of the text. That is the case here. We think it is important for students taking research methods courses to know something about program evaluation, archival research, and meta-analysis, but please be aware that our coverage of these topics is somewhat brief.

Consider the following questions:

Is this new enrichment program for inner-city kids doing what it was designed to do?

Are insurance companies justified in exacting higher premiums from young male drivers than from young female drivers?

When we examine the hundreds of studies of the frustration-aggression hypothesis, some supporting and some refuting the hypothesis, what can we conclude?

PROGRAM EVALUATION

Several years ago, one of us was hired to evaluate the effectiveness of a government program designed to help disabled people learn basic living skills. Imagine her surprise when she learned that the frontline workers did not really know what the goals of the program were, and so no data on whether those goals were achieved were available.

Program evaluation is a crucial process. After all, how can you justify spending taxpayers' money on a program without having put in place ways to evaluate the effectiveness of it? Program evaluation (sometimes called *evaluation research*) is a kind of applied research, the goal of which is to determine if a policy or specific program is doing what the creators of the policy or program intended it to do.

Program evaluation is not a research design but instead indicates something about the motivation of the research. It is applied research with a focus on evaluation. The researchers might ask questions such as the following:

Has the Breakfast Program at Sunnyside Elementary met its goals of improving performance of third graders?

Has the First Year Scholarship program at Yale met its goals of increasing first-year enrollment and student satisfaction?

Has the At Home Care program in Tampa, Florida, met its goals of reducing the number of hospital beds occupied by people diagnosed with early Alzheimer's disease?

Program evaluators typically do more than assess whether a program is meeting its goals. They will also determine if the program is truly needed, is cost-effective, and is being run efficiently, and they will offer suggestions for improvement. Ideally, program evaluation is considered in advance of offering a new program so that problems such as the one described at the beginning of this section do not occur. When people create a program, they must think about not only the goals but also how they will determine if those goals are being met. Moreover, if evaluation is built into the program, then ongoing improvements can be made.

Let's look at the process involved in creating a program.

> ## FYI
>
> Program evaluation is also called evaluation research because the evaluation may be of something other than a program. For example, needs assessment research is research with the purpose of evaluating needs. *Formative research* is evaluation research that is conducted as part of the creation or formative stages of a program. *Summative research* is evaluation that is focused on assessing the summed benefits of a program. These are just some of the terms used to refer to the broad area of evaluation research. But what unites these endeavors is the common motivation to use research procedures for evaluation.

Determining Need

Obviously, we would not institute a program unless there was a need. A **needs analysis** is a way of determining whether there are enough people who would benefit from and use the program and whether the program would meet the needs of those people. Imagine a headline in a local newspaper such as the following:

Baby found toddling down Main Street at midnight!!

We would not immediately begin designing a program to educate parents about the dangers of letting their babies out at night, would we? Not without determining if this is a widespread problem.

Determining need might involve examining available data (archival research), surveying potential users of the program, and/or conducting focus groups within the target community. Once it has been determined that a need exists, that the program can be expected to meet that need, and that people will use the program, program evaluators must make decisions about what kinds of measures should be taken so that the program can be properly evaluated.

Selecting Outcome Measures

Most programs have several goals and subgoals. Measures of whether those goals have been met must be determined in advance. It is particularly important that those measures be as objective as possible because often the people who collect the data are the frontline workers or others who have a vested interest in the success of the program. The more objective these measures are, the less likely it is that bias can be introduced by the data collector.

Most social programs have goals that include improvement in the life of the individuals using the program, and many include broader goals such as improvement in the community as a whole. User satisfaction is another measure that is often taken. Care must be taken to match the outcome measures with the goals of the program and to minimize any bias that might be introduced by the people doing the measuring.

Conceptual Exercise 12A

Some Seattle residents became concerned about motorcycle safety following a summer in which eight riders died in crashes. There was a call to change laws to restrict the size of bike a new rider could own, and there were also suggestions to legislate mandatory riding lessons. If you were called to evaluate the situation, what would you do?

Ethical Constraints on Program Evaluation Research

Like a lot of applied research, there are limitations on the kind of research design that can be ethically used in program evaluation. Imagine we want to evaluate a program designed to help teens with substance abuse problems. From a *design* point of view, a good approach would be to randomly assign troubled teens to the program and to a nontreatment control group. From an *ethical* point of view, of course, this is not a good approach at all. Program evaluation researchers tend to use other designs that might lack some experimental control but are ethically more acceptable such as nonequivalent control group, time series, and pretest-posttest designs.

Let's look at some program evaluation research that focused on youth crime.

The Research Problem. Intervening with young offenders is becoming more of a concern these days. It seems prudent to "nip the problem in the bud" rather than to wait until the offender is a more hardened criminal. This was the interest of Claire Nee and Tom Ellis of the United Kingdom (Nee & Ellis, 2005).

The Needs Analysis. In 1996, a report (Audit Commission Report) was published. The authors of this report determined that there was a need in the United Kingdom to create programs to reduce criminality in children and youth. The report recommended that programs focus on more intensive supervision of chronic young offenders and on crime prevention strategies for youth at risk of offending. In response to this report, the Persistent Young Offender Project (PYOP) was developed.

Nee and Ellis (2005) wanted to evaluate the effectiveness of PYOP with a targeted group of youth. They recommended that an initial risk/needs assessment be conducted. An instrument called the Level of Service Inventory–Revised (LSI-R) was used to do this. With this instrument, criminogenic risks and needs of the target (intervention) group and a non-intervention group of child and juvenile offenders were measured. The LSI-R assesses risk factors such as antisocial associates, attitudes, personality, and criminal history.

The Program. The PYOP was designed to help young chronic offenders, offenders with special needs such as sex offenders, and children between 7 and 12 deemed to be at risk for offending.

The program differed from other programs in the following ways:

- It served much younger children.
- It served children at risk who, at the time, were not yet involved in the criminal justice system but who had been referred by social workers, parents, or other concerned individuals.

The program strategies included the following:

- One-on-one mentoring in areas of education, anger management, and constructive use of time
- Group work in areas of antisocial behavior, problem solving, victim awareness, substance abuse, and so on
- Music, art, and drama workshops
- Outdoor activities

The Goals. The primary goal of the PYOP was to reduce reoffending among chronic young offenders. A secondary goal was proactive: to prevent youth at risk from offending.

The Outcome Measures. The LSI-R was the primary measure for determining risk of reoffending. Participants in the program were assessed every 6 months for change in their risk levels for a period of 30 months.

Other measures were taken, but we will discuss only the primary LSI-R measure.

The Results. Forty-one youth comprised the PYOP intervention group. A group of 19 youth referred to the program but who dropped out within the first 2 weeks was used for comparison. Nee and Ellis (2005) noted that the comparison youth, although likely to have been initially different from the intervention youth, were similar in age, background, and eligibility for the program with similar LSI-R scores at the outset.

Conceptual Exercise 12B

What are the problems with the comparison group that Nee and Ellis (2005) used? How and why might that group be a poor control group?

We will describe only some of the findings here. In terms of descriptive statistics, the overall LSI-R scores at the outset for the intervention group* (PYOP) were $M = 17.48$, $SD = 8.5$ and after 6 months of treatment were $M = 14.53$, $SD = 8.6$.

Inferentially, the mean LSI-R score improved significantly with treatment, t [df not provided] $= 3.60$, $p < .001$.

Because Nee and Ellis (2005) were not interested in age as a factor but thought it might influence the effectiveness of the program, they used a 2×2 analysis of covariance

---

*Comparable statistics for the comparison group were not provided.

(ANCOVA) to assess the effect of the program on LSI-R measures with age as a covariate. One factor was time of testing. Nee and Ellis compared the LSI-R measures at the start of the program and 6 months later. The second factor was group: PYOP and comparison. A significant interaction between time of testing and group was found, $F(1, 57) = 10.51$, $p < .002$, as was a significant effect of the covariate age, $F(1, 57) = 5.95$, $p < .01$. Further comparisons (adjusted with Bonferroni's t) determined that there was no significant difference between the two groups at the outset of the program, but 6 months later, the PYOP group improved significantly, whereas the comparison group worsened ($p = .039$). The authors reported that the effect size ($\eta^2 = .16$) was similar to previous studies of intervention with juvenile offenders on recidivism.

Further analysis showed that the positive effect of the program was greatest in the first 6 months but was maintained over time.

The Conclusions. Nee and Ellis (2005) concluded that intervention with young offenders is more likely to be successful if it is longer term and with more attention to individual needs in noncustodial settings. They indicate that more research is needed on the effectiveness of programs for child offenders.

> **FYI**
>
> Evaluation research is not really a research design. It is named such because of the motivation for the study. Various designs can be used by evaluation researchers, and they may be qualitative and/or quantitative. The inclusion of some qualitative measures can have a lot of impact on funding agencies. For example, if you are evaluating a program that helps prostitutes get off the street, then a measure of the number of individuals helped makes sense as a quantitative measure. But powerful stories of how individuals have been helped (a qualitative measure) can reinforce the decisions made by funding agencies.

ARCHIVAL RESEARCH

Earlier, we showed you some research by Nakonezny, Reddick, and Rodgers (2004) on the effects of the Oklahoma City bombing on the divorce rate of residents of that state. They did not collect the divorce rate data themselves; rather, they obtained data that had already been collected by others for different purposes. Information that has been collected for some reason other than the research project at hand is archival information, and researchers using such data are conducting **archival research**. There are many kinds of archival data available to researchers, including census data, opinion polls, crime statistics, population demographics, health information, and so on. The term **archive** refers to both the information itself and where it is housed. Universities, governments, and corporations are all sources of archival information. Of course, probably the fastest growing archives are located in electronic databases, many of which can be accessed online.

> ### FYI
>
> Sources for archived questionnaire data include
>
> - General Social Survey from the National Opinion Research Center (NORC): http://www .icpsr.umich.edu/gss/
> - The Roper Center for Public Opinion: http://www.ropercenter.uconn.edu/
> - Polling the Nations: http://www.pollingthenations.com/

A great strength of archival research is that the information base is huge; there is information available on just about anything. Another strength is that this kind of research has no problems with participant reactivity. You will recall that reactivity refers to changes in behavior when participants know that they are being observed. This, of course, is not an issue with many forms of archival research. Experimenter bias, on the other hand, is a potential problem with archival research, and researchers must take steps to reduce the probability of this kind of bias.

Archival researchers might ask questions such as

Has the recidivism rate declined since the introduction of the three-strikes policy in California?

Has the number of people going to the ER changed since walk-in mediclinics were opened in New York City?

Has the rate of gay men seeking psychological therapy declined since the *DSM* removed homosexuality as a category of disorder?

Collecting Information From an Archive

Don't expect to walk into a university library, government building, or newspaper office and start gathering information without planning your visit beforehand. Many archives require that you register first before you will be permitted to access the archives. Always find out in advance what the archive needs from you. Students are usually accommodated, but you will probably need student ID and an explanation of your project. And many archives require that you book time in advance. So again, don't just show up!

Find out if the information you need is restricted in any way or kept in another location.

Rules and Regulations

Many archives contain documents that need to be carefully preserved. The rules for preserving documents will vary, but we include some general rules that are common to many archives.

- Use pencils, not pens, for note taking.
- Do not bring food or beverages into the reading areas.

- Knapsacks and coats are often not allowed, to prevent theft.
- Cell phones are often not allowed.
- Documents must be handled in such a way to minimize the risk of damage or loss.

If you intend to bring a laptop to record your data, make sure this is allowed in the reading area.

Planning Your Research

You should plan in advance what kinds of data you need to extract, but keep an open mind. You may find when you start reading that there are data that are interesting but that you had not thought about. Familiarize yourself with the catalog system used at the archive so that you do not waste time when you get there. Ask in advance for any information the archive makes available about its collection and study it.

At the Archive

Carefully note the full reference for each document you intend to use so that you do not have to return for that information. Make sure you understand the reason that the document was created. This will help you interpret the information in the document. Who created it and why?

Researchers certainly still visit archives and read original documents, but the Internet has reduced the need for this in many cases.

Collecting Archival Information Online

Many archives have put or are now putting their information in electronic databases accessible through the Internet. This makes it easier for researchers and eliminates the risk of damage to original documents.

Probably the first thing you should do is *Google* the archive. Many archives have their own Web sites where you can find out what online services they have and if any fees are involved with using those services. When you search a database online, you will use keywords to find documents. Be careful. If your keywords do not match the words keyed into the database by the person doing that work, you may miss important documents. Check to see if a thesaurus of keywords is available.

Do not rely on personal Web sites created by unknown people or average citizens. Just because the information is online does not make the information accurate, complete, or even true. We often tell our students, "The fact that you read it somewhere doesn't make it true." Find out if the Web site was created by an expert or, better yet, an official institution such as a university or government.

Conceptual Exercise 12C

In a previous conceptual exercise, we described a project where there was a concern about motorcycle safety. What archives would you use to conduct research on this question?

A Word of Warning

Just because your online search did not locate a document or some information, don't assume it does not exist. Sometimes you have to go to the source.

Have you ever noticed that people who experience the same event will often have very different versions of what happened? Eyewitnesses to crimes are often called upon to testify about the crime when it comes to trial. But are witnesses reliable? This is the question addressed by Fahsing, Ask, and Granhag (2004) of Norway in their archival study.

The Research Problem. Fahsing et al. (2004) noted that although there has been a lot of research into eyewitness memory for criminal events and identification of offenders, there has been little research on the recall and description of offenders by witnesses. These researchers decided to examine archival data to determine the validity of the descriptions of perpetrators given by eyewitnesses to the crime.

The Archives. The researchers collected their data from archived case files kept by the Robbery Squad at the Oslo Police Department. They targeted bank and post office robberies between 1999 and 2001, finding 48 cases that included appropriate information for the study. In particular, they needed video footage of the events.

The Predictions. The researchers made several predictions based on previous research. Some of their predictions were the following:

A positive correlation would be found between crime duration and the completeness and accuracy of the description of the perpetrator.

Witnesses to crimes involving firearms would provide less complete and accurate descriptions of perpetrators than witnesses to crimes involving knives.

Witnesses to crimes with larger numbers of perpetrators would provide less complete and accurate descriptions than witnesses to crimes with fewer perpetrators.

The Measured Variables. The researchers were interested in factors that might predict completeness and accuracy of the description of the perpetrator. They included several predictor variables, but we will discuss three: duration of crime, number of perpetrators, and type of weapon.

Two criterion variables were selected. Completeness of description was categorized into two types of attributes: basic attributes such as the offender's height, gender, build, age, and ethnicity and details that included all the other features of the offenders that the witnesses reported.

The second criterion variable was accuracy of the description, which was determined by comparing the description to the video footage. This comparison was made by two raters so that interrater reliability could be measured. An accuracy measure ranging between 0 and 1 was calculated, with 0 indicating no agreement and 1 perfect agreement.

The Results. Two hundred and fifty offender descriptions were available from witnesses to the robberies. Here are some of the descriptive statistics regarding the criterion variables of completeness and accuracy followed by their respective inferential statistics:

- **Completeness of descriptions: Descriptive statistics.** Gender of the offender was reported more often (99.6%) than any other basic attribute. The five attributes identified by the researchers as basic were among the 10 most frequently reported.

  On average, witnesses reported 9.4 attributes ($SD = 2.3$) in total and 3.9 ($SD = 1.0$) of the attributes called basic by the researchers.

- **Accuracy of descriptions: Descriptive statistics.** The overall accuracy of the individual descriptions ranged from 0.31 to 1.00 ($M = 0.74$, $SD = 0.13$). The accuracy of the descriptions of basic features ($M = 0.75$, $SD = 0.19$) was similar to the accuracy of the description of the details ($M = 0.73$, $SD = 0.21$).

  Witnesses' accuracy varied from 100% accuracy on some attributes to 20% on others. Interestingly, witnesses tended to overestimate the age of the youngest offenders (by about 3 years) and underestimate the age of the oldest offenders (by about 10 years).

  Multiple regression analyses on the completeness and accuracy measures were used to assess the researchers' inferential predictions.

- **Completeness of descriptions: Inferential statistics.** No relationship between event duration and description completeness was found. The first hypothesis was not supported.

  When the perpetrators used firearms, the descriptions of basic attributes were less complete than when the perpetrators used knives ($\beta = -0.33$, $p < .05$).* This finding supported the second hypothesis of the researchers.

  As the number of perpetrators increased, the completeness of the description decreased but only for details ($\beta = -1.51$, $p < .01$). This finding partially supports the third hypothesis.

- **Accuracy of descriptions: Inferential statistics.** The expected correlation between duration of the crime and accuracy of descriptions was found for details ($\beta = -.03$, $p < .05$) but not for basic attributes. Thus, the first hypothesis was partially supported by this finding.

  The researchers' expectation that number of perpetrators would be negatively correlated with accuracy of description was supported for both basic attributes ($\beta = -0.09$, $p < .05$) and details ($\beta = -0.23$, $p < .01$).

  Although the researchers expected that accuracy of descriptions when guns were involved would be poorer than when knives were involved, this was not the case. In fact, witnesses tended to be more accurate in their descriptions of robbers using firearms ($\beta = 0.04$, $p < .05$) than of robbers with knives, at least when it came to the description of basic attributes. No relationship was found for details.

The Conclusions. The researchers noted that many of their findings were similar to those of previous archival research. For example, they too found that typically, eyewitnesses' descriptions of robbers are general, with few useful details, and therefore they suggested that these descriptions might be helpful in eliminating suspects but less helpful in identifying perpetrators.

---

*In case you missed the description of beta weights in Chapter 2 and our note in Chapter 10, β indicates the relative importance of a variable in regression analysis. The sign (positive or negative) indicates the direction of the relationship, and the value indicates the strength of the relationship.

They noted that although the descriptions lacked useful details, they tended to be quite accurate.

They acknowledged that their predictor variables accounted for very little variance in the criterion variables but noted that some relationships were nevertheless significant.

Archival research has some true advantages over other kinds of methods. For one thing, someone else has gathered the data for you. And there is a huge amount of data available. Of course, you are limited to the variables that were of interest to the people developing the archive. They may not have recorded that crucial piece of information you need.

Whereas archival research involves the use of data that have already been collected, there is research that uses the results of previously published research. This research is called **meta-analysis** and is our next topic. Meta-analysis can be very complex. Our intention here is to introduce you to the topic.

META-ANALYSIS

A friend of one of us, Judy Cameron, was curious about the belief of many educators that rewarding children for doing things they intrinsically enjoy serves to reduce their interest in that activity. This is the *extrinsic-intrinsic motivation* debate. The idea is that extrinsically reinforcing an intrinsically motivated activity takes away its intrinsic value in some way. Many educators believe this partly because a lot of research supports the idea. Judy decided to examine the research on this problem. Instead of reviewing the literature, she conducted a meta-analysis. A meta-analysis is a measure of the *combined effect size* in many studies of the same variables. The variables may be different in terms of their operational definitions, but the underlying construct is considered the same. And this is what Judy did. She examined the extrinsic-intrinsic effect sizes in several studies and combined them to determine if the extrinsic-intrinsic hypothesis was supportable from a statistical point of view across all the studies. She concluded that it was not. The debate, however, continues.

Meta-analysis and a literature review may seem similar, but the approaches are very different. The objective of a literature review is to summarize, integrate, and critically evaluate the research that has been published on a specific topic. The idea is to make a comprehensive overview of a research area, make recommendations for further studies, and formulate and/or modify theories. In meta-analysis, you are combining the results of a number of studies to statistically evaluate an area of research.

Meta-analysis is a statistical technique that allows us to combine the effect sizes reported in experimental and correlational studies of the same underlying variables. In this way, we can better estimate the true relationship among variables than each study does alone. Various statistical procedures are used in a meta-analysis. Interested students should consult an upper-level statistics text for the details of meta-analysis.

Meta-analysis might be used for topics such as

An analysis of techniques used for teaching reading and writing skills to children with dyslexia

A meta-analysis of treatments for procrastination

A meta-analysis to evaluate the effectiveness of exercise in the treatment of depression

Let's look at a meta-analysis of sexual harassment research.

The Research Problem. Have you ever been harassed sexually or otherwise on the job? Harassment has become an issue of increasing concern in universities, schools, hospitals, government offices, corporations, retail outlets, and other places where people work or study.

Lapierre, Spector, and Leck (2005) of the Universities of Ottawa and South Florida focused on two kinds of harassment: sexual and nonsexual.

The Research Problem. Lapierre et al. (2005) noted that although there is a lot of research on the effects of both sexual and nonsexual harassment on employees in the workplace, little has been done to determine if these two forms of harassment affect victims differently. They decided to conduct a meta-analysis of the existing research on sexual and nonsexual harassment in the workplace in terms of their effects on overall job satisfaction.

The Results. Overall, the researchers found that job satisfaction was negatively related to employees' perceptions of being victims of harassment. This means that employees who felt they were being more harassed were less satisfied in their jobs than employees who felt they were less harassed ($r = -.31, p < .05$).

The researchers then meta-analyzed the sexual-nonsexual harassment findings. Although there were complexities with the findings, mainly as a result of missing data, it appeared that nonsexual harassment was more strongly negatively related to job satisfaction ($r = -.41$) than sexual harassment ($r = -.32$), at least for women.

The Conclusions. The researchers concluded that although sexual harassment has been the primary focus of the media and legislators, attention to the negative effects of nonsexual harassment in the workplace should be given.

As we mentioned at the beginning, this chapter covers three research approaches that you may not think belong together. We could argue that archival research and meta-analysis are similar in that they both deal with existing data. Program evaluation is a kind of meta-analysis of many goals, perhaps. In any case, all three types of research are important, and we felt that it was important to include them.

CHAPTER SUMMARY

Program evaluation is used by applied researchers to determine if a policy or program is meeting its goals. Program evaluation methods and criteria should be determined in advance. The first step in program evaluation is to conduct a **needs assessment** to determine if there is a need and if the proposed program would meet that need. The next step is to **specify objective outcome measures.** Typical outcome measures in program evaluation include improvement in the lives of the participants, improvement in the community as a whole, and participant satisfaction.

Archival researchers examine existing data, gathered for some other reason, to answer their research questions. Census, health, opinion, crime, and population information are managed by universities, governments, and corporations. In addition, a lot of electronic data are accessible via the Internet. Visiting archives requires advance preparation, and rules and regulations must be followed for the protection of the documents.

Meta-analysis is a statistical technique used to estimate the relationship between variables by analyzing the results of many existing studies. By including several studies, the true relationship can be better determined.

ANSWERS TO CONCEPTUAL EXERCISES

Conceptual Exercise 12A

First determine the need. Evaluate if there really is a problem. Look at the number of deaths that occurred in previous years. Perhaps eight deaths do not represent an increase; this could just reflect normal fluctuations. Examine whether the individuals who died had taken riding lessons. Examine crash rates for riders who have taken lessons compared to those who have not. Examine the size of the riders' bikes to see if this is related to crashes.

Conceptual Exercise 12B

In this study, the comparison group was composed of youth who dropped out of the program. This is a problem for two reasons. First, the fact that they dropped out may be a clear indication of their lack of motivation to change. This could be a serious confound and threaten the internal validity of the study. Second, it may be useful to identify the reasons they dropped out. It may be that the program could be changed to reduce the dropout rate. The problems in this research highlight that sometimes it is impossible to conduct perfectly controlled research, and you need to be willing to compromise. Indeed, much evaluation research uses quasi-experimental designs such as time-series and nonequivalent control groups.

Conceptual Exercise 12C

The state keeps records of motor vehicle accidents. Generally, when locating data, try to identify the stakeholders involved in the issue. By contacting them, you can probably find where the data are located and how to obtain access.

FAQ

Q1: Don't people get anxious and annoyed when they know they are being evaluated?

A1: This is definitely a possibility. People may feel anxious, particularly if they feel their jobs are threatened. It is a good idea to meet with people at all levels and do so early in the process. It is better to have them informed of the purpose of the evaluation and involved in the process. It is guaranteed that if you do not provide the information, it will be created through rumors.

Q2: What if I'm hired to evaluate a program and I determine that there really is no need for the program?

A2: Depending on who is paying for the evaluation, this may be good news or bad. Ultimately, whether your findings are used or not may be out of your control. Be objective in your research and make your recommendations, but just because the program is evaluated does not mean that action will follow.

Q3: Why wait until a program is up and running to evaluate it; can't evaluation be an ongoing process?

A3: Absolutely! Most organizations (both corporate and not-for-profit) require that programs have ongoing evaluation built in. This information is essential for decisions about when and how to alter the program and how success can be measured.

Q4: I know that my research will require archive data, but I don't know where I should look for it.

A4: As we described, the best first step is to do an Internet search. This search may indicate who is holding the information, and if you are very lucky, it may be available online. A second step is to contact your various levels of government. They may have published reports available or databases that can be accessed.

Q5: Isn't using available data sort of plagiarism?

A5: If you are claiming that you gathered the data, then it is plagiarism. Archival research is not plagiarism as long as you clearly state the source of the data. The research is your own. You are testing your hypothesis, the analysis is yours, and so, too, are the conclusions.

Q6: Will I have to pay to use someone's data?

A6: Many government sources are available free of charge, and there are other sources operating within universities that offer the data to researchers for a small fee or no cost.

Q7: How does meta-analysis differ from archival research?

A7: They differ in the level of analysis. In archival research, you are analyzing data that have already been gathered, but in meta-analysis, your analysis is of research results from previous studies. Meta-analysis is an analysis of previous analyses, whereas archival research is an initial analysis using previous research data.

Q8: How does a meta-analysis study differ from a review article?

A8: A review article does not include an analysis of data (or previous analyses). The goal of a review article is to provide an overview of a research area. It does not include a statistical analysis and consequently has no results section.

CHAPTER EXERCISES

1. For each of the following, indicate whether you think the researcher should take a program evaluation, archival, or meta-analytic approach.
   a. Teenage sexual behavior and STDs: Has there been a change?
   b. Does AA work?
   c. Modeling and aggressive behavior: What is the overall connection?

2. How are ethical concerns more salient in evaluation research?

3. What are some of the special problems associated with archival research?

CHAPTER PROJECTS

1. Visit a local daycare or other suitable facility. From your observations and discussions with the staff, determine several needs that are not being met. Design a program for meeting those needs. Include what you would measure to evaluate the effectiveness of your program and your definition of program success.

2. Select a simple question that could be answered doing archival research using online material. Do the research and write your report indicating the data you examined, the measures you took, and the answer to your question.

3. Find a meta analytic study from the existing literature. Report the following: problem, number of studies examined, results, and conclusions.

REFERENCES

Fahsing, I., Ask, K., & Granhag, P. (2004). The man behind the mask: Accuracy and predictors of eye-witness offender descriptions. *Journal of Applied Psychology, 89*(4), 722–729.

Lapierre, L. M., Spector, P. E., & Leck, J. D. (2005). Sexual versus nonsexual workplace aggression and victims' overall job satisfaction: A meta-analysis. *Journal of Occupational Health Psychology, 10*(2), 155–169.

Nakonezny, P. A., Reddick, R., & Rodgers, J. L. (2004). Did divorces decline after the Oklahoma City bombing? *Journal of Marriage and Family, 66,* 90–100.

Nee, C., & Ellis, T. (2005). Treating offending children: What works? *Legal and Criminological Psychology, 10,* 133–148.

Visit the study site at www.sagepub.com/evansmprstudy for practice quizzes and other study resources.

CHAPTER 13

Your Research Project

Analyzing, Interpreting, and Presenting Your Research

OBJECTIVES

After reading this chapter, students should be able to do the following for a research project they have conducted or proposed:

- Select and calculate an appropriate measure of central tendency
- Select and calculate an appropriate measure of variability
- Conduct and interpret the outcome of several tests of significance suitable for many student projects
- Choose the appropriate test of significance for their specific project
- Report descriptive and inferential statistics following APA guidelines

If you are a typical student taking a course in research methods, you will be expected to either *do* or *propose* the following:

- Find a topic that interests you
- Search the literature in the area
- Design a study to assess a specific hypothesis or hypotheses
- Collect your data
- Analyze those data
- Interpret the analysis
- Make conclusions about the research you have done

This chapter is for you!

We begin this chapter with a refresher on basic descriptive and inferential procedures. We think this information will help you to complete your own research project or research proposal. We assume that you have completed an introductory statistics course but, like our students, would benefit from a review.

Often students ask us why psychology students and students in many other disciplines have to study statistics. We hope you know the answer we give them. Psychology is a research-based discipline, and much psychological research requires the use of statistical techniques. If you plan to do research, you must have a solid background in statistics. But a good understanding of statistics is equally important for those of you who will become consumers of research (and that includes everyone). In Chapter 2, we focused on what you need to know to read and understand the research literature (i.e., to be *consumers of research*). In this chapter, we focus on what you to need to know to be *doers of research*.

WHAT ARE STATISTICS AND WHY ARE THEY NECESSARY?

Before talking about what statistics are, we would first like to convince you why they are necessary. The short answer is variability. If there were no variability of characteristics or behavior (and no variability in measurement), then everyone would have the same IQ and the same level of education. Everyone would be the same age and, for that matter, we would all have to be the same gender. In this uniform world, why would we waste our time calculating an average? Everyone is the same. And we would not worry whether our samples were representative of the population because any measure taken from the sample would be identical to the population. Actually, we would not have any variables because nothing would vary. We would have only constants: Remember that a *constant* is a characteristic of events, people, animals, or objects that does not vary. A *variable*, of course, is a characteristic of events, people, animals, or objects that take on different values, that is, varies. If our world had no variability, then we would not talk about variables, and we would not need statistics.

But that is not our world. People have different characteristics and backgrounds and behave differently. People behave differently in the same situations, and the same people behave differently in different situations; indeed, the same people may behave differently on different occasions in the same situations. Variability among people is a problem for researchers and is the main reason that we need statistics. It is precisely because people are different that psychology and the other social sciences have focused on describing and explaining general patterns of behavior. In order to look at how people behave *in general,* we often conduct research on groups of people.

NOTE: When we use the term *behavior,* we include both observable behavior and mental processes: Both are the subject matter of psychology.

Why is variability such a problem? Well, often we conduct research to determine if one variable has an effect on another (i.e., a *causal* inference). Or we may be trying to figure out if two or more variables are related (i.e., looking for relationships that *might* be causal). Sometimes, our goal might be to describe general patterns or trends in behavior (i.e., descriptive research). If behavior varies wildly, it is difficult to assess these questions. This is where statistics come in. Statistical techniques help us discover general trends in behavior, describe the degree of variability, and determine how much variability is due to chance factors and how much is a result of other important factors.

How we measure behavior will determine in part what kinds of statistical analyses we can do and what kinds of questions we can ask.

There are two goals of statistics: (1) to summarize our data and (2) to make inferences about the nature of populations by examining samples drawn from them. Therefore, there are only two types of statistics: descriptive and inferential. We use **descriptive statistics** to summarize data and communicate our research results to others. Imagine a large pile of completed surveys. What do you do with these surveys? How do you organize them? How do you summarize the findings so they make sense to you and others? Descriptive statistics help us do these things. We use **inferential statistics** to make statements about whole populations when we have only included a sample of individuals in our study. You may have sampled 100 individuals in your research, but you will want to generalize your findings to the entire population. Inferential statistics help us do this.

Let's consider an example close to home. You come into class and find your last exam on your desk. You got 64%. What questions would you ask your professor? Probably you would ask about the class **average** (the mean). You might ask what the high and low scores were (the range). If you had taken an introductory statistics course, you might ask a more sophisticated question about **variability** (the standard deviation). Many professors provide the **frequency distribution** (the shape). These are all descriptive statistics. They summarize, in just a few numbers, how the class did on the exam.

Have you heard that Crest users have 25% fewer cavities? "Fewer than whom?" probably comes to mind. But let's say fewer than Colgate users. Were you in the study? Did someone from Crest talk to your dentist? Probably not. Yes, you are no doubt correct that Crest used a sample and did not measure everyone. How many people do you think Crest may have included in the study? How would you interpret the result if only four Crest users were compared with four Colgate users? The finding that the Crest users had 25% fewer cavities than the Colgate users could have been a fluke, don't you think? So do we. The inference by Crest is that Crest users, *all Crest users,* have fewer cavities than non-Crest users. But this inference is only valid if the sampling procedure and research procedures in general were valid.

What is an inference? According to one source (www.m-w.com), it is the following:

1: the act or process of inferring: as **a:** the act of passing from one proposition, statement, or judgment considered as true to another whose truth is believed to follow from that of the former **b:** the act of passing from statistical sample data to generalizations (as of the value of population parameters) usually with calculated degrees of certainty

Consider the following: A person passing you on the street smiles at you. From that you infer that he or she likes you. Are you right? You do not have much information on which to base your decision, and you cannot be certain, but are you probably right? Inferential procedures help us determine if our inferences are *probably* correct.

When we infer something about a population from a sample drawn from that population, we are using inferential statistics. These procedures tell us how probable it is that our inference is correct. We need to use these procedures when the population that we are interested in is not available to us to describe. Psychologists are interested in the behavior (both observable behavior and mental processes) of humans (the population). Psychologists cannot study and describe all humans; they can only study some of them and hope to learn from samples of humans, things about all humans. And they use inferential statistics to do this.

Early in the planning stage of your study, you need to carefully consider how you will analyze your data. There is nothing worse than spending a lot of time and effort collecting data only to discover that there is no statistical analysis that can help you answer your research question. So as you are considering how you will measure your dependent variable, how you will manipulate your independent variable, and how you will control for extraneous variables, you need to keep in mind what statistics you can use.

To help you understand your results and to help you communicate those results to others, you will need to summarize the data. Let's look at the statistics researchers typically calculate when they are describing their results. These, then, are common descriptive statistics.

Every year, we have students who study sex differences in some variable or another. When presenting their results, they dutifully report their *t* test results and talk about the difference between their groups but forget to state what the group means were. Consequently, we have no idea of the direction of the outcome. Did the men score higher than the women or the women higher than the men? Remember, you must always include descriptive statistics in your report.

Summarizing Your Data With Descriptive Statistics

Describing Central Tendency

You will recall that the three most common measures of central tendency, or average, of a distribution of numbers or values are the mean, the median, and the mode. The **mean** is the arithmetic average and takes into account every score in the distribution. The **median** is the middle score and separates the distribution in half. Half the scores fall above the median and half fall below. The **mode** is the most frequently occurring score.

Calculating Measures of Central Tendency. Imagine that we have measured heart rate (number of beats per minute) of highly anxious people; half have received stress management training and half have not. Our data are shown in Table 13.1.

Let's first use the mean as our measure of average beats per minute for our two groups. You will recall that to calculate the mean, we simply sum the scores and divide by the total number of scores. The formula is as follows:

$$M = \frac{\sum X}{n}.$$

(Mean)

TABLE 13.1	Heart Rate (Number of Beats per Minute) for Trained and Untrained Groups	
Training		**No Training**
86		88
85		87
84		86
83		86
82		85
81		85
78		80
78		80
78		80
76		80

The sum for the training group (T) is 811, and the sum for the no-training group (NT) is 837. There were 10 people in each group, and so our group means are as follows:

$$M_T = \frac{\sum X}{n} = \frac{811}{10} = 81.1$$

$$M_{NT} = \frac{\sum X}{n} = \frac{837}{10} = 83.7$$

Let's calculate the median as our measure of average. Once the scores are sorted from highest to lowest, the median is the middle value, the one that divides the distribution in half. In our example, the median is the value above which lie half the scores (i.e., 5) and below which lie half the scores. If we have an even number of scores, which we do in our example, the median will be halfway between the two middle scores. Our medians are as follows:

$$Mdn_T = 81.5$$

$$Mdn_{NT} = 85$$

You can see that the medians are close but not identical to the means. This is because the mean uses the exact scores, but the median does not.

Now, let's report the mode as our measure of average. The mode is the score that occurs most often. Our modes are as follows:

$$Mo_T = 78$$

$$Mo_{NT} = 80$$

The mode is the crudest measure of average and has limited practical value in statistics, but the mode is the only measure we can use when we have nominal data. Modal eye color, modal college major, and modal gender make sense, but mean eye color, mean college major, and mean gender do not.

 Of the three measures, the mean is the most often reported measure of average in research reports. However, be sure to look at the frequency distribution of your data before deciding to use the mean. Remember that for very skewed distributions, it may be more appropriate to report the median.

Conceptual Exercise 13A

Which of the three measures of average would you choose for each of the following variables?

1. GPA of freshman students

2. Number of children per family in rural America

3. Height of basketball players in the NBA

Describing Variability

There are two common measures of variability (the range and the standard deviation). The **range** is quite a crude measure of variability and is simply the span of the distribution. If the highest score was 10 and the lowest score was 0, the range would be 11 because the span of the distribution is 11 values. You can see that the range depends on only two values, the highest and the lowest.

 The **standard deviation** is the average distance of the scores from the mean and, unlike the range, uses all the values in its calculation. The mean IQ on the Stanford Binet test is 100, and the SD is 15. We know then that, on average, IQ scores tend to vary about 15 points from 100.

Calculating Measures of Variability. Let's calculate the variability of our heartbeat data.

 The range is easy to find. We simply subtract the lowest value from the highest and add 1. The formula then is as follows:

$$H - L + 1 = \text{Range}$$

We would report the ranges for our two groups as

$$R_T = 86 - 76 + 1 = 11$$

$$R_{NT} = 88 - 80 + 1 = 9$$

Let's calculate the standard deviation for our two groups.

Recall that the formula for the standard deviation is as follows:

$$SD = \sqrt{\frac{SS}{n}} = \sqrt{\frac{\sum(X - M)^2}{n}}$$

(Standard deviation)

SS is the sum of the squared deviations of the scores from the mean. You can see that we need to subtract the mean of the distribution from each score, square each difference, sum the squares, divide by *n*, and finally take the square root to obtain the standard deviation.

To compute the *SD* for our two groups, untrained and trained, we need the information in Table 13.2.

We have all the bits we need for our standard deviation formula, and our measures are as follows:

$$SD_T = \sum \sqrt{\frac{SS_T}{n}} = \sqrt{\frac{106.9}{10}} = 3.27$$

$$SD_{NT} = \sum \sqrt{\frac{SS_{NT}}{n}} = \sqrt{\frac{98.1}{10}} = 3.13$$

We can see that, on average, the trained group varies 3.27 points from its mean, and the no-training group varies 3.13 points from its mean. As you can see, this measure is sensitive to the value of each score in the distribution.

Which measures of central tendency and variability we use depends, in part, on the level of measurement of the variable and, in part, on the shape of the distribution (see Chapter 5 on measurement). In the social sciences research literature, you will find means and

TABLE 13.2   Calculating the Standard Deviations: Untrained Versus Trained Group

	Training	*X ~ M*	*(X ~ M)²*	*No Training*	*X ~ M*	*(X ~ M)²*
	86	4.9	24.01	88	4.3	18.49
	85	3.9	15.21	87	3.3	10.89
	84	2.9	8.41	86	2.3	5.29
	83	1.9	3.61	86	2.3	5.29
	82	0.9	0.81	85	1.3	1.69
	81	−0.1	0.01	85	1.3	1.69
	78	−3.1	9.61	80	−3.7	13.69
	78	−3.1	9.61	80	−3.7	13.69
	78	−3.1	9.61	80	−3.7	13.69
	76	−5.1	26.01	80	−3.7	13.69
Sum	**811**		**106.9**	**837**		**98.1**
n	**10**			**10**		

standard deviation reported most often, but let's see how level of measurement must be considered when choosing the appropriate measure of average and variability.

Describing Central Tendency and Variability of Levels of Variables

Describing Nominal Variables. The values of a nominal variable, even if assigned numbers, reflect only qualitative differences. The only measure of average or central tendency for nominal variables that makes any sense is mode. We can report that modal eye color is blue. But median or mean eye color makes no sense. Describing the variability of eye color would best be done by creating a frequency distribution by listing the values of the variable (i.e., the different eye colors) and indicating the frequency for each. If we wanted to create a graph of this kind of nominal information, we would choose a **bar graph** because nominal variables are discrete. In Chapter 14, we discuss graphing techniques for various kinds of data in detail.

Describing Ordinal Variables. Ordinal variables, unlike nominal variables, do differ in quantity. But because they provide no information about distance between values, arithmetic and statistical operations are limited. The mode is probably the only sensible measure of average of an ordinal variable. The range of the variable is a reasonable measure of its variability. As was the case for nominal variables, it would be best to show the variability in a frequency distribution table or a bar graph.

Let's imagine that we had socioeconomic status information for residents in the state of Washington. We could prepare a table to describe this ordinal information.

SES	*% of Washingtonians*
Upper	14
Middle	76
Lower	10

SES is an ordinal variable because the values differ in quantity, but the distance between the values cannot be assumed to be equal. In other words, the difference between upper and middle class may not be the same as the difference between middle and lower class.

If we wanted to describe the average SES of Washingtonians, we would report the mode as middle class. We would say that SES has a range of 3 (i.e., the variable ranges across three values).

FYI

The range is found by subtracting the lowest from the highest value of the variable and adding 1, giving us the span of the variable. Statistical packages such as SPSS do not calculate the range this way. They simply subtract the lowest from the highest value.

Describing Interval Variables. Interval variables provide information about the distance between values. The distance is assumed to be the same. This may seem to you to be a subtle difference, but in fact it is important. Because the distance between values is the same, we can treat these variables much like ratio variables in terms of arithmetic and statistical operations. The median or the mean can be used to describe average, and the range or the standard deviation can be used to describe variability. IQ is an interval variable, and researchers typically report mean and standard deviation when describing IQ populations.

Describing Ratio Variables. In most cases, the best measures of central tendency and variability for ratio variables are the mean and standard deviation, respectively. But remember, the mean, or arithmetic average, unlike the median and mode, is calculated by summing all the values. Each value affects the mean. Let's consider the ratio variable, income. What if one of us, let's say Bryan, told you that the average income in Canada is $35,000. What if Annabel told you the average income in Canada is $54,000. Could you resolve this apparent discrepancy? We hope so. The key is the shape of the distribution. Examine Figure 13.1.

Income is a positively skewed distribution, of course, with only a small group of people earning huge incomes. These extraordinarily high numbers pull the mean toward them. As a result, mean income will be high. But the median is not influenced by the actual values of these high incomes—only by their frequency. And the mode is only sensitive to the single income most often earned. So we could both be correct. You have to ask, "What measure of average was used?" Unless the distribution is fairly symmetrical, the mean may not be the best measure of average; median might be a fairer description of the central tendency of the distribution.

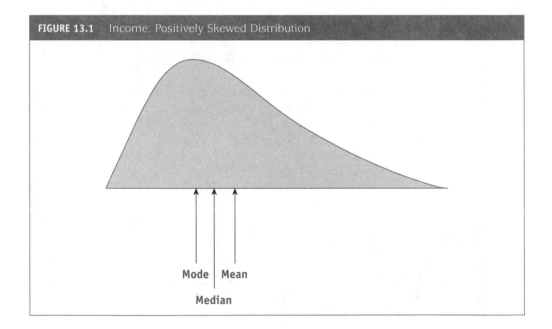

FIGURE 13.1   Income: Positively Skewed Distribution

Mode | Mean

Median

The variability of ratio variables is best described by their standard deviation. Remember, range is computed on only two values—the highest and the lowest. The standard deviation takes all the values of the variable into account and better describes the spread or variability of a ratio variable.

You should always report measures of average and variability, and usually you will report these measures at the beginning of the results section of your report. In our example study of stress management training, we chose the mean and standard deviation for our measure of average and variability of our two groups of highly anxious people.

What next? Probably you are asking yourself, "Did the stress management training help our highly anxious people?" To answer that question, we need the help of inferential statistics.

Conceptual Exercise 13B

For each of the following, determine the best measure of central tendency and variability, if appropriate:

1. IQ

2. Salary of female academics in Britain

3. Salary of professional soccer players in South Africa

4. Student evaluations of professors

5. Dress size

MAKING INFERENCES FROM YOUR DATA

How do North Americans feel about global climate change? Does stress management training help highly anxious people lower their heart rate?

These kinds of questions about whole populations cannot be answered with absolute certainty unless you ask all North Americans or train all highly anxious people. Because that is not reasonable, we must turn to inferential procedures.

When we do research, we ultimately want to generalize our findings. We want to make statements that can be applied to all individuals in a population. The problem is that we do not include everyone in our study; we only work with a sample. Although it is important to compute summary statistics to describe what happened to our sample, we really want to make inferences to corresponding values in the population. The most common inferential technique in psychological research is hypothesis testing. Researchers in psychology often have hypotheses about their research questions. These hypotheses are educated guesses about the effects of a variable on behavior or how variables are related.

They are generated from theories, from previous research, or sometimes from logic. Consider the following:

"People work harder when they think they are being evaluated."

"Outgoing people are happier than people who keep to themselves."

"Highly anxious people trained in stress management are less anxious than those not trained."

These are hypotheses that might have been generated from theories or previous research.

Inferential statistics can be used for testing hypotheses such as the ones above to determine if they are reasonable. In statistics, by *reasonable,* we mean likely to be true.

FYI

Another inferential technique is called confidence interval estimation. This is a post hoc, or after the fact, technique used when researchers do not have a priori, or before the fact, hypotheses about the values of the parameters. Rather, they use sample statistics to estimate the value of those parameters. We discuss this approach in Chapter 2.

Testing the Statistical Significance of Your Research Findings

In the section that follows, we present tests of significance that are well suited to a student research project. These simple statistics are covered in most introductory statistics courses, and the discussion that follows is provided only as a review. Keep in mind that details of research design are not included here; that's what the rest of the book is about. The following is presented as a refresher on how to conduct some simple tests of significance.

t Tests

t Test: Independent Groups Design. The simplest experiment involves two groups, an experimental and a control group. The researcher treats the groups differently (the independent variable [IV]) and measures their performance (the dependent variable [DV]). The question then is, did the treatment work? Are the groups significantly different after the treatment? If the dependent variable is an interval or ratio measure, the *t* test may be the appropriate test of significance. You will recall the *t* ratio is as follows:

$$t = \frac{M_1 - M_2}{SE}$$

(*t* ratio: Independent groups)

The numerator is the mean difference between groups, and the denominator is the unbiased estimate of the standard error of the difference. The obtained *t* value is compared to the critical value of t with $n_1 + n_2 - 2$ df. Although the example below is experimental, it is important to note that the t test can also be used in quasi-experimental and nonexperimental research. For example, a t test would work well if you were interested in comparing freshmen and seniors on some measure of study behavior.

Here is an example of a simple study with two levels of the independent variable. Suppose we wanted to test the claims that some oxygenated drink enhanced cognitive ability. We could operationally define cognitive ability in a variety of ways, but we decide to use the score on a timed math test. We recruit 40 students and randomly assign 20 participants to receive the special oxygenated drink (O group) and 20 to receive plain water (C for control group). Five minutes after consuming the drink, all participants are given 10 minutes to complete the math test. Their scores are shown in Table 13.3.

We can see that the O group ($M = 76.65$, $SD = 4.06$) did indeed perform better than the control group ($M = 68.35$, $SD = 6.38$). But the real question is, can we conclude that the population means are significantly different? In other words, can we generalize our sample outcome with our 40 participants to people in general? To answer that question, we could use a t test. To do that, we need both sample means and the unbiased estimate of the standard error. We already have the two sample means.

TABLE 13.3	Math Scores for Two Independent Groups	
	C	**O**
	56	70
	80	80
	63	79
	62	83
	67	77
	71	75
	68	84
	76	78
	79	75
	67	75
	76	78
	74	82
	67	74
	70	81
	62	72
	65	70
	62	75
	62	72
	69	76
	71	77
M	**68.35**	**76.65**
SD	**6.38**	**4.06**

To calculate the standard error, we use this formula for groups that are the same size:

$$SE = \sqrt{\frac{SS_1 + SS_2}{n(n-1)}}$$

(Standard error for t test: Independent groups)

You can see that to calculate the standard error for the denominator of the t ratio, we have to calculate the sum of squares for each group. To do that we use this formula:

$$SS = \Sigma X^2 - (\Sigma X^2)/n$$

Table 13.4 presents the bits and pieces we need to do this.

TABLE 13.4	Scores for t Ratio Calculation: Independent Groups		
Scores		**Squares**	
X_c	X_o	X_c^2	X_o^2
56	70	3,136	4,900
80	80	6,400	6,400
63	79	3,969	6,241
62	83	3,844	6,889
67	77	4,489	5,929
71	75	5,041	5,625
68	84	4,624	7,056
76	78	5,776	6,084
79	75	6,241	5,625
67	75	4,489	5,625
76	78	5,776	6,084
74	82	5,476	6,724
67	74	4,489	5,476
70	81	4,900	6,561
62	72	3,844	5,184
65	70	4,225	4,900
62	75	3,844	5,625
62	72	3,844	5,184
69	76	4,761	5,776
71	77	5,041	5,929
Sums 1367	1533	94,209	117,817
Means 68.35	76.65		

We calculate the *SS* for the control group and for the oxygenated group:

$$SS_C = \sum X^2 - \frac{\left(\sum X\right)^2}{n} = 94,209 - \frac{1369^2}{20} = 774.55$$

$$SS_O = 117,817 - \frac{1533^2}{20} = 312.55$$

We calculate our unbiased estimate of the standard error to use in the denominator of our *t* ratio:

$$SE = \sqrt{\frac{SS_C + SS_O}{n(n-1)}} = \sqrt{\frac{774.55 + 312.55}{20(19)}} = 1.69$$

Now we can calculate our *t* statistic:

$$t = \frac{M_O - M_C}{SE} = \frac{76.65 - 68.35}{1.69} = 4.91$$

What now?

If the obtained *t* value is larger (ignoring the sign) than the critical value, the null hypothesis is rejected. The researcher reports that the group means were significantly different. Critical *t* values can be found in any statistics book, but first you will need the degrees of freedom. For this example, the degrees of freedom are $(20 - 1) + (20 - 1) = 38$. But before you go look up a critical *t* value, we need to review the difference between a **one-tailed** and **two-tailed *t* test.** When we conduct a *t* test, we need to specify whether we believe our treatment will produce a change in a particular direction, a one-tailed test of our hypothesis; if we are not sure of the direction of the difference, we use a two-tailed test of our hypothesis.

Researchers usually specify a particular direction of effect, often basing their decision on previously published research. The advantage of a one-tailed test is that you have more statistical power (i.e., you increase the probability of rejecting a null that is false). For example, if you examine a table of critical *t* values (provided in all stat texts), you will note that the critical *t* value is larger for a two-tailed test than for a one-tailed test even when degrees of freedom and the alpha level are the same. In other words, your obtained *t* value will have to be larger to be significant for a two-tailed test than for a one-tailed test.

In our drink example, we hypothesized that the oxygenated drink would increase math performance, so we would use a one-tailed test.

Our obtained *t* of 4.91 is larger than the critical value, which is approximately 2.42 at $\alpha = .01$ and 38 degrees of freedom, and so we would reject the null and state in our published report something like the following: The math performance of participants who drank the oxygenated beverage was significantly better than the performance of those who drank the nonoxygenated beverage, $t(38) = 4.91, p < .01$.

We would accompany our statistic with an effect size estimate. Cohen's *d* is appropriate in this case. Using the formula for Cohen's *d* that we showed you in Chapter 4, let's calculate this effect size estimate for our example. We need to calculate the pooled standard deviation to use in the denominator of the formula. We do that as follows:

$$SD_{pooled} = \sqrt{\frac{(n_1 - 1)SD_1^2 + (n_2 - 1)SD_2^2}{n_1 + n_2 - 2}}$$

$$= \sqrt{\frac{(19)4.06^2 + (19)6.38^2}{38}}$$

$$= 5.347$$

Now we can calculate our effect size estimate.

$$d = \frac{M_1 - M_2}{SD_{pooled}} = \frac{76.65 - 68.35}{5.347} = 1.54$$

As you can see, the oxygenated drink had a large effect on performance.

FYI

Many students have access to Excel, part of the Microsoft Office package. Excel will do several tests of significance. We cannot provide instruction on the specifics of Excel, but if you know how to enter your data into the spreadsheet, you can select your specific test from the Tools menu. If we used Excel to calculate our t for our oxygenated drink study, we would choose from the menu t test: two sample assuming equal variances, and our output would look like Table 13.5.

TABLE 13.5 t Test: Two Sample Assuming Equal Variances

	Control	Oxygenated
Mean	76.65	68.35
Variance	16.45	40.76578947
Observations	20	20
Pooled variance	28.60789474	
Hypothesized mean difference	0	
df	38	
t Stat	4.90721564	
P(T< = t) one-tail	8.8663E-06	
t Critical one-tail	2.428567627	
P(T< = t) two-tail	1.77326E-05	
t Critical two-tail	2.711557598	

Excel reports the obtained t value as t Stat. You can see that the critical value for a one-tailed test at our alpha level of .01 is reported by Excel as t Critical one-tail. But it also reports the actual probability of obtaining this t statistic if the null hypothesis is true. This is the value that we want to be less than .05 or .01. The computer reports p as 8.8663E-06, which means move the decimal place six spaces to the left or .0000088663, but we can just report it as $p < .001$.

This simple example demonstrates how we would statistically compare two groups of randomly assigned participants after we have treated them differently in some way, an independent groups design. Because we have randomly assigned participants to groups before we apply our treatment, we are confident that the groups are initially equivalent. As we have said probably countless times, initial equivalence of groups is critical if we wish to assess the effects of an IV. How else could we be confident that groups are initially equivalent?

Well, what if we matched participants on the dependent measure before we treat them? Or maybe better yet, how about we use the same people in all conditions? If we have matched pairs of participants, one member of each matched pair serving in each treatment condition, or if we have one group of participants, all of whom serve under each of two treatment conditions, we have a dependent groups design, and a t test for dependent groups might be the analysis we would choose to analyze our data.

***t* test: Dependent Groups Design.** A dependent groups t test is the significance test we would use when participants serve in both of two treatment conditions, a **repeated-measures design,** or when pairs of participants have been matched on some measure related to, or identical to, the dependent measure and are treated as if they were the same individual, a **matched groups design.** A major statistical difference between an independent groups and a dependent groups design is seen in the calculation of degrees of freedom.

If the groups are independent (i.e., different participants in each group), degrees of freedom for the t test are $n_1 + n_2 - 2$.

If the same participants serve in both treatment conditions or if the participants are matched, then the degrees of freedom for the t test are $n_p - 1$, where n_p is the number of pairs of scores.

Let's return to our oxygenated drink study and think about how we could test our hypothesis about the effect of oxygenated drinks on math performance using a dependent groups design. Let's redesign our study to be a repeated-measures design. We might recruit 20 participants with the intention of having all do the math test after drinking the oxygenated drink and again after drinking the control beverage. Of course, we are concerned about order effects, so we will have half our participants drink the control beverage first (and the oxygenated beverage second after some delay), and we will have the other half drink the oxygenated beverage first (and the control beverage second). Let's assume we have addressed other possible carryover issues in our design.

The data are shown in Table 13.6.

We can see the improved performance when people drank the oxygenated water ($M = 73.85$, $SD = 7.85$) over their performance with plain water ($M = 68.35$, $SD = 6.38$). Clearly,

TABLE 13.6	Math Scores: Repeated-Measures Design	
Participant	C	O
1	56	56
2	80	88
3	63	68
4	62	69
5	67	74
6	71	80
7	68	75
8	76	82
9	79	86
10	67	77
11	76	80
12	74	81
13	67	72
14	70	76
15	62	63
16	65	68
17	62	67
18	62	68
19	69	74
20	71	73
M	**68.35**	**73.85**
SD	**6.38**	**7.85**

for our group of 20 participants, we did see improved performance from the oxygenated drink, but if we want to generalize our results beyond our sample, we will need to do a significance test—in this case, we will chose a t test for dependent groups.

The **direct difference method** for calculating a dependent t value uses difference scores as the data in the calculation, essentially operating as if there is only one group (i.e., one group of difference scores).

The formula for the t ratio for a dependent groups design is as follows:

$$t = \frac{M_D}{SE_D}$$

(t ratio: Dependent groups)

The numerator is the mean of the difference scores, and the denominator is the unbiased estimate of the standard error of the difference. The obtained t value is compared to the critical value of t with $n_p - 1$ df.

The formula we will use to find the standard error is as follows:

$$SE_D = \sqrt{\frac{\sum D^2 - (\sum D)^2 / n_p}{n_p(n_p - 1)}}$$

(Standard error for t test: Dependent groups)

You can see that to calculate the standard error of the denominator of the t ratio, we have to find the difference scores. Let's subtract each control score from each experimental score. The data we need are shown in Table 13.7.

Now we can calculate the standard error of the difference.

$$SE_D = \sqrt{\frac{\sum D^2 - (\sum D)^2 / n_p}{n_p(n_p - 1)}} = \sqrt{\frac{728 - 110^2 / 20}{20(19)}} = 0.569.$$

TABLE 13.7   Scores for t Ratio Calculation: Dependent Groups

Participant	C	O	D	D²
1	56	56	0	0
2	80	88	8	64
3	63	68	5	25
4	62	69	7	49
5	67	74	7	49
6	71	80	9	81
7	68	75	7	49
8	76	82	6	36
9	79	86	7	49
10	67	77	10	100
11	76	80	4	16
12	74	81	7	49
13	67	72	5	25
14	70	76	6	36
15	62	63	1	1
16	65	68	3	9
17	62	67	5	25
18	62	68	6	36
19	69	74	5	25
20	71	73	2	4
Sum			**110**	**728**
M_D			**5.5**	

And our t is easy to calculate:

$$t = \frac{M_D}{SE_D} = \frac{5.5}{0.569} = 9.67$$

As we did for the independent groups t test, we need to compare our obtained t value against the tabled critical t. The degrees of freedom for this t test are $20 - 1 = 19$ because we have 20 pairs of scores. Our research hypothesis was that the oxygenated drink would increase performance, so we will use a one-tailed test. We consult our statistics book to find a table of critical values, and we find that the critical value of t for our example is 2.539 at an alpha level of .01.

Because our obtained t value of 9.67 is larger than the critical value, we can report that we found that the oxygenated drink significantly increased performance, $t(19) = 9.67, p < .01$. We should provide an effect size estimate as well. We can use Cohen's estimate for this example. The formula for the paired t test uses the standard deviation of the difference scores in the denominator. Our calculations are as follows:

$$d = \frac{M_1 - M_2}{SD} = \frac{73.85 - 68.35}{2.544} = 2.16.$$

As you would expect, our treatment had a large effect on performance.

FYI

To do a t test for dependent groups for our oxygenated drink study with Excel, we would select t test: paired two sample for means from the Excel menu.
    Our output would look like Table 13.8.

TABLE 13.8 t Test: Paired Two Sample for Means

	Oxygenated	Control
Mean	73.85	68.35
Variance	61.60789474	40.76578947
Observations	20	20
Pearson correlation	0.956802935	
Hypothesized mean difference	0	
df	19	
t Stat	9.667227346	
P(T< = t) one-tail	4.5263E-09	
t Critical one-tail	2.539483189	
P(T< = t) two-tail	9.0526E-09	
t Critical two-tail	2.860934604	

NOTE: One last note about ignoring the sign in calculations of *t*. Be sure that you are clear about which condition you subtract from which when you report your data. In this example, we subtracted the performance in the plain water condition from the performance in the oxygenated drink condition. Therefore, better performance under the oxygenated drink condition would translate into a positive difference score and a positive *t* value. It is easy to make an embarrassing mistake here (particularly if you are using a computer) and report an opposite effect because you did not pay careful attention.

The *t* test, a parametric test of significance, is quite robust and powerful. The *t* test is a good test when you want to compare two sets of scores provided by different participants, the same participants, or matched participants. Remember that the American Psychological Association (APA) expects researchers to provide an estimate of their effect sizes in the report. See Chapter 2 for details on estimates for various tests.

But what if we want to compare more than two groups? Maybe we have drinks of various levels of oxygenation, or maybe we want to assess the effects of several dosages of a drug designed to treat depression. The *F* test might be the statistical choice for these kinds of research questions.

F Tests

As with the *t* test, we use the *F* test of significance when we have interval or ratio data. With the *F* test, we are not limited to comparing just two groups or levels of an independent variable; rather, we can compare any number of levels of an independent variable and also more than one independent variable at a time.

Like the *t* test, the *F* test can be used in quasi-experimental research as well as experimental research. For example, an *F* test could be used to compare freshmen, juniors, and seniors on some measure of study behavior.

In earlier chapters, we presented examples of numerous experimental and quasi-experimental designs, known as analyses of variance (ANOVAs), which were analyzed with the *F* test. Our intention here is to provide a few simple examples to help you with your research project. If you require a more detailed review, we suggest you consult the textbook you used in your introductory statistics course.

The null hypothesis tested with ANOVA is similar to the null for the *t* test—there is no difference among group means.

Let's extend our oxygenated beverage study to include a super-oxygenated beverage. We now have three groups or levels of our independent variable: plain water control (C), oxygenated (O), and super-oxygenated (S). Essentially, the **F statistic** is a ratio between the variability between treatment groups and the variability within each group. If there is no treatment effect, this ratio will be close to 1, but if there is a treatment effect, then the variability between groups will be larger than the variability within groups. Consequently, the *F* ratio will be larger than 1. Because the *F* statistic is a ratio of two measures of variability, it is always positive, and therefore there is no one-tailed and two-tailed *F* test. The alternative hypothesis is that the null is false: No direction is specified.

One-Way ANOVA. The term *one-way* in one-way ANOVA means that there is only one independent variable. A **one-way ANOVA** has only one independent variable, but that variable may have any number of different levels. In our beverage example, the independent variable is the type of drink, and we have three levels of that variable: a control group that drinks water, a group that drinks the oxygenated water, and a third group that drinks the super-oxygenated water. We will again be investigating the effects on cognitive performance using our timed math test as the dependent variable. This time, to save paper and space, we will randomly assign only 10 participants to each group. The data are shown in Table 13.9.

A calculation of the group means shows that the S group scored highest ($M = 77.6, SD = 4.17$), followed by the O group ($M = 74.6, SD = 6.87$), and the lowest scores were for the C group ($M = 68.9, SD = 7.72$). This describes the performance of our samples, but we need to do an F test to determine if our outcome is statistically significant so that we can generalize to the population.

Recall that the F test compares the between-group variability with the within-group variability. If the treatment had an effect, then the between-group variability will be larger than the within-group variability. Let's go ahead and see just how the F test does this for our beverage study. Remember that our intention here is to show you, with a simple example, how you would conduct such a test, but we urge you to consult your statistics textbook before you begin your analysis of the data from your research project.

The formula for the F ratio for a one-way ANOVA is as follows:

$$F = \frac{MS_{BG}}{MS_{WG}}$$

(*F* ratio for one-way ANOVA)

You will remember, we hope, that *MS* stands for **mean square,** an unbiased estimate of the population variance, which is found by dividing a sum of squares (*SS*) by the appropriate degrees of freedom. The *F* ratio compares two unbiased estimates of the population variance, one based on between-group variability and the other based on within-group variability. If the treatment had no effect, then these two estimates are estimating the same thing, basically variation due to individual differences. But if the treatment had an effect, then the estimate between groups will include that variability caused by the treatment, and so this estimate will be larger than the estimate within groups, and the *F* ratio will get larger.

TABLE 13.9	Math Scores: One-Way ANOVA Design		
	C	*O*	*S*
	56	60	70
	80	75	80
	63	78	79
	62	85	83
	67	72	77
	71	73	75
	68	70	84
	76	80	78
	79	80	75
	67	73	75
M	68.9	74.6	77.6
SD	7.72	6.87	4.17

So to calculate our F ratio, we need to first compute the sum of squares between groups and the sum of squares within groups.

The formula for SS between groups for a one-way ANOVA is as follows:

$$SS_{BG} = \frac{(\sum X_1)^2}{n_1} + \frac{(\sum X_2)^2}{n_2} + \cdots + \frac{(\sum X_k)^2}{n_k} - \frac{(\sum X_{tot})^2}{n_{tot}}$$

(Sum of squares between groups: One-way ANOVA)

where k is the number of groups.

This formula indicates that we need to

1. sum the scores for each group in our study, square each sum, and divide by the group size (n);
2. sum the values found in 1;
3. sum all the scores of all groups, square that sum, and divide by the total number of scores;
4. subtract the value found in 3 from the value found in 2.

The formula for SS within groups is as follows:

$$SS_{WG} = SS_1 + SS_2 + \cdots + SS_k$$

where $SS = \sum X^2 - \dfrac{(\sum X)^2}{n}$

(Sum of squares within groups: One-way ANOVA)

This formula indicates that we need to compute the sum of squares within each of our groups and then add them together.

Let's compute these two sums of squares for our beverage study. For our three-group study, the formulas we need are as follows:

$$SS_{BG} = \frac{(\sum X_1)^2}{n_1} + \frac{(\sum X_2)^2}{n_2} + \frac{(\sum X_3)^2}{n_3} - \frac{(\sum X_{tot})^2}{n_{tot}}$$

$$SS_{WG} = SS_1 + SS_2 + SS_3$$

The bits and pieces we will need to compute our sums of squares are seen in Table 13.10. Let's compute SS between groups.

$$SS_{BG} = \frac{(\sum X_1)^2}{n_1} + \frac{(\sum X_2)^2}{n_2} + \frac{(\sum X_3)^2}{n_3} - \frac{(\sum X_{tot})^2}{n_{tot}}$$

$$= \frac{474721}{10} + \frac{556516}{10} + \frac{602176}{10} - \frac{(689 + 746 + 776)^2}{30}$$

$$= 163341.3 - 162951 = 390.6.$$

TABLE 13.10	Scores for One-Way ANOVA Calculation					
	C (X_1)	O (X_2)	S (X_3)	X_1^2	X_2^2	X_3^2
	56	60	70	3,136	3,600	4,900
	80	75	80	6,400	5,625	6,400
	63	78	79	3,969	6,084	6,241
	62	85	83	3,844	7,225	6,889
	67	72	77	4,489	5,184	5,929
	71	73	75	5,041	5,329	5,625
	68	70	84	4,624	4,900	7,056
	76	80	78	5,776	6,400	6,084
	79	80	75	6,241	6,400	5,625
	67	73	75	4,489	5,329	5,625
Sum	**689**	**746**	**776**	**48,009**	**56,076**	**60,374**
Sum²	**474,721**	**556,516**	**602,176**			

Now we need the *SS* within groups. We will calculate each *SS* for each group and then sum the three values.

$$SS_1 = \sum X_1^2 - \frac{\left(\sum X_1\right)^2}{n_1} = 48009 - \frac{689^2}{10} = 536.9$$

$$SS_2 = 424.4$$

$$SS_3 = 156.4$$

$$SS_{WG} = 1117.7$$

Whew, the hardest part is done. All we need to do now is compute the two mean squares by dividing each sum of squares by its associated degrees of freedom. Do you remember what the *df* are?

- Between-groups $df = k - 1$, where k is the number of groups or levels of the IV.
- Within-groups $df = n_{tot} - k$.
  For our study, then, we have three groups, so *df* between groups is 2.
  We have a total of 30 participants, and so *df* within groups is 30 − 3 = 27.

Now we can compute our *F* ratio by dividing the *MS* between groups by the *MS* within groups.

$$MS_{BG} = \frac{SS_{BG}}{df_{bg}} = \frac{390.6}{2} = 195.3$$

$$MS_{WG} = \frac{SS_{WG}}{df_{wg}} = \frac{1117.7}{27} = 41.4$$

$$F = \frac{MS_{BG}}{MS_{WG}} = \frac{195.3}{41.4} = 4.72$$

Now we can compare our obtained F value with the critical value. The critical value of F at $\alpha = .05$ with 2 df for the numerator and 27 df for the denominator is 3.35.

Our F value is larger than the critical value, and we can report that our outcome was statistically significant, $F(2, 27) = 4.42$, $p < .05$. We would include an effect size estimate. In this case, eta-squared is appropriate. We need the total sum of squares for the denominator, and we obtain this simply by adding the between-groups and the within-groups sums of squares. In a one-way ANOVA, the treatment sum of squares is the between-groups sum of squares.

$$\eta^2 = \frac{SS_{treatment}}{SS_{total}} = \frac{390.6}{1508.3} = 0.259.$$

We have a large effect, as you can see.

The F statistic tells us that the groups differ but not specifically which groups differ from which. For example, it could be that the control group differs from the two treatment groups but that the difference between the oxygen drink group and the super-oxygen drink group is not statistically significant. To make this determination, we perform a post-ANOVA test.

FYI

If we wanted to use Excel to conduct our F test, we would choose ANOVA: single factor from the menu. Our output would look like Table 13.11.

TABLE 13.11   ANOVA: Single Factor

SUMMARY

Groups	Count	Sum	Average	Variance
Control	10	689	68.9	59.66
Oxygenated	10	746	74.6	47.16
Super-oxygenated	10	776	77.6	17.38

ANOVA

Source of Variation	SS	df	MS	F	p Value	F Crit
Between groups	390.6	2	195.3	4.72	0.02	3.35
Within groups	1,117.7	27	41.3962963			
Total	1,508.3	29				

There are a variety of tests we can use to find out which pairs of means are significantly different after we have done our ANOVA. Two of the most commonly used are Tukey's and Scheffé's tests. We will use the Tukey test for our example, and we direct you to your introductory statistics text for details on the other post-ANOVA tests.

Tukey's test involves finding the difference between each pair of group means and comparing those differences against what Tukey called the **honestly significant difference** (*HSD*). If the difference between a pair of means is greater than the *HSD,* you can report the result as a statistically significant difference. Tables of *HSD* values can be found in any introductory statistics text. To find the value, you need know your alpha level, the degrees of freedom associated with the error variance used in your ANOVA (for a one-way ANOVA, this is the within-groups *df*), and the number of groups you have. For our example, using an alpha of .05, 27 degrees of freedom, and three groups, we find in the table that the *HSD* value is 3.53. The exact value may differ from one table to another, so if you find a slightly different value, do not be concerned. The mean differences we have with our beverage study are as follows:

$$\text{Control} - \text{Super-oxygen} = 68.9 - 77.6 = -8.7$$

$$\text{Control} - \text{Oxygen} = 68.9 - 74.6 = -5.7$$

$$\text{Super-oxygen} - \text{Oxygen} = 77.6 - 74.6 = +3.0$$

Comparing these mean differences (ignore the sign) against the *HSD* of 3.53, we see that two of the comparisons are statistically significant and one is not. Both the super-oxygen group and the oxygen group performed significantly better than the control group. However, there is no significant difference between the two types of oxygenated drink.

You will recall that we ran a *t* test to compare the oxygenated group with the control group when the groups were different, or independent. And then we looked at how we would analyze our data if participants served in both conditions, a dependent groups design.

We went on to extend our study to include a third group, and we did an *F* test, a one-way ANOVA, much like an independent *t* test but for more than two groups. Is there an *F* test for dependent groups? You bet, and it is called a *one-way ANOVA with repeated measures.*

One-Way ANOVA With Repeated Measures. How would we conduct our beverage study using a repeated-measures design? Well, we would have to be concerned with various things such as carryover effects (see Chapter 8), but our purpose here is to show you how the analysis would be done.

Imagine that we have 10 participants, and all of them sample each of our three drinks (we would carefully control for order effects) and we measure math performance.

You might think that the analysis for this study would be the same as, or similar to, the analysis we just did when the groups were different people, but it is not. The mean squares that we use in a repeated-measures design are quite different from those we use for the independent groups design.

The formula for the *F* ratio for a **one-way ANOVA with repeated measures** is as follows:

$$F = \frac{MS_T}{MS_{P \times T}}$$

(*F* ratio for one-way ANOVA with repeated measures)

You can see that the numerator and the denominator for this F ratio are different from the ones we used in our earlier F test.

Because we use different mean squares in our F ratio, even if the data for our three conditions are identical to the data we used when we had three different groups, you will see that our ANOVA calculations cannot be the same. We will prove this to you by using the same numbers that we did earlier. But first, let's look at what we have to calculate for our F ratio when we have repeated measures.

The repeated-measures F test requires that we compare the *treatment mean square* with the *participant-by-treatment mean square*. Of course, we need to calculate the sums of squares first.

First, we find the sum of squares within participants (SS_{WP}). Next we partition or separate the within-participants sum of squares into two parts: the treatment sum of squares (SS_T) and the participant-by-treatment sum of squares (SS_{PxT}). Once we have done this, we can compute the treatment mean square by dividing the SS_T by the appropriate df for the numerator of the F ratio and the participant-by-treatment mean square, again by dividing the sum of squares by df, for our denominator.

The calculations for a repeated-measures ANOVA are a bit more complicated, and again we suggest you go back to your statistics textbook before you begin a repeated-measures analysis.

The formula for the within-participants sum of squares is as follows:

$$SS_{WP} = \sum X_{tot}^2 - \frac{\left(\sum P_1\right)^2 + \left(\sum P_2\right)^2 + \ldots + \left(\sum P_n\right)^2}{k}$$

(Within-participants sum of squares for one-way ANOVA with repeated measures)

This formula tells us to

1. Square all the scores in the study and sum the squares
2. Sum the scores of each participant and square each sum
3. Sum the squares from 2 and divide this sum by k, the number of conditions
4. Subtract the value you got in 3 from the value you got in 1

The bits and pieces we need for this sum of squares are also found in the previous sum of squares, so we just put those bits in the right places and our work is done.

Now we need to separate the within-participant sum of squares into the two sums of squares we will need for our F test, the treatment sum of squares and the participant-by-treatment sum of squares.

The formula for the treatment sum of squares is as follows:

$$SS_T = \frac{\left(\sum T_1\right)^2 + \left(\sum T_2\right)^2 + \ldots + \left(\sum T_k\right)^2}{n} - \frac{\left(\sum X_{tot}\right)^2}{kn}$$

(Treatment sum of squares for one-way ANOVA with repeated measures)

This formula tells us to

1. Sum all the scores in each condition and square the sums
2. Sum the squares from 1 and divide by the number of participants, n
3. Sum all the scores in the study, square the sum, and divide by kn
4. Subtract the value you got in 3 from the value you got in 2

We are almost there. We have the numerator of our F ratio. Finding the denominator is very easy. Remember that we are separating the within-participants sum of squares into two parts, the treatment sum of squares and the participant-by-treatment sum of squares, which we need for the denominator. To find the participant-by-treatment sum of squares, we only need to subtract the treatment sum of squares from the within-participant sum of squares.

$$SS_{PXT} = SS_{WP} - SS_{T}$$

(Participant-by-treatment sum of squares for one-way ANOVA with repeated measures)

Here are the data we used in our earlier ANOVA with different people in each beverage group. But now, all participants have served under each condition, and so we will run a repeated-measures ANOVA (see Table 13.12).

The first thing to do is to compute the within-participants sum of squares.

TABLE 13.12	Math Scores: One-Way ANOVA With Repeated Measures		
	C	**O**	**S**
	56	60	70
	80	75	80
	63	78	79
	62	85	83
	67	72	77
	71	73	75
	68	70	84
	76	80	78
	79	80	75
	67	73	75
M	**68.9**	**74.6**	**77.6**
SD	**7.72**	**6.87**	**4.17**

We have three conditions in our study, so the formula we will use to compute the within-participant sum of squares is as follows:

$$SS_{WP} = \sum X_{tot}^2 - \frac{(\sum P_1)^2 + (\sum P_2)^2 + \ldots + (\sum P_{10})^2}{3}$$

The leftmost part of our formula indicates we need to square all the scores in our experiment and sum the squares. We did this in our earlier analysis and we found the following:

$$\Sigma X_{tot}^2 = 164,459.$$

For the rest of the formula, we need to find the sum for each participant, and we need to square each sum. Table 13.13 has the scores we need.

Okay, now let's go ahead and calculate our within-participants sum of squares.

$$SS_{WP} = 164,459 - \frac{490,759}{3} = 872.67$$

Now we need to partition this sum of squares into the two bits we really care about, treatment and participant by treatment. Let's calculate the treatment sum of squares. For our three treatment condition study, the formula is as follows:

$$SS_T = \frac{(\sum T_1)^2 + (\sum T_2)^2 + (\sum T_3)^2}{n} - \frac{(\sum X_{tot})^2}{kn}$$

Let's create a simplified table showing the sums and squares we will need (see Table 13.14).

TABLE 13.13   Scores for One-Way ANOVA
With Repeated-Measures Calculation

Participant	Sums (P)	Squares (P²)
1	186	34,596
2	235	55,225
3	220	48,400
4	230	52,900
5	216	46,656
6	219	47,961
7	222	49,284
8	234	54,756
9	234	54,756
10	215	46,225
Sum		**490,759**

	C **T_1**	**O** **T_2**	**S** **T_3**	**Sum**
Sums (T)	689	746	776	2211
Squares (T^2)	474,721	556,516	602,176	

TABLE 13.14 Treatment Sums and Squares for Treatment Sum of Squares Calculation: One-Way ANOVA With Repeated Measures

We have what we need, so let's calculate the treatment sum of squares for our study:

$$SS_T = \frac{474,721 + 556,516 + 602,176}{10} - \frac{2,211^2}{30} = 390.6.$$

We need one more sum of squares, the participant by treatment sum of squares. This is a breeze.

$$SS_{P \times T} = SS_{WP} - SS_T = 872.67 - 390.6 = 482.07$$

We have the two sums of squares we need for our F ratio. All we have to do now is find the mean squares by dividing each sum of squares by its appropriate degrees of freedom. The formulas for the mean squares for a one-way repeated-measures ANOVA are as follows:

$$MS_T = \frac{SS_T}{k-1}$$

$$MS_{P \times T} = \frac{SS_{P \times T}}{(n-1)(k-1)}$$

(Means squares for one-way ANOVA with repeated measures)

The mean squares for our study are as follows:

$$MS_T = \frac{390.6}{2} = 195.3$$

$$MS_{P \times T} = \frac{482.07}{18} = 26.78$$

And finally, our F ratio is as follows:

$$F = \frac{MS_T}{MS_{P \times T}} = \frac{195.3}{26.78} = 7.29$$

The critical value of F with 2 df in the numerator and 18 df in the denominator is 6.01 at the .01 alpha level.

We can report that there was a significant difference between groups, $F(2, 18) = 7.29$, $p < .01$. The total sum of squares and treatment sum of squares are the same as in the one-way ANOVA we did on these data earlier, and so our effect size estimate is also the same ($\eta^2 = 0.259$, a large effect).

In order to specify which pairs of means are significantly different, we will follow our F test with a post hoc test such as the Tukey test. The *HSD* for our study at alpha = .05 is 5.92. Remember that for a pair of means to be significantly different, the difference must be larger than the *HSD*. Let's see which means are different according to the Tukey test.

Condition	Mean
Control	68.9
Oxygenated	74.6
Super-oxygenated	77.6

Oxygenated – Control $\quad\quad = \quad 5.7$, *NS*

Super-oxygenated – Control $\quad = \quad 8.7, p < .01$

Super-oxygenated – Oxygenated $= \quad 3$, *NS*

So our post hoc test tells us that the participants performed significantly better on the math test after drinking the super-oxygenated beverage than they did after drinking plain water and that no other differences were statistically significant.

FYI

Sadly, we cannot show you the output you would get from doing this analysis with Excel because Excel does not include a repeated-measures one-way ANOVA. But if Excel did do a repeated-measures one-way ANOVA, we think the output for our analysis should look something like Table 13.15.

TABLE 13.15 One-Way ANOVA With Repeated Measures

Source of Variance	SS	df	MS	F	p
Treatment	390.60	2	195.30	7.29	< .01
Participant × Treatment	482.07	18	26.78		

We have now taken you through the computations required to run a t test for independent groups when you have two levels of one IV and an F test for independent groups (one-way ANOVA) when you have more than two levels of one IV.

And we have run a *t* test for dependent groups when you have the same or matched participants serving under two levels of one IV and an *F* test for dependent groups (one-way ANOVA with repeated measures) when you have the same or matched participants serving under more than two levels of one IV.

As you can see, we have been talking about significance tests for studies with one independent variable. But what if we have two or three or more independent variables?

Maybe we should look at how food in the stomach might affect our beverage results. Maybe differences in math performance between groups who drink plain, oxygenated, or super-oxygenated water might depend on whether our participants have empty or full stomachs. Or perhaps we might want to see if the volume of beverage affects the performance on the math test. In both of these examples, we are interested in *not one but two* independent variables. In the former case, our second IV would be stomach content, and in the latter, our second IV would be volume of drink. When our dependent measure is on an interval or ratio scale and we have more than one independent variable, we may find that the appropriate statistical analysis is a two-way ANOVA.

Two-Way ANOVA. You may be wondering how many ANOVA designs there are. There are a lot. *ANOVA* is a general term for a large family of statistical analyses for dozens of designs. We will discuss a simple **two-way ANOVA,** an analysis we might use when we have two independent variables each with a number of levels and where different participants have been randomly assigned to each treatment condition.

The null hypothesis for a two-way ANOVA is the same as it is for any ANOVA: The population means are equal. And the alternative is also the same for all ANOVAs: The null is false.

But the two-way ANOVA has an interesting twist. You will recall that the *F* test for a one-way ANOVA allowed us to answer one question: Did the IV affect the DV? But with a two-way ANOVA, we actually do three *F* tests. One *F* test will answer the following question: Did our first IV affect the DV? A second *F* test will answer this question: Did our second IV affect the DV? And a third *F* test will answer the following question: Did the different combinations of levels of the two IVs affect the DV?

When we look at the effect of each IV on the DV in a two-way ANOVA, we are examining what are called **main effects.** When we look at the effect of different combinations of levels of our two IVs on the DV, we are examining what is called an **interaction effect.**

So let's imagine that we indeed are interested not only in our three types of beverages—plain water, oxygenated water, and super-oxygenated water—but we are also interested in the effect of stomach content, full versus empty stomach. There are three questions we can ask:

1. Overall, does type of drink make a difference in math performance?
2. Overall, does stomach content make a difference in math performance?
3. Does type of drink interact with stomach content in terms of math performance? In other words, does the effect of type of drink depend on stomach content?

Let's hypothesize a bit about these three questions.

1. Maybe we think that in general, people will do better on a math test the more oxygen there is in the drink they consume—in other words, we think there will be a main effect of type of drink.

2. Maybe we think that in general, people do better on a math test when they are hungry—in other words, we think there will be a main effect of stomach content.

Let's consider the third question carefully.

3. Maybe we think that the benefits of oxygenation of the drink that our people consume will be different when they have an empty stomach than when they have a full stomach. Maybe we think that on an empty stomach, the super-oxygenated drink will have a much stronger beneficial effect on math performance than it will when taken on a full stomach. In other words, we are hypothesizing an interaction between drink type and stomach content.

Three questions—three F tests.

For our study, we recruit 60 people and randomly assign 10 participants to each of our six conditions. The data are shown in Table 13.16.

We have three F tests to do, one for each main effect and one for the interaction. The three F ratios we will compute are as follows:

$$F_A = \frac{MS_A}{MS_{WG}}$$

$$F_B = \frac{MS_B}{MS_{WG}}$$

$$F_{A \times B} = \frac{MS_{A \times B}}{MS_{WG}}$$

(F ratios for a two-way ANOVA)

A is our first independent variable: type of drink, and
B is our second independent variable: stomach content.

We will need to compute the sum of squares for each independent variable, the sum of squares for the interaction, and the within-group sum of squares, which we will use in the denominator of all three F ratios.

TABLE 13.16	Math Scores: Two-Way ANOVA				
Full Stomach			**Empty Stomach**		
C	*O*	*S*	*C*	*O*	*S*
56	58	60	58	59	84
80	69	70	79	74	85
63	70	75	65	68	83
62	69	72	63	70	83
67	70	72	68	71	80
71	70	73	70	72	80
68	70	70	70	71	84
73	72	78	75	73	82
70	70	76	65	75	80
67	66	73	65	72	78

NOTE: We have assumed that sample sizes are the same for all conditions. The calculations for a two-way ANOVA with unequal sample sizes are more complicated, and we will not discuss them here.

The first thing we will do is compute the between-group sum of squares, which we will then partition or separate into the three bits that we actually want for our *F* tests, the sum of squares for *A,* the sum of squares for *B,* and the sum of squares for $A \times B$.

The formula for the between-group sum of squares is as follows:

$$SS_{BG} = \frac{\left(\sum A_1 B_1\right)^2 + \left(\sum A_1 B_2\right)^2 + \ldots + \left(\sum A_a B_b\right)^2}{n} - \frac{\left(\sum X_{tot}\right)^2}{n_{tot}}$$

(Between-group sum of squares: Two-way ANOVA)

where *a* is the number of levels of the first independent variable, and *b* is the number of levels of the second independent variable.

This formula tells us to

1. Sum the scores of the participants in each condition in the study and square each sum

2. Sum the squares from 1 and divide by *n,* the number of participants in each condition

3. Sum all the scores in the study, square the sum, and divide the total number of scores in the study

4. Subtract the value you got in 3 from the value you got in 2

The *SS* between groups can now be separated into the three sums of squares we will use in our *F* tests, *A, B,* and $A \times B$.

The formula for the *A* sum of squares is as follows:

$$SS_A = \frac{\left(\sum A_1\right)^2 + \left(\sum A_2\right)^2 + \ldots + \left(\sum A_k\right)^2}{bn} - \frac{\left(\sum X_{tot}\right)^2}{n_{tot}}$$

(*A* sum of squares for two-way ANOVA)

This formula tells us to

1. Sum all the scores in each of the *A* conditions (i.e., sum across all levels of *B*) and square each sum

2. Sum the squares from 1 and divide by *bn*

3. Sum all the scores in the study, square the sum, and divide the total number of scores in the study

4. Subtract the value you got in 3 from the value you got in 2

Next we find the sum of squares for our second main effect.

The formula for the B sum of squares is as follows:

$$SS_B = \frac{\left(\sum B_1\right)^2 + \left(\sum B_2\right)^2 + \ldots + \left(\sum B_k\right)^2}{an} - \frac{\left(\sum X_{tot}\right)^2}{n_{tot}}$$

(B sum of squares for two-way ANOVA)

This formula tells us to

1. Sum all the scores in each of the B conditions (i.e., sum across all levels of A) and square each sum
2. Sum the squares from 1 and divide by an
3. Sum all the scores in the study, square the sum, and divide the total number of scores in the study
4. Subtract the value you got in 3 from the value you got in 2

Because the between-group sum of squares is composed of the A, B, and $A \times B$ sum of squares, we will get the interaction sum of squares by subtraction.

The formula for the $A \times B$ sum of squares is as follows:

$$SS_{A \times B} = SS_{BG} - SS_A - SS_B$$

($A \times B$ sum of squares for two-way ANOVA)

We will use the within-group sum of squares for the denominator of all three F ratios, and this sum of squares is calculated in the same way it is for the ANOVAs we have done previously. We find the sum of squares within each group and sum them.

Let's do a two-way ANOVA on our beverage data.

First we compute the between-group sum of squares. For our six-group study, the formula is as follows:

$$SS_{BG} = \frac{\left(\sum A_1 B_1\right)^2 + \left(\sum A_1 B_2\right)^2 + \left(\sum A_2 B_1\right)^2 + \left(\sum A_2 B_2\right)^2 + \left(\sum A_3 B_1\right)^2 + \left(\sum A_3 B_2\right)^2}{n}$$
$$- \frac{\left(\sum X_{tot}\right)^2}{n_{tot}}$$

Table 13.17 has the bits we need to do the computations.

A is type of drink
  A_1: Control
  A_2: Oxygenated
  A_3: Super-oxygenated

B is stomach content
B_1: Full
B_2: Empty

TABLE 13.17 Scores for Two-Way ANOVA Calculation

Stomach Content		B_1			B_2		
Type of Drink	A_1	A_2	A_3	A_1	A_2	A_3	Sum
Sum	689	697	737	696	742	806	4,366
Sum^2	474,721	485,809	556,516	484,416	550,564	633,616	3,185,642

We can now compute the between-group sum of squares.

$$SS_{BG} = \frac{474,721 + 485,809 + 556,516 + 484,416 + 550,564 + 633,616}{10} - \frac{4,366}{60}$$
$$= 307,061.6 - 305,592.07 = 1,469.53$$

Now let's compute the three sums of squares we actually want to test.

We first calculate the sum of squares for the A main effect. We have three levels of A, and our formula is

$$SS_A = \frac{\left(\sum A_1\right)^2 + \left(\sum A_2\right)^2 + \left(\sum A_3\right)^2}{bn} - \frac{\left(\sum X_{tot}\right)^2}{n_{tot}}$$

The data we need for this calculation are in Table 13.18.

TABLE 13.18 Sums and Squares for A Main Effect Calculation: Two-Way ANOVA

	A_1	A_2	A_3	Sum
Sum	1,355	1,389	1,538	4,282
Sum^2	1,836,025	1,929,321	2,365,444	6,130,790

And our sum of squares is

$$SS_A = \frac{1,836,025 + 1,929,321 + 2,365,444}{20} - 305,592.07$$
$$= 306,539.5 - 305,592.07 = 947.43$$

To find the B sum of squares, we use Table 13.19.

$$SS_B = \frac{4,326,400 + 4,848,804}{30} - 305,592.07$$

$$= 305,840.13 - 305,592.07 = 248.07$$

TABLE 13.19   Sums and Squares for B Main Effect Calculation: Two-Way ANOVA

	B_1	B_2	*Sum*
Sum	2,080	2,202	4,282
Sum²	4,326,400	4,848,804	9,175,204

Because the between-group sum of squares is composed of the A, B, and $A \times B$ sum of squares, we can find the $A \times B$ sum of squares by subtraction:

$$SS_{A \times B} = SS_{BG} - SS_A - SS_B = 1,469.53 - 947.43 - 248.07 = 274.03$$

Finally, we need the within-group sum of squares to use in the denominator for all three F tests. We compute the sum of squares within each group and sum them, and our sum of squares is

$$SS_{WG} = 1,302.40$$

We can now compute the mean squares we need and do our F tests.

We use the within-group mean square for our three tests. We calculate the mean square within groups by dividing the sum of squares within groups by the appropriate degrees of freedom. For this ANOVA, degrees of freedom within groups are equal to the total number of participants × the total number of groups.

$$MS_{WG} = \frac{SS_{WG}}{n_{tot} - k} = \frac{1,302.40}{54} = 24.12$$

We find the MS_A by dividing the SS_A by df. The degrees of freedom are $a - 1$, the number of levels of the A independent variable minus 1. We have three levels of A, and so $df = 2$.

$$MS_A = \frac{SS_A}{df_a} = \frac{947.43}{2} = 473.72$$

We can now compute the F ratio for the main effect of type of drink, A.

$$F_A = \frac{MS_A}{MS_{WG}} = \frac{473.72}{24.12} = 19.64$$

Degrees of freedom are $b - 1$, number of levels of B minus 1.

$$MS_B = \frac{SS_B}{df_b} = \frac{248.07}{1} = 248.07$$

$$F_B = \frac{MS_B}{MS_{WG}} = \frac{248.07}{24.12} = 10.28$$

We finish our analysis by computing the interaction F ratio using $(a - 1)(b - 1)$ degrees of freedom to find the interaction mean square.

$$MS_{A \times B} = \frac{SS_{A \times B}}{df_{a \times b}} = \frac{272.03}{2} = 137.01$$

$$F_{A \times B} = \frac{MS_{A \times B}}{MS_{WG}} = \frac{137.01}{24.12} = 5.68$$

Let's put all our calculations into an ANOVA summary table.

FYI

Although Excel seems to have a two-way ANOVA in its menu, we have not been able to get it to work. Table 13.20 shows what the output from Excel should look like.

TABLE 13.20 ANOVA Summary Table

Source	SS	df	MS	F	p
A	947.43	2	473.72	19.64	< .001
B	248.07	1	248.07	10.28	< .01
A × B	274.03	2	137.01	5.68	< .01
Within groups	**1,302.403333**	**54**	**24.12**		

We can see that there is a significant main effect for type of drink, $F(2, 54) = 19.64$, $p < .001$; a main effect for stomach content, $F(1, 54) = 10.28$, $p < .01$; and a significant interaction effect, $F(2, 54) = 5.68$, $p < .01$. Post-ANOVA Tukey tests show that the superoxygenated group ($M = 76.9$) performed significantly better than the control group ($M = 67.75$) and the oxygen group ($M = 69.45$) but that the control group and oxygen group were not significantly different.

We would want to include effect size estimates for our three treatment effects, and we will use eta-squared again to do this. We use the sum of squares for A, B, and $A \times B$ in the numerator and sum of squares total (sum of squares between groups plus sum of squares within groups) in the denominator. Our effect size estimates are as follows:

$$\eta_A^2 = \frac{SS_A}{SS_{tot}} = \frac{947.43}{2771.93} = 0.312$$

$$\eta_B^2 = 0.089$$

$$\eta_{A \times B}^2 = 0.099$$

The *A* effect was large, and the *B* and *A* × *B* effects were small.

We think that the best way to see what went on in a two-way ANOVA is to look at graphs of the main effects and the interaction. To graph these, we will use a table of group means (see Table 13.21).

Let's first look at the main effect of type of drink, which was significant at an alpha level of .001.

Clearly, the scores were highest for the O group and lowest for the control group (see Figure 13.2).

Now let's graph our second main effect, stomach content (see Figure 13.3).

Participants who were hungry did better those who were not.

The real value of a two-way ANOVA is our ability to examine an interaction effect (see Figure 13.4).

We know from our *F* test that the interaction was significant, and we can see that interaction by examining the figure. It is when participants are hungry that the super-oxygenated drink really improves math performance.

If we were to only look at the two main effects, we would overlook the most interesting finding in our study—the interaction effect.

Remember that the APA expects researchers to provide an estimate of their effect sizes in the report. See Chapter 2 for details on estimates for various tests.

As we have said, ANOVA is a family of statistical analyses suitable for assessing differences among group means. And a great deal of research in psychology involves doing just that. But not all.

Sometimes, researchers are looking at nominal or ordinal variables and have classified things into categories. In these cases, a nonparametric analysis, such as a chi-square, might be the appropriate test of significance.

TABLE 13.21	Group Means: Two-Way ANOVA			
	A_1	A_2	A_3	*Means*
B_1	67.7	68.4	71.9	69.33
B_2	67.8	70.5	81.9	73.4
Mean	**67.75**	**69.45**	**76.9**	

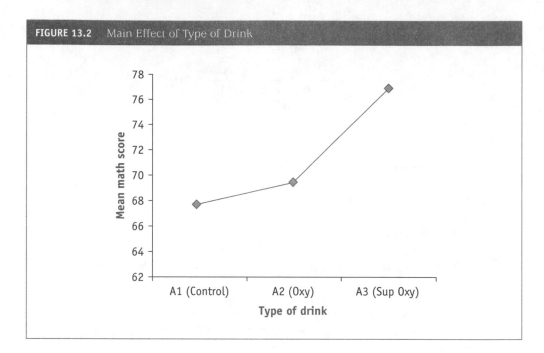

FIGURE 13.2   Main Effect of Type of Drink

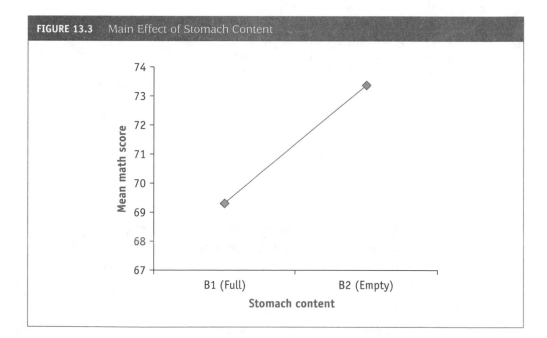

FIGURE 13.3   Main Effect of Stomach Content

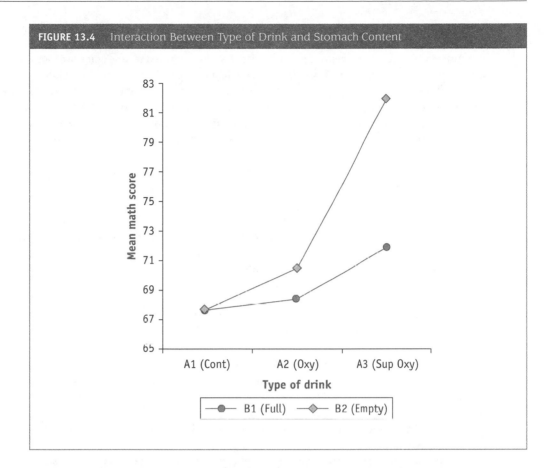

FIGURE 13.4   Interaction Between Type of Drink and Stomach Content

Chi-Square Tests for Frequency Differences

Do dentists really prefer Crest? How would we do a study to answer this question? First, we would be more specific in our question. Let's ask whether dentists prefer Crest over Colgate. We should randomly select a sample of dentists and ask each dentist to declare his or her preference. We count the number of people preferring each brand. These data are not measures, and means cannot be calculated. If dentists do not have a preference, we would expect about the same number of people to pick each brand of toothpaste, and we could use a chi-square test, called the **goodness-of-fit test,** to test our hypothesis. In chi-square, our null hypothesis is that our observed frequencies will not be different from what we expect from chance.

The chi-square ratio is as follows:

$$\chi^2 = \sum \frac{(O - E)^2}{E}$$

(Chi-square ratio)

The obtained value of chi-square is compared to the critical value where degrees of freedom are the number of categories – 1. If the obtained value is larger than the critical value, the null is rejected. The researcher concludes that the obtained frequencies are significantly different from the expected frequencies. This test compares the frequency distribution of obtained scores with the frequency distribution that is expected, if the null hypothesis were true. Chi-square is a nonparametric test because the test does not make the assumption that the population is normal in shape. Indeed, the inference that is made is *about the shape* of the population distribution. The null says it has a certain shape, and the alternative says it has a different shape.

So let's randomly select 100 dentists from a listing of all dentists across the country and ask them to indicate whether they prefer Crest or Colgate. Our null is that there is no preference, and so we would expect about 50 dentists to choose each brand, and 50 is the expected frequency we would use in our test. Suppose 55 of our sample of 100 dentists chose Crest, and the rest chose Colgate. To conduct our chi-square test, we would create a table such as the one in Table 13.22.

And now we can compute our chi-square:

$$\chi^2 = \sum \frac{(O-E)^2}{E} = \frac{(55-50)^2}{50} + \frac{(45-50)^2}{50} = 0.5 + 0.5 = 1$$

We will compare our obtained value with the critical value of chi-square. We have only two categories, so $df = 1$, and at an alpha level of .05, the critical value of chi-square is 3.84. You can see that our obtained value is smaller than the critical value, and we cannot reject the null.

We would say that there is no statistical evidence that dentists prefer Crest over Colgate, $\chi^2 (1, N = 100) = 1$, *NS*.

For an outcome such as this, we would not report an effect size calculation because there is no evidence of an effect, but had the chi-square been statistically significant, we would proceed as follows. Effect size for a chi-square goodness-of-fit test is reported either as Cohen's *w* or as pairwise comparisons using odds ratios. We will calculate both with this example.

TABLE 13.22   Brand Preference: Expected and Obtained Frequencies

	Crest	*Colgate*
O	55	45
E	50	50
O – E	5	–5
$(O - E)^2$	25	25
$(O - E)^2/E$	0.5	0.5

Cohen's w is calculated in the same form as a chi-square, except proportions are used instead of actual frequencies.

$$w = \sum \frac{(P_O - P_E)^2}{P_E} = \frac{(.55 - .50)^2}{.50} + \frac{(.45 - .50)^2}{.50} = 0.005 + 0.005 = 0.01$$

According to the guidelines we included in Chapter 4, this is a small effect. Odds ratios are calculated as follows:

The odds of a dentist recommending Crest over Colgate is 55/45 = 1.22.

The odds of a dentist recommending Colgate over Crest is 45/55 = 0.82.

As you can see, the goodness-of-fit test is easy to use and suitable when you have frequency data on one variable.

Perhaps we have categorized on two variables simultaneously and are interested in the relationship between these two categorical variables. In this case, we might use a **chi-square test for independence.** Let's extend our toothpaste study to include two variables. Do you think amount of exposure to advertising might influence dentists? Let's ask another sample of dentists (we will ask 200 this time) to tell us how much TV they watch per week and what toothpaste they prefer. And let's include an *Other* category for our toothpaste variable. What we are doing, then, is simultaneously classifying our dentists on two variables: brand of toothpaste preferred and amount of time spent watching TV. In a chi-square test for independence, the null is that the two categories are indeed independent, and the alternative is that they are dependent. In other words, the alternative for our toothpaste example is that preference for brand of toothpaste depends on the amount of TV our dentists watch.

The chi-square ratio is computed in the same way for this test as for the goodness-of-fit test. If our obtained chi-square is larger than the critical value with $df =$ (number of categories of variable 1 – 1) (number of categories of variable 2 – 1), then we will conclude that the variables are dependent.

Table 13.23 shows our frequency data.

When we did our chi-square test for goodness of fit, the expected frequencies were determined by the null hypothesis beforehand, or a priori. For a chi-square test for independence, you may recall that the expected frequencies are found post hoc. The formula we use to calculate the expected frequency for each cell is

$$E = \text{(Row Sum)(Col Sum)/Total.}$$

TABLE 13.23   Obtained Frequencies

TV Hours/Week	Brand			Row Sum
	Crest	*Colgate*	*Other*	
> 14 hours	30	20	10	60
8–13 hours	25	25	20	70
< 8 hours	20	25	25	70
Column sum	**75**	**70**	**55**	**200**

TABLE 13.24	Expected Frequencies			
	Brand			
TV Hours/Week	**Crest**	**Colgate**	**Other**	**Row Sum**
> 14 hours	22.5	21	16.5	60
8–13 hours	26.25	24.5	19.25	70
< 8 hours	26.25	24.5	19.25	70
Column sum	**75**	**70**	**55**	**200**

Our expected frequencies for our toothpaste study are in Table 13.24.
Our chi-square value is as follows:

$$\chi^2 = \sum \frac{(O-E)^2}{E} = \frac{(30-22.5)^2}{22.5} + \dots + \frac{(25-19.25)^2}{19.25} = 8.42$$

We have 4 degrees of freedom, and so the critical value of chi-square at $\alpha = .05$ is 9.49. Again we fail to reject the null. We have no statistical evidence that preference for brand of toothpaste depends on amount of TV watched per week, $\chi^2 (4, N = 200) = 8.42$, *NS*. We will go ahead and calculate Cramer's *v*, as an effect size estimate, for this analysis so you can see how it is done.

$$v = \sqrt{\frac{\chi^2}{N_{tot}}} = \sqrt{\frac{8.42}{200}} = 0.205$$

According to the guidelines we included in Chapter 4, this is a small effect.

Chi-square is easy to compute and suitable for categorical data. We think it is always better to use parametric tests of significance rather than nonparametric tests, and so we encourage our students to collect interval or ratio measures if they can. Of course, sometimes that is not possible, and so nonparametric analyses must be used. We will mention some of the additional common nonparametric tests here, but students should refer to a statistics text for more information about these tests.

A nonparametric alternative to a *t* test for independent groups is the **Mann-Whitney** *U* **test,** which detects differences in central tendency and differences in the entire distributions of rank-ordered data.

The **Wilcoxon signed-ranks test** is an alternative to a *t* test for dependent groups for rank-order data on the same or matched participants.

A nonparametric alternative to the one-way ANOVA is the **Kruskal-Wallis** *H* **test,** which is used when the data are rank orders of three or more independent groups. When those groups are dependent (i.e., repeated measures), a nonparametric test is the **Friedman** *T* **test.**

These statistics are quite easy to compute, and again we refer you to any general statistics text for details.

We have found that students in our methods courses are often interested in how variables are related. Are richer people happier people? Do more attractive students get better grades than less attractive students? These are questions about correlations, and we will discuss two tests of significance that can be used to answer these kinds of questions.

Correlation Tests of Significance

When we have measures on two **continuous variables** and we want to know if these variables are systematically related, we might choose Pearson's r test. If we have rank-order data on two variables, we might choose Spearman's rank-order correlation test.

Pearson's r test. Pearson's r test is used to determine if there is a **linear relationship** between two continuous variables. Values of r can range from +1 to –1. The sign indicates the direction of the relationship, and the value tells us the strength. If there is no relationship between the variables, $r = 0$; if there is a perfect correlation, then $r = +1$ or -1. Of course, perfect correlations do not occur in the real world, so if you get one, you have probably correlated two variables that are measuring the same thing. Such would be the case if you correlate height measured in inches with height measured in cm. As with the other tests of significance, if your obtained r value (ignoring the sign) is larger than the critical value with $n_p - 2$ df, you will conclude that there is a statistically significant relationship between the variables. The null hypothesis for r is that there is no relationship between the variables in the population.

Pearson's coefficient is useful for determining relationships between continuous variables. But there are some things we want to bring to your attention. Pearson's r is only appropriate if the relationship between the variables is **linear.** By this, we mean that the best way to describe the relationship is with a straight line. Pearson's r is not useful if the relationship is curvilinear, for example. Performance on a cognitive task, such as writing a tough exam, depends in part on arousal. If you are asleep, you probably will not do well. Likewise, if you are totally freaked out, you will not do well either. A moderate level of physiological arousal is best for cognitive tasks such as exam writing. So the relationship between arousal and exam performance is curvilinear, not linear, and calculating Pearson's r would not give a result that reflects this relationship.

Pearson's r also assumes what is called **homogeneity of variance.** This means that the variability around the regression line (or straight line of best fit) is more or less equal from top to bottom. If there is a lot more variability in Y for high values of X, for example, than for low values of X, Pearson's r will underestimate the strength of the relationship between X and Y for low values of X and overestimate the relationship for high values of X. It is best to examine a **scattergram** of the bivariate distribution to make sure that the variability in Y along the regression line is about the same.

Another problem arises when there are a few wildly extreme points, called **outliers.** These can have big effects on the size of the correlation. How to treat outliers is a matter of debate, and interested students should consult an upper-level statistics text for more information on this debate.

Perhaps our research of the literature leads us to think that there might be a negative correlation between criminality and income. In other words, we believe that for people who have been convicted of crimes, those who are poorer commit more crimes than those who are less poor. From databases kept by our local police department, we are able to find measures of both income level (average over 5 years) and number of criminal convictions (over 5 years) for 30 men between the ages of 18 and 25. Both variables are ratio variables, and so we can use Pearson's r test to measure the relationship between them.

The formula for Pearson's r is

$$r = \frac{\sum XY - (\sum X)(\sum Y)/n}{\sqrt{SS_X SS_Y}}$$

(Pearson's r coefficient)

This formula indicates that we need to multiply each pair of measures that we have for each participant and sum those products. We also need the sums and sums of squares for each variable.

Table 13.25 has the bits and pieces we need to do our correlation test.

Let's compute Pearson's r for our data.

$$r = \frac{\sum XY - (\sum X)(\sum Y)/n}{\sqrt{SS_X SS_Y}}$$

$$r = \frac{3,917,738 - (573,172)(237)/30}{\sqrt{(36,550.31)(26.51)}} = -.63$$

As usual, we compare our obtained value with the critical value found in any statistics text. The critical value of r at alpha = .01 and 28 df is .463.

Our value (ignoring the sign) is larger than the critical value, and we may reject the null and say that there is a significant correlation between income level and number of convictions, $r(28) = -.63$, $p < .01$. We would report the coefficient of determination as our effect size estimate in this case ($r^2 = .397$), and once again we have a large effect.

As you may have gathered, we are both visual people and like to graph things. Figure 13.5 presents the scattergram of our data.

As you can see, as income increases, number of convictions decreases.

Pearson's correlation test is suitable for assessing the linear relationship between two continuous variables. Pearson's correlation test has been adapted for various kinds of measures. One of these is suitable for rank-order data.

Spearman's Rank-Order Correlation Test. Imagine that we have rank-ordered 10 occupations from highest to lowest in terms of average income. And we conduct a survey asking people to rank-order the 10 occupations in terms of prestige. We wonder if those occupations with higher income ranks are the ones that people rank as more prestigious. Both variables are rank orders, and **Spearman's rank-order correlation test** will answer our question.

The formula for Spearman's rho is

$$rho = 1 - \frac{6 \sum d^2}{n(n^2 - 1)}$$

(Spearman's rho coefficient)

where d is the difference between each pair of ranks, and n is the number of paired ranks.

TABLE 13.25	Income and Number of Convictions: Pearson's r Test				
Participant	**Average Income**	**Convictions**	X^2	Y^2	XY
1	12,000	22	144,000,000	484	264,000
2	12,500	20	156,250,000	400	250,000
3	14,000	10	196,000,000	100	140,000
4	14,200	15	201,640,000	225	213,000
5	14,300	10	204,490,000	100	143,000
6	15,000	15	225,000,000	225	225,000
7	15,400	10	237,160,000	100	154,000
8	15,600	10	243,360,000	100	156,000
9	16,000	8	256,000,000	64	128,000
10	16,000	8	256,000,000	64	128,000
11	16,300	8	265,690,000	64	130,400
12	16,500	10	272,250,000	100	165,000
13	17,000	5	289,000,000	25	85,000
14	17,450	5	304,502,500	25	87,250
15	17,500	6	306,250,000	36	105,000
16	17,600	6	309,760,000	36	105,600
17	17,650	8	311,522,500	64	141,200
18	17,650	8	311,522,500	64	141,200
19	17,700	7	313,290,000	49	123,900
20	17,800	3	316,840,000	9	53,400
21	17,800	8	316,840,000	64	142,400
22	18,000	5	324,000,000	25	90,000
23	18,500	4	342,250,000	16	74,000
24	20,222	4	408,929,284	16	80,888
25	20,500	9	420,250,000	81	184,500
26	22,000	3	484,000,000	9	66,000
27	26,000	3	676,000,000	9	78,000
28	35,000	1	1,225,000,000	1	35,000
29	37,000	4	1,369,000,000	16	148,000
30	40,000	2	1,600,000,000	4	80,000
Sum	**573,172**	**237**	**12,286,796,784**	**2,575**	**3,917,738**

To calculate this correlation, we will need to find the rank differences, square the difference, and sum the squares. Table 13.26 contains the information we need.

Let's compute Spearman's *rho*.

$$rho = 1 - \frac{6(10)}{10(100 - 1)} = 0.94$$

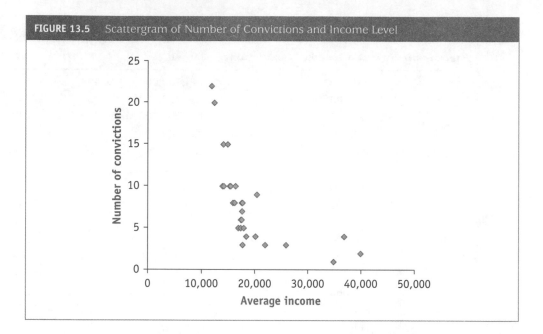

FIGURE 13.5   Scattergram of Number of Convictions and Income Level

TABLE 13.26   Prestige and Income for 10 Occupations:
Ranks, Differences, and Squares for Spearman's *rho*

| | Ranks | | | |
Occupation	Prestige	Income	d	d²
Physician	1	1	0	0
Lawyer	2	2	0	0
Banker	3	3	0	0
Professor	4	4	0	0
Engineer	5	7	−2	4
Hairstylist	6	6	0	0
Computer technician	7	5	2	4
Secretary	8	9	−1	1
Server	9	8	1	1
Laborer	10	10	0	0
Sum				**10**

When we consult a table of critical values of *rho,* we will see that our obtained value is significant at the .001 level. And we may conclude that there is a significant positive correlation between prestige and income ranks, *rho* ($n = 10$) = .94, $p < .001$, and that the

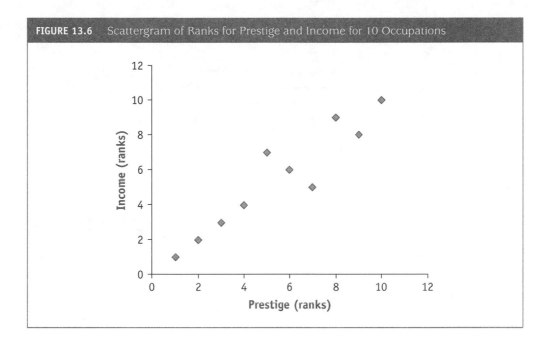

FIGURE 13.6   Scattergram of Ranks for Prestige and Income for 10 Occupations

effect is a large one ($rho^2 = .88$). And to inspect our relationship visually, we would plot our data in a scattergram (see Figure 13.6).

As Figure 13.6 clearly shows, occupations with higher incomes are perceived as more prestigious.

Our primary objective in this chapter was to go through in a step-by-step fashion the typical kinds of statistical analyses that our students use to analyze the data they gather for various research projects that they do in our research methods course. And we have shown you how those analyses should be reported. You may find that we have not covered the particular statistical analysis that you need for your research project. We wish that we could anticipate all the possible analyses that students taking research methods courses might use, but alas, we cannot do that. And once again, we will have to refer you to your statistics textbook for specifics on analyses that we did not cover here. But perhaps we can offer some help to you as you consider your choices.

Choosing the Appropriate Test of Significance

Deciding which test of significance will most appropriately and best answer a research question is often very difficult for students. And this is a skill that cannot be acquired without a solid understanding of statistics. We include two flow diagrams in Figure 13.17 that we hope might help.

FIGURE 13.7 Choosing the Appropriate Test of Significance

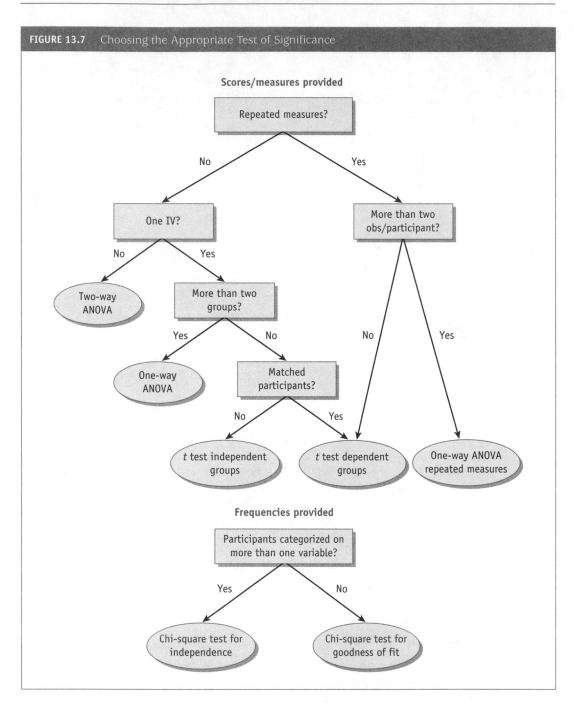

Conceptual Exercise 13C

Which test of significance would you recommend for the following research problems?

1. You wish to compare the effectiveness of three different training approaches on gymnastic performance. Individuals are randomly assigned to one of three training programs, and you measure mean performance using judges' scores.

2. You wish to compare the popularity of four different styles of underwear: briefs, bikinis, boxers, and thongs. You are also interested in whether the popularity differs between men and women. Your approach is to simply ask an equal number of men and women what they are wearing today. To control for age, you restrict your sample to individuals who are 18 to 24 years of age.

3. Many students hold part-time jobs while attending university. You think the amount of time a student works will have a negative effect on his or her academic performance. You test this by obtaining a sample of students and asking them how many hours, on average, they worked per week for the last academic term. You use their GPA at the end of term as your measure of academic performance.

4. A new drug has been released. The pharmaceutical company claims it is better than any other drug on the market to control hallucinations in patients diagnosed with schizophrenia. You decide to test the drug. You randomly select a number of patients diagnosed with schizophrenia and randomly assign them to two conditions. The treatment group will be prescribed the new drug, and the others will be given their usual drug treatment. For 3 months, the participants record the number of hallucinations they experience. You are interested in comparing the mean number of hallucinations reported by the two groups.

5. A new drug has been released. The pharmaceutical company claims it is better than any other drug on the market to control hallucinations in patients diagnosed with schizophrenia. You decide to test the drug. You randomly select a number of patients diagnosed with schizophrenia. Half the participants take the new drug for a 6-month period and then take their regular drug for the next 6 months. The other half take the drugs in reverse, the regular drug for the first 6 months and the new drug for the subsequent 6 months. All participants record the number of hallucinations they experience during each 6-month period. You are interested in comparing the mean number of hallucinations when participants are on the new drug with the mean number of hallucinations when they are on their regular prescription.

More on Data Analysis With Computers

Computers have fundamentally changed data analysis. The computer has meant that we do not have to worry about embarrassing arithmetic errors or looking up critical values in tables, and even the most complex analyses take only seconds to calculate. On the other hand, just because you can complete a complex statistical analysis with a few mouse clicks does not mean that you are using the correct analysis or that you are able to interpret the analysis. At our university, we offer an intermediate statistics course that includes how to use SPSS (Statistical Package for the Social Sciences), but we are not going to cover computer use here. However, it is important to note that t tests (for independent groups and dependent groups), Pearson's r, one-way and two-way ANOVA, and several other simple statistical tests are built into Microsoft Excel. Also, we encourage our students to use a very educational (and free) package on the Web from Vassar College in New York state (search word: VassarStats).

CHAPTER SUMMARY

This chapter was designed for students doing or proposing research projects, and it begins with a refresher of basic descriptive and inferential procedures.

Descriptive statistics are used to summarize data, and **inferential statistics** are used to generalize from samples to populations. Descriptive statistics that summarize the **central tendency** of distributions include the mean, the median, and the mode. The **mean** is the arithmetic average, the **median** is the middle value, and the **mode** is the most frequently occurring value in a distribution.

Descriptive statistics that summarize the **variability** of distributions include the range and the standard deviation. The **range** is the span of a distribution, and the **standard deviation** is the average distance of scores from the mean.

Selecting the appropriate descriptive statistics depends in part on the level of the measured variables. The mode would be the measure of central tendency suitable for **nominal variables. Ordinal variables** can be described by mode and range. Median and/or mean and range and/or standard deviation can be reported for **interval variables. Ratio variables** should be described by the mean and standard deviation.

The t **test** is a parametric test of significance that can be used to test for the difference between the means of two sets of **interval** or **ratio** measures. If those measures have been provided by participants who were randomly assigned to groups, a t **test for independent groups** may be used. If those measures were provided by one group of participants (a **repeated-measures design**) or by matched pairs of participants (a **matched groups design**), a t **test for dependent groups** may be used.

The F **test** is a parametric test of significance that can be used to test for differences among means of more than two sets of interval or ratio measures. A **one-way ANOVA** can be used to test for differences among means when participants have been randomly assigned to several levels of one independent variable. A **one-way ANOVA with repeated measures** can be used to test for differences among means when participants serve under each level of one independent variable.

A **two-way ANOVA** can be used to test for differences among means when participants have been randomly assigned to all combinations of the levels of two independent variables. Three F **ratios** are calculated in a two-way ANOVA, one for each **main effect** and one for the **interaction effect.**

Chi-square is a nonparametric test of significance that is used to compare frequency counts on categorical (nominal or ordinal) variables. The **goodness-of-fit test** is used to compare obtained with expected frequencies on one variable, and the **test for independence** is used to compare obtained with expected frequencies on two variables. The chi-square test compares the shape of the obtained frequency distribution with that specified in the null hypothesis.

To determine the **linear relationship** between two **continuous variables**, the **Pearson r test** may be used. **Spearman's rank-order correlation,** *rho,* can be used to test for the linear relationship between the ranks of two variables (i.e., ordinal). Both correlation tests produce a correlation coefficient ranging from -1 to $+1$. The closer the correlation is to -1 or $+1$, the stronger the relationship.

ANSWERS TO CONCEPTUAL EXERCISES

Conceptual Exercise 13A

1. Probably mean is the best measure of average GPA.

2. Perhaps mode would be the best measure here because it would be the "typical" number of children

3. Well, some basketball players are really tall, so perhaps median might be the best measure of average height.

Conceptual Exercise 13B

1. IQ is an interval variable, and the mean and standard deviation would be appropriate.

2. Salary is a ratio variable that is typically positively skewed. Perhaps median is the best measure of central tendency. Standard deviation should be reported.

3. Again, median and standard deviation are appropriate for salary.

4. Student evaluations are on an interval scale, at best. Median or even mode could be used, and range should be reported.

5. Modal dress size and range should be reported.

Conceptual Exercise 13C

1. Mean performance is the dependent measure, so we know that a parametric test of significance is in order. There is one IV, type of training, with three levels. We should choose a one-way ANOVA.

2. Presumably, we are going to count the number of people who report wearing each type of underwear and classify them by gender. Our research question is, does type of underwear worn by our group depend on gender? This question could be assessed with a chi-square test for independence. Any inference we make could only be generalized to the population from which we sampled (i.e., people between 18 and 24 years of age).

3. This research question is best answered with a correlation test. Because the variables, GPA and average number of hours worked per week, are both ratio variables, Pearson's r is a good test to use to see if the variables are related.

4. Participants have been randomly assigned to groups, and the dependent measure (number of hallucinations) is a ratio variable. The appropriate test of significance is a t test for independent groups.

5. Well, let's assume that any carryover effects that might arise with a design such as this have been addressed. Because all participants served in both conditions, a repeated-measures design, the appropriate test is a t test for dependent groups.

FAQ

Q1: If variability is such a problem, why not use lab rats for everything?

A1: Well, we sure can use lab rats to study many kinds of behavior. Lots of research in basic learning processes has relied on the lab rat. Rats are probably not going to help us understand the complex mental processes that we humans have.

Q2: Which average is best?

A2: It is not really a matter of best. The choice of which measure to use depends on the nature of the variable and, in some cases, the shape of the distribution.

Q3: What's the difference between standard deviation and variance? Why do we need both?

A3: The variance is the square of the standard deviation. Standard deviation is the measure of variable we use descriptively. Variance is used in inferential analyses.

Q4: How do I determine what inferential statistics to use?

A4: The short answer is that it depends on your variables (i.e., nominal, ordinal, interval, or ratio) and your research hypothesis. Many statistics books provide decision flowcharts for determining which test to use, and we would suggest you go back to your statistics text to review this.

Q5: Why is regression called regression?

A5: It is a reference to regressing to the mean. A regression line is fitted as closely as possible to the mean of the values of Y for any given level of X. The fit is one that minimizes the sum of the squared distances between the actual Y values and the predicted Y values (i.e., the regression line). This method of best fitting the straight line to a bivariate distribution is called the least squares criterion, developed by Karl Pearson.

Q6: What do I do if my correlation data form a curve and not a straight line?

A6: It is always a good idea to plot your data so you can see what the relationship looks like. If it is not a linear relationship, then do not use linear regression. There are nonlinear procedures that fit a curve to the data instead of a straight line. For example, the equation for a line is $y = mx +$ constant, but a curve with one bend uses a quadratic equation (remember this from high school?) $y = ax^2 + bx +$ constant; a curve with two bends is a cubic equation $y = ax^3 + bx^2 + cx +$ constant, and so on.

NOTE: We have not included chapter exercises and projects here. This chapter is intended for students who are conducting or proposing a research project for their methods class.

Visit the study site at www.sagepub.com/evansmprstudy for practice quizzes and other study resources.

CHAPTER 14

Communicating in Psychology

OBJECTIVES

After studying this chapter, students should be able to

- Describe the difference between scientific and literary writing
- Prepare an organized summary of the literature on a particular topic following APA style requirements
- Define plagiarism and describe how to avoid it
- Describe the difference between a primary and secondary source
- Recognize common errors in writing and correct them
- Prepare a formal research report following APA requirements
- Give an effective oral presentation
- Create an effective poster

First we want to say that we sympathize with you. We know you are probably frustrated because professors of different courses have different writing and formatting styles that they expect you to follow. We also find this frustrating and wish everyone would use a consistent style, preferably APA, of course. But sadly, this is not likely to happen any time soon. The writing portions of this chapter focus on the style requirements of the American Psychological Association, the style manual followed by most psychologists.

WRITING IN PSYCHOLOGY

Writing in science is very different from literary writing. **Scientific writing** has one objective: to communicate information. **Literary writing** has a second objective: to entertain. It may be perfectly acceptable in literary writing to change voice and tense abruptly, use flowery language, use amusing or unusual sentence construction, and even to write grammatically incorrect but interesting sentences. None of this is acceptable in scientific writing. The goal is to inform the reader as concisely and clearly as possible. As you read this chapter, you may notice that we, in writing this textbook, have violated some of the very rules we recommend. That is partly because a secondary objective to our primary objective of communicating information clearly in this book is to make the material interesting and even fun at times. Textbooks in psychology, unlike research reports published in academic journals, do not always follow the rules of APA because the goals are somewhat different and the book publisher controls various aspects of the style and design of the book. So, do as we say—not as we do.

> **FYI**
>
> Students often become confused when the format rules they learn in class are not the same as the format they see in published articles. The confusion arises because the format rules of the American Psychological Association are used to guide the preparation of a manuscript. A researcher submits a manuscript to the editors for publication. The published version that appears on the glossy pages of the journal has completely different formatting than the original manuscript.

Plagiarism

Recently, a student of ours said, "But I didn't mean to plagiarize. I cited the source." And we said, "Intention is irrelevant, and citing the source is not necessarily enough."

Plagiarism is borrowing the words or ideas of another without crediting the source for those words or ideas.

- When you write about an idea of another without crediting that person as the source of the idea, you are indicating that the idea was yours. This is plagiarism.
- When you use the exact words of another without putting quotation marks around those words, you are plagiarizing, even if you have cited the source.
- When you paraphrase someone else's words by making minor changes in word choice or sentence structure, you are still plagiarizing even when you cite the source.
- When you summarize even using your own words and structure without citing the source, you are plagiarizing.

We tell our students the best way to avoid the temptation to paraphrase too closely is to read all the material you want to summarize and then close the books, put the papers away, and then write using your own words and sentence structure and cite the source.

This is difficult for students to do. Many students do not write as well as authors of published work or think they don't, and so the temptation to change a word here and there and basically use the author's words and structure is strong. The electronic thesaurus makes this even easier. DO NOT DO THIS. It is dishonest and can have serious consequences not only to your academic career but also to your life after school.

> **FYI**
>
> Although the existence of the Internet makes it much easier these days for students to plagiarize, it is even easier for professors to catch them. Professors these days have amazing tools to detect plagiarized materials.

Conceptual Exercise 14A

Original source statement made by Evans: "Raters in the behavioral label group appeared to attribute less responsibility to the child for the negative behavior than did raters in the DSM group."

Student statement: The behavior group raters assigned less accountability to the child for the bad behavior than the DSM raters did (Evans, 2006).

Do you think this is or is not an example of plagiarism?

References and In-Text Citations

The reference list is so named because each entry has been *referred to* in the text of the paper. There should be no items in the reference list that do not appear in the body of the paper, and there should be no citations in the paper that cannot be found in the reference list. In our classes, we discourage students from using secondary sources. A **secondary source** is a book or paper in which primary sources are cited. If you wish to cite a primary source that you have found in a secondary source, you have two options:

- The best option is to get the primary source and read it yourself.
- The poorer option is to trust that the secondary source has accurately interpreted the primary source.

If you choose to discuss a research paper that you have not read but has been discussed by another writer, you *must not* cite the primary source in your reference list. Doing so indicates that you have read the primary source document. If you have not, you should write something like the following:

Jones reported that . . . (as cited by Brown, 2007), or

Brown (2007) discusses an experiment conducted by Jones.

Only Brown should be included in your reference list. If Jones is in your reference list, you have indicated that you have read Jones's original paper.

We discourage students from using secondary sources in research papers because doing so suggests to us that they are too lazy to read the primary source. In addition, relying on someone else to interpret the research is risky.

APA Primer

The APA style manual, as you probably know, is a comprehensive and often tedious tome. We would not even begin to try to summarize it here, but instead we will discuss the basics that our students have found helpful. We also include discussion of topics that our students have difficulty with. But always consult the manual for detailed explanations of style and format.

Avoiding Sexist Language and Stereotypy

The APA is particularly sensitive about sexist and other derogatory language. Habits are hard to change, but here are some tips on avoiding problems:

- Avoid using *he/she* and *him/her;* use the plural form instead.
- Eliminate the terms *man, manpower, man hours, mankind, chairman,* and so on from your writing and speaking vocabulary. Practice using substitutes such as *people, labor force, staff, worker hours, humankind, chair,* and so on. Avoid use of the term *mothering.* Substitute *nurturing* or *parenting.*
- Do not use stereotypical or sexist language in your speech or writing. For example, a student who writes or says, "Women are more emotional, more nurturing, less spatial, etc., than men" is a student who is bound to be challenged by his or her classmates and professors to provide empirical support for such statements.
- The terms *male* and *female* are adjectives used to modify nouns. Neither is a noun by itself. For example, men and women may have participated in your study, but males and females did not, although male and female participants may well have.
- Do not specify gender unless it is relevant to the discussion. For example, *female lawyer* should only be used if *male lawyer* would also be appropriate to the discussion.

The term *woman lawyer* or *woman doctor* is not acceptable under any circumstance. You would never say *man lawyer* or *man doctor,* would you? *Woman* and *man* are nouns, not adjectives.

Don't write or say *girls* or *boys,* unless you are referring to children. Adult humans are *women* or *men.* They are not guys or gals either!

Conceptual Exercise 14B

What is wrong with the following statement?

The children diagnosed with ADD spent more time out-of-seat than did normal children.

Common Problems With Student Writing

We find students make the same errors year after year. In this section, we will discuss the most common errors. But always consult with the **APA manual** for specific details.

Personification. Many students have trouble with personification. And we do too sometimes. Do not attribute human capabilities and qualities to lower animals, inanimate objects, theoretical constructs, or concepts. Your professor may call this animism or anthropomorphism. For example:

Behaviorism does not believe; behaviorists do.

The data do not suggest; the researchers do.

The theory does not claim; the theorist does.

Conceptual Exercise 14C

Rewrite the following incorrect sentence with as few changes to the structure as possible:

Pavlov's dogs knew the meat powder was coming and so they salivated.

***That* Versus *Which* Clauses.** To understand when to use *that* and when to use *which,* you must know the difference between a restrictive and a nonrestrictive clause. We use the following example, and our students rarely forget it (J. Watkins, personal communication, 1996).

A. The teacher, *who arrived late,* smoked dope.
B. The teacher *who arrived late* smoked dope.

In A, the italicized clause is nonrestrictive. A **nonrestrictive clause** adds extra, but nonessential, information to a sentence. In this example, the focus is on the dope-smoking teacher. The fact that she arrived late is additional but not essential information. This sentence implies that there was only one teacher.

In B, the italicized clause is restrictive. A **restrictive clause** is essential to the sentence. This example is referring to a specific teacher—the one who arrived late. This sentence implies there was more than one teacher.

That clauses are restrictive and should not be set off with commas. *Which* clauses are nonrestrictive and should be set off with commas.

Restrictive: The meal that was served by the woman was low calorie: A specific low-calorie meal is being discussed—the one brought by the woman. This sentence implies that the low-calorie meals are restricted to those served by the woman, and presumably the meals served by other people are not low calorie.

Nonrestrictive: The meal, which was served by the woman, was low calorie: In this case, the fact that the woman brought the meal is not essential. In this sentence, all the meals may be low calorie, not necessarily just the one served by the woman.

Conceptual Exercise 14D

Rewrite the following sentence correctly:

The database which I consulted did not include the paper I needed.

Noun-Pronoun Disagreement. Noun-pronoun disagreement is almost always a disagreement in number. Typically, a singular noun and a plural pronoun are used to refer to the same subject. Consider the following sentence:

Each child was brought into the room and asked to take their seat.

The subject of the sentence is the singular noun *child*. The pronoun *their* is plural. To avoid this problem, use *his or her* or change the noun to the plural form. Rewrite the sentence as follows:

Each child was brought into the room and asked to take his or her seat (or *a seat* would be even better).

The children were brought into the room and asked to take their seats.

Ambiguous Referents. Using ambiguous referents is a common problem with student writing. This means that the subject to which the writer is referring is unclear. Consider the following:

Psychologists typically adhere to the doctrine of empiricism. This has led to more objectivity by researchers.

The word *this* is referring to something, but we are not sure what that something is. The referent is unclear. Is it the *adherence* of psychologists to the doctrine that has led to more objectivity, or is it the *doctrine itself* that has led to more objectivity? We just don't know.

Conceptual Exercise 14E

Rewrite the following sentence correctly:

After everyone filled out their reports, they were taken to another room.

Run-On Sentences. There are two types of run-on sentences.

A **comma splice** occurs when two (or more) independent clauses are joined by a comma. An independent clause has a subject and a verb and can stand alone.

Here is an example of a comma splice:

John went fishing, he caught six fish.

This is a comma splice because the independent clause, "he caught six fish," could stand alone as a sentence.

A **fused sentence** occurs when two (or more) independent clauses are strung together with no punctuation. Here is a fused sentence:

John went fishing he caught six fish.

This is a fused sentence because the independent clause, "he caught six fish," could stand alone as a sentence.

Run-on sentences of either type can be fixed in four ways.

1. Rewrite as two sentences. John went fishing. He caught six fish.
2. Punctuate with a semicolon. John went fishing; he caught six fish.
3. Add a comma and a conjunction before the independent clause. John went fishing, and he caught six fish.
4. Add a conjunction before the dependent clause. John went fishing and caught six fish.

All are grammatically acceptable, but the latter two are preferred.

Sentence Fragments. A sentence must have at least one independent clause. Most errors of this type are clause or phrase fragments.

Here is an example of a **fragmented clause:**

Mary found many errors. Whereas I found only one.

Although the clause has a subject (*I*) and a verb (*found*), it cannot stand alone. It is a subordinate clause.

Rewrite as:

Mary found many errors, whereas I found only one.

Here is an example of a **fragmented phrase:**

We took a walk. *Enjoying the fresh air as we went.*

The italicized part is a phrase, not a sentence.

Rewrite as:

We took a walk, enjoying the fresh air as we went.

Conceptual Exercise 14F

Rewrite the following sentences correctly:

Genevieve believed that her report was fine, her teacher did not. Causing Genevieve much distress.

Wrong Word. Our students have a lot of difficulty with the use of **transition words** such as *since, while,* and *as.* One reason for this confusion is that other style manuals do not fuss about these words, but the APA manual does. (You may have noted that we just committed person-ification by saying that style manuals fuss; again, do as we say when you write—not as we do.)

According to the APA, *since* must be used only to refer to time passed. Students often use this word when they mean *because.*

Consider the following:

Since I agree with most of your arguments, I will not argue with you.

The word *since* is incorrect here. It should be replaced with the word *because.*
The following is a correct use of the word *since*:

I have been depressed since last Christmas.

Our students make a similar error using the word *as* when they mean *because.*
Read the following sentence:

As Mary is on academic probation, she must attend all her classes.

As we hope you can guess, *as* must be replaced by *because.*

Another frequent error is using the word *while* to contrast things when *whereas* is cor-rect. The APA specifies that *while* also refers to time.

Correct: While I was waiting for the bus, my backpack broke.

Incorrect: John got a goal, while Bob played poorly.

In the incorrect example, the word *while* has been used to contrast two things. The sentence should be:

John got a goal, whereas Bob played poorly. (You could also use *but* or *although.*)

Conceptual Exercise 14G

Rewrite the following sentence correctly:

Freddie could bowl up a storm while Billie could only throw gutter balls as he was not athletic.

Amount Versus _Number._ Use *amount* to refer to things you cannot count and *number* to refer to things that you can.

Incorrect: We tested a large amount of babies.

Correct: We tested a large number of babies.

We can count babies.

Incorrect: We waited a large amount of days.

Correct: We waited a large number of days.

We can count days.

Incorrect: We gave the participants a small number of water.

Correct: We gave the participants a small amount of water.

We cannot count water.

***Affect* Versus *Effect*.** Usually *affect* is used as a verb, and it means "to influence." An example of the correct use of the word *affect* is as follows: "We wondered how temperature would affect the mood of our group."

Effect is usually used as a noun. An example of the correct use of the word *effect* is the following: "The McCulloch effect can be demonstrated easily in the classroom."

FYI

Psychologists use *affect* as a noun to refer to emotion or mood. We might say, "She has flat affect."

Also, sometimes *effect* is used as a verb, meaning "cause." An example is as follows:

"We used our influence to effect a change in school policy."

***Then* Versus *Than*.** The word *then* refers to the time when something occurred, as in

"We waited for everyone to relax and then we read the instructions."

The word *than* is used to make comparisons, as in

"The first group was larger than the second."

Other Assorted No-Nos We Find Particularly Aggravating. Never write *try and,* as in "I will try and find the directions." It is *try to,* of course.

Do not use the words *impact, interface,* or *network* as verbs. These are nouns notwithstanding the apparent opinion of many journalists!

Do not write *anywheres, anyways, being as, being that, could of, should of, would of, irregardless, in regards to,* ever!

Do not ever write, *The reason is because,* as in "The *reason* I failed *is because* I missed so many classes."

> ### Conceptual Exercise 14H
>
> Rewrite the following sentence correctly:
>
> The reason we networked with the people from IBM was because we would of been excluded from the post meeting gathering had we not.

In this section, we have discussed common errors we find in our students' writing. We have not begun to discuss all the errors we see. The APA manual is an excellent source for information about grammar and style. Other useful sources include the following:

Hacker, D. (2003). *Rules for writers* (5th ed). Boston: Bedford Books.

Strunk, W., & White, E. B. (2000). *The elements of style* (4th ed.). Boston: Allyn & Bacon/Longman.

PRESENTING RESEARCH IN WRITING

Psychology students typically will prepare two kinds of **research papers:** term papers and research reports. The term paper is typically a systematic review of the current literature on a particular topic in psychology. A research report is a report on research that the student conducted.

The Term Paper/Literature Review

A **term paper** is an organized summary of the research on a particular topic. It should be logically organized. The organization depends on the objective of the writer. Some term papers will be organized chronologically, tracing the research on a problem from a historical perspective. Other term papers may be organized from general to specific. And yet other term papers may be organized by subtopics within the larger topic. Whatever the objective of the writer is, there must be logic to the organization of the paper.

We find that many term papers are poorly organized. Students will often summarize the studies they have read in no apparent order, jumping from one study to another. Begin the writing process by creating an outline of the topics you wish to address. Spending your time organizing and reorganizing your thoughts will make the writing process much easier. Then organize your material by listing the papers that are relevant to each topic and the point that each paper brings to the topic. By following an outline, you know what you need to write in each section, you know which papers are relevant, and the large task is now broken down into much smaller ones. Finally, don't be afraid to reorganize your outline. You may find that you have forgotten to include something, need to break a topic down into subtopics, or that a section can be omitted.

Term papers typically have one prime objective: to summarize the research on a topic so that the reader is up to date. Research reports also bring the reader up to date on a problem or topic, but usually to a lesser degree. In addition, the research report informs the reader about a new study conducted by the writer.

The Research Report

A **research report** is the most common way that researchers communicate their findings to others. After you have a general idea of what your topic will be, reading the literature is the next step in a research project. As discussed in Chapter 2, you need to know what has been done already and what has been found before you design your own research.

Before research is published, it is sent to the journal editor as a **manuscript.** The research report in manuscript form looks very different from the final published report. A manuscript typically contains a cover page, abstract, introduction, method section, results section, discussion section, and a reference list. It may include appendices as well. The checklists we give our students for preparing their research reports are included in the appendix to this chapter.

Cover Page

The cover page is the first page. It includes a **short title** and page number in the upper right-hand margin. The title of the report, the name of the researcher, and the affiliation of the researcher (i.e., your institution) are centered. The **running head** is included somewhere on the left-hand side and may be the same as the short title. For example, if the title of the report is "The Effects of Domestic Violence on Later Offending in Young Adult Men," the running head and short title might be "DOMESTIC VIOLENCE AND LATER OFFENDING."

FYI

Students often confuse the running head with the short title. The short title of the manuscript is always the first couple of words of the title. It simply identifies the manuscript to the journal editors. It will not appear in the final published article. The labeled running head that appears in capital letters on the top left of the title page is the running head that will appear in the final published journal article. It is an abbreviated title no longer than 50 characters.

Abstract

The abstract is the first thing most people read when they are doing a literature search. This is the information available online. From the abstract, you can determine if the article is relevant and should be read in its entirety. The abstract is a brief summary of the article. It informs the reader what was done, to whom, and what was found. It should be no longer than 120 words. Unlike the rest of the research report, the abstract is not indented. It is the second page of the report and begins with the heading "Abstract" centered.

Introduction

The introduction starts on the third page and has the title of the paper as the heading (centered). The introduction is where you review the existing literature relevant to the study being reported.

Your first job is to describe the general problem that you are addressing. Then you should inform your reader about the relevant research that has been done in the area. You need to bring your reader *up to speed* in the area. The research articles to which you refer should be found in scholarly journals. Most professors requiring research reports will not accept references to review articles, books, or popular media.

Finally, you should describe the point of your own study. Tell your reader what you investigated and what you expected to find.

Describe your specific study in general terms. Do not describe your results here.

Method

Replicability of psychological research is important. The method section continues from the previous section, is headed by the word *Method* (centered), and should be clear and detailed enough so that another researcher can replicate your research elsewhere.

The method section should more or less stand alone. By this, we mean that someone should be able to read the method section without having read the introduction and still understand what was done and how. The method section is often best broken down with subheadings. Typical subheadings include *Participants, Materials, Apparatus,* and *Procedure* (each flush left and in italics).

Participants. Describe the number of participants and relevant demographic information (e.g., age, gender, ethnicity). Either here or in the procedure section, describe how the participants were recruited and how they were assigned to groups if appropriate.

Materials. Describe any stimulus materials, tests, questionnaires, and instructions that you used. Examples of stimulus items can be included, but long lists should be put into an appendix.

Apparatus. Describe any machinery or instruments used in the study.

Procedure. There is an art to writing the procedure section. There must be enough detail so that the study can be replicated but not so much that the reader falls asleep. Begin by describing the procedure common to all groups. Then describe the differences in procedure between groups.

Results

The results section continues from the previous section and is headed by the word *Results* (centered). In general, you should first report your descriptive statistics and then any inferential statistics that you used. Means and standard deviations for all groups are a must. These are usually presented in a table.

Be sure to introduce the table in the text by referring to it. For example, you might write the following: Table 14.1 contains the descriptive statistics for each group in the experiment. Do not refer to the "Table above, below, or on page X." Use the table number. Here is an example.

TABLE 14.1			
Summary of Descriptive Statistics			
Group	*Number of Participants (n)*	*M*	*SD*
[Name of gp] [Name of gp]			

The table number should appear above the table with no period. The table caption appears below the table number in italics.*

You should briefly describe the data that are in the table. Don't describe every item in the table. If you do so, the table is unnecessary. Just describe the highlights.

Following the descriptive statistics, you should present your inferential statistics. These are typically included in the text unless there are too many to report, in which case a table is better. You must include the *t* value, the *df,* alpha level, and the *p* value. Here are some examples:

An alpha level of .05 was used for all statistical tests. We conducted an independent *t* test on the mean BDI ratings and found that the Prozac group participants ($M = 28.0$, $SD = 2.45$) were significantly less depressed than the placebo group participants ($M = 33.5$, $SD = 3.14$), $t(23) = 2.63$, $p < .05$.

We used an independent *t* test to compare the mean depression symptoms as measured by Beck's Depression Inventory. The two groups were significantly different (Prozac: $M - 28.0$, $SD - 2.45$; Placebo: $M - 33.5$, $SD - 3.14$), $t(23) = 2.63$, $p < .05$.

A statement such as "An alpha level of .05 was used for all statistical tests" must appear beforehand. You should consult with your professor to see if an effect estimate is also required.

However you choose to report your inferential statistics, you must report the significance test result, and you must use words to describe what it means. Do not speculate here but make sure you interpret the inferential analysis as statistically significant or not.

NOTE: Tables, figures, and appendices DO NOT EXIST if they are not introduced in words in the text of the paper.

It is often helpful to present data graphically. This makes it easier for the reader to see what went on. Which type of graph you choose will depend in part on what you are trying to show and in part on the kind of data you have.

Bar Graphs for Discrete Data. If your data are categorical (i.e., discrete), then a bar graph is often the best way to show your results. Perhaps you want to present some data describing the number of patients diagnosed with various disorders who reside in an assisted living complex. A simple bar graph such as Figure 14.1 would be a good way to do this.

---

*NOTE: Because this is a book, not an APA manuscript, these rules have not been followed here. Our publisher uses its own style.

Usually the values of the variable (categories) are on the abscissa (*x*-axis), and frequency is on the ordinate (*y*-axis). Notice that the bars are not connected. This tells your reader that your data are discrete. We can see that 25% of the patients were classified in the other psychological disorder category.

The figure number appears below the figure in italics (use a period). The figure caption follows the figure number in roman type followed by a period.* When including figures in your manuscript, do not worry about where they should be placed. All your figures are placed at the very end of your manuscript. Yes, the very end, after the references and appendices. Also, all your figure captions are written on one page, in order, and the page is placed at the beginning of your pages of figures.

Histograms for Continuous Data. When the data are continuous, a **histogram** can be used to present them graphically. Perhaps we want to present data showing the amount of perseverative behavior of 38 children with autism during treatment sessions. We could use a histogram such as Figure 14.2.

Notice that the bars are joined to indicate that the data are continuous. We can see that six of the children engaged in 3 to 5 minutes of perseverative behavior per session.

Bar graphs and histograms can be used to present **univariate** data. By this, we mean there is one variable. When we have two variables to describe graphically, we would choose a scattergram.

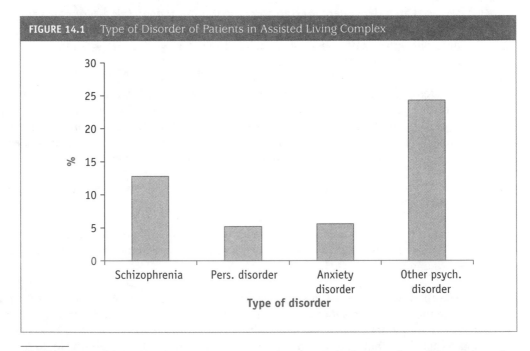

FIGURE 14.1   Type of Disorder of Patients in Assisted Living Complex

NOTE: Because this is a book, not an APA manuscript, these rules have not been followed here. Our publisher uses its own style.

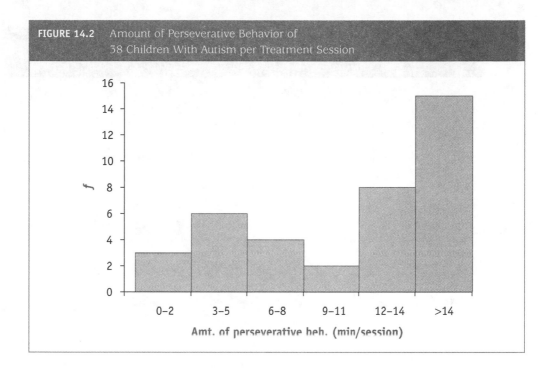

FIGURE 14.2 Amount of Perseverative Behavior of 38 Children With Autism per Treatment Session

Scattergrams for Bivariate Data. In a correlational study, there are two (or more) variables of interest. To present bivariate data, we would choose a scattergram. Imagine that we are interested in the relationship between the amount of time in treatment and depression symptoms of patients diagnosed as clinically depressed. We have two scores for each patient, and we could present these data in a scattergram as in Figure 14.3.

Notice that each point represents the patient's score on the depression scale and the number of months of therapy received. For example, the single patient who had received 3 months of therapy had a score of 12 on the depression scale. There appears to be a negative correlation between the two variables. In other words, as number of months in therapy increases, depressive symptoms decrease. To determine if the relationship was statistically significant, we would compute a correlation coefficient appropriate to the measurement scale of the two variables.

Other Ways of Graphing Data. Sometimes graphing rules must be violated for a higher cause—communicating clearly. Such is the case when you want to show interaction and main effects from an analysis of variance (ANOVA). Often researchers will use line graphs as we did in Chapters 7 and 8, even though the data points may be discrete. This is a case where communicating the pattern of results is the primary objective.

Presenting data in graphs is often desirable because many people find graphs easier to understand than tables. You should choose the method of data presentation that is clearest and most accurate.

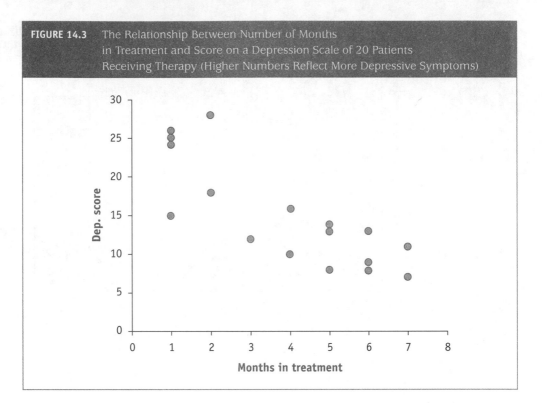

FIGURE 14.3   The Relationship Between Number of Months in Treatment and Score on a Depression Scale of 20 Patients Receiving Therapy (Higher Numbers Reflect More Depressive Symptoms)

Discussion

This section continues from the previous section and is headed by the word *Discussion* (centered). The discussion section is the place to speculate about the implications of your findings, discuss how your findings relate to other research, discuss improvements that could be made to the study, and suggest further research that could be done. Although there is room for some speculation, wild speculations that go way beyond your data and study are not appropriate.

FYI

We find that students often beat themselves up in their discussion. It is important to suggest improvements that could be made to your study, but don't go overboard. Discuss your research objectively. If you find that your data did not support the theories presented in the literature, perhaps the theories are wrong!

Reference Page

The **reference list** begins on a new page headed with the word *References* (centered).

Consult the APA manual for details about referencing various sources. All in-text citations must be in the reference list. The references must be in alphabetical order by the surname of the first author of each source. *Do not alphabetize the authors' names within the paper.* They are ordered by their status or their contribution to the research. The order of entries in each reference is as follows:

Surname of first author, initials, surname of second author, initials, etc. (year of publication); title of paper using uppercase for the first word, proper nouns, and the first word after a colon; title of journal in italics using uppercase for major words in journal title; volume(issue) in italics; and page numbers.

Use a hanging indent (all lines but the first are indented).

Here is an example of a journal article reference. Don't look for this article; we made it up!

Evans, A., & Rooney, B. (2008). Research methods in psychology. *The Journal of Research and Statistics for the Social Sciences, 12*(3), 212–245.

Appendices

Each appendix begins on a new page and is headed by the word *Appendix*. If there is more than one appendix, they should be labeled A, B, and so on. Tables in appendices can be labeled A1, A2, B1, B2, and so forth.

You should include in the appendix any information that is not necessary for understanding your research report but needs to be included for completeness. This might include a copy of your questionnaire, a list of words used as memory items, computer programs, and so on. Remember that appendices must be referred to in the text.

General Typing Guidelines for Term and Research Papers

- Set the spacing on double space and leave it there.
- Do not insert an extra line space between paragraphs.
- Always use left justification for the text.
- Use a **serif** font such as Times set at 12 points.
- Set all margins at 1 inch.
- Type a manuscript header, five spaces, and insert page numbers in the right header and justify right.
- Leave the footer blank.
- Do not staple your report; use a paper clip.
- Do not use boldface type anywhere (except symbols for vectors).
- Always introduce tables, figures, and appendices in the text of the paper: If you do not refer to these things in the text, *they do not exist.*
- Indent three to six spaces for text paragraphs. Use a hanging indent for the reference list.

A Sample Experimental Report

One of our statistics students was interested in the treatment of soldiers suffering from post-traumatic stress disorder (PTSD), and he decided to design an experiment to evaluate two treatments for the disorder as a course project. We include his final experimental report here as our sample.*

---

*Sample is from Nye, K. (2005). Effect of cognitive behavioural sleep therapy: REM density change in combat veterans with PTSD. A paper submitted in partial fulfillment of course requirements. Paper included with permission of the author.

Effect of cognitive   1

Note manuscript head, five
spaces, and page # in margin

Running head: EFFECT OF COGNITIVE BEHAVIOURAL SLEEP THERAPY

This is the running head of the
published paper, all capitals, no
longer than 50 characters

Effect of Cognitive Behavioural Sleep Therapy:

REM Density Change in Combat Veterans with PTSD

Keith Nye

Concordia University College of Alberta

Title with main words capitalized, your
name, and institutional affiliation
The entire manuscript is double spaced

Abstract

No indent for abstract

Forty male soldiers aged 20 to 25 years with recent combat-related post-traumatic stress disorder (PTSD) were assessed for sleep disturbances. Twenty were treated with cognitive behavioural relaxation therapy and twenty were treated with cognitive behavioural sleep therapy and cognitive behavioural relaxation therapy. Rapid eye movement (REM) density was measured using polysomnography and PTSD was rated using a standardized test. The sleep therapy group demonstrated significantly decreased REM density, $t(38) = 4.24$, $p < .001$ and PTSD scores, $t(38) = 3.22$, $p < .01$ compared to the relaxation group. Therefore, lower PTSD scores and a reduction in REM density followed sleep therapy treatment.

120 words or fewer

Effect of behavioural therapy   3

Effect of Cognitive Behavioural Sleep Therapy: REM Density Change in Combat Veterans with PTSD

One of the hallmark features of post-traumatic stress disorder (P̶ is sleep disorders, including frequent nightmares (Krakow et al., 2001). Although slee̶ traditionally viewed as secondary to PTSD (Krakow et al., 2001), associated with PTSD can impair coping ability, which worsen symptoms of PTSD during the waking hours (Lavie, Hefez, Halperin, & Enoch, 1979).

> Title is centered and major words are capitalized

Research of PTSD sleep disturbances w̶ revealed that soldiers exhibit significantly reduc̶ have been replicated and it has been further four̶ higher eye movement (REM density) during REM̶ Nolan, 1995; Mellman, Nolan, Hebding, Kulick-Bell, & Dominguez, 1997): a mean of 5.0 compared to̶ non-PT̶ ̶f 2.9. A correlation between the severity of PTSD and the REM den̶ ̶stablished (Mellman et al., 1997). In addition, an association has been ̶ awakenings and periods of REM sleep (Mellman et al., 1995).

> Use ampersand inside brackets and *and* outside brackets; use *e.g.,* and *i.e.,* inside brackets and *for example*, and *that is*, outside

> or PSG) has ̶ese findings ̶nificantly ̶ock, &

> The year is included in this citation within this paragraph because this is a second paper with the same first author

High REM density̶ ̶ctor in the "specific occurrence of stereotypical, repetitive nightmares" that are so debilitating to soldiers with PTSD (Mellman et al., 1997, p. 47). REM density has also been found in non-pathological adaptations to bereavement̶ ̶eynolds, et al., as cited in Mellman et al., 1997), suggesting that REM de̶ ̶n in processing emoti̶ ̶his natural process is disrupted̶ ̶ellman et al., 1997)̶

> Cite only the first author if there are six or more

> You must include the page number with a quotation

Sleep̶ ̶n cognitive behavioural therapies (CBT) have been effective in reducing frequency of nightmares as well as significantly reducing PTSD symptoms in studies with crime victims (Krakow et al., 2001). These findings have been replicated with fire evacuees diagnosed with PTSD (Krakow et al., 2004)̶ ̶sleep therapy have also been documented with rape victims wh̶ ̶rbances including frequency of nightmares, improved REM sleep,̶ ̶symptoms (Nishith et al., 2003). These studies have utilised a form of CBT̶ ̶involves imagery rehearsal, specifically targeting distressing dreams (Krakow et al., 2001; Nishith et al.).

> You don't need to include the year if the paper has already been cited in the paragraph

No studies of CBT sleep therapy on soldiers with PTSD have been undertaken prior to this study. Furthermore, no previous study has examined the effects of sleep therapy on REM density.

This study involved 40 randomly selected combat veterans diagnosed with PTSD. Participants were recent returnees from the war̶ ̶ ̶her psychological disorders, substance abuse, and medication usage. For et̶ ̶received treatment of some form: The control group received standard CBT̶ ̶ ̶whereas the experimental group received

> Use numerals for numbers larger than 10

CBT-based sleep therapy in addition to CBT relaxation techniques. Using PSG, sleep disturbances including REM density and frequency of awakenings were measured for both groups for the duration of their treatment. In addition, PTSD symptoms were rated before and after treatment using the Post Traumatic Stress Diagnostic Scale (Foa, 1995). The independent variable was the exposure to sleep therapy, and the dependent variables were REM density and Post-Traumatic Stress Diagnostic scores. I expected both dependent variables to improve moderately for the control group and significantly for the experimental group.

Method ———————⌐ Centered ⌐

Participants ————⌐ Flush left in italics ⌐

Forty participants, aged 20 to 25 years, took part in this study. All were male returnees from the Iraqi War, diagnosed with PTSD for less than six months. Participants were recruited from the U.S. Department of Ve[Always use words]entre for Post-Traumatic Stress Disorder and were randomly selected and [for numbers that] disorders and substance or alcohol abuse. None were receiving treatment or [begin a sentence] medications at the time of this study. Participants were randomly assigned to either a control or experimental group.

Materials

Cognitive Behavioural Therapy (CBT) relaxation techniques and CBT-based sleep therapy were provided by specialists with experience working with soldiers with PTSD and were customized for relevancy to combat exposure PTSD. CBT-based sleep therapy was provided by sleep specialists and included imagery-based techniques based on Neidhardt, Krakow, Kellner, and Pathak's (1992) model. Therapy was provided at the Department of Veteran Affairs' Medical Centre.

The Post Traumatic Stress Diagnostic Scale (Foa, 1995) has been shown to be a successful tool for recording changes in PTSD after treatment (Krakow et al., 2001). PTSD is diagnosed according to the following five categories: no PTSD (score of 0), mild PTSD (1–10), moderate PTSD (11–20), moderately severe PTSD (21–35), and severe PTSD (35 or greater).

Polysomnograph assessments were conducted with electroencephalograph (EEG), electrooculograph (EOG), and electrocardiograph (EKG) leads, monitoring brain wave patterns, eye movements, and heart rate, respectively. Data were collected according to standard procedure and analyzed by computer program at the Department of Veteran Affairs' Medical Centre.

Procedure

Participants were habituated to a standard sleep schedule before baseline data were collected and maintained this schedule throughout the treatment period. For both baseline and final testing, a total of two nights were spent in the sleep laboratory. Data were collected on the second night but not for the first night, following standard habituation procedures with sleep monitoring. EEG leads

Effect of behavioral therapy   5

were used to determine time in REM sleep. EOG leads provided data for REM density, defined by Krakow et al. (2001) as the number of eye movements during REM divided by minutes in REM sleep. The Post Traumatic Stress Diagnostic Scale is a self-report measure and was carried out before and after treatment by both groups under standardized conditions.

The relaxation therapy group (RT) received CBT relaxation therapy for a period of three weeks. The relaxation and sleep therapy group (RST) also received CBT-based sleep therapy concurrently for the same three-week period. In CBT-based sleep therapy, participants described their trauma-related nightmares in detail, were taught how to change aspects of the nightmare, and then rehearsed these changed dreams while awake, using visualisation techniques.

Results

Descriptive statistics for each group in the experiment are presented in Table 1. The experimental group displayed lower score means and slightly higher stand eviations for both REM density and the PTS Diagnostic Scale. All partic program.

> Tables and figures are on separate pages at the end of the document.

An alpha level of .05 was used for all statistical t the mean REM density reve led that the experimental g as significantly lower than th control group (*M* = 4.35, *SD* = 0.25), *t* (38) = 4.29, *p* < .001. There is statistical dence that participants who receive sleep therapy have lower REM density than inants who do not receive sleep therapy. Similar results were found es. An independent *t*-test computed on the mean PTS diagnostic scale treatment indicated that the experimental group (*M* = 28.30, *SD* = 2.5 wer than the control group (*M* = 30.85, *SD* = 2.50), *t* (38) = 3.22, *p* < .01. Statistical evidence exists to support the hypothesis that participants who receive slee herapy have lower than participants who do not receive sleep thera

> A statement like this must be included with your results

The ra for REM de dix A; those for PTS Diagnosti dix B. Computations of the t-tests by hand are included in Appendix

> Use italics for statistical symbols; insert spaces between terms

> Use two decimal places; do not include a zero in front of the decimal when the value cannot exceed 1, e.g., *p* and *r*

   *Note: ed for this course project and are not typical of published research reports.

Discussion

Although the sleep therapy group demonstrated significantly decreased REM density and PTSD scores compared to the relaxation group, the majority of both groups remained at moderately severe PTSD classification post-treatment

Effect of behavioural therapy   6

(Control $n = 19$, Experimental $n = 20$). Both groups also continued to demonstrate REM densities comparatively higher than normal range; mean REM density for typical men has been reported as 2.9 by Mellman et al. (1997).

I would like to suggest some future directions for research in this area. Earlier research on sleep therapy has been completed exclusively for cases of single incident trauma. To clarify whether PTSD arising from multiple incident combat trauma responds differently to sleep therapy than PTSD caused by single incident trauma, a 2×2 between subjects ANOVA using an experimental group that receives sleep therapy and a control that does not may be helpful. An additional challenge in using sleep therapy to treat combat-related PTSD includes the design of Neidhardt et al.'s (1992) sleep therapy, which depends on identifying and vividly visualising a single traumatic event related dream. For this reason, further 2×2 between subjects ANOVA studies that compare length of treatment, allowing some participants time to work through successive traumas, may be particularly worthwhile for multiple incident PTSD.

ANOVA can be abbreviated

All references have a hanging indentation

Centered and on a new page

Effect of behavioural therapy   7

References

Foa, E. B. (1995). *Posttraumatic Stress Diagnostic Scale.* Lawrence, KS: National Computer Systems.

This is a published test; the reference is similar to a book except the major words in the title are capitalized. With books only the first word of the title is capitalized

Krakow, B., Haynes, P. L., Warner, T. D., Santana, E., (...4). Nightmares, insomnia, and sleep disordered breathing (...) nt for posttraumatic sleep disturbance. *Journal of Traumati(...)*

Krakow, B., Johnston, L., Melendrez, D., Hollifield, M., (...)., et al.. (2001). An open-label trial of evidence-based (...) nightmares and insomnia in crime victims with PTSD. *American Journal of Psychiatry, 158,* 2043–2047.

Lavie, P., Hefez, A., Halperin, G., & Enoch, D. (1979). Long-term effects of traumatic war-related events on (...) p. *American Journal of Psychiatry, 136,* 175–178.

Journal title and volume (issue) in italics

Mel(...), R., Ashlock, L., & Nolan, B. (1995). Sleep events among veterans with (...) osttraumatic stress disorder. *American Journal of Psychiatry, 152,*

Mellman, T., Nolan, B., Hebding, J., Kulick-Bell, R., & Dominguez, R. (1997). A polysomnographic comparison of veterans with combat related PTSD, depressed men, and non-ill controls. *Sleep, 20,* 46–51.

Neidhardt, J., Krakow, B., Kellner, R., & Pathak D. (1992). The beneficial effects of one treatment session and recording of nightmares on chronic nightmare sufferers. *Sleep, 15,* 470–473.

Nishith, P., Duntley, S., Domintrovich, S., Uhles, M., Cook, B., & Stein, P. (2003). Effect of cognitive behavioral therapy on heart rate variability during REM sleep in female rape victims with PTSD. *Journal of Traumatic Stress, 16,* 247–250.

Effect of behavioural therapy   8

Appendix A

> Only called Appendix A if there are others. Just use Appendix if there is only one

Table A1

Raw Data for REM Density Scores

Control Group	Experimental Group
4.5	4.1
4.6	4.2
4.0	4.3
4.5	3.9
4.4	3.9
4.0	3.6
5.0	4.2
4.5	4.5
4.4	3.7
4.3	3.4
4.2	3.8
4.0	4.5
4.1	4.1
4.2	4.0
4.6	3.8
4.6	4.1
4.4	4.2
4.3	3.5
4.2	3.6
4.2	3.9

Effect of behavioural therapy 9

Appendix A Continued

Table A2

Statistical Data for REM Density

Control Group		Experimental Group	
Mean	4.35	Mean	3.965
Standard Error	0.056429	Standard Error	0.069689
Median	4.35	Median	3.95
Mode	4.2	Mode	4.1
Standard Deviation	0.252357	Standard Deviation	0.311659
Sample Variance	0.063684	Sample Variance	0.097132
Kurtosis	0.784182	Kurtosis	−0.65092
Skewness	0.633148	Skewness	−0.03161
Range	1	Range	1.1
Minimum	4	Minimum	3.4
Maximum	5	Maximum	4.5
Sum	87	Sum	79.3
Count	20	Count	20

Table A3

t-Test: Two-Sample Assuming Equal Variances

	Control Group	Experimental Group
Mean	4.35	3.965
Variance	0.063684	0.097131579
Observations	20	20
Pooled Variance	0.080408	
Hypothesized Mean Difference	0	
df	38	
t Stat	4.293499	
p (T<=t) one-tail	5.86E-05	
t Critical one-tail	1.685953	
p (T<=t) two-tail	0.000117	
t Critical two-tail	2.024394	

Appendix B

Table B1

Raw Data for PTS Diagnostic Scale Scores

Control Group	Experimental Group
31	30
32	27
30	29
29	30
36	26
34	27
34	28
31	31
27	27
26	25
30	26
31	30
27	29
32	25
30	32
30	35
31	27
31	28
31	26
34	28

Effect of behavioural therapy   11

Appendix B Continued

Table B2

Statistical Data for PTS Diagnostic Scale Scores

Control Group		Experimental Group	
Mean	30.85	Mean	28.3
Standard Error	0.558546045	Standard Error	0.56242
Median	31	Median	28
Mode	31	Mode	27
Standard Deviation	2.49789385	Standard Deviation	2.515217
Sample Variance	6.239473684	Sample Variance	6.326316
Kurtosis	0.188326212	Kurtosis	1.178632
Skewness	−0.013451512	Skewness	0.98965
Range	10	Range	10
Minimum	26	Minimum	25
Maximum	36	Maximum	35
Sum	617	Sum	566
Count	20	Count	20

Table B3

t-Test: Two-Sample Assuming Equal Variances

	Control Group	Experimental Group
Mean	30.85	28.3
Variance	6.239473684	6.326315789
Observations	20	20
Pooled Variance	6.282894737	
Hypothesized Mean Difference		
Difference	0	
df	38	
t Stat	3.217068354	
p (T<=t) one-tail	0.001323677	
t Critical one-tail	1.685953066	
p (T<=t) two-tail	0.002647353	
t Critical two-tail	2.024394234	

Effect of behavioural therapy   12

Appendix C

List of tables and figures

Table 1

All tables and figures on separate pages

Descriptive Statistics for Each Experimental Group

| | Treatment group | | | |
| | PTS score | | REM density | |
	RT	RTS	RT	RTS
Mean	30.85	28.3	4.35	3.96
Standard Deviation	2.50	2.52	0.25	0.31
Number of Participants	20	20	20	20

OTHER WAYS OF PRESENTING RESEARCH

Oral Presentations

Most psychology students are required to make in-class presentations in upper-level classes. Good presentation skills are important because most if not all psychologists will present information of some sort in front of an audience at some point in their careers.

Typically, oral presentations require that a large amount of information be condensed into a small amount of time. Researchers at conferences often have only 15 or 20 minutes to present their material. The art is determining what can be communicated clearly in such a limited period of time. Many oral presenters use computer software these days to organize their presentations. Here are some hints for creating an effective oral presentation:

- Use a large font size—26 points or more.
- Programs such as PowerPoint have default font sizes that are suitable—don't go much smaller.
- Do not put a lot of text on slides—include only major points and elaborate each.
- Avoid presenting tables of data.
- Use graphs if appropriate for presenting data.
- Slow down when presenting a graph and define the axes before discussing the content.
- Begin with an introduction of the problem or purpose; often, this will include a brief description of a couple of key research papers.
- Include general method or procedure—integrate the information in a method section to describe what you did and how you did it.
- Describe your data, choosing the most important findings.
- Discuss the implications of your research—how it fits with current theory or research.
- Do not apologize for results that do not support your research hypothesis—that's science.
- Do not waste time on statements such as "if we had more participants" or "if only we had controlled this variable."
- End your talk with a discussion of directions for future research.

Here are some more tips:

- Time your talk and remember to leave time for questions.
- Practice your talk in advance, preferably with an audience.
- Videotape yourself giving the talk.
- Practice your talk until you have eliminated all the "ums" and "ahs."
- Make sure you have a plan if you run short; students are nervous and typically they will speak much faster in the actual presentation than they did when practicing. Have a backup plan.
- Do not run long. Pace yourself.
- Have water available.

Don't think that you cannot do an oral presentation because you get too nervous. Most of us are nervous when speaking to a group. The secret to a successful presentation is to be well prepared and to harness your anxiety. Preparation requires giving yourself time to practice and edit your talk. Harnessing your anxiety means taking that nervous energy and directing it outward. When we get anxious, we take all our energy and direct it inward. We tighten up and get stiff or we overcompensate and project an appearance of disinterest and boredom. What you want to do is project the appearance of enthusiasm and confidence. You are well prepared, you have practiced your talk, and you know the material better than anyone in the audience. You have every reason to be confident and relaxed.

For some, being fully prepared and highly practiced is not enough to counter the fear. There are techniques available. We suggest that our students shake. Yes, whole-body shakes help to release the muscle tightness and help to project that energy out.

Another technique is to loudly say the entire alphabet by combining all the consonants and vowels (e.g., AEIOU, BA BE BI BO BU, CA CE CI CO CU, etc.). This is a great way to warm up your voice and it sounds so silly that you must relax.

Another way to conquer fear is through practice. Toastmasters International is an organization that helps people develop their public speaking skills. You probably have Toastmasters or a public speaking club on your campus.

Here are a few useful resources:

- O'Hair, D., Rubenstein, H., & Stewart, R. (2004). *A pocket guide to public speaking.* Boston: Bedford/St. Martin's.
- http://www.toastmasters.org/
- The APA Web site has instructions for preparing talks and posters. Go to http://www.apa.org and follow the links to the annual convention.

Writing up your research in a formal paper is a daunting but satisfying exercise. Presenting your research in person to a group is also daunting and also satisfying. There is another way of communicating your research findings to others that is not so daunting; you can present your findings on a poster.

Poster Presentations

Many students first participate in scholarly conferences by submitting a poster. The more professional looking the poster, the better. As with oral presentations, a lot of information must be condensed. Typically, the presenter is nearby the poster to answer questions from viewers. Therefore, the poster must contain all the important information but not all the details of the method and results. Handouts with more detail can be prepared and given to interested viewers.

Organize your poster in columns. It is easier for readers to scan down a column than it is to move across rows. There is no standard size for posters, so check with the organization (APA allows up to 3 feet high and 7 feet 6 inches wide). When formatting figures, remember that people will be standing about 3 feet from your poster.

Here is a sample poster that our student, Keith Nye, might have used to present his experimental study reported earlier.*

---

*Sample is from Nye, K. (2005). Effect of cognitive behavioural sleep therapy: REM density change in combat veterans with PTSD. A paper submitted in partial fulfillment of course requirements. Paper included with permission of the author.

A Combination of Two Therapies for Veterans with PTSD

Keith Nye

Concordia University of Alberta

E-mail: knye@condordia.ab.ca

Fall, 2005

The Research Problem

To investigate the effectiveness of behavioral sleep therapy in combination with cognitive behavioral relation therapy in treating PTSD.

Participants

Forty randomly selected combat veterans diagnosed with PTSD. Participants were recent returnees from the war in Iraq.

Measured Variables

PTS diagnostic scale score

REM density score

Treatment

The control group (RT) received standard CBT relaxation techniques, whereas the experimental group received CBT-based sleep therapy in addition to CBT relaxation techniques (RTS) for a period of 3 weeks.

Conclusions

Behavioral sleep therapy can improve the therapeutic outcome of cognitive behavioral relaxation therapy for combat veterans experiencing posttraumatic stress disorder.

Results

Dependent Measure	PTS		REM density	
Treatment group	RT	RTS	RT	RTS
M	30.85	28.30**	4.35	3.96*
SD	2.50	2.52	0.25	0.31
n	20	20	20	20

$**p < .001$
$*p < .01$

We hope you now appreciate the importance of communicating your research findings with others. Effective communication between researchers is necessary for any science to move forward.

CHAPTER SUMMARY

Writing in science differs from **literary writing.** The primary goal of **scientific writing** is to communicate information clearly and accurately.

Students in psychology must conform to the rules of the **APA publication manual** when writing term papers and research reports.

Borrowing the words or ideas of others without crediting the source is **plagiarism,** a very serious offense. Tips to avoid plagiarism include closing all source material before writing and refraining from using a thesaurus when paraphrasing. All referenced material must be cited in the text, and writers should avoid citing secondary source material if possible.

The APA publication manual specifies style and format for APA **manuscripts. Sexist** and **stereotypical language** is not permitted.

Common problems with student writing include **personification,** confusion of **restrictive** and **nonrestrictive clauses, noun-pronoun disagreement, ambiguous referents, run-on sentences, sentence fragments,** and improper use of **transition words.** Other difficulties include the correct use of *amount* and *number, effect* and *affect,* and *then* and *than.*

Students of psychology typically prepare **term papers,** organized summaries of the research on a topic, and **research reports.** Term papers can be organized chronologically or from general to specific. Research reports in psychology typically include the **cover page, abstract, introduction, method section, results section, discussion section, references,** and **appendices.**

Other ways of communicating in psychology include **oral presentations** and **poster presentations.**

ANSWERS TO CONCEPTUAL EXERCISES

Conceptual Exercise 14A

We think it is plagiarism. The writer has altered the sentence structure a bit and substituted some similar words, but basically the sentence is too close to the original. Either use the original sentence, enclosing it with quotes, or paraphrase in a way that is clearly different from the original.

Conceptual Exercise 14B

The use of the word *normal* in this context is not a good idea. It has a judgmental connotation that would not be approved of by the APA.

Conceptual Exercise 14C

Pavlov's dogs salivated before the meat powder came.

Conceptual Exercise 14D

Either of the following would work:

> The database, which I consulted, did not include the paper I needed.

> The database that I consulted did not include the paper I needed.

Conceptual Exercise 14E

After everyone filled out his or her report, the reports (or the participants) were taken to another room.

Conceptual Exercise 14F

Genevieve believed that her report was fine; her teacher did not, which caused Genevieve much distress.

Conceptual Exercise 14G

Freddie could bowl up a storm but Billie could only throw gutter balls because he was not athletic.

Conceptual Exercise 14H

The reason we associated (mingled?) with the people from IBM was that we would have been excluded from the postmeeting gathering had we not.

FAQ

Q1: Do I alphabetize the authors in each paper in my reference list?

A1: NO NO NO—Leave the order of authors as it appears on the paper. The authors are listed in terms of importance or amount of contribution. Only alphabetize the list of papers by the surname of the first author.

Q2: How do I cite a personal communication?

A2: A personal communication is the exception to the rule, "what you cite in the text must also appear in your reference list." A personal communication is cited, either directly or indirectly, in the text and does not appear in your reference list. Here is an example:

> Eating ice cream can enhance self confidence (I. Robbins, personal communication, November 16, 2005).

Q3: How do I reference an online source?

A3: Online sources include a wide variety of materials. Some sources may also be available in print, but others are available only online. Proper format depends on the type of material—consult the APA manual.

Q4: When can I use et al.?

A4: Never use et al. with one or two authors. When citing a paper for the first time with more than two authors but fewer than six, use the full citation. After that you may use et al. If the paper has six or more authors, you may use et al. the first time you cite it.

Q5: Why do I need to learn APA formatting?

A5: APA format is the style used in psychology. You will need to know these rules for future course work, graduate school, or if you pursue a career in research. Also, learning the rules of good writing is a valuable investment no matter where your future leads.

Q6: Why does APA change the indent for the reference page?

A6: The hanging indent makes it easier to scan down the list for an author's name.

Q7: What's wrong with using a lot of quotes?

A7: The reader is interested in *your* thoughts. Too many quotations give the impression that you have no thoughts of your own.

Q8: If I don't understand a quote, should I still use it?

A8: Not unless you are presenting the quotation in a discussion of how difficult it is for you to understand. Of course, you run the risk that your reader will understand it and think less of your intellectual ability.

Q9: How can I tell if a research article is an experimental one?

A9: An empirical research article will have a method and results section. A review paper will not. To determine if the research uses an experimental design, check the method section for a manipulated independent variable.

Q10: Can I use *Psychology Today* as a reference?

A10: You can cite any source you use in your paper, but keep in mind that *Psychology Today* is *not* a peer-reviewed publication. Without peer review, there is no verification that the information is even correct!

Q11: Do I have to include all the articles I read in the reference list?

A11: Absolutely not. Include in your reference list only those articles that you cite in your paper. And be sure if you cite a source in your paper that you include it in your reference list.

Q12: What is a split infinitive? Does APA object to them?

A12: An infinitive consists of "to" and a verb (e.g., to run, to eat, to write). You split an infinitive when you place a modifier in the middle (e.g., to quietly run, to neatly eat, to slowly write). Yes, they are often awkward and APA does object to them. However, sometimes it is less awkward to split than not to split—APA is okay with some split infinitives.

Q13: What do I do if the quote I want to use is from an HTML article and the page numbers don't match the published version in the journal?

A13: If the source shows paragraph numbers, use them. For example, "median interpolation is a simple calculation" (Evans, 2007, ¶ 32). If paragraph number is not available, cite the heading and paragraph number of the material. For example, "median interpolation is a simple calculation" (Evans, 2007, The Median, ¶ 3).

CHAPTER EXERCISES

1. Below are examples of sentences we have taken from papers written by students. Rewrite each such that it is grammatically correct with the goal of changing as little as possible and retaining the writer's probable intent.
   a. Watson's Little Albert study, has been considered unethical in the way they treated an enfant.
   b. This type of behavior is unethical and morally wrong, by examining experiments such as this we can use it as an example of what not to do.
   c. Apparently, from reading the study, all Milgram was concerned about was to clarify any misconceptions of the experiment.
   d. Determinism claims that all events can be explained in terms of natural laws of cause and effect.
   e. The results were clear, girls were less aggressive than boys.
   f. Being that the data were conclusive.
   g. Professors seem to use their wives and children as examples.
   h. The reason that the deception was unethical is because significant discomfort and emotional trauma could occur as a result.
   i. Even though the subjects were told prior to the experiment that they would receive electrical shock and that they were free to withdraw from the experiment at any time.
   j. The materials which were used were obtained from the APA manual.

2. List the sections of a research report and list the essential components of each.

3. Create a bar graph for the following data that shows the percentage of students choosing the type of population they prefer to study. Because there are two variables, you will need to decide how to best show the difference between graduate and undergraduate choices. You decide.

The ACME Anxiety and Depression Scale: Anxiety Scores Measure of Patients Prior to Surgery

Preferred Population	Graduate Students	Undergraduate Students
Children	15	20
Elderly	20	15
Disabled	35	15
Undecided	30	50

4. Create a histogram for the following data.

Patient Number	Score
1	44
2	72
3	64
4	54
5	98
6	73
7	75
8	95
9	74
10	77
11	52
12	91
13	45
14	64
15	80
16	74
17	60
18	92
19	99
20	88
21	75
22	53
23	67

5. Create a scattergraph for the following data to show the relationship between age and sleep onset.

Age	Sleep Onset Latency (min)
75	40
23	5
28	7
30	10
47	20
36	13
39	16
43	18
60	30
50	30
57	27
62	32
21	3
70	45
32	14

CHAPTER PROJECTS

1. Select a simple experiment or study from the literature and create a poster to present the research.

2. Select a simple study from the literature and create a 12-minute talk to present the research.

3. Conduct a simple survey of consumer or student attitudes about some issue such as gay marriage. Write a report of your research following the APA requirements. Include graphs and tables of your results.

APPENDIX: RESEARCH REPORT CHECKLIST

Cover Page

	Yes	No
Running head of paper all in capitals (50 characters max)		
Manuscript header including the first two or three words of the title, five spaces, and p #		
Title, name, affiliation centered and double spaced		

Abstract

	Yes	No
No indent		
Separate page		
Header = Abstract		
100–120 words		
What was done		
To whom		
What was found		

Introduction

	Yes	No
Starts on new page		
Title of report is main head (A Head)—centered uppercase and lowercase		
Proper citation style		
All citations in reference list		
Brief description of your study indicating hypotheses at end of intro		

Method

	Yes	No

Head is the word *Method*—do not start on new page
Subheads properly formatted in italics
Description of participants
Description of materials and apparatus
Description of procedure

Results

	Yes	No

Head is the word *Results*—do not start on new page
All tables and figures properly introduced in words before inserted
Table number and caption above table
Figure number and caption below figure
Figures have both axes labeled
All tables and figures briefly described after insert
Descriptive and inferential statistics reported properly including *df* and *p*
Alpha level reported
Appendices are introduced in words—remember appended material not referred to in text DOES NOT EXIST

Discussion

	Yes	No

Head is the word *Discussion*—do not start on new page
Discuss possible problems or limitations, implications of research for theories and applications
Relate your discussion back to your introduction
Suggest further research

References

	Yes	No
On new page		
Properly formatted and ordered		
All references cited in body of paper		
All citations included in reference list		

Appendices

	Yes	No
On new page		
Labeled and titled		
Tables labeled and titled		
All appended material introduced in the text		

Visit the study site at www.sagepub.com/evansmprstudy for practice quizzes and other study resources.

Glossary

ABA withdrawal design. Single-participant operant design where behavior is measured during baseline, treatment, and withdrawal of treatment phases.

ABAB withdrawal design. Single-participant operant design where behavior is measured during a baseline, a treatment, a withdrawal of treatment, and a second treatment phase.

Abstract. A brief description of a study or experiment, including information about the participants, the procedure, and the results.

Alpha levels. Also called levels of significance; probability level for rejecting the null hypothesis.

Alternating treatment design. Single-participant operant design where more than one treatment is assessed with a given individual.

Alternative hypothesis. A hypothesis that specifies something different than what is stated in the null and is the hypothesis the researcher hopes to confirm.

ANCOVA (analysis of covariance). A general linear model with one constant variable and one or more factors. ANCOVA is a combination of ANOVA and regression for constant variables.

APA Manual. The publication manual of the American Psychological Association.

Applied research. The use of basic research findings to improve conditions in real-world settings.

Archival research. The study of existing data, gathered for some other reason, to answer research questions.

Archive. Both the information itself and where it is housed.

Authority-based belief. A belief that something is true because an "expert" said so.

Bar graph. A figure used to present frequency data for a categorical or discrete variable.

Baseline. Natural level of a behavior.

Basic or pure research. Research conducted to increase the body of knowledge of a discipline.

Beneficence. Maximizing benefits.

Between-participants experimental designs. Designs where comparisons are made between groups of independently assigned participants.

Carryover effects. Changes in the dependent variable caused by the order of presentation of the levels of the independent variable.

Case studies. Detailed studies of a single individual.

Categorical variables. Discrete variables whose values are mutually exclusive, such as sex (female, male) or age (young, middle, old).

Central tendency. Average score in a distribution; examples are mean, median, and mode.

Changing criterion design. A single-participant operant research design where the target behavior is trained in a stepwise fashion.

Changing phase. In single-participant operant research where an independent variable is introduced, changed, or withdrawn.

Chi-square tests. Nonparametric statistical tests that compare theoretical or expected frequencies with obtained frequencies.

Cluster analysis. Methods used to group similar objects into categories or clusters.

Cluster sampling. A probability sampling method where the unit of sampling is a cluster of participants.

Coefficient of determination. r^2; an estimate of the treatment effect size often used with a correlation test.

Cohen's d. An estimate of the treatment effect size often used with a t test.

Competence. Being educated and skilled in areas that you are researching.

Complete counterbalancing. A scheme for assigning participants to conditions in a repeated-measures design such that all treatment conditions precede and follow each other the same number of times.

Completely randomized design. An experimental design where participants are randomly assigned to different levels of one independent variable.

Conceptual hypothesis. A statement about the expected relationship between conceptual variables.

Confidence interval estimation. A range of values with a known probability of containing a parameter.

Confidentiality. Guarding any information collected so that it is used only for purposes agreed to by the participants and is not disclosed to anyone other than the researchers.

Confounding variables. Variables that systematically vary with the independent variable and may cause changes in the dependent variable.

Construct validity. A measure that truly reflects the theoretical construct.

Content validity. A measure that includes all the dimensions that are part of a concept.

Continuous variables. Variables that can take on an infinite number of values in theory.

Control group. A comparison group that received a different level of the independent variable (often no treatment) than the experimental groups.

Controlled experiments. Experiments conducted in a laboratory.

Convenience sampling. A nonprobability sampling method where participants are selected based on their easy availability.

Correlation. A relationship between two variables.

Correlational research. A nonexperimental approach that assesses the relationship between two or more variables.

Criterion validity. Also called predictive validity; the extent to which a measure correlates or is predictive of an outcome measure.

Critical thinking. The ability and willingness to assess claims and make objective judgments on the basis of well-supported evidence.

Cross-sectional research. The study of people of different ages.

Debrief. To inform participants of the purpose of the research, particularly when deception is used.

Deception. Any information or action on the part of the researcher that is intended to mislead the participants about the true nature of the research.

Dependent groups designs. Experimental designs where the same participants or matched participants are assigned to groups.

Dependent variables. Measures of behaviors or mental processes expected to be affected by independent variables.

Descriptive research. Research where the goal is to describe characteristics of a population (i.e., not test a hypothesis).

Descriptive statistics. Numerical summaries of samples or populations. Examples of descriptive statistics are frequency distributions and measures of average (i.e., mean, median, mode), range, and standard deviation.

Determinism. A doctrine of belief that events have natural causes.

Differential order effects. Occurs in repeated-measures designs when the carryover effect from condition A to B is not the same as the carryover from B to A.

Disclosure. Revealing confidential information to others.

Discriminant function analysis. A method used to determine which variables discriminate between two or more categorical dependent variables.

Discrimination. Bias, favoritism, prejudice, unfairness, and inequity.

Effect size. The size of the relationship between two variables.

Empiricism. Beliefs based on experience.

Empiricist. A person who relies on real observations to assess claims.

Eta-squared. A measure of treatment effect.

Experiment. A design where the researcher has control of the independent variable.

Explanatory research. Research where the goal is to explain the relationship between variables (i.e., to test a hypothesis).

External validity. The extent that a research finding can be generalized to different participants or different settings.

Extraneous variables. Variables that may affect the outcome of a study but were not manipulated by the researcher.

Face-to-face interview. An interview that is conducted in person (i.e., not by phone).

Face validity. A measure that seems to be reasonable.

Factor analysis. A multivariate statistical technique that forms factors from groups of variables that are correlated.

Falsifiability. Hypotheses and theories that can be shown to be false.

Fidelity. Being loyal, faithful, and trustworthy.

Field experiments. Experiments conducted in the natural setting.

Fixed alternative questions. Questions where the respondent selects his or her answer from a set of specified responses.

Focus group. A facilitated interview of a small group of people.

Frequency. Rate of responding.

F **test.** Also known as analysis of variance, a statistical test that compares means of two or more groups.

General ethical principles. Suggested guidelines meant to guide psychologists in their research and practice.

Goals of science. Description, explanation, prediction, and control.

Goodness-of-fit test. Chi-square test used to compare obtained with expected frequencies on one variable.

Group-administered questionnaire. Data collection by administering a questionnaire to a group of participants.

Histogram. A figure used to present frequency data for a continuous variable.

Hypothesis. A prediction of how concepts are related that is often deduced from a theory.

Hypothesis testing. Research conducted to test the validity of a hypothesis.

Incomplete counterbalancing. A scheme for assigning participants to conditions such that each condition occurs equally often in each position.

Independent groups design. An experiment where different groups of participants are independently assigned to treatment groups.

Independent variable. The variable manipulated by the researcher and expected to influence the dependent variable.

Inference. A probability statement about a parameter(s) that is based on a statistic from a sample.

Inferential statistics. Procedures used to generalize from samples to populations.

Informed consent. A participant's consent to participate after he or she has been given all the information necessary to make that decision.

Institutional Review Board (IRB). A group of people from various backgrounds whose mandate is to apply guidelines to assess the ethics of research proposals.

Integrity in research. Striving to be truthful, accurate, objective, and fair in all parts of the research process.

Interaction. The effect of combinations of levels of independent variables on the dependent variable.

Internal validity. The extent to which the change in the dependent variable was due to (or caused by) the change in the independent variable.

Internet questionnaire. Administering a questionnaire via the Internet.

Interrater agreement. Method used to determine reliability of observational measures.

Interrupted time-series design. A design where several pretest measures are taken before the occurrence of some event, often a naturally occurring event, and then several posttest measures follow.

Interval scale. Scales or variables that have equal-sized intervals between values but with an arbitrary zero point.

Interval variables. *See* Interval scale.

Interview. Collection of data by asking questions verbally.

Intuition-based belief. A belief that something is true because it feels true.

Inventory. A measure that indicates, from a wide variety, which characteristics an individual possesses.

Justice in research. Being aware of your limitations and biases and taking steps to ensure they do not interfere with the rights of others.

Laboratory observation. Systematic observation of behavior conducted in a controlled setting (lab).

Likert scale. A set of statements where people indicate their agreement or disagreement by selecting a numerical value.

Linear relationship. The relationship between two variables that is best described by a straight line.

Literary writing. Writing with the goal of entertaining as well as communicating information.

Literature review. An article that summarizes, integrates, and critically evaluates the research that has been published on a specific topic.

Logistic regression. A variant of standard regression used when the dependent variable is dichotomous, such as success/failure.

Longitudinal research. The study of the same people over time or at different stages in their lives.

Mail-out questionnaire. Administering a questionnaire by mail.

Main effects. In ANOVA, the effects of each independent variable on the dependent variable.

Manuscript. The form of a paper sent to a publisher for consideration.

Matched groups design. A dependent groups experimental design where participants are matched or made equivalent on a variable(s) that is correlated with the dependent variable.

Matching variable. In dependent groups designs, a variable that correlates with the dependent variable.

Mean. A measure of central tendency; the arithmetic average.

Median. A measure of central tendency; the middle value.

Mediating variable. A variable that is assumed to be a predictor of one or more dependent variables and, at the same time, is predicted by one or more independent variables.

Meta-analysis. A statistical technique used to estimate the relationship between variables by analyzing the results of many existing studies.

Mixed design. An experimental design using between- and within-participants variables.

Mode. A measure of central tendency; the most frequently occurring value in a distribution.

Moderating variables. Variables that increase, decrease, or reverse the relationship between the independent and dependent variables.

Multiple baseline design. A single-participant operant design where replication is made in another behavior, another individual, or another setting.

Multiple regression analysis. A correlational technique for evaluating the relationship between several predictor variables and one criterion variable.

Multiple relationships. Having more than one role or relationship with clients or research participants.

Multiple time-series designs. Designs that are similar to interrupted time series designs but include a comparison group.

Multistage sampling. A probability sampling method where cluster sampling is done in more than one stage.

Naturalistic observation. The observation of behavior in its natural environment.

Needs assessment. First step in program evaluation used to determine if there is a need and if the proposed program would meet that need.

Negative correlation. An inverse linear relationship between two variables.

Nominal variables. Variables whose values differ qualitatively.

Nonequivalent groups design. A nonexperimental design where changes in behavior among groups that differ at the outset of the study are compared.

Nonmaleficence. Minimizing harm.

Nonprobability sampling methods. Methods of participant selection where the probability that a participant will be selected for inclusion in the sample is not known.

Nonrestrictive clause. A clause that adds extra, but nonessential, information to a sentence.

Null hypothesis. A statistical hypothesis about the value of a parameter, the relationship between two or more parameters, or the shape of a distribution and is the hypothesis that the researcher hopes to reject.

Observational research. Systematic observations of behavior.

One-way ANOVA. A statistical test for differences among means when participants have been randomly assigned to several levels of one independent variable.

One-way ANOVA with repeated measures. A statistical test for differences among means when participants serve under each level of one independent variable.

Open-ended questions. Questions where the respondents are allowed to create their own answers.

Operant. Behavior that operates on the environment to produce effects or consequences.

Operationalized variables. Measurable variables.

Ordinal variables. Variables whose values differ in quantity, but intervals between values are not assumed to be equal.

Parsimony. The simplest explanation for a phenomenon.

Partial correlation. A correlation between two variables with the effect of a third variable that is statistically controlled.

Participant observation. Observational research where the researcher is part of the group being observed.

Pearson product-moment correlation. *See* Pearson *r* test.

Pearson *r* test. Statistical test for the linear relationship between two continuous variables.

Perfect correlation. A correlation of 1 (either positive or negative).

Phase. Periods of time in which the individual is studied to see how his or her behavior changes when different treatments are introduced, withdrawn, or changed.

Plagiarism. Borrowing the words or ideas of others without crediting the source.

Population. All the observations of interest.

Positive correlation. A linear relationship between two variables.

Power of the statistic. $1 - \beta$; the probability that a false null hypothesis will be detected.

Predictive validity. *See* Criterion validity.

Probability sampling techniques. Methods of participant selection where the probability that a participant will be selected for inclusion in the sample is known.

Program evaluation. Research designed to determine if a policy or program is meeting its goals.

Qualitative research. Studies of differences in the kind or quality of behavior.

Quantitative research. Studies of differences in the amount of behavior.

Quasi-experiment. A nonexperimental design where comparison groups are not formed by the researcher and therefore not under the control of the researcher.

Questionnaire. Collection of data by having respondents read the questions and write their responses.

Quota sampling. Like convenience sampling, but participants with particular characteristics are selected until a specified number is reached.

Random assignment. Independent assignment of participants to groups.

Randomized factorial design. An experimental design where participants are randomly assigned to all levels of more than one independent variable. Each participant is assigned to only one condition.

Random sampling. A procedure for selecting participants whereby each participant has an equal probability of being included in the sample.

Range. The span of a distribution.

Rating scales. Scale often used in survey research to quantify a response to a question.

Rational thought. Thinking with reason.

Ratio variables. Scales or variables that have equal-sized intervals between values and a true zero point.

Reasoning. Beliefs based on logic and empiricism.

Referral sampling. A nonprobability sampling method where participants have been referred by other participants.

Reliability. The extent to which a measure produces the same result when repeated.

Repeated-measures design. In experimental design, a dependent groups design where more than one measure has been taken on the same individuals.

Replication. Duplication of a research outcome in another setting, with different participants, or at a different time.

Research hypothesis. A statement about the expected relationship between measurable, or operationalized, variables.

Research paper. A report on research that was conducted.

Response set. The tendency to respond to all questions in a similar way.

Responsibility. Being dependable and accountable.

Restrictive clause. A clause that is essential to the understanding of the sentence.

r^2. *See* Coefficient of determination.

Sample. A subset of a population.

Sampling frame. A list of the members of the population.

Sampling methods. Techniques for selecting samples from populations.

Scale. A measure that provides a number for specific characteristics.

Scattergram. A graph used to present bivariate continuous data.

Science. A way of acquiring knowledge through the continual interaction of empiricism and reasoning.

Scientific method. Method used by scientists for testing hypotheses.

Scientific writing. Writing with the goal of communicating information.

Secondary source. A book or paper in which primary sources are cited.

Semantic differential. A rating scale where respondents indicate, on a continuum between opposite adjectives, the meanings they associate with a word.

Semipartial correlation. A measurement of the correlation between two variables that remains after controlling for the effects of one or more other predictor variables.

Serif. A typesetting term for the small tails on letters (e.g., those in Times font).

Single-participant research design. An operant approach involving the experimental analysis of behavior of a single individual.

Size of the effect. *See* Effect size.

Skepticism. A healthy reluctance to accept new information without sufficient evidence.

Social desirability. The tendency for people to provide answers that make them look good.

Spearman's rank-order correlation. *Rho,* a test for the linear relationship between two ordinal variables.

Split-half method. A method for evaluating the internal reliability of a test by correlating one half of the test items with the other half.

Standard deviation. A statistical measure of the average distance of scores from the mean.

Statistical hypothesis. A statement about the relationship between statistical properties of data.

Statistical inference. *See* Inference.

Statistical significance. An outcome that leads to rejection of the null hypothesis; it indicates that the outcome was unlikely due to chance.

Stratified sampling. A probability method of sampling where the population is divided into strata based on some population characteristic and participants are randomly selected from each stratum.

Structural equation modeling. A method consisting of confirmatory factor analysis, path analysis, and regression used for determining the extent to which data on a set of variables are consistent with hypotheses among the variables.

Survey. A method of data collection where questions are asked in an interview or with a questionnaire.

Systematic sampling. A probability method of sampling where every *k*th individual is included in the sample.

Telephone interview. An interview conducted over the phone.

Term paper. A systematic review of the current literature on a particular topic.

Test. A measure that produces a single score.

Test for independence. Chi-square tests used to compare obtained with expected frequencies on two variables.

Test-retest method. A method for evaluating the consistency of a measure over time.

Theory building. Devising a hypothesis, applying empiricism to the hypothesis, abandoning hypotheses that are not supported by further empirical evidence, and constructing new hypotheses. In this way, general principles and predictions can be made.

Time-series designs. Quasi-experimental designs in which measures are taken both before and after a treatment or event has occurred.

Tradition-based belief. A belief that an idea is true because it has been accepted as true for a long time.

t **test.** A statistical test of significance used to compare two means.

Two-way ANOVA. A test for differences among means when participants have been randomly assigned to all combinations of the levels of two independent variables.

Type I error. Rejection of a true null hypothesis.

Type II error. Failure to reject a false null hypothesis.

Validity. The extent to which a measure actually measures what it is supposed to measure.

Variability. Spread of scores in a distribution; examples include the range, variance, and standard deviation.

Within-participants designs. Also called repeated measures, experimental designs where the same participants serve in all conditions.

Within-participants factorial designs. Experimental designs where participants serve under all combinations of all levels of each independent variable.

Index

About the Authors

Annabel Ness Evans received her PhD in Cognitive Psychology from the University of Alberta in 1979. She is currently Professor and Chair of the Department of Psychology at Concordia University College of Alberta, where she has taught since 1975. She teaches introductory Statistics and directs the BA programs in psychology at Concordia. She has written two previous texts. Her *Using Basic Statistics in the Social Sciences* (fourth edition) is now available from Pearson Education, Canada. With Lyle Grant, she published *Principles of Behavior Analysis* (1994). She believes that a large part of her job is to provide an instructional environment that supports undergraduate students in their endeavor to acquire the skills and information they need to be successful students and citizens. She does outside consulting work of various kinds, including graphic design, statistical analysis, and content editing for private and government agencies.

Bryan J. Rooney is an Associate Professor of Psychology at Concordia University College of Alberta. Bryan earned his PhD in psychology from Carleton University in Ottawa and his MSc and BSc from the University of Calgary. He enjoys teaching research methods and finds the process of helping students design and implement their own research projects particularly rewarding. When students learn about research by developing their own projects, they experience the frustration, excitement, and occasional disappointment that are part of the process. They also discover how fun it is to seek answers to questions that pique their curiosity. Bryan has taught research methods for 9 years and also teaches statistics and biopsychology. His research background is in visual and auditory perception, and more recent interests include the efficacy of teaching technologies, such as online course delivery. When he is not involved in the lives of his busy family, you can find him skiing or riding his motorcycles depending on the season.